636.009 Kat
Katz, Jon
Soul of a dog : reflections on the
spirits of the animals of Bedlam Fa

34028072124754
ATA $24.00   ocn176952250
08/26/09

3 4028 07212 4754
HARRIS COUNTY PUBLIC LIBRARY

W9-AKB-806

DISCARD

DISCARD

ALSO BY JON KATZ

Izzy & Lenore

Dog Days

A Good Dog

Katz on Dogs

The Dogs of Bedlam Farm

The New Work of Dogs

A Dog Year

Geeks

Running to the Mountain

Virtuous Reality

Media Rants

Sign Off

Death by Station Wagon

The Family Stalker

The Last Housewife

The Fathers' Club

Death Row

SOUL OF A DOG

SOUL OF A DOG

Reflections on the Spirits of the Animals of Bedlam Farm

JON KATZ

VILLARD Ⓥ NEW YORK

While all of the incidents in this book actually happened, some of the names and personal characteristics of some of the individuals have been changed. Any resulting resemblance to persons living or dead is entirely coincidental and unintentional.

Copyright © 2009 by Jon Katz

All rights reserved.

Published in the United States by Villard Books, an imprint of The Random House Publishing Group, a division of Random House, Inc., New York.

VILLARD BOOKS and VILLARD & "V" CIRCLED Design are registered trademarks of Random House, Inc.

LIBRARY OF CONGRESS CATALOGING-IN-PUBLICATION DATA

Katz, Jon.
Soul of a dog: reflections on the spirits of the animals of Bedlam Farm / Jon Katz.
p. cm.
ISBN 978-1-4000-6629-2
eBook ISBN 978-0-345-51536-0
1. Domestic animals—Anecdotes.   2. Bedlam Farm (West Hebron, N.Y.)—Anecdotes.   3. Farm life—New York—West Hebron—Anecdotes.
I. Title.
SF416.K38 2009   636.0092'9—dc22   2009020152

Printed in the United States of America on acid-free paper

www.villard.com

2 4 6 8 9 7 5 3 1

First Edition

Photographs by Jon Katz

Book design by Susan Turner

For Maria,
who always came through the door

THE SOUL OF A DOG

Dog, n.   A subsidiary Deity designed to catch the
overflow and surplus of the world's worship.

—AMBROSE BIERCE,
The Devil's Dictionary (1911)

I F I DIDN'T HAVE A DOG LIKE ROSE, I WOULDN'T KNOW OR
care that a big fat ugly goose had lost her mate to a coyote
attack and was wandering the roads of a small town nearby,
hiding away in a swamp at night, at risk of being eaten by a
coyote herself, or flattened by a speeding car or truck.

Because I did have Rose, word of such problems came to
me quickly. Somebody was sure to call. It turned out to be
my friend Becky, from Argyle, who got upset driving past the
goose every morning on her way to work.

The first line of defense for animals in distress was Annie,
my farm helper, a.k.a. the Bedlam Farm Goddess. Annie, rescuer of many species—birds, bunnies, bats—tried to coax the

goose into her pickup, but the bird ran off into the swamp. Annie told me she didn't know what else to try.

Time to call in Rose. By the end of the day, I had no doubt, that goose would be in custody.

Rose is my right hand—my entire right arm actually. On my farm, the clarion call is: "Rosie, let's go to work." That's all it takes for this ferociously energetic and whip-smart border collie to spring into action.

Rose doesn't play much, or cuddle much. She doesn't even care much about eating, and pays scant attention to treats, rightly dismissing them as bribes. Unlike most dogs I have owned, Rose doesn't crave the warm body of a human at night, preferring to patrol the farmhouse, checking through the windows on the pastures and the barns. She doesn't appreciate being cooed over, or having her belly rubbed. Apart from me, she isn't all that crazy about humans in general; she doesn't grasp the point of pleasing strangers, as they don't lead her to work. When we're not working, she isn't even all that interested in me.

She's always working, or waiting to work; it's deep in her bloodlines, the result of generations of service. Anything that doesn't have to do with work is extraneous to her, an interruption, an annoyance.

When Rose approaches me, it's not a bid for a pat or a biscuit, but a signal that something is wrong. A gate is open, perhaps, or a predator is about.

There's a vulnerability about Rose, even a sweetness in her eyes, but there's no mistaking her priorities. Smart, tough, determined, she is essential, but rarely the dog that people melt over or want to take home. Yet she's a great dog.

She moves sheep, separates sick animals, alerts me to the

birth of lambs, fends off stray dogs, rounds up errant goats, helps the shearer, the large-animal vet, the farrier.

Over our years together, she's proved invaluable not only to me, but to others as well. Rose regularly gets calls from panicky farmers trying to round up recalcitrant cows, collect sheep who have gone through a fence, quell barnyard riots. She's worked in blizzards, downpours, heat waves, and bitter cold. She has never failed to get the job done. We charge a flate rate of $10 per emergency call.

Except for one late-night visit to Salem, where some sheep went wandering just before a snowstorm was expected. Rose stuck her head out the car window, all it took to persuade the sheep to hustle into the barn. No charge.

"ROSIE, let's go to work!" I yelled that spring afternoon, and she came flying. The goose was being sighted on Route 47 in Argyle, a densely wooded, thinly populated stretch of country road. She was a domesticated African Grey, Annie told me; her wings had been pegged, so she couldn't fly off to protect herself or find another mate. It's unusual to see a goose alone; they mate for life. The pair had probably been dumped by people who were moving or just didn't want them.

She was big and white—a good forty pounds, I guessed—and loud. She honked and squawked furiously, one of her protections against predators, when we pulled up on the shoulder of the road, where Annie was already on the scene. Geese are notoriously ill-tempered, and they're hardly helpless: They have powerful bones in their wings and peck with their beaks. But this one seemed more anxious and confused than aggressive.

Unfortunately, she had acres of marshy wetlands for shelter. Smelly, mucky, crisscrossed with vines and brush, and an incubator for flies and mosquitoes, this swamp was a good place for her to hide from humans—but it wouldn't protect her from predators.

It was a hot, humid day. The bugs were on us in minutes. Nobody would have much energy for long, not even Rose, especially if we wound up tromping around in the muck.

Sure enough, the goose, running along the roadside ahead of Annie, made for the water when she saw Rose hop out of the car. This was not going to be easy.

Rose looked around for sheep, gave Annie and me a look when she couldn't see any, and then locked in on the goose. Now she knew what she'd come for. She grasped the mission.

But it was going to be a tough one. We could hear the goose shrieking and splashing in the swamp, hidden by tall grasses. Rose didn't swim, so far as I knew. When I pushed a long branch into the marsh bottom to gauge whether we could walk into it, the stick went down about four feet. No way.

Rose began pacing, looking around, glimpsing the swimming, retreating goose, looking at me. She seemed stumped, glancing from me to Annie, eyeing the goose and the murky water.

In theory, we were defeated. A broad expanse of non-navigable swamp lay between us and this hapless, frightened—and unnervingly large—creature. She was in her element, and we were out of ours.

Rose looked at me, and I looked at Rose and shrugged, as if to say, I wish I could tell you what to do, but I don't know. And I didn't, other than to call her back, get into the car, and head home.

I had no commands for this conundrum. "I don't see how we can do this," Annie lamented, already sweating and muddied. All I could do was shrug.

But Rose, still pawing and peering, loped off down the road, away from the goose. It startled me, but Rose never ran away from a mission, so I waited and watched as she covered several hundred yards, then veered into the woods and disappeared.

Unlike me, she wasn't nearly ready to give up.

I worried about her plunging through the thick underbrush. It can be dangerous for dogs in the country. Rose had twice had her belly ripped open by old pieces of barbed wire hidden in thickets; once her collar snagged and she was stuck for hours until she could chew through a branch. She came home still dragging it.

In a few minutes, pacing the bank myself, I glimpsed her circling the swamp to come around opposite me, as herding dogs do with sheep. The goose was loudly squawking at Annie—who was still hoping to persuade it that she meant no harm—then retreating and hiding.

Suddenly, Rose popped up behind the goose, who seemed stunned and confused. Rose plunged into the water and began swimming toward it. Annie and I stood amazed.

Rose had come along many times when I took my Labradors to lakes and creeks, where they swam enthusiastically; she had never shown any interest in joining them. The goose, possibly also amazed, began backing away. Rose advanced, staying well out of range of the bird's beak and flapping wings. It turned into a strange water ballet.

All I could see was Rose's muddy head across the swamp as she paddled toward the goose, then retreated; the goose moved menacingly toward her, then backed off. Annie,

meanwhile, clambered back along the edge of the swamp—
a pincer movement.

The goose stopped flapping and squawking. She looked at
Rose, looked at Annie coming up behind her. Forced to
choose between this obsessive and determined dog, charging
at her again and again in the water, and Annie, calling gently
from the rear, the goose seemed to surrender. She swam
toward Annie, who swooped down and grabbed her, holding
her firmly against her chest. Rose, almost black from mud
and panting heavily, climbed out of the ooze and, in her effi-
cient and businesslike way, shook herself off and headed back
around the swamp.

At the road, she encountered Annie, lugging the goose
through the woods.

The creature was exhausted, clearly spent, and apart from
some final hisses at Rose, who came over for a curious sniff,
she allowed herself to be steered into a large dog crate in the
back of Annie's truck and carted off to her farm, where she
resides in comfort and ease to this day. Christened Sophia, the
goose sits happily next to Annie in the backyard, eating special
goose treats, and honking intermittently just for the hell of it.

Rose came over to me, ignoring all our praise and comments. She was no longer interested in the goose; that job was
done. She was ready to go back to Bedlam and find more
work to do.

This had been just another job. "What a dog," Annie said,
after loading the mud-covered Rose onto her truck. Yes, indeed.

WHEN I THINK ABOUT ANIMALS and souls, I often think of
Rose, of what she does for me, how I value her, what she
makes possible.

She's not the sweetest dog, not the kind most people want. She doesn't live to show me unconditional love; I doubt she could care less about making a sick person feel better, or charming a small child. Rose is a working dog, the kind bred to perform tasks with humans.

I treasure working dogs, and currently have three—Rose, Lenore, and Izzy. Conditioned to attach to humans, highly trainable if they're well bred, their instincts have been honed over generations. Rose came from a working line out of Texas and Colorado, bred not for looks, geniality, or even temperament, but for energy, instinct, and drive.

Since she was six months old, just a scrawny little pup, Rose has lived on my farm. She was pressed into service her first week in residence—and mine—when my sheep and donkey bolted from the fenced pasture and headed into the woods.

I was alone on a farm in a remote corner of upstate New York with no experience or assistance, and no idea what to do. Rose, even then intense and businesslike, was still a novice, a herder in training.

But she gamely set out into the woods, corralled the animals, and marched them back, and I knew I wasn't alone anymore.

Rose waits to work, lives for work. She watches me constantly for the signals that mean a task at hand, even before I can say, "Let's go to work." She knows the working door—we always head out the back when we work—from the others. She knows which shoes I put on for work, which walking stick I take. If she's in the yard and I'm inside the house and reach for my cell phone, another portent, she'll be waiting by the front door.

Rose is undistractable, indefatigable, a problem solver.

Work is her essence, her animating spirit, and the core of her impact on me. Her dedication to it helps make my life possible, connects the two of us in this powerful way.

Rose is, in some ways, the perfect animal to help me consider the soul of a dog. She is heroic, determined, and her life is in service to me.

I am fortunate to live with some other animals as well, and they all, in their own way, have enriched my life and shaped my understanding of one of the most debated and compelling questions in the long history of human beings' relationships with animals: Do they have souls, and if so, what might they be?

SOUL OF A DOG

Chapter One

DOGS AND SOULS

If I have any beliefs about immortality, it is that
certain dogs I have known will go to heaven,
and very, very few persons.

—JAMES THURBER

U NTIL RECENTLY, I'D NEVER SPENT MUCH TIME WITH ARIS-
totle, one of the world's pioneer thinkers. When I finally sat down with him, I found his essays tough going but
rewarding; his ideas came as something of a jolt.

Like many of the early philosophers and scholars, Aristotle took a hard, clear line when it came to animals and
souls. He exalted the rational being that a human had the potential to become. There was nothing like it, he wrote. A
human could develop morality and responsibility. Since animals aren't widely believed to possess those traits (not even in
our contemporary animal-worshipping culture, although that's
changing), he argued that humans had a higher status, that

human values and attributes—including the soul—couldn't and shouldn't be attributed to animals.

What made humans distinct from other living things, Aristotle believed, was that very ability to reason about ethics, to be held morally accountable for their decisions. Our ability to perceive what was right, and to struggle to do right rather than wrong, was our most distinguishing characteristic.

Animals (and children) weren't able to determine right from wrong, Aristotle believed, and thus existed on a different plane. One could no more attribute human consciousness to animals than to trees.

Religious scholars, sorting out questions of faith and the afterlife, carried these arguments further and codified them. In the thirteenth century, Thomas Aquinas established Aristotle's ideas as part of Christian doctrine, which states clearly that animals, lacking reason, don't have immortal souls. Animals couldn't read the Bible, accept God, or worry about heaven and hell. Therefore, they bore no responsibility for their choices. They were beasts, under our control, subordinate.

Mainstream Christianity, writes contemporary theologian Andrew Linzey (who believes that animals *do* have souls) remains "firmly humanocentric."

Maybe so, but in the United States at least, the faithful are creating their own animal theology. Society's broader view of animals has shifted radically. Scientists' investigations suggest more intelligence and consciousness among animals than Aristotle or Aquinas could have perceived. Animals, particularly dogs and cats, are moving toward the center of our emotional lives. It sometimes seems that our love, even adoration, of animals is approaching the dimensions of religion itself.

A number of studies in recent years have indicated that

the occasional border collie, elephant, or chimpanzee shows signs of self-awareness, some ability to see itself as an individual apart from the others of its species, though most researchers are candid about this work being far from conclusive.

Meanwhile, liberal theologians like Linzey, animal-rights activists like philosopher Peter Singer, and many millions of pet owners and lovers profoundly attached to their animals are reshaping the way we view other species, and are developing their own theologies.

I've been asking dog and cat lovers for years if they believed their animals had souls. By now I've met few dog owners who would consider their companions thoughtless, subordinate beasts, incapable of reason or self-awareness. Quite the opposite—I meet people all the time who tell me in considerable detail what their dogs and cats are thinking, feeling, and planning, and who find the very idea that their companion animals might be barred from heaven heretical.

Anthropomorphizing isn't merely a trend in our culture but an epidemic. Some animals who have not learned to live with and love humans (raccoons, for example) do not seem to be benefiting from this new consciousness. But dogs and cats, who've lived among us for thousands of years and have us figured out, are on a roll.

Though I know better, I attribute human emotions to dogs myself, all the time. It's almost impossible not to anthropomorphize, if you love and live with animals.

Consider the way that Rose, who usually spends the night in distant corners of the farmhouse—I rarely know where—occasionally comes to wake me, hopping up onto my bed to look at me or, if necessary, lick my face or ear.

At first, I shooed her away, annoyed at having my sleep interrupted. But I came to realize that this behavior meant something was amiss. Rose moves around at night, looking out the windows, keeping an ear and eye on things. When something isn't right, she knows it.

It might be a fox or coyote on the prowl, or a broken fence, or a sick animal crying out. Once, a goat had escaped from its enclosure and was wandering around the driveway. Once, a rabid raccoon was trying to get into the barn. Another time, the donkeys had nosed open the gate and were heading for the road.

What is Rose doing when she wakes me in the night? Does she intend to warn me of danger, or is she just reacting to her finely honed working instincts? And how would I know the difference?

Animals generally *do* react out of instinct, genetics, environment, and experience, if you accept what vets and behaviorists tell us. We want our dogs to love us madly because we're wonderful, but most of us who spend a lot of time around dogs come to understand that they love us because we feed them—and that's one of the reasons we do.

They certainly have strong spirits, emotions, perhaps imaginations—the truth is, we still really don't know a lot about what's going on inside those furry heads—but an ethical self seems a human trait. Humans possess the ability to use narrative, language, and self-consciousness to reason, to struggle with right and wrong and make good decisions, to ponder questions of a spiritual nature. These are not things dogs can do.

I've never seen a dog, cow, or chicken resolve to be a better dog, cow, or chicken and work on improving itself. Domesticated animals seem to live the opposite way, following instincts and training, accepting their roles.

Aristotle wasn't calling animals inferior to us. He was saying they were different, not comparable, and that we ought not diminish people *or* animals by assuming they have the same qualities, capacities, and emotional constructs we do. The human conscience is unique in all biological life, and there is no evidence, beyond our tendency to romanticize other species, that such an extraordinary trait exists in the animal world. The fact that that's become a somewhat controversial notion is remarkable.

Aristotle's philosophical and theological heirs, Augustine and Aquinas, did believe, for different reasons, that humans were inherently superior to animals. If anybody in Aquinas's time had claimed that dogs were just like children, he would have been shunned.

Our values have changed. Rationality was an almost sacred trait to thinkers like Aristotle, whose culture had emerged from darker, more primitive times when little was understood about the natural or scientific world.

Rationality was the groundwork for learning, morality, even democracy. To Aristotle, it formed the core of what it meant to be a human being, and the human soul was uniquely precious. Animals weren't idealized or personified; they were valued as workers—or food.

Aquinas, also enormously influential in shaping notions about animals and souls, further theorized that since animals lacked all reason and self-consciousness, humans couldn't be cruel to them. They existed, were created, for our benefit and had no awareness of their condition beyond instinct. The reason to treat animals well, Aquinas argued, was primarily to foster compassion toward other humans.

It's important to remember the context of those much harsher times, marked by starvation, war, disease, suffering, and superstition. Pets existed, even then. Dogs were used for protection and companionship, and cats prized as rodent sentries, but other animals were on the periphery of our families and emotional lives, not so central. They were rarely seen as childlike or as possessing human-style emotion.

The number of domestic dogs in this country has exploded in the last generation, from roughly 15 million in 1960 to more than 75 million today, according to the Humane Society of the United States. Figures for cats, rodents, birds, reptiles, and fish are less reliable. In the past, owning a dog was simpler. They were rarely purchased, often ate human food, and were not generally walked, cleaned up after, or permitted to sleep in our beds. They didn't have human names, and expensive health care for them was almost unheard of. Bites were common, leashes rare, gourmet snacks and play groups unimaginable.

There was little discussion of animals and souls, or much expectation of them joining us in the afterlife.

Certainly they weren't as emotionally engaged with their human owners. Dogs sometimes provided companionship, but more often assisted with hunting, herding, and guarding.

Largely beasts of burden, animals were useful—vital—for pulling carts and plows, for hauling and transporting and fighting, for providing wool and meat and soap. Few people in Aquinas's time had the resources to feed companion animals or spend money on their health care. The notion that they might have human-style thoughts, motives, or reasoning was centuries away.

Now and then, pushing a cart through the aisles at a pet superstore, I like to imagine Aristotle or Aquinas at the mall with me, gawking at the overwhelming variety of toys, beds, collars, scoopers, shampoos and deodorizers, exotic foods and snacks. I suspect both men would be horrified.

What would I say to them if, after shopping, we had a chance to sit on the front porch of my farmhouse, enjoying that comparatively new invention—the rocking chair—and talk about animals?

Having lived with pets for decades, I might point out that my dogs and other animals learn all the time. They adapt and react to one another, to me, to members of other species. They change routines, get acclimated to people and noises, track the movement of anything that might be food. They're not so dumb. Yet I don't see them as much like me. I don't see a capacity to make moral decisions, change their lives, promote freedom, justice, or other human values. The animals on my farm don't have free will; they're dependent on me for almost everything they need to survive.

We don't have an equal relationship. To me, that signifies a great responsibility to treat them well. I can take care of myself, but they need me to take care of them. As much as anything, that reality shapes our relationship and underscores the differences between us.

Aristotle's were among the first known words on the subject of animals and souls, and even though our views of animals have changed—deepening, even hardening—the line Aristotle drew stands up pretty well, I would have to acknowledge to him. Not surprisingly, I find his logic difficult to change.

But to many people, dogs are perfect, loving, unassailable creatures. They can do no wrong, even if—Aristotle had a point—they can do no right either, at least not consciously.

RELIGION IS NO LONGER CLEAR about animals and their souls; science is even more muddled. Scientists and behaviorists are increasingly intrigued by animal intelligence and cognitive process, and studies increasingly suggest that our dogs and cats are smarter, deeper, and more spiritual than we have previously imagined. Yet these studies are oddly inconclusive, and I often get the sense that we are being told what we wish to hear, perhaps want to believe. Animals have alien minds, and no serious behaviorist believes they think the way we do.

If you are convinced that your spaniel has a soul, perhaps he does.

There is something very personal about this question of animals and souls, perhaps an issue to be determined by the particular mix of emotion, chemistry, spirituality, and experience that defines our individual experiences with our animals. I have acquired a lot of that experience, and a lot of ideas about this question of souls, more than I would ever have guessed, and I'd like to share those stories, my own experience.

I'm in a good position to contemplate the question. My own soul, my spiritual life, is by now quite enmeshed with the souls of dogs—and of donkeys and several large bovines as well. I live on a 110-acre farm with an impressive roster of animals—three dogs, two steers and a cow, four donkeys, three goats, a rooster and a small tribe of hens, two barn cats, twenty-eight Tunis sheep, plus countless wrens, barn swallows, and chickadees, hawks and bats, chipmunks, moles, mice, raccoons, bobcats and coyotes, foxes and deer.

I'm not sure I'll ever know where the spirit of a dog begins and mine leaves off. I think the souls of dogs and of humans often interact; they couple, shaping and changing one another at times and in ways that aren't always visible or per-

ceptible. That can be an extraordinary, and efficacious, encounter.

Dogs have surely changed my life, more than once. My
first border collie, Orson, led me to life on this farm. Rose
makes my life here possible. Izzy, my other border collie,
came out of absolutely nowhere and eventually brought me
to work as a hospice volunteer, one of the most moving and
spiritual experiences of my life. Lenore, an irresistible black
Labrador, helped me learn how to feel and express love at a
time when I needed it.

My other animals also shape my life and spirit, almost
daily, though less distinctly. Communing with donkeys, who,
like dogs, have a time-honored history and—it seems to
me—a rich understanding of humans, is grounding, soothing. Hanging out with Elvis, my enormous Brown Swiss
steer, has affected my own humanity, and introduced me to
the spirits and lives of animals I previously paid little attention to.

The irresistible goats spark my humor and test my patience. Barn cats have more than once led me to ponder the
question of good and evil. Even my grumpy old rooster,
Winston, has taught me much about fidelity, bravery, and responsibility.

I SUPPOSE of all my dogs, past and present, Rose may be the
simplest to describe in terms of spirit. Rose is about devotion
to work, about service; she possesses the kind of independent
spirit that helps a human live his chosen life. That's no small
thing.

Lenore, who joined us as a squirming puppy, is about love;
she demonstrates a fierce determination to show and receive
affection.

And Izzy, well, he's permitted me to grow not only as a writer, but as a photographer, and, most important, as a human being. Izzy has changed my life, even as Rose helps define and support it.

I think the question of dogs and souls can best be approached for my purposes not by scientists, pastors, or Ph.D.s, but through the animals themselves, through stories about Rose and her remarkable work on my farm, through the shenanigans of Lenore, who has become best friends with one of my rams, through Izzy, who seems to see deep into the human psyche. Researchers are amassing evidence about what animals can think, sense, and do, but so are the rest of us.

ONE BOILING, sticky July day, Izzy and I drove to a nursing home far out in farm country. It was a one-story brick-and-mortar building, neglected outside and grim inside. Most of its residents suffered from deepening dementia, and many of them were crying or shouting out as we walked inside to visit hospice patients.

Every nursing home is different. Some are quiet, almost serene; others, like this one, are difficult places to be, filled with troubled patients, and severely challenged staffs.

Edith was nearly ninety, and no one had been able to speak to or communicate with her for months. She was angry and confused, repeatedly pushing her wheelchair in one direction, then another. If you got too close, the nurses cautioned, she might lash out, turn her wheelchair away, complain loudly that she had something to do, or simply shout, "Get away!" Even the hospice workers, always so attentive and persistent, had nearly given up on getting through to her.

I approached Edith in the hallway, calling her name. She

ignored me, refused to look at Izzy, backed her wheelchair into the wall, and then abruptly wheeled around and almost ran over Izzy's paw. He backed up just in time, and so did I.

I consulted the hospice social worker, then a nurse. We all shook our heads, uncertain that we could do much. Izzy, meanwhile, approached from one side of the chair, which caused Edith to yell at him, and then from the rear. "Get out, get away," she shouted at him and at all of us.

I was about to do just that when Edith happened to lower her hand by the side of her wheelchair. Izzy, seeing his chance, darted forward and slid his head under her palm, fixing his eyes on hers.

Edith froze. She stared back down at Izzy, meeting his gaze, appearing to actually see him for the first time. She took his head in both her hands, and she smiled a bit, for what was probably just seconds. To those of us watching, though, it seemed a much longer time. It was stunning to see, the perceptible bond Izzy was making with this woman whose soul had appeared to be buried, perhaps lost for good, a spirit no human had been able to reach in recent memory.

The nurse started to weep; the hospice social worker, who'd seen so much, was already wiping her eyes. Izzy's spirit was so focused, generous, and loving that the hallway seemed to almost glow, to fill with light. Edith stroked him with a tenderness that, given her earlier agitation, was breathtaking.

Flash forward a few weeks to a very different location: I had to buy a new truck and I drove to Glens Falls and parked outside the Toyota dealership. Izzy, off-leash, hopped out of the car, walked beside me onto the sales floor, and lay down under a salesman's desk.

After a few minutes of chitchat and paperwork, I got up,

shook hands, and turned to go see my new pickup. That's when one of the salesmen called out, "Hey, there's a dog under the desk over there."

It was true; I had forgotten that he'd come in with me. That happens now and again. I once took Izzy into my doctor's office. He lay on the examining table while I sat in a chair, and when we were done with the exam and the conversation, he trotted out through the waiting room with me and into the car. It seemed so natural for him to be there, he was so at ease, that the doctors and nurses hardly bothered to comment on his presence. He was simply where it seemed he ought to be: with me.

This, then, may be Izzy's soul, the part of his spirit that fits so easily and completely into my life that it's sometimes hardly noticeable or worth mentioning, and that can enter other people's existences, too, and bring joy just by his presence.

As for Lenore, whose soul seems to involve a determination to bestow on and receive affection from any and all sources, she has crossed all boundaries. She gives and demands love from me, her trainer and feeder and—I admit—bedmate. But also from any human who crosses her path, intimate or stranger. And from the other dogs, even Rose, who thinks playing and romping a silly distraction from what really matters: sheep. Lenore, we'll see, even evokes affection from other species.

I think the stories of these dogs, and of the other animals on my farm, will speak for themselves. People can reach their own conclusions.

Besides, I'm surely not in Aristotle's league. I'm a storyteller, and, having lived with several excellent dogs on this farm, I have stories to tell. I want to explore that mysterious, powerful space where animal and human link and affect one another. Perhaps these stories will help people reach some clarity of their own about the spirits, souls, and meanings of dogs and other animals in their lives.

No dog has affected my life more than Rose, or done more to make my life possible each day. No dog has brought me more joy than Lenore. No dog has introduced me to deep human relationships, or woven himself more thoroughly into my life, than Izzy has.

Every dog is unique, and so is our relationship with him or her. We each know our dog in a different way, in the context of how we live or work with them, what they mean to us, how our own lives have shaped our perceptions of them. If no two dogs are exactly alike, neither is there a universal relationship with them.

One of the wonders of the human–dog experience, often lost in generalizations from gurus and "experts," is that each relationship is one of *individual* experience and meaning.

Chapter Two

SNICKERS FOR THE KING

The problem of sanctity and salvation is in fact the
problem of finding out who I am and of discovering
my true self. Trees and animals have no problem. God
makes them what they are without consulting them,
and they are perfectly satisfied. With us it is different.
God leaves us free to be whatever we like.
We can be ourselves or not, as we please.
We are at liberty to be real, or to be unreal.
We may be true or false, the choice is ours.

—THOMAS MERTON,
Seeds of Contemplation

I WAS OUT IN THE PADDOCK, CHECKING ON THE COWS—
Elvis, Harold, and Luna—when I saw a blue pickup truck
suddenly stop on the road below, then back up into my driveway.

Soon, an older man in overalls and a John Deere cap appeared by the gate and introduced himself as Jim, owner of a

slaughterhouse near Schuylerville. "That's a big steer," he said, a common observation when people spot Elvis, my gentle giant.

"Can I ask you a question? Did he come from the Hanks farm? I think I might know him."

It says something about Elvis that somebody merely driving by can recognize him, after having seen him once in a dairy barn nearly two years earlier. Partly it's his enormous size, of course, but there's also his curious, alert, amused expression; it catches humans' attention.

Jim had been buying cows from Peter Hanks, my dairyman friend, and it came time to discuss a price for this steer. He was the only animal to approach Peter and then Jim, to nuzzle them both, and to shy away from the truck bound for the plant.

"Truth is, I offered him a low price, less than he was worth," Jim recounted. "And Peter seemed relieved. We both agreed later that neither one of us wanted to put him on the truck."

Wow. I wondered how many cows had charmed their way off that truck before. None he could readily think of, Jim acknowledged.

So that made three humans, at least, that Elvis had gotten to spare his life or otherwise do his bidding: Peter, a farmer for more than four decades; Jim, owner of a meatpacking plant, and no squish when it came to the fate of livestock; and me, a guy who'd never known a steer before but couldn't abide the thought of sending this guy to his death. Not a bad record for a beast supposedly less intelligent than we were.

Jim came over and scratched Elvis's broad neck. "You are one lucky guy," he said, in some wonder. Elvis gazed at Jim and drooled genially.

OF ALL THE CHALLENGES, joy, surprises, and tribulations of farm life, nothing is more bewildering or difficult to explain than my instant and deepening love for a two-thousand-pound Brown Swiss steer.

From the moment I met him in Pete's barn, Elvis touched me with his affectionate nature and interest in humans. He seemed to somehow be connecting with me. The dozens of other cows were milling around the Big Green Farms' concrete barn, but this big brown one came clomping over, stretched his head over the railing, and pressed it against my chest.

Peter told me that Elvis (whom he called "Brownie," in the best tradition of dairy farmers) was the first animal he'd ever been unable to send to market. Still, he wasn't about to keep Elvis as a pet—that's taboo among dairy farmers, feeding a steer for years and years—and perhaps it raised too many questions for people whose livelihood depends on sending cows to slaughter.

Elvis experienced a different fate: Peter sold him to me for $500, with various complicated provisos and understandings, should I ever send Elvis to market myself (ha). That's a lot of money for a steer who won't do anything in life but eat pricey hay. But less than Elvis was worth as hamburger or steak, as Pete kept pointing out.

Elvis isn't conventionally lovable. The size of a mobile home, he doesn't always move gracefully. He trails clouds of steam, drool, flies, manure. He smells. His cow pies dot the pasture like land mines, and you don't want to be anywhere nearby when he takes one of his enormous whizzes. He has no sense of his own size or strength, so far as I can tell, so I have to be wary when he tiptoes up behind me for a snuggle or swings his head over for a scratch. More than once I've found myself lying a dozen feet away while he looks around for me, puzzled.

It was interesting to see how Rose reacted to the new arrival. One of the rules of the farm is that she's present for every arrival and every departure. I believe she keeps a running inventory of the farm and its creatures in her head, a secret map she's constantly updating. So when a truck pulls up with a new animal, Rose is there to oversee; when an animal dies or is given away, Rose watches it leave.

Through close attention, I think, she knows where things ought to be, or not be—even intimate things. I frequently drop my cell phone while herding or walking in the woods, or sometimes a camera lens cap. The next time Rose is out, she will almost invariably approach the lost object and touch her nose to it, because it wasn't there the day before and thus merits her time and investigation. Rose finds keys, sunglasses, even coins sometimes.

But when Elvis arrived, strangely, Rose didn't seem to even see him. She didn't look at him, react to him, or try to herd him. As massive as he is, he seemed quite invisible to her, and did not enter her long list of responsibilities.

Even now, when I go into the pasture to visit Elvis, Rose waits by the gate; if I call her to join me, she sits about a hundred yards away and looks everywhere but at Elvis. It tells me that Rose knows what isn't her work, as well as what is. My theory is that Elvis is beyond her sense of work, her self-defined job description, so she just makes him go away.

In this way, too, Elvis is a creature apart.

I would do nearly anything for Elvis. Sometimes, I do too much.

In the summer, Elvis and his best beloved, Luna, and their

compatriot, Harold, graze on the steep hillside behind the paddock. In winter, when the grass withers, we feed them hay, the rougher, "first-cut" bales harvested early in summer.

Annie, my helper, totes out two or three bales in the morning and again at dusk. On cold winter days, she adds buckets of grain for energy. In between, the trio take in the sun, or nose around for edible grass, or stare meditatively into the distance. I thought they had everything they needed.

A couple of months after Elvis arrived, though, he stuck his head over the paddock gate late one morning and seemed, for the first time, to notice me sitting in my office directly across the driveway, maybe fifty yards away. In summer, with the windows open, he could probably hear me talking on the phone, or maybe the bings and bongs of my computer caught his attention. He lowered his head and stared intently, as if he'd spotted a fresh tub of grain. He was there the next morning, and the next.

I took to greeting him, yelling, "Yo, Elvis," or "Morning, dude, how's it going?" This seemed to fascinate him further, and he began lowing in response. We got into the habit of chatting a bit around eleven. I'd come to cherish this monster, for whatever reason, and I enjoyed our hailing each other as I worked.

After a couple of weeks, Elvis leaned his head over the gate one early fall day, fixed his enormous eyes on me, and launched a mournful round of moos and bellows. Was he in trouble or in pain? It definitely struck me as an unhappy call.

My animals usually are not shy about making noise—raising hell, in fact—if they haven't been fed on time. If I attempt to sit down at my desk before breakfast has been served in the barnyard, I'll be looking out my window at a gaggle of braying donkeys, bleating sheep, squawking chickens, and yowling barn cats, all clustered along the gate right across from my study. Woe to anybody who tries to eat before they do.

Hearing Elvis's lament, I left the computer and hustled outside with Rose and Izzy (I'm forever rushing somewhere with Rose and Izzy, the harried commandant with his aides). Elvis was waiting for me, drooling and sniffing and lowering his head, the signal to scratch him behind the ears.

"You okay, big guy?" I asked. What could be the matter? Izzy and I went into the barn, grabbed a bale of hay, and dragged it out to the feeder. Elvis came loping over and started wolfing down mouthfuls of hay, soon joined by Luna and Harold.

I felt a surge of satisfaction to see them chowing down, especially Elvis, who'd apparently been making a personal appeal for sustenance. I closed up the barn, called the dogs, and went into the house and back to the computer, at ease and ready to work. All was well in the world. No sad cow eyes were fixed on me, no lowing directed toward my window.

A couple of hours later, Annie came and, as scheduled, fed Elvis and the others again.

Annie misses nothing. The strewn-about fresh hay was a clue that Elvis was having a midday snack. "Why is all this hay lying around?" she asked, eyeing me suspiciously.

Cornered, I went on the offensive. "They aren't getting enough food," I argued. "They were hungry. You're starving the cows."

"They get plenty," she said. "Elvis is playing you. You can't refuse him anything."

Annie and I take turns playing hard-ass. With the sheep, I'm the tough one, always muttering about whether they really need the peanuts Annie likes to distribute by hand. But

Annie is tougher with cows, muttering about waste, chastising them for not going outside the paddock to graze. "If you give them less," she scolded, "they'll eat more of what they already have. Believe me, they're fine."

But I didn't quite believe her. A bale or two of hay didn't seem like much of a meal for this crew. Elvis had been pleading with me for food, so he must have needed it. He was hardly smart enough to manipulate me.

Even the eagle-eyed Annie didn't grasp, for a while, that I was secretly ferrying hay to Elvis every day. In fact, I denied it. "Just once in a while," I said, "when you don't give him enough."

To be candid, it's very difficult to look at Elvis—from any angle—and conclude that he's undernourished. But he induced me to believe it. We fell into a secret routine: around noon, he came to the gate, stared for ten or fifteen minutes, then began his piteous call. I came out, hauled over a bale of hay, then returned to work. With hundreds of bales of hay stacked in the barn, nobody—not even Annie—noticed the disappearance of one a day.

Sometimes, I had to thwack Elvis on the nose to make him wait while I lifted the hay into the feeder and cut the baling string with my pocketknife. He didn't seem to mind these swats, or even really notice them.

Otherwise, in his enthusiasm, he'd grab the bale and pull it and me halfway across the paddock while I shouted and cursed. I began training him, more or less successfully, to stay.

Between meals, I visited often, usually toting carrots, apples, or chunks of stale bread, all of which he enjoyed, plus some less organic treats. A farmer from Cossayuna who stopped to admire Elvis shortly after he came to the farm told me he had a favorite steer a few years back to whom he of-fered a Baby Ruth from time to time. "He sure loved that candy bar," he said.

Elvis, it turned out, loved Snickers. Merely unwrapping one within earshot caused him to swivel his head and make a beeline for me, a sometimes unnerving sight.

Once or twice, after inhaling the candy (king-sized, of course), he sneezed, showering me with globs of chocolate drool. Now I stand to the side while he munches. After he's done, he lowers his head and I scratch his head and shoulders.

SOMETIMES, in ice storms or heavy rain, I feel guilty about leaving the cows outside. Perhaps I should usher them into the barn? But vets and bovine experts all agree that cows don't need to be indoors, and if they're not being milked, it's neither necessary nor, in most cases, good for them.

Besides, as I've learned the hard way, it's difficult for a small farmer to handle the mélange of straw, water, manure, and muck that ensues when cows spend time in barns. Within a day or two, the interior is a fetid mess—a mess that grows rank in summer, freezes in winter, and is very difficult in any season to move without a tractor.

So Elvis, Luna, and Harold, a black-and-white Holstein, stay outside. We built a large tin-roofed feeder to keep the hay dry, but also to shelter them from the worst of the ele-ments.

Of all the creatures I know, on my farm or off, Elvis lives most in the moment, his world bounded by hay feeder and fence, trees and grass, and whatever materializes in front of him to look at. Unlike the donkeys, he's not a curious crea-ture, not that I can see. He's mostly interested in things that affect him—the other cow and steer, people carrying hay or grain, me and the contents of my pockets. He seems drawn to life on the farms in the valley below, staring intently at them and whatever movement of tiny animals and tractors he can see.

Sometimes he puts his head down to sniff Izzy or one of the other dogs. When people enter the pasture, I see him check them out and, if he thinks they have food, amble over.

He does radiate a sense of contentment. Since he spent the first few years of his life almost entirely indoors, I like to think that he appreciates the view.

As Thomas Merton suggests, Elvis seems perfectly satisfied with the way he's made. He doesn't seem to miss anything, to aspire to something beyond.

Does he have bovine thoughts as he grazes? Who knows? Unlike dogs, cows are rarely given much stimulation— exercise, games, human socialization, work—that can increase intelligence, interaction, and alertness. Domesticated since foregone times, cows are now mostly confined, fed, then milked or slaughtered. Local farmers can't even tell me how old cows live to be, since few can afford to let them live very long.

We don't bring cows into our homes, speak to them or train them, or take them to play groups.

Nor have cows learned to manipulate humans the way dogs have, to worm their way into human homes, social lives, and beds.

Or have they?

THE MORE I PAID ATTENTION, the more it seemed Elvis had more going on inside that great head than might appear.

Over the few months I'd had him, I'd noticed changes. He'd lost his skittishness around people, for instance. When he first arrived, he backed away from most humans, as if he expected to get whacked.

Now he invariably ambled over to visitors for a sniff and a scratch. In fact, I had to be careful: Elvis seemed so sociable that people wanted to pat him, but one swing of that head could do significant damage. And when Elvis got excited and danced around a bit, you wanted visitors in flip-flops to be on the opposite side of the fence.

Still, he liked people, and associated them with good things. And why not? This animal was no fool.

Plus he'd really begun to focus on me. One of my bedrock principles of animal acclimation—the way I introduce new creatures to the farm—is to make sure I bring them food the first time they see me, and every time for months. It's a principle I first learned in training a puppy: If a dog learns to associate you with food, if you hand feed to him and say his name while he eats, he will pay attention to you, bond with you.

Food, after all, is not a gourmet experience to a cow or a donkey; it's survival. Bring a donkey a cookie every morning, month after month, and the donkey will come to see you as a source of nourishment, safety, satisfaction—as life itself.

Bringing Elvis his king-sized Snickers, calling his name, stroking his neck and shoulders, touching and handling him wasn't just indulging him. I wanted him to be as relaxed and people-friendly as the other animals on the farm.

Food is underrated in the human-animal bond, because so many people want their dogs and other pets to love them out of choice or preference, not for baser reasons. Food doesn't feel personal enough. We want other explanations for their attachment to us. *He understands me. He loves me unconditionally. He needs me.*

How tempting to write the Elvis story that I and everybody else would love: A cow confined to a lonely barn is fated to go to market. I save him, and in gratitude he loves and trusts me. A neat parable. I would prefer it myself to what I see, day by day, as the more likely truth: Elvis is savvy about manipulating humans, much savvier than his barnmates.

He understands on some instinctive level that if he pays attention to humans, reacts to them, draws close to them, lets them touch him and admire him, then they will bring him food and other sustenance, and they won't put him on that somehow scary truck.

Elvis, I suspect, is a gifted animal. His talent lies not in strategizing or reasoning but in just the sort of highly developed social skills that anthropologist Brian Hare writes about: Elvis has learned how to manipulate humans, how to read their behavior, to latch on to those who show some interest or attachment, and to get them to save his life. That social skill is, in many ways, his soul.

Like a lot of nonfarmers with farms, I tended to overfeed my animals at first. I'm learning not to; it's expensive for me and unhealthy for them. I'm still a sucker for the donkeys, if they bray mournfully at me, but I'm trying to steel myself.

Curiously, I'm impervious to the importuning stares of dogs, even Labs, better understanding their blatant panhandling and the dangers of overfeeding. But Elvis had become master of the whiny moo.

It was a couple of months later that Sarah Bagley, the large-animal vet, came by to give the sheep their rabies shots.

While Sarah readied her syringes, Rose rounded up the sheep, moved them into the training pen, then lay down by the gate to prevent escapes.

Sheepherding on TV is lovely, civilized-looking, all those people with nice clothes and whistles, all those beautiful, skilled dogs. Real work with sheep is rarely so picturesque. The ground in the pen, already muddy, grew far messier as the sheeps' hooves dug it up and their droppings got mixed in.

Annie and Sarah and I caught the sheep with hands and crooks, wrestled them into positions where they couldn't move, gave each its shots and X'ed its forehead with a marker so we knew which had been inoculated. Sheep have only one weapon for dealing with trouble—flight—and will try to run, kick, or jump, so this was intensely physical, sometimes even dangerous, work. After a couple of hours, we were exhausted, sore, and covered in crud. Rose was her usual stellar self, holding the sheep in a corner of the pen, chasing down the occasional escapee, escorting the sheep out when we were done. As I did almost daily, I gave thanks for her.

Before she packed up her truck Sarah said she wanted to take a look at the cows and give them rabies shots, too. Scraping the top layer of mud from our boots and clothes, we walked through the barn and into the paddock. Sarah went out to pat Elvis, who looked at her and lowered his head for scratching.

"Hey, sweet guy," she said, then turned to Annie and me. "He's getting a bit tubby, though. Maybe cut back on the grain for a while."

Busted.

I got a ten-minute lecture from Dr. Bagley about the dangers of obesity in cows. Elvis, she assured me, wasn't obese, but we wanted to keep it that way.

Ha! Annie was triumphant.

So I stopped catering Elvis's lunch.

BUT WHAT WAS REALLY GOING ON in my pasture? If Elvis was getting enough food, why was I feeding him more? Why did I feel the *need* to feed him more?

James Serpell, who teaches at the University of Pennsylvania Veterinary School and is one of my favorite writers about the human-animal bond, knows a lot about anthropomorphism—the attribution of human thoughts, feelings, motivations, and beliefs to nonhuman animals—and its implications for our relationships with animals.

On the human side, Serpell writes in "Anthropomorphism and Anthropomorphic Selection—Beyond the Cute Response" (published in the journal *Society and Animals*), anthropomorphic thinking enables us to see animal behavior in human terms, using our own language, our own motivations and thought processes.

The attribution of human-style emotions to animals isn't just about our seeing them as "cute," Serpell argues. It's much more significant, explaining not only why Elvis seems to have bonded with me, but also why I'm drawn to giving him more food than he needs.

On the animal side, anthropomorphism contributes enormously to animals' evolution, molding the behavior, even the anatomy and appearance, of companion-animal species, says Serpell, "so as to adapt them to their unusual and growing niche as our social support providers."

What's interesting about Elvis isn't his sweet nature, but the fact that he has done so much better for himself than most steers. Steers are not normally considered "companion animals," like dogs and cats. But Elvis has managed to become one, and is being treated accordingly. Neither Luna nor Harold pay much attention to me, or to other humans. It costs them a lot of Snickers bars.

Admittedly knowing better, I've come to see Elvis as cute, loving, needy, and grateful. In reality, he's a crafty steer who's moved further up the evolutionary chain than most of his buddies, and has figured out how to get the human in his life to hop up and fetch him hay bales, even though he's already well fed, even though the human has many better things to do. Not only that, but other humans, with the exception of real farmers, think the whole thing's adorable.

Pet keeping is odd—Serpell calls it "an anomalous activity"—from an evolutionary standpoint. It's easy to see why we raise sheep or chickens or pigs, who pay their way in wool, eggs, meat, and hides. But why, he asks, do we need Siamese cats or miniature schnauzers? Or, he might have added, giant steers who drool and consume staggering amounts of hay?

Pets are expensive; they belong to a different species; they can't remember or return past favors or debts; they may even bite or scratch.

And Elvis is a particularly burdensome pet, if you can call him that. Rose earns her keep every day. Izzy is my companion on the farm. Even the affable donkeys play a useful role, guarding the sheep from coyotes and the chickens from foxes. Elvis makes no such contribution.

Yet I have seen him, from the first, as a steer with spiritual dimensions, perhaps even a soul. So, obviously this relationship does something that *I* need, that's beneficial to me.

Actually, it does a number of things, as researchers have found. Pet owners are more resistant to the stressful effects of trauma and "negative life events." They have fewer health problems and go to the doctor less often than non–pet owners. The acquisition of pets, studies show, often results in less stress, lower blood pressure, and longer life spans.

Moreover, pets represent a form of social support. Different researchers define this term differently, but in general, "social support" is whatever leads people to believe that they're cared for, that they're loved and valued, that they're connected to others and have the ability to nurture and protect them in turn.

For humans, social support is critically important, as has been acknowledged throughout human history, notes Serpell. A relationship in which a person believes that he is cared for, loved, esteemed, part of a network of mutual obligations, is helpful to him, both physically and emotionally.

"The socially supportive potential of pets," Serpell writes, "should therefore hinge on their ability to produce similar effects by behaving in ways that make their owners believe that the animal cares for and loves them, holds them in high esteem, and depends on them for care and protection."

Serpell's analysis, a big idea that speaks to the lives of millions of animal lovers, was revelatory for me. I was reading about Elvis, understanding with sudden and belated clarity why I was dragging hay to him in the middle of the day.

It seemed good for him, at least at first, but it was even better for me. It let me believe that Elvis cared for me, that he was more attached to me than to any other human, even Annie, and that he depended on me.

Elvis had somehow come to grasp what my dogs, and so many dogs, rely on: Because humans often feel isolated and undervalued, the prospect of unconditional love, the sense of being needed, the opportunity to be affectionate and compassionate, not only *feels* good to me, it *is* good for me. And good for the animals who maneuver, and perhaps even strategize in some primal, instinctive way, to keep those impulses alive in us. This is the reason we love dogs so much and treat them so well.

Elvis is nothing if not a good learner. His head still appears over the gate around noon, he still fixes those huge brown eyes on me and moos mournfully. Hey, it's worth a try. I continue to greet him in return, saying hi, calling his name.

After the vet visit, though, there were no more noon hay runs.

I understood that I was being manipulated. I understood that Elvis was acting not out of need but opportunistically, though instinctively. I was, after all, a human and Elvis was a large and dumb beast—just not as simple as I'd thought.

"The hell with you," I shouted from the study one frosty January day. "You're not getting any more hay." But I went out anyway with a huge Snickers bar.

It was cold. I thought he might need the energy.

Chapter Three

HENRIETTA,
HEN OF ENTITLEMENT

To me, animals have all the traits indicative of soul.
For soul is not something we can see or measure. . . .
No one can prove that animals have souls. Asking for
proof would be like demanding proof that I love my
wife and children, or wanting me to prove that
Handel's *Messiah* is a glorious masterpiece of music.
Some truths simply cannot be demonstrated. But if
we open our hearts to other creatures and allow
ourselves to sympathize with their joys and struggles,
we will find they have the power to touch and
transform us. There is an inwardness in other creatures
that awakens what is innermost in ourselves.

—THE REVEREND GARY KOWALSKI,
The Souls of Animals

FIRST A WORD ABOUT HENRIETTA'S LINEAGE. HER MOTHER
is one of my hens, a tawny variety known as a Buff Or-
pington, a none-too-bright eating and pecking (and, on oc-

casion, laying) machine. If this chicken has a soul, personality, or identity beyond scratching for bugs and birdseed, it's not apparent to me.

Her father, on the other hand, is a major figure hereabouts. Winston, a big, speckled rooster, was injured on a neighboring farm in the line of duty, defending his hens against a hawk attack. For his troubles, Winston's left leg was mangled, and he hobbles on it like a proud veteran.

A serious rooster who crows at odd times for no apparent reason, he isn't nasty or violent, like some, but keeps a close eye on his hens, racing over (he can move pretty fast, even with his bad leg) if there's any trouble. When a visiting beagle rushed out of a car and headed for one of the hens last summer, Winston came hurtling across the barnyard before the dog could get too close. Like some demonic fury, the rooster was crowing and clamoring, wings outstretched, all puffed up and ready for battle.

I joke that Winston and I may end up together in a South Florida trailer park one day, hobbling around and taking in the sun. I also remind myself that it's not that much of a joke.

TWO YEARS AGO I found Winston near death, lying stiffly on the concrete floor of the barn in deep winter. I went to get my rifle, intending to put him out of his misery, and my friend Peter Hanks, dairy farmer, set off to fetch his ax. "You don't waste a bullet on a chicken," he explained. But Annie, my helper and a true animal lover, swept the frozen Winston into her arms, fed him soup and potions, installed hay beds and heatlamps, and restored him to health. Now he's not only alive, but a proud dad.

Henrietta hatched last summer. From the half dozen eggs

her mother was sitting on (the hen had hidden away in the garden, and it was some time before we found her), Henrietta was the only hatchling.

Annie promptly whisked her and her squawking mother out of the garden and into the tiny old milkhouse, installing a heatlamp, waterer, and generous supplies of corn, grain, vitamins, and special baby-chick feed.

Annie intended to keep Henrietta in the nursery, as I called it, for a year or so. She was concerned about Mother, the barn cat, who'd been eyeing the chick lustfully for days. Mother is sweet and agreeable, as long as you aren't a chipmunk, squirrel, mole, rat, or mouse, all of which she stalks. Their dismembered corpses litter the grounds.

But Mother shares the barn amicably with the chickens; they apparently enjoy some sort of exemption. Besides, I've learned the hard way that chickens are tougher than they look. Maybe Winston had persuaded Mother that coexistence was the wisest course.

So Annie and I squabbled about when Henrietta could leave the milkhouse. In the time-honored tradition of men pushing their kids out to make their way, I argued that Henrietta was ready to take on the world, or at least the barnyard. Annie reluctantly agreed.

We put heavy gloves on and tackled the outraged, squawking mom until we got her chick out into the barn. Annie outfitted one of the stalls with a feeder, water, and nesting box.

Mother circled the newcomers but somehow categorized Henrietta correctly—"chicken"—and both she and Annie relaxed. As for Henrietta, she greatly relished her newfound freedom, scuttling past Mother and outside into the barnyard, where she pushed the sheep and donkeys aside and went to work, pecking at spilled hay and feed, seeking out the good stuff.

The animal population is in constant flux here, as newcomers and departees change the character of the place. Carol, my first donkey, was a major presence until she died suddenly at the onset of our second winter here. So was Orson, my first border collie, whom I sorrowfully put down the following summer.

When Jeannette, the oldest donkey, joined the clan, she seemed to immediately take charge, dominating the barnyard with her noisy bray, unquenchable appetite, and pushy ways. "Bossy boots," Annie huffed, as Jeannette routinely elbowed the others aside while Annie attempted to distribute carrots and brush the donkeys' shaggy coats. (They eventually reached an accommodation.) Myself, I'd call Rose the farm's most dominant creature. But early last winter, just after she emerged from protective custody, I began to notice that Henrietta was different. Chickens are highly predictable creatures, usually—I can't recall one surprising me before—but this one was strange.

WHAT CAN I SAY about chickens?

I admire them because they're industrious, always busy— the only truly useful creatures on the farm. They eat bugs and ticks; they supply our eggs; and if they're not too complex or expressive, that's fine with me.

At first light, accompanied by imperial bugling from Winston, they march purposefully out of the barn and make their regular circuit: They hoover up the scattered seed beneath the bird feeder, then try to raid Mother's dish of dry cat food, then circle the farmhouse, pecking for grubs, worms, and other things I can't see.

They march up the pasture and then down, over to the hay feeder and around again, covering a lot of ground, all the while muttering and exclaiming, perhaps critiquing the menu.

Chickens don't seem bright to me, but, like most animals, they're smart about food. When they see me opening a can of birdseed, or bringing them bread crumbs, they come toddling over at full speed. When they see Annie, they come squawking double-time, as they've learned that her pockets are filled with treats.

They appreciate dietary supplements—stale bread, cold spaghetti, the bits of potato chips from the bottom of the bag, and leftover homemade chili. But nothing slows their rounds for long. They're unfazed by nearly everything— cows, donkeys, dogs, me.

Winston, venerable and proud, sometimes accompanies the hens and sometimes sits off by himself, keeping an eye on things. He is the only animal on the farm, other than Rose, who ever got close to Orson. The two of them often sat side by side, napping or taking in the view. Sometimes, I see Winston up the hill near Orson's grave and wonder if he's visiting.

At dusk, led by Winston, the chickens all file into the barn, fuss a bit, then hop onto their roosts and veg out.

The hens lay an egg apiece every other day or so—unless it's too hot or too cold. Or they're too old. Or something has been moved around. Simple organisms, they aren't picky or demanding. Creatures of habit and devotees of routine, they rarely cause trouble and are surprisingly self-sufficient.

So it came as a surprise to see young Henrietta flap her

wings one December day and hop right up onto Jeannette's broad back. Jeannette can be grumpy about assaults on her dignity or invasions of her space (just try taking her temperature with a rectal thermometer), but she seemed to enjoy hosting Henrietta. At least she took no action to shake her off. This practice continued.

Sometimes Henrietta, who carries Winston's speckled gray coloring, pecked away at bugs or specks of hay and dried manure that collected on Jeannette's back. Sometimes she just soaked up the warmth of her shaggy fur and dozed, or surveyed the barnyard.

I looked up at various times to see Henrietta aboard other animals—a good-natured ewe known only as Number 57, the older ewe named Paula, enormous Elvis, and his daintier companion, Luna.

Henrietta carried herself differently from the other hens. Perhaps because of her status as Winston's only child, she had an air of entitlement, a willingness to be apart from the flock and to do things other chickens don't.

I looked out my study window one morning to see Henrietta amid the huddle of the sheep around the hay feeder, perched atop the bale as the sheep munched away.

The other hens pay absolutely no attention to my dogs. But Henrietta marched right up to Izzy one afternoon as he lay quietly outside the pasture gate and peered down quizzically, staring at him for so long that he grew unnerved. Unlike Rose, Izzy has no ambition to run a farm and no taste for conflict with any creature. He got up and skittered off.

NOTHING MUCH on the farm happens without Rose's scrutiny or approval. She's always watching, constantly taking inventory. If a ewe drifts out of sight, Rose will seek her out; if a lamb is lying up in the field by herself, Rose will go investigate. My name might be on the deed, but the farm is clearly Rose's place.

So it was only a matter of hours before Rose noticed this strange new chicken behavior. Henrietta was settled comfortably aboard Number 57, and when Rose came outdoors, she did a double take. Rose has a manual in her head at all times for how sheep are supposed to behave and where they are supposed to be. Clearly, no chicken is mentioned in the regulations. She shot over to chase the chicken away.

Number 57, who has known Rose for several years now, bolted toward the flock, just up the hill. The young hen squawked and shrieked—she made a strangely high-pitched sound, almost like a turkey—and then hopped down to the ground.

Rose dislikes deviations from the ordinary, especially when they happen without her knowledge or consent. "Whoa, Rosie," I yelled, from a few feet away. "Leave her alone."

Normally, when Rose gives a chicken—or anything—her famous piercing border collie "eye," the animal moves. But Henrietta merely looked indignant, stalked over to Rose, and got in her face, clucking and squeaking like a rubber toy.

I doubted the outcome of this face-off would be good news for Henrietta, but I'd also learned over the years to trust Rose, who as a rule didn't injure other living things (except for belligerent rams and the occasional small bat she pulled out of the night air). Nor did she back down.

As Rose stared, poised to move, Henrietta flounced around behind her and simply sat down on the ground. Now Rose was truly befuddled. Henrietta settled in, complaining still about the loss of her woolly resting place; then she closed her eyes and went to sleep. Winston came lurching over to see if there was trouble, but he and Rose had a longtime understanding and never messed with each other.

So Rose backed up a few feet, still staring at Henrietta, perhaps wondering, as I was, exactly what this odd bird was up to.

Rose paused for a few seconds, then skirted Henrietta and went off to push the sheep around. I told Paula later that I'd encountered my first empowered hen.

THIS *WAS* ONE UNUSUAL HEN. One morning as I brought Mother a can of cat food (though she found plenty of rodents to kill, she was more likely to present them to me as trophies than to actually eat them, so I still fed her), Henrietta watched me intently. Then before Mother could have more than a mouthful, she quickly swooped over to Mother's bowl. I half expected Henrietta's speckled head to join the next delivery of body parts deposited at the back door, but, to my surprise, Mother backed off. A moment later, Henrietta hustled her right out of the barn.

I surveyed the farmers I knew: Had they ever known a chicken who rode on donkeys or sheep, or who pushed a barn cat right off her bowl? They were unanimous: Never.

Ordinarily, I'd fall solidly in the chickens–don't–have–souls camp. I might land there yet. But Henrietta certainly had an animating spirit.

Day by day, her distinct personality slowly emerged as she evolved from a protected chick to an imperious hen. She was curious, explorative, alert, experimentally inclined, and fearless.

I don't know if Henrietta understood how different she was from others of her kind, nor did it matter all that much. It was enough to enjoy her funny, beguiling presence.

STILL, the question lingers: Did she have a personality? A consciousness? Did she choose in some instinctual or other way to behave differently? Is self-awareness a uniquely human attribute, or can other animals, like Henrietta, also develop a sense of self?

Hard to say, conclude researchers Marc Bekoff and Paul Sherman, professors of ecology and evolutionary biology at the University of Colorado in Boulder. "Although laypersons and researchers from many disciplines have long been interested in animal self-knowledge, few unambiguous conclusions are available," they wrote in a paper titled "Reflections on Animal Selves."

In social animals, they note, the demands of living—cooperation, competition, the maintenance of bonds, and the avoidance of being cheated or bested—have fostered increased mental intricacy.

And chickens *are* social animals. They travel together, co-exist with larger, more dominant species, and have to find ways to evade or defend against numerous predators—foxes, coyotes, badgers, raccoons, hawks. Cats. Dogs. Humans.

Of course, multiple explanations are possible for my feisty hen. Winston navigated the farm with great confidence and skill, so perhaps Henrietta inherited his boldness. She was also the first chicken to be born on the farm. Perhaps because she grew up here, and the other animals were familiar to her from the first, she had less fear of them.

So she immediately took advantage of their presence, hopping onto a ewe on a cold morning and nestling into five inches of cozy fleece. I believe the other hens would have frozen to death before thinking to do that.

The animals' backs also provided tasty buffets; Henrietta

found lots of good stuff to eat there, from bits of hay and grain to parasites and smudges of manure.

If any other animal had tried to ride Jeannette, it would have gotten kicked halfway to Vermont. Why didn't the donkeys mind Henrietta? What did they and the sheep pick up from her that caused them to accept her? I chalked it up to her confidence: Henrietta acted as if she belonged everywhere, and perhaps that made it so.

Researchers say animals "know" they are similar to, but distinct from, others of the same species. For example, they rarely try to mate with another species (although I have seen new lambs nursing from donkeys). They travel as a coordinated unit, without collisions. But, Bekoff and Sherman concede, "There is no agreed-upon, objective way to assess the degree of self-cognizance of an individual."

I wondered too, why the other chickens didn't notice—and adopt—Henrietta's innovative warming and feeding techniques. They seemed utterly unaware of her individuality.

Contrast these birds with Rose, whose animating spirit is so much more evident. Henrietta, however amusing, didn't function at anywhere near that level.

While it's equally impossible to say just what's going on inside her head, it seems almost inconceivable to me, watching Rose work—day after day, on my farm and others, for years now—that she doesn't have a sense of herself as different from other animals, and of the others as distinct from one another.

She treats sheep differently from donkeys. She won't herd, or even notice, a hulking steer, correctly assessing that he can't be herded and that it would be folly to try. Her presence, authority, and work ethic are all distinct traits; she seems to grasp her role in the complex social system of a farm.

EVERY NIGHT before bed, Rose and I make the final rounds of the farm. I bring a powerful lamp whose beam can reach all the way to the top of the pasture. Rose and I have made these bed checks literally a thousand times by now, so we know the drill. We can both sense anything out of the ordinary— a donkey in the wrong place, an urgent bleat from a ewe or lamb.

I pull on a jacket. Rose heads for the door. I check my cell phone; sometimes I have needed it out there at night.

I sweep the meadow with the lantern, see that the sheep are huddled together on the hill, that the donkeys have gathered in the pole barn for the night.

Unlatching the gate, I walk over to the barn and slide the door open. Rose is alongside me at every step, her eyes sweeping along with the lantern light, taking in things I haven't begun to see or even suspect.

I look in on the chickens' roost to make sure no raccoons or other predators are lurking. On this particular December night, I spotted Winston and the two golden hens, but no Henrietta, which was slightly alarming.

"Heads up, Rose," I hissed, her signal to pay attention. Her ears went up and she tensed, then skittered off ahead, deeper into the barn. If something was amiss, Rose would let me know.

Meanwhile, where was Mother? She always greeted me when I entered the barn, balancing on the rafters, literally climbing the walls, purring and meowing for food and ear-scratching. Did Mother change her mind about tolerating

Henrietta? Did Henrietta wander off and meet a coyote or fox? Rose circled and sniffed as I moved farther into the darkened barn.

I heard purring and shone my lantern toward it.

Mother was curled on a pile of straw in the stall, eyes half closed, making sounds of contentment. Henrietta had perched right nearby on the wooden wall that separated the stalls, settled into the vegetative trance chickens enter at night.

Rose stared at this duo, but there was nothing to involve us further. Mother seemed pretty vegetative herself. I'd never seen behavior quite like this, but that was becoming par for the course.

I turned off the light, closed up the barn, and went to bed.

A FEW MORNINGS LATER, I went out to the barn. Rose usually heads like a rocket to the pasture gate, but this time she veered off sharply to the right, heading for the road. Something was wrong.

I walked to the edge of the driveway and froze. Henrietta was lying dead in the road. I could remember hearing a car speed by in the night, then hit its brakes, and I had wondered, sleepily, about it. Henrietta had almost surely dashed across the road and been hit.

She did dart across the road too quickly sometimes, unlike my other chickens, who seemed to know to stay away.

Rose came up to Henrietta and sniffed her, perhaps crossing the hen off her farm inventory list. Rose didn't waste time on sentiment.

I felt Henrietta; her body was already stiffening in the cold.

I picked her up and carried her back to the farmhouse door. I got a trash bag and put her body inside. Then I called Rose and I climbed onto the four-wheeler and ran out to the woods about half a mile.

Rose loped alongside. As always, she was present when an animal came to the farm, and present when one left.

She watched curiously as I stopped, walked out into the woods, and dumped Henrietta out of the bag, onto the ground.

I left her as a gift to the coyotes and the other woodland predators. I didn't wish to bury a chicken, nor hold a ceremony for her; it didn't seem appropriate.

"Goodbye, Henrietta," I said. "You were a pretty interesting chicken."

Chapter Four

MURDEROUS MOTHER

Ultimately, I fear, the question of whether
consciousness, forethought, reasoning, imagery and
rational planning exist in species other than our own
simply can't be answered conclusively until we have
gathered a lot more scientific data. What is more,
in animals, where language is not possible,
it is difficult even to know what evidence would be
sufficient to prove or disprove the existence of
consciousness and all its trappings.

—STANLEY COREN,
The Intelligence of Dogs

MOTHER, THE BARN CAT, MAY BE THE SINGLE MOST AF-
fectionate animal on Bedlam Farm, apart from the dogs.
Whenever I go into the barn or the pasture, she pops up, meowing and wrapping herself around my leg, or leaping onto
a convenient fencepost or stump so I can scratch her ears.

Mother often strolls along with me at night, darting

through the brush to keep up as I make my final rounds. Sometimes she even comes onto the front porch to yowl and draw me outside, where she takes possession of my lap while we stare out at the valley below, the farmhouses and barns bright pinpricks of light in the vast dark.

She's delighted when I pick her up and rub her head, which I do, faithfully. She's particularly delighted when I bring her special treats like a can of sardines.

She makes contact with me at no small risk. Rose has never fully accepted a cat's presence in her realm. Rose has had her nose raked and bloodied more than once by this tough little cat but won't acknowledge defeat. Mostly, the two of them maintain a wary truce.

Mother came to me as a young cat, a ratty wisp of a thing. A tortoiseshell with lovely black and white and ginger fur, she'd gotten her name because she watched out for everybody's kittens, not just her own. But the farmer who gave her to me had enough cats, and had no use for her. I did; my barns were overrun with rats and mice—what farm isn't?—and I didn't want to turn to pesticides.

I had Mother spayed, gave her the proper shots, and brought her a steady stream of kibble and canned food to help her fill out. It didn't seem to quell her desire to hunt, however. I don't have a rodent problem anymore.

I love Mother. She's my first cat, and she's taught me about the wildness cats retain, their indirect ways of loving, their intelligence, and their determination—unlike that of dogs—to live life on their own terms, not yours.

She has other fans, too. My friend Maria, the artist who works in my studio barn, is happy to have her company. Mother often materializes—especially on cold or stormy nights—and curls up in an old leather chair, purring for hours by the woodstove while Maria works.

Mother also adores Annie, following her around whether Annie is mucking out stalls or feeding sheep.

"Mother," Annie calls early every morning when she arrives and climbs out of her truck. Within seconds, the cat emerges from some crevice, tail up, meowing, and stays beside her, batting at dead leaves or baling wire to amuse herself. When Annie goes into the barn to move hay, Mother follows her, hopping from bale to bale.

The dairy barn is Mother's Palace; she rules with complete authority. She moves around the space like Spider-Man, hurtling straight up posts and across beams, diving behind hay bales, lazing way up in the rafters to soak up the late-afternoon sun. One wall, rising five feet from the floor, and thus safe from the vigilant Rose, is where Mother usually waits for me, purring and batting her enticing golden eyes. What a mysterious creature, I often think, so gentle and affectionate, yet so ferocious and undomesticated.

She has been a barn cat all her life—a tough job, marked by short life spans—and has never spent a night in a human dwelling. On the bitterest, snowiest nights, I invite her inside the farmhouse, but she never accepts.

Barn cats are mythic creatures hereabouts. They're hardy, and they have to be: Farmers can rarely pay for their immunizations or veterinary treatments. So barn cats fall prey to all kinds of trouble—they get felled by disease, hit by cars, attacked by predators, including people who shoot them for sport. Those fates, I'm determined, won't befall Mother. She does get medical treatment. She doesn't have to roam, because I feed her every day. And since she'll never come inside,

Annie has made a hay igloo for Mother that I wouldn't mind sleeping in, most nights.

Still, Mother is a barn cat. Every couple of months, she vanishes, for reasons I never know, and I worry that a coyote has gotten her, or that one of the pickups that zoom up and down the hilly road in front of my farm has hit her. After two or three days, she always returns. But one day, I suspect, she won't. That, too, is the lot of the barn cat.

HOWEVER LOVINGLY Mother greets me, she's also the most deadly creature I've ever known.

Mother is all about mayhem and violence. When she isn't cuddling with one of her many human friends and admirers, she is killing things. She kills mice and rats, of course, but also birds—any kind she can. She kills moles and chipmunks and eviscerates frogs, toads, and snakes.

When I come outside each morning, I find dismembered animals, or parts thereof, left as gifts for me: rodent limbs, birds' heads and wings, unidentifiable organs.

I frequently look out my study window to see Mother stalking or playing with a corpse, tossing mice or birds in the air and catching them, batting them around. Most of my farm animals are placid vegetarians. Not this one.

UNTIL I HAD BACK TROUBLE one winter, I'd been caring for the swelling population of Bedlam Farm largely by myself, hauling hay and water, tending to hooves, dispensing grain and feed.

Even after treatment helped relieve my pain, I knew I couldn't handle all the chores any longer. Square bales of hay look light, but they weigh fifty pounds each. I sometimes lean more heavily than I used to on my walking sticks.

I hired Annie to haul the hay and grain buckets around on weekdays. Maria, a restorer of old buildings as well as an artist, helps out on weekends in exchange for the use of the studio barn.

So I was looking forward to Christmas, an unseasonably warm day, when Annie would be off duty and Maria away, and I was once again alone with my animal charges. My only plans were to bring some friends their Christmas presents, then hang around the farm and read by the kindly wood-stoves, walk with the dogs. It was a bittersweet holiday; my wife, Paula, and I had separated earlier in the year. Emma, my daughter, was covering a New York Giants game and would arrive in a few days with Pearl, the sweet-tempered yellow Lab she'd borrowed (with no real intent to return her) for fledgling-writer support.

So Christmas was very quiet—no phone calls, no visitors, no plans. It was a good day to hang around with the sheep and donkeys, cows and chickens, species that were some of the original participants in that long-ago manger scene (well, except for the chickens).

I got up early, took Rose and Izzy out to the barn. Rose's role is to hold the hungry sheep at bay while I drag out the hay and fill the feeders. Izzy, still useless when it comes to farm tasks, merely lies down and looks appealing. I spent a long time watching Mother, who jumped onto my shoulder, purred as I stroked her, then headed off to slay something.

This is what Aristotle and Aquinas were trying to get at, in the harsher, more limited contexts of their own times. This is what they were trying to say. As I watched Mother, things grew clearer.

Mother is not loving or good, I thought. Nor is she evil. She's the embodiment of animal instincts, not of the sensitive rational soul Aristotle goes on and on about. She represents the very thing so many people don't want to believe about their pets—that they don't think like us, don't choose us consciously or rationally, are not able to make moral decisions, and so can't be held responsible for what they do. In certain central respects, in fact, Mother is the antithesis of what people mean by souls.

If dogs and cats are like us, think like us, have souls like ours, then Mother is the Khmer Rouge, a brutal killer who massacres indiscriminately. She's no sweet soul bound for heaven.

But I suspect that, instead, she's a remarkable animal, bristling with instinct, acting out genetically encoded impulses while keeping my farm remarkably free of rats. She's amazing, admirable.

I love the birds that visit the feeder hung outside my study window. Blue jays, woodpeckers, chickadees, sparrows, swallows, cardinals, robins—one or two have even landed briefly on my outstretched arm or shoulder on occasion. They fill the day with song and color and beauty.

It's not easy to sit at my desk day after day and watch them get slaughtered, especially when my own feeders are helping to lure them to their deaths. Mother, it turns out, hides behind the garbage cans below the feeders and when her prey come for sunflower seeds and suet, she pounces. I moved the trash cans, but Mother merely found another hiding place behind the adjacent stone wall. I've raised and moved the feeders, but wherever they are, seed spills out onto the ground, birds swoop down on it, and Mother routinely picks them off, one after another.

Mother doesn't just murder; she seems to enjoy prolonging her victims' suffering. She maims before she kills. Drawn by awful screams, I caught her torturing baby rabbits one afternoon in the big barn across the street, and briefly wanted to kick her. I caught myself, of course, reminding myself it was just her instinct, her genes being true to her history.

Watching her stalk a field mouse on Christmas Day, I reflected that while our dogs and cats have grown ever more domesticated, while we've become affluent, needy, or perhaps generous enough to treat them extraordinarily well, Aristotle's argument has held up.

If Mother were equal to or superior to humans in her self-awareness, consciousness, soul, and spirit; if she were, as so many people say of their pets, "just like a child," then probably I should call the police, have Mother arrested or committed.

For that matter, if that were really my view—that she was a sentient, self-conscious, self-aware, and moral being—shouldn't I punish her severely, or even kill her myself?

Mother wasn't killing in self-defense or for food. She had ample nourishment without these victims. Yet in just a day she'd slaughter two or three or more small, defenseless creatures, simply because it was her nature. And while nobody, surely not I, knows what goes on inside an animal's head, she sure seemed to be having a good time doing it, batting her victims around like Ping-Pong balls.

I'm working to gain some perspective on this conundrum. This killing is, I know, natural for cats. I love Mother anyway, and she shows great affection for me. I not only cherish her, I depend on the very brutality that sometimes startles me. She has vanquished the rats that invaded my farm and barns, stealing food, possibly spreading disease and menacing the other animals. She keeps the mice at bay. An exceptional animal, she teaches me much.

But when notions of good and evil get kicked around, Mother reminds me not to apply them to animals. What

Aristotle argues—that the most precious aspect of the human soul is the ability to reason and make choices, and that since animals can't do that, they can't be compared to us—is so true of Mother that it shocks me. It doesn't mean she is inferior to me, but it bracingly reminds me how different she is. Human-like notions of good or bad can't be applied to her and, for both her sake and ours, they ought not be. We're responsible for the choices we make; she isn't.

Think how many cats, dogs, and other pets suffer from being measured against human notions of good behavior, of how many animals get beaten, abused, even killed, because we judge them by human terms.

IN THE MOST IRONIC of situations, therefore, I was bringing a Christmas gift to my bizarrely contradictory barn cat, offering her a can of yummy, oily sardines while looking warily around the barn floor for any fresh kills.

"Mother," I said, "you are a butcher, an indiscriminate slaughterer of living things that pose no threat, give no food or sustenance, mean you no harm. How can you be so loving to me?"

She meowed in her squeaky way, hopped flirtatiously up onto her favorite post, and—keeping an eye out for Rose—leaped into my arms, purring constantly. We cuddled for a few minutes, our reverie interrupted by bellowing from Elvis, who'd heard my voice and was awaiting his own snack.

"Can't keep Elvis waiting," I told Mother, giving her the last of the sardines. If he got annoyed, he could probably stroll right through the (closed) barn door. Mother hopped down, to accompany me on the rest of my rounds. She was a friend of my cow and steers.

A few minutes later, back in the house, I was watching the songbirds flitting about the feeder. I saw Mother's agile form slink across the driveway and disappear behind the trunk of the tree from which the feeder hung. I banged on the window and yelled, which prompted Rose to bark, and the birds took off. Mother, looking betrayed, trotted back to the barn, but they'd be back, and so would she.

Don't I owe them protection? Shouldn't Mother be stopped, somehow? I could probably find other ways to get rid of rats. But living on a farm is a model for dealing with nature and its simple, unwavering, and sometimes lethal realities. There are no animal rights on a farm, really, only the intricate, intertwined web of species, instinct, and survival.

Every day, the birds and mice and rats still come. They don't understand what awaits them, nor do the experiences of their peers seem to alter their behavior. They—and Mother—act out their timeless rituals. Minutes after a bird is dismembered outside my window, a score more will appear to dine, their lost comrade in full view.

If animals lack human-style consciousness, if they act purely out of instinct, why do we have so much trouble accepting that? Why do we need so badly to remake them in our own image?

In earlier ages, people generally agreed that animals had been placed in the world to be at man's disposal. Genesis taught that man had been given dominion over nature, just as Aristotle insisted that "nature has made all the animals for the sake of men." Human superiority, he wrote, lay in the fact that while plants possessed a "vegetative" soul and animals a "sensitive" soul, humans alone could boast a rational soul.

Today, such notions sound arrogant, outdated. In an on-

going reassessment, animals have become romanticized, emo-
tionalized, humanized. In fact, one hears all the time that animals are our superiors—simpler, more honest, loving,
dependable. We've been demoted, while they're increasingly
considered to have, and deserve, rights, protections, legal
status—and, possibly, an afterlife.

Consider this Milan Kundera poem, meant to express
how much our animals mean to us, but also illustrating how
rapidly humans have lost ground since Tudor times:

> *Dogs are our link to paradise.*
> *They don't know evil or jealousy or discontent.*
> *With a dog on a hillside on a glorious afternoon is to be back in*
> *   Eden,*
> *where doing nothing was not boring—it was peace.*

The curious thing about that poem is that I've not only read
it, but felt it. A couple of days before Christmas, in this lovely
but freakishly warm winter, Rose and I took the sheep across
the road to the meadow. It was sunny, the grass still green, and
I was awash in wonderful dogs.

Rose was overseeing the sheep down in the meadow,
keeping them in line. Izzy had flopped down next to me,
lying on his back, awaiting belly scratches.

Mother appeared behind us, popping out of the tall grass
as she often does when we are herding—I can't imagine how
she moves so quickly and covers so much ground with such
stealth. Sizing up where Rose was, she tiptoed up behind me,
purring, and flopped onto her back, too.

To me, these animals *were* a link to paradise, and I *was* back
in Eden, far from the ugly headlines of the day. Mother, like
the dogs, did not know "evil or jealousy or discontent." Nor

did she know that she had no reason any longer to kill and torture birds and rabbits.

Watching her, meeting her eyes, responding to her demand for attention, I could see why this argument was so important to people trying to make sense of the world. Good people were supposed to be rewarded, bad people punished, and reason was the means by which they made their choices. If animals lacked that capacity, how could they be punished or rewarded in this or any world? Why should they bother to be good or bad, as we are constantly training and imploring them to be?

Liberal-minded contemporary theologians grasp that many of the old, cruel views of animals need updating. We've learned that some animals are more involved and intelligent than Aristotle could possibly have known. And many of us have also come to see the human race as less entitled to its dominion, since we're making such a rotten job of it.

Walking around, visiting with my animals on Christmas— after I brought Elvis his candy bar, fed the donkeys and sheep stale bread and apples, and treated the dogs to basted bones— I felt grateful to be able to walk among these sweet and simple creatures, and to learn from them. A life in Boston or Philadelphia, New York City or suburban New Jersey—all places I have lived—no longer felt possible, mostly because *they* couldn't be there with me.

So, certain philosophers and theologians strike a chord with me when they challenge us to include animals in our notions of mercy and love, to pay greater attention to them as sentient beings. The question, really, is how far to take those arguments, and how much of the earlier ones to keep.

Watching Mother later that Christmas afternoon as she

stalked yet another bird, I did wonder—for her sake—if we weren't doing animals a disservice by believing they had our style of souls, perhaps misunderstanding them in the process, even putting them at risk.

Mother traveled low to the ground, silently, bloodily effective at what she did. There was no way, I thought, that I was looking at a good creature, or a bad one. Only at one that I respected and loved, and that, in some indefinable way, seemed to love me back.

And that was good enough.

Chapter Five

BRUTUS AND LENORE

I think we turn so much to our pets because they
remind us of our deeper nature, of what is truly
important. And also in a strange way of what we can
be. They rest us deeply and give us sudden joys
that we have forgotten.

—JEAN HOUSTON

THE SPRING HAD BEGUN WITH A LONG DRY SPELL. THEN,
even after the rains came, the main pasture behind the
farmhouse didn't spring into its usual lush greenness. It produced more weeds than grass, which would have made a fine
diet for goats, but wouldn't sustain my hungry sheep.

I recognized, with chagrin, that I'd allowed this field to
become overgrazed, that I should have reseeded it. I would
arrange that next spring, but now, either I had to order many
more bales of hay to feed the sheep for some weeks—an expensive solution—or I had to take them into the farther
meadows to graze each day.

Accordingly, Rose and I began each morning—early, before the sun got too strong—by herding the flock through the gate and escorting them to literally greener pastures.

Sometimes we went up the hill, sometimes across the road. Then we sat and kept vigil for an hour or so while the sheep crunched happily at the abundant grass, and later escorted them back, repeating the procedure in early evening. It was a hot, buggy, and time-consuming routine, though not without its quiet pleasures.

Rose, of course, was delighted to have additional opportunities to boss her flock around. She kept a judicious eye on the sheep at all times. Since she did, I was free to listen to music on my iPod, read a book, mull on the larger meaning of life. Lenore was also a good muller, though of little use as a herder, so I took to bringing her along for company.

At first she was anxious, staying back, even hiding in the tall grass when the sheep approached. Then, day by day, she became bolder, more curious.

I was sitting on a rock and reading one morning when, in my peripheral vision, I noticed Lenore sidling over toward the grazing Brutus, one of my wethers (neutered rams). I dropped my book and sprinted over. Sheep don't like dogs much. Even Rose has been kicked, butted, and charged at, especially by rams, who are notoriously grumpy.

Lenore, just eleven months old, had in her young life encountered few animals or people that didn't respond to her genial nature. She didn't seem to grasp the idea of inherent hostility, either in humanity or in the animal world.

Labs are famously affectionate and outgoing, but Lenore had an especially charismatic personality, even by Labrador standards. I got her when I was in the midst of a gripping depression; I needed a love dog, and she obliged. I suspect I re-inforced her tendency toward affection. It had been bred into her, but it also developed and was strengthened by my rela-tionship with her, my work with her.

It showed, not only with me and with other people but, curiously enough, with the other animals on the farm. Lenore began courting the no-nonsense Rose, who rarely deigned to play, and Izzy, who was focused on people and didn't seem to care much about other dogs. She greeted Mother, the barn cat, who ran from her at first, then drew closer. She went nose-to-nose with the goats and the donkeys through the pasture fence; she seemed eager to befriend every animal on the place.

I expected that Brutus would run, or perhaps butt her. My own attitude toward sheep is mixed: I like and care for them, but they always seem too uniform to be interesting, with their elemental concern about food and rest and not much else. Besides, I'm almost never near a sheep without a border collie next to me; sheep are unlikely to find that endearing.

But Lenore was focusing on Brutus, and he wasn't run-ning away. He stared at her, somewhat exasperated, as if as-suming he was going to have to move, but Lenore dropped to the ground, a submissive position. Brutus looked at her for a long while, then lowered his head.

Uh-oh. I was close now, about ten feet away, ready to res-cue Lenore, when she reached up and, astonishingly, licked Brutus's nose. And he let her.

It was the beginning of one of those interspecies animal friendships you see in movies but rarely in life. In fact, I'm often struck by how closely species stick together. The cows are always within a few feet of each other; the donkeys are inseparable; and I've never seen the sheep show much curiosity about creatures without fleece.

Either Lenore's charms were especially persuasive, or Brutus was a very strange sheep. Or both.

Brutus had been born on this farm, pulled out of his mother by me on a brutally cold morning the first winter we had lambs. He's easy with people, mostly even-tempered, though it's not unheard of for him to charge or butt another sheep—or even me, if I'm not looking. Rose has tangled with him several times—she brooks no rebellion from sheep—so he's generally well behaved.

Still, the sight of Brutus and Lenore meeting in the meadow was striking. I laughed out loud, and reached for my camera.

I didn't see that any good could come from this relationship. He isn't good for you, I told Lenore, adopting a protective paternalism. The other sheep will turn on you. Rose will never accept it. This can't go anywhere.

Rose, in fact, was already staring incredulously as Lenore curled up next to Brutus, gave him another lick, and took a nap while he grazed a few feet away.

But the ritual continued over the next couple of weeks. The two would find each other, bump noses. Brutus lowered his head for a slurp, then grazed while Lenore sat or lay beside him.

Once in a while, another sheep—especially Brutus's mother, Paula—drifted over to try to figure out what was going on.

Rose did seem to have a rough time of it. This fraternization undermined the sense of order she always strove to maintain. Sheep did what they were told, period, and dogs didn't commune with them, linger with them in a far corner of the pasture, or lick them on the nose. That wasn't the way Rose worked.

Here, I thought, were the souls of two dogs colliding. Lenore loved every creature she met. Rose lived for work.

Yet the two of them seemed to work it out over the next few weeks. Rose got nervous whenever Lenore and Brutus drifted too far from the rest of the sheep and would go fetch Brutus, making him return to the flock, without Lenore. So they learned to stay closer to the flock.

Lenore made a few other friends, too—another ram, a couple of ewes—but Brutus remained her main squeeze. After a while, he automatically lowered his head when she approached, presenting his nose and ear for licking.

Eventually, Rose came to accept this odd couple in her midst, and either worked around them or simply ignored them. Lenore, after she'd visited awhile with Brutus, would come over to lie by Rose—another transgression. Rose hadn't permitted Lenore near her when she was working, as if she sensed that this less disciplined creature would bring chaos.

But now, Rose seemed to enjoy it, and the sight of these two beautiful working dogs, each faithful to her own nature, was touching, even calming.

I loved, too, that all this had happened with no involvement by me, beyond my experience, commands, or control. All sorts of things were going on in the pasture daily—between Lenore and Brutus, Rose and the sheep, Rose and Lenore, the dogs and me. Some of it I was aware of, some of it I wasn't; I had no clear idea of what anybody was up to, or why.

The best theory I could come up with was that Lenore had been rewarded for her loving nature from puppyhood. I needed it at the time, I reveled in it, and beamed when she approached people or other animals in her joyous, enthusiastic way. Rose has no such agenda.

Each dog responds to what's innate in them, and also to what I ask of them. Rose works for me and Lenore loves me. That's where our souls converge.

IT WAS A HOT, sticky July afternoon. A haze had settled over the valley, and the farm was very still. My dogs lay in the shade near the garden.

Suddenly, I heard them bark. A car had overheated on the road right in front of my farmhouse. A young couple emerged, the guy fiddling under the hood, muttering, and the mother comforting two fussing girls.

It was oppressively humid. The black flies that torture my animals were swarming everywhere, as they do around farms in summer. The kids—one seemed about three or four, the other perhaps six—looked and sounded miserable.

I went and asked if anybody needed help, but the young parents seemed shy, anxious not to disturb. The father, hard at work under the hood, had the air of somebody who didn't like asking for help.

The border collies, Izzy and Rose, were still barking through the fence; Lenore had her paws up on the fence, her tail wagging furiously. I got some bottled water out of the refrigerator, called Lenore, and walked back down the driveway. "Can I bring you some water?" I called.

The father, peering out from under the hood, nodded. The mother looked apprehensively to her girls, who had stopped whimpering and were staring at Lenore, making a beeline down the driveway, her tail going a mile a minute.

"They aren't really used to dogs," the woman said hesitantly, eyeing this big black dog trotting toward them. But I said that Lenore was very gentle and loved children, and was it okay to bring her over? The mother said, well, okay, and waved us across.

Lenore wiggled over to the girls—Chrissy and Katie, we learned. At first, the girls backed away, fascinated but wary. Then Lenore plopped down next to them and rolled over on her back, exuding so much unthreatening pleasure that, almost instantly, both girls were on their knees on either side of her, laughing and squealing and leaning over for Lenore's licks. She sat up and happily accepted more pats and hugs.

Lenore radiated affection, but she also seemed to know, instinctively, not to jump on the little girls or knock them over, not to overwhelm them. This, it struck me, was also a dog at work, a dog with boundless heart whose instincts led her to share it.

Watching her work, I saw her joy spread through this harried family. The two girls were leaning over her to hug her; the father looked out from under the hood and laughed. "We need to get the girls a dog," he said. The young mother, hot and weary, was smiling, joining in the Lenore lovefest.

Lenore presented herself appropriately to the children, charmed the mother, and when she was done with that, came around the car to lick the father's shoe and wiggle her tail at him. When I went back into the house, all four were laughing, joking, drinking their water, talking about getting a puppy. "Goodbye, Lenore!" I heard the kids shout from the road.

SHE CERTAINLY HADN'T consciously decided to do what she'd done. To some extent, she didn't have to: Lenore is well bred, of a good-tempered lineage; she was already inclined to like people and be sociable.

I've bolstered this behavior, no doubt, by continually taking her to stores, friends' houses, book events, hospice visits, bringing her into unfamiliar situations, giving her the opportunity to meet all kinds of people. I've made it clear to her that affection is welcomed, and she gets praise for it, further helping to develop a natural trait.

It can seem like a tiny thing, walking across the road to amuse some children, yet to me, it was a big thing. The power to bring smiles to four uncomfortable and anxious people, to introduce children to the pleasure of a canine companion, to promote the love of animals—none of those was a small thing.

And Lenore did it all the time, multiplied the impact of that little visit by hundreds of encounters with hundreds of people. She went with me to a local high school and helped nervous students in a writing course I taught relax and feel easier with me, with one another. She goes into one hospice home after another, sad places sometimes, where suddenly there is a bit of laughter. Here and there, in this interaction and that, fifty times a day, she turns on the lights.

If there's magic in the relationships between humans and dogs, it might be that mysterious interdependence, the ways in which we sometimes need our dogs greatly, and some of them can read that and become the dogs we need. In this way, they steady us, buoy us, especially in dark times.

This love, the impact it has on human beings, is Lenore's work. Whether it will get her into heaven or not rests in much more knowing hands than mine. It's not really a question someone like me can answer.

But I can see why so many people find almost ludicrous the idea that dogs lack souls and might therefore be barred from the afterlife. God made them, after all. God loves us, and we love dogs. The scene on my road this summer day shows one reason why.

One summer night, not long after that, when I was tired and my back hurt and I was feeling discouraged, I crawled into bed early, with a good book. I took a deep breath and tried to settled myself. It had been a rough day.

I knew that in a minute or two, though, I would hear a clacking and a panting as Lenore barreled up the stairs, and I was right. A black shadow entered the bedroom. Her big, smooth, squarish head appeared by the bedside; I could feel a breeze from the wagging tail.

I bent over and leaned my forehead against hers. "Hey, Love Hound," I said, and she slurped at my face. Then she hopped up, curled herself into a ball, and nestled herself against my ribs.

I smiled.

Chapter Six

THE SOUL OF ROSE

The gate opens	I'm good at this
my heart awaits, limbs taut	crouch and wait
I hear Jon's command	give them time
"get the sheep"	round in back
hugging the meadow	down the hill
knowing my mission	through the gate
there you are sheep	now settle you sheep
I will make you move	I'll lie and watch

—MARY KELLOGG

I HAD A FEW FRIENDS OVER FOR DINNER ONE NEW YEAR'S Eve. Among the guests was Maria the artist. Apart from Annie and me, Maria may be the only human Rose loves.

This makes a certain amount of sense. Like Rose, Maria has a ferocious work ethic. It's as common to see her up on ladders in broiling heat or brutal cold, restoring old buildings to service and beauty, as it is to see Rose moving the sheep in mud, ice, or midsummer sun. Like Rose, Maria is loving and loyal, with a sense of vulnerability, a self one can never see completely.

Normally, when Rose is working, humans barely exist. Even when she's not herding, people aren't of much interest. She doesn't charm, the way Izzy and Lenore do; she's rarely in anyone's lap. When she sees Maria, though, she comes running over, full of tail wags and kisses, almost Lab-like.

On this holiday eve, though, Rose hopped up onto the couch next to Maria despite all the other guests nearby. She showed Maria her belly. "What's wrong, Rose?" Maria asked, stroking her. I mentioned that Rose hadn't been eating much for a day or two—probably she'd ingested some decaying thing. Rose licked Maria's hand.

It startled me, and Maria as well, this submissive posture. It's rare for Rose to appear at all when there's company, uncharacteristic. Rose doesn't care for New Year's Eve celebrations any more than I do. Something unusual was passing between these two.

Maria felt it, too. Rose was sending someone she loved and trusted a message of some sort, perhaps one I'd been slow to pick up on: She needed help.

Rose had been herding as usual, but afterward, she'd been sluggish. Her appetite, never hearty, was off. I'd been thinking of taking her to see our vet.

After a few moments, as people drifted into the living room, Rose left the couch, walked into my office, and crawled beneath the printer, one of her favorite spots. I didn't see her again until everyone had left. But I knew we'd be at the vet's on January 2.

ROSE POSES A PERENNIAL CHALLENGE when it comes to health care. She's been kicked by donkeys, butted by rams. She's torn her paws in rocky pastures and on tangles of old wire in the woods. She once ran underneath the tires of the ATV. Her folder at the vet's is fattening to telephone-book dimensions.

She's lucky to be alive, and I am luckier still.

Often, she'll scarf down some dubious food when her prey drive is high—donkey or sheep manure, maybe part of a dead animal carcass. A day or two of vomiting generally follows, after which her digestive system recovers.

You hardly ever know, if you're not paying strict attention, when Rose is truly sick. The vet calls her stoic; I'd say she's astonishingly indifferent to pain. Once, while she was herding sheep, I noticed a slight limp (her right leg was broken). Another time, she lay on the bed next to me, and only when she got up did I notice bloodstains on the sheets (she'd impaled herself on a stone or possibly a shard of glass, the vet said).

I often fear that Rose won't live to reach old age, and that's troubling for many reasons: I love her, but I also doubt that I could keep this farm functioning without her.

Probably I could keep her safer by confining her more, but that's not the life Rose is destined for, it seems to me. She's a working farm dog, from a proud tradition; she needs—deserves—to be free to do her job, watch the sheep, cover my back.

I do take precautions. Rose never goes outside alone, out of my sight. I've fenced several areas around the farmhouse, so that she can hang out and observe her sheep when I'm busy or away. But she's never left to run unsupervised. Still, she manages to injure herself with some frequency.

ON NEW YEAR'S DAY, Rose was up and ready to run as always. Whatever had been bothering her the night before seemed to have eased.

When I feed the dogs in the morning, Rose keeps an eye on the mudroom, where I leave my shoes. If I put on sneakers, she'll eat her kibble. If I choose rubber pasture boots, she knows we are going out to the sheep. In that case, I put her bowl on the counter for later, knowing she won't bother with breakfast until her herding's done. Given the choice, Rose would much rather work than eat.

This day I pulled on my rubber boots because rain had rendered the countryside a boggy mess. So I had no opportunity to gauge Rose's appetite.

We—Rose, Izzy, and I—were about to usher in the new year with one of our favorite things: an ATV ride through the woods, border collie nirvana.

I crank up the ATV and putt-putt down the driveway.

When I reach the dirt road in front of the farm, I hold up my arm and yell, "Stay!" Rose and Izzy go into their best border collie crouches and freeze. When I've checked the road for traffic, I look over my shoulder. Izzy is usually about ten feet off on my left, Rose poised up on the hill behind me, both tensed for action.

If all is clear, I yell, "Go!" and the two dogs shoot ahead like bullets from a rifle, catapulting down the dirt path across the road, into the woods. I motor after them, but I can never quite keep pace.

Every quarter of a mile or so, they spin around and crouch, facing me, waiting until I'm just a couple of hundred feet away. Then they turn and sprint off again. When I catch up to them a mile or so up the path, both are lying in a clearing, waiting for me, their tongues long. In warm weather, I bring a jug of water and a collapsible bowl. I turn off the ATV and sit on a tree trunk, offer a drink.

I may have brought a book to read, or the three of us may

just stare out into the woods, collecting ourselves. Izzy will eventually sniff about a bit. But however speedily Rose has been running, she doesn't move as long as I'm sitting with her, reading or thinking.

After fifteen minutes or half an hour, by which time the dogs are no longer even breathing heavily, I start up the ATV and Rose takes off ahead of me. I've never passed her.

Few dogs are as well adapted to sheer joyful running as border collies, who can travel long distances at high speeds without damaging their joints or limbs the way Labs might. It helps calm and settle them.

It isn't the only exercise Rose gets, but she especially loves flat-out running, and it's done her good. Jeff Meyer, the vet, says she has one of the strongest heartbeats he's heard in a dog, and that she's remarkably healthy and fit. (So is Izzy, though he doesn't go quite as far or as fast.)

It helps her with herding, too. Even when the flock takes off, Rose easily outflanks the sheep, heads them off, turns them around. If they're balking, she can scamper up and down hills all day, rarely tiring or even slowing.

On New Year's, after our morning outing, I put the ATV in the barn, walked with Izzy and Rose back into the house, and put her untouched food bowl on the floor. No dice. She wouldn't even give breakfast a sniff.

Then she followed me into my office and put her head on my knee, another unusual gesture. So whatever had been bothering her hadn't resolved itself. I got onto the floor and cradled her in my arms. "What's the matter, sweetie?" I asked. She vomited.

JEFF SHOWED ME THE X-RAY. Something had lodged in her stomach, blocking food, and our ATV run might have caused further damage. I felt stricken as he gestured at the squarish object at the bottom of her stomach; even I could see that it shouldn't be there. Jeff couldn't identify what it was, but he needed to find out and scheduled surgery for the next morning. Meanwhile, Rose had to stay at his clinic; she'd become dehydrated and needed intravenous fluids.

At home, I tended to farm chores, took the other dogs for a walk, tried to work. Izzy kept looking around for Rose. I'd planned to move the sheep, so that Annie could bring the grain out unmolested, but I couldn't. All of us were off balance without Rose.

I called the vet's office to see if I could come visit Rose in the evening, before her surgery. Sure, the tech said, come on by. I brought Izzy along, and the two of us threaded through the back rooms to the presurgical area. Rose, lying in a large crate with an IV tube taped to one foreleg, was happy to see us, wriggling and sticking her nose through the crate's bars to lick me. I reached my fingers through to scratch her nose.

"Hang in there," I told her. "And get your ass back on the farm. The sheep will run amok, the donkeys will misbehave, and I ain't living there without you, period." We sat with her for a few minutes.

I talked with Jeff, then with the techs, who sounded reassuring. But back out in the parking lot with Izzy, my eyes filled with tears.

At such times, dogs seem to act like spigots, opening up hidden parts of ourselves. Jeff was a great vet and had performed such surgery many times. Rose was probably not in real peril.

I was frightened and sorrowful. We'd been through so much together; she'd been so true to me. I hoped our ATV romp hadn't made her condition more dangerous.

Sitting on the concrete steps in the parking lot, I wiped my eyes. Izzy sat behind me, waiting and silent.

Two day later, she was home, back at work.

THE SUMMER BEFORE, an enormous crew of people had descended on Washington County to shoot a movie of one of my earlier books, *A Dog Year*. Producers, actors, caterers, grips, drivers, production assistants—they were everywhere.

In my barn, residents for several weeks, were five border collies, assembled from Hollywood and other points around the country, who would play Orson. Every morning after they were fed and exercised, they were made up—complete with tinted contact lenses, hair extensions, and fur coloring—so they'd all look alike. They were gorgeous dogs, cute and perky and well trained; they tolerated such cosmetic fussing the way any star would. They weren't, in other words, like my dogs. Rose, in particular, seemed disgruntled by their presence in her barn.

On almost the same day the movie people arrived, as if by some secret signal, my ewes began lambing. By my calculations, the lambs weren't due for two months, but I'd been off before. The first time I bred the sheep, the lambs were born in February, in the midst of the worst winter in decades. This time, blessedly, it was summer, so weather was not a factor; no lambs were in danger of dying from the cold.

Still, chaos threatened. Once I saw what was happening, and told the movie crew, they graciously insisted on building a temporary lambing pen inside the dog fence behind the house. A few sheets of plywood nailed together was what I had in mind, but that wasn't substantial enough for the film carpenters. Big white trucks began depositing wood, tin roofing, and other supplies, and construction started. But the carpenters were pulled off the job to work on sets, and the lambs had already begun dropping.

We went into emergency lambing mode. Annie and I hauled out syringes, towels, tail-dockers, medicines, and milk supplements. Rose went from alert to hypervigilant.

When I saw two or three ewes still circling and straining one late afternoon, I knew we were headed for an all-nighter. I brought out biscuits and granola bars, bottled water and dog food, and set up a little encampment next to what we'd started calling the HBO Memorial Lambing Pen—so far, still a depression in the ground and a pile of plywood. I erected some temporary fencing under the apple tree; on a warm night, the lambs and ewes would be fine there.

After sunset, as the ewes were still doing their Lamaze breathing, Rose and I settled on a blanket with a powerful electrical torch and a cell phone (to call for reinforcements) and waited, Rose's eyes fixed on the mothers-to-be. She and Annie and I had painstakingly collected the pregnant ewes, the humans grabbing them with hands and crooks as Rose pushed the flock through the gate, so we were now in the dog run with about a dozen sheep, the rest nestled at the top of the pasture.

We watched as ewe Number 96 (only two or three of the sheep had names) began more active labor, lying on her side, her head upraised, straining visibly. She had a long and difficult labor, groaning and bleating for two hours. There was little we midwives could do to help but wait and watch. I brought 96 a bucket of water, which she gulped eagerly.

This was taking too long. One of my biggest and oldest ewes, she was growing exhausted, and I worried that her lamb might be in trouble. I moved behind her and looked beneath her tail. She tried to bolt, but Rose kept her in place.

I thought I saw the lamb's large head beginning to appear, though the area around it was swollen and dry. But it was hard to see clearly in the darkness, and I couldn't hold the ewe completely still for a good look. Should I call the large-animal vet? But I'd seen in previous years that the vets often couldn't do much more than I could; besides, I'd learned a lot from them, namely how to reach in and properly position a lamb's head and legs, and then pull.

The ewe, too weary to remain standing, lay down to rest. So did I, Rose beside me. But her eyes stayed locked on 96.

Sometime later, I woke up. Rose was sitting across from the ewe, who was on her feet again. Suddenly, as she gave a grunt, her water broke. At this point, if I'd had a lambing pen, the ewe would have been in it, rather than in this large fenced dog run.

Now time became critical. Within a half hour or so after the water breaks a lamb can die, and so can the ewe. "Rose, get the sheep," I said quietly. She had an uncanny ability to grasp a task; having been raised as a farm dog, rather than trained for herding trials, she almost always seemed to intuit what I needed. She'd been focusing on this ewe—ignoring the others on the far side of the run—all night.

Rose followed my command, staying in front of the ewe and backing her slowly toward me. I saw the lamb's head beginning to emerge, gray and cold, the eyes closed and swollen. I called Annie on my cell; she said she'd be right over.

The ewe suddenly scrambled away, but Rose circled ahead of her. I got a crook around her neck and wrestled her onto her side, quietly asking her forgiveness for the rough treatment. In a few minutes Annie came zooming into the driveway in her truck.

I wasn't able to hold the ewe at that point, my back complaining loudly; she struggled to her feet and took off. Rose cornered her, though, at the long end of the run. Annie came rushing up and, with Rose's help, we took up positions on either side of the ewe, and I grabbed her by the shoulders. We rolled her onto her side. She was too tired to put up much of a fight at this point. Rose backed away and watched.

As Annie held the ewe's head and shoulders, I got behind her with the torch. The lamb's head was protruding, but it felt lifeless. Clearly the lamb had gotten stuck in the birth canal. I regretted having waited so long to call Annie. Still, the lamb had to come out, or we'd lose the mother, too.

I reached inside and slid my right hand under the head, feeling for the legs to make sure they were pushed back. There was still fluid inside; it felt warm. I moved my hand behind the lamb's feet and then, with my other hand, got a grip on its jaw and pulled as hard as I could, the ewe moaning, and Annie pulling in the opposite direction.

I was almost too tired to move; I could only imagine what the poor ewe was feeling. Suddenly, the lamb's body came sliding out and I fell backward onto the grass with it. It lay unmoving and cold, eyes shut.

The first casualty of the lambing season, I remarked to Annie. She looked stricken, but pointed out that at least the mother was alive. We tended to her, bringing her some hay and fresh water laced with molasses, for energy. For some minutes she lay perfectly still, resting.

Suddenly, Annie's eyes widened; she pointed over my shoulder. "Look!" The lamb's chest was heaving, and Rose was licking at its wet body.

We rushed over to towel the baby's face; it opened both its

eyes and began to struggle to its feet. We brought it quickly to Number 96, who recognized it instantly and began to clear its eyes and mouth, nosing it to stand up. In a few minutes, we'd nudged the pair into the fenced area beneath the apple tree. The lamb was nursing, the ewe sipping her molasses water. If mother and baby couldn't occupy the HBO Memorial Lambing Pen, at least they could be snuggled together, apart from the rest of the maternity ward. Annie made them a bed of straw.

Three more lambs were born that night, the other births uneventful and by-the-numbers: a set of twins and another female. Annie headed back to bed. All Rose and I had to do was watch, wait for the licking and nuzzling, and administer vitamins and other shots.

It was a happy and successful night, but also filthy, grinding, and chilly. I fell asleep leaning against the pasture fence, Rose curled up a few feet away.

I was awakened by her low growling and felt something licking at the back of my head. The movie-star dogs, out for their morning stroll, had come over to the dog run and were sitting in a row, eyes wide, ears up. Cute and clean, they looked like curious spectators at a sporting event. Rose and I, on the other hand, were covered in manure, amniotic fluid, blood, and milk, and were surrounded by all sorts of debris. Towels, syringes, and bottles were strewn about.

"Morning, guys," I said to the perky onlookers. But something seemed to snap in Rose. She wriggled through a gap below the fence, went straight at the movie dogs, and chased them back into the barn, where they would soon be picked up and ferried to the set, ready for their close-ups.

This was not like Rose, who ignored almost all other

dogs, especially if she was working. But who says dogs lack self-awareness? Maybe she couldn't stand that they were so clean.

THOMAS AQUINAS SHAPED THE LIVES of many generations of animals when he wrote that irrational creatures like animals are not "god-possessors" and, thus, not fitting beneficiaries of good deeds. They cannot be equated with us, in his view—or mistreated.

When I went to visit Rose in the veterinary hospital, I was expressing concern for her, worrying about her—things she couldn't do for herself and couldn't do for me. In mainstream Christian theology, Rose had no status as a moral being. She could not possess the cornerstone element of a soul: the ability to make moral choices.

Rose's guidance through this tricky night, one of many, and her pardonable annoyance with the movie stars—great dogs all, and working dogs themselves—highlighted again just how remarkable she is. But it isn't the same thing as a friend's deciding to wade through a snowstorm to help plow me out, or Annie's coming out to serve as midwife in the small hours. Rose's actions arise from a different motive.

The hundreds of times—lambing is just one of many—that Rose served me, stood by me, helped me to achieve the life I wanted, all that gave her a very particular status, to my mind.

Yet I understood what Aquinas was getting at. Rose was not choosing to serve me and do good, not consciously.

So we aren't the same.

Rose can accomplish many feats that I can't; in that sense, she is my superior. But while I can appreciate the good she does for me, she cannot. That is a large part of what distinguishes us from each other.

And yet, so often we share moments when what I need and what she can do fuse perfectly.

Eventually, when lambing was nearly over, the crew completed the HBO Memorial Lambing Pen. A magnificent structure, it never housed a lamb. I wasn't sure what ought to be done with it, and it is now a dormitory for my three goats, but I considered it a monument to Rose, a reminder of that night and so many others when her presence made it possible, literally, for me to live this life.

Sometimes it saddens me that Rose will never truly understand the contribution she's made. Sometimes, though, I'm happy for her, an animal free to do the work her instincts command, relieved of the burden to figure out what's good, who's deserving, and other conundrums that prey on the human mind.

Chapter Seven

THE JEERING GALLERY

A dog has the soul of a philosopher.

—PLATO

I GO OUT TO DO THE BARN CHORES EVERY MORNING, AND AS soon as I open the back door, I am hooted at—by my goats, Murray, Ruth, and Honey.

Their jeering is sharp, loud, a quick nasal *maah* that's impolite and annoying. The goats, short agile beings with furry coats and luminous yellow eyes, a Boer-Saanen cross, inhabit a large pen right behind the house, so they get to see and hear everything.

They're not reserved in their commentary. The cable talk show panelists of the animal world, they're always ready to interject; they have something to say about everything, little of it complimentary. They're the most impertinent animals I know.

They are impish, curious, and, worst of all, bright enough

to carry out their impulses. It is a cardinal principle of farming not to have animals more intelligent than you are. I've already screwed up, because the donkeys are smarter than me. And the goats are smarter than the donkeys, though not nearly as agreeable.

"Nuts to you, goats!" I jeer back each morning. "You don't know anything. Bug off. Be quiet."

They won't be quiet; they can't be. You might as well tell the wind to stop blowing. They don't care what I think, have no desire to please, and their spirits are brimming over with mischief.

The daily ridicule continues as I feed the donkeys, check on the cows, walk the dogs. It abates when I bring the goats the leftover microwaved popcorn I've saved from the previous evening, but resumes when I head for the car.

Goats are not like the other farm residents. Sheep, peaceable creatures, have no interest in me or my activities, unless I'm coming at them accompanied by a border collie or carrying a bale of hay. Even then, once they've been moved to another pasture or polished off the hay, they have little to say.

The cows are even more laissez-faire. If I am bringing them apples or stale Dunkin' Donuts, they appear very concerned about me. Otherwise, they gaze out at other farms, perhaps contemplating the harder fate of other cows; they're not about to move their big bottoms to see what I'm up to.

The donkeys are curious, but also quiet and reflective. They're not rude. I sometimes think I amuse them, but they're discreet enough to keep that to themselves.

My goats, on the other hand, are the farm's Greek chorus, watching me closely and reminding me that I am ridiculous.

Rose has tried several times to herd them. They respond

confoundingly by prancing and playing, and running around in circles. Rose has taken on sheep, cows, other dogs, even pigs, but goats are beyond her authority. They wear her out.

About two years old now, the three all came from the same farm in Shushan, New York. The 4-H'ers who'd raised them passed along this bit of wisdom, regarding their habits: "Sheep eat low, goats eat high."

True enough. Sheep eat grass. Goats eat not only the scrubby brush I hoped they'd clear, they also strip the lower branches of trees I want to survive. That old saw that they'll eat anything? Untrue—when it comes to nonplants, my goats appreciate Paul Newman's low-fat popcorn (including the bag), oat cookies, and Cheerios; they turn up their noses at almost anything else.

The 4-H'ers didn't tell me they mind everybody's business but their own. They stick their noses into your pants pockets. They hop up on rocks, picnic tables, and car hoods. They can open gates, and wriggle under or through fences. Then, having no use for the freedom they've achieved, they hang around, complaining bitterly until you let them back into their pen.

They jeer not only when I'm outdoors, under their scrutiny, but even when I move around inside the house. I hear their contemptuous bleats when I turn on the kitchen light, for instance. Or if I drop a frying pan with a clatter. I sometimes get additional ridicule when I get out of the shower and slam the glass door.

The cows couldn't care less if I'm hauling trash out to the cans. To the goats, it's like a presidential inaugural; they offer a running commentary.

They're always together. Murray is the ringleader, the first one to poke his nose through the wire-mesh fence, the one who kicks off the vituperation, the loudest and most insistent. But Ruth and Honey are not much quieter.

So I've begun jeering back.

GOATS' SPIRITS—part curiosity and intelligence, part refusal to submit to authority—are an odd combination. They're domesticated, useful to humans for eons, but without that sense of service and partnership that dogs have. I'm unable to discern any spiritual bent, the kind donkeys exude. Nor are they contemplative, like cows.

They are virtually untrainable, driven to investigate and disturb. If you don't have a sense of humor, if you're not patient, don't have goats. You'll have to get rid of them, as many people do; I had to let Annie take home an earlier pair of rambunctious Nubians who just didn't fit in, even on a farm called Bedlam. These three are working out better, happily, and that may have as much to do with me as with them.

Goats put us in our places. They're not devoted to serving us, cuddling with us, or meeting our expectations. They are beyond us. Yet they have the gift of making us laugh, during those moments when they are not actively attempting to annoy us.

I'm not proud of the fact that, late in middle age, I'm exchanging insults—largely unfit for a family audience—with these insolent creatures, but there it is.

Unlike dogs, goats are indifferent to what you want or think, almost viscerally incapable of obedience even when it's in their interest.

I admit that I love their imperious personalities, their anti-authoritarianism, their alertness. Surrounded by animals that seem to cherish me—largely because I bring them food—I find it refreshing to have a few that regularly taunt the hand that feeds them.

I wouldn't call them completely without affection. Last spring, I decided to spend some quality time with my goats. I brought some oat cookies, opened the gate, came into their goat pen, sat down at the picnic table that Ruth has turned into her personal Matterhorn.

This was unusual. All three came up to investigate. They nosed me, sniffed my pockets, stared at me as if to say, Just what are you up to? Who do you think you are, anyway? You didn't bring any more than that?

Eventually, Murray and then Ruth put their heads in my hand, even though it was empty. For once they were quiet, practically affectionate. It was nice.

After a few minutes of this uncharacteristic calm, I got up to leave—and was instantly taunted and derided.

"The hell with you, goats!" I yelled back, and went into the house.

Chapter Eight

FLY

Primitive man must tame the animal in himself and
make it his helpful companion; civilized man must
heal the animal in himself and make it his friend.

—CARL JUNG

MY FRIEND SARAH CALLED LAST SPRING TO SAY THAT SHE
thought Fly missed me. You ought to come see her,
she said.

I missed Fly, too. But it was painful to see her. This border collie had known trouble her whole life, and it had been
difficult to let her go. I'd gotten deeply involved in her rescue,
I'd watched her nearly die and then return to life before my
eyes. However one defines soul, ours were joined.

Sarah's farm was just a few miles away. The minute I
walked into the house, Fly came zooming into the room and
threw herself onto the sofa next to me, crawling almost inside
me. I held her for many minutes, kissing her on her nose as
she licked my hands and face.

Animal rescue is very complicated. I'm drawn to it, yet afraid of it. I'm never sure exactly who's being rescued, whether I am doing more for the animal or for myself. I sometimes think the soul of a dog can only be seen in its human mirror—in us, and the boundless way we love these creatures.

When Patsy Beckett, a longtime dog rescuer, first saw Fly tethered to a tree in front of a farmhouse in northern Florida, she pulled her car over for a closer look.

Fly was a gray-and-white border collie of indeterminate age, racing back and forth as much as a short length of clothesline permitted. When border collies don't have real work, they tend to make their own—running fences, chasing cars, obsessing over balls. Untrained and unrestrained, they can become anxious, even a bit mad.

Fly was such a border collie, wild-eyed and wired. Even from the car, Patsy could see that her fur was matted, with bits of dirt and who-knew-what clinging to her coat. The dog was scarecrow-skinny and hyper, dashing one way, then the other.

Most people would have just driven by—hundreds did every day—but it was the sort of scene a dog rescuer notices. Fly's was a breed Patsy often encountered. People get border collies because they're supposed to be smart, then find them too intense, too fixated on work. Such dogs often wind up in deep trouble.

Here we go again, Patsy thought. Why don't I just look the other way this time? Let this one go?

She knew where this would go even before she pulled to the side of the road. Depending on what she saw and how the owner reacted, this border collie would likely join the vast dog rescue underworld, wending her way north.

Over the next few days, Patsy got to know the dog—her neck was wreathed in rope burns, and she had lots of fleas and ticks in her fur and skin—and her suspicious owner. The farmer, when Patsy approached him politely, barked that he'd paid $200 for a watchdog, and no, he wasn't about to put her in a dog run instead of on a rope. And no, he didn't want to sell her. And would this nosey woman please leave his property and mind her own business?

"He didn't want to talk to me," Patsy told me later, with a sigh. She hated these discussions, often tense, with owners. "I didn't get the sense he was cruel, just out of gas. That's often the case with these dogs, really—people are busy, or broke, or just overwhelmed."

But of course Patsy couldn't leave it at that. Fly was outside day and night, in rain, heat, or cold. Apart from the branches of the tree, she had no shelter. She put her head in Patsy's lap when she came, and licked her hand. "She had no reason to love people, but she did," Patsy said.

Patsy also noticed that the dog looked listless and had a disturbing cough, which could mean heartworms. Perhaps there wasn't as much time to wait as Patsy had thought.

She left the owner a few phone messages, again offering to buy the dog or help with vet care; they were never returned. It was becoming unbearable for her to drive by the farm, hard not to think of Fly while she was at work. Patsy was passing the point where she could draw back, remain disengaged.

So, late one evening, Patsy and her friend Jeanine, a member of the same rescue group, parked their creaky Windstar on the road out of sight, crept up to the front lawn, cut Fly's rope with scissors, and walked off with the startled but friendly dog. Patsy's visits had made her no stranger, so the dog didn't bark, and the farmhouse remained dark.

"You will never be treated this way again," Patsy told Fly. "I promise you." They left a note for the farmer, explaining what they'd done and leaving a post-office-box address; he could send a letter if he wanted to be compensated for the dog or was willing to discuss treating her more humanely.

A few hours later, Fly's picture went up on the Web, along with those of thousands of other dogs available for adoption. And I got an email message: Could I help?

THE GROWTH of the dog rescue movement is closely tied to the digital age. Rescuers flourish online. They're obsessive emailers and networkers—it's hard to rescue dogs single-handed—and the growth of the Net has made every dog a national adoptee.

Some of these groups are highly organized, experienced, well funded, and professional. Others are amateur operations run out of garages and backyards.

It says much about the lives dogs lead in America, and about the country itself, that in an age when politicians compete to define how little government should do, there's no comparable rescue movement for people.

Humans who find themselves laid off, in urgent medical trouble, or homeless in America have no such safety net. No van will pull into their driveways to whisk them off to doctors; no one will screen potential homes for them, resettle them with loving caretakers, then visit regularly to make sure they're okay.

But when Fly's rope was cut, she entered an underground that eventually involved individuals and groups from Florida to New York.

She went first to a private home in Jacksonville for a night or two. Meanwhile, messages requesting help and transport were posted on craigslist and Yahoo bulletin boards where dog rescuers congregate and organize.

Next, a "transporter" in a battered old pickup met Fly at an interstate rest stop near Jacksonville and drove her to Atlanta. The better-funded rescue groups can reimburse members for gas and expenses, but most can't. This transporter had spent thousands of her own dollars ferrying dogs.

In Atlanta, she took Fly to a vet tech. Vets vary in their attitudes toward rescue animals; most help when they can, some a lot, some a little. Since few rescuers can afford standard veterinary care, they grow adept at finding alternatives. The lowest-paid of veterinary office staffers, techs attend to sick dogs, collect samples, draw blood, work brutal hours. Yet they're often the most fervent animal lovers in a practice.

In Fly's case, the tech had agreed to tend to rescue dogs at night and on weekends for little or no money. She treated Fly's neck sores, dispensed medication for worms and fleas, vaccinated her against rabies and distemper. A nonprofit mobile veterinary service spayed her for a bargain $60.

As it turned out, though, the would-be helpers nearly killed Fly. Despite repeated warnings from Patsy and me, after we'd consulted our own vets, the mobile service anesthetized Fly without having tested her for heartworm. When the heartbeat slows in a dog with heartworm, the worms cluster around the blood vessels near the heart. The result is often fatal, and even if it doesn't kill the dog, it almost surely weakens the heart and lungs. That's what happened to Fly, apparently inadvertently. Rescuers are almost always well-meaning, but not always saintly, or well organized. Who knew whether our warnings ever reached the people who spayed Fly—or anyone?

Fly then proceeded to Charleston with a different transporter, where another volunteer met her and brought her to a "fosterer."

This Carolina group, I later learned, belonged to a religious sect that didn't believe in traditional medical care, for animals or people. The fosterer treated Fly with herbs, and didn't want to release her without assurances that she wouldn't end up in the hands of conventional vets.

It was starting to look like Fly might have to be rescued from her rescuers. There ensued much emailing, many phone calls, even a discussion with an attorney. Fly disappeared for a week before she was tracked down, then reacquired by conventional rescuers. She resumed her journey north.

Being shuttled about so much can be traumatic for a frightened, unsettled dog. But Fly, who'd been tied to a tree for a long time, seemed to find life on the road interesting. She enjoyed the treats, the attention, the opportunities to chase a Frisbee in the fosterer's yard. Nobody yelled at her. Quite the contrary; everybody loved her.

As volunteer transporters and fosterers passed Fly along, online schedules and notes helped them know what to feed her, how to play with and socialize her. At each stop, people posted progress reports on how her sores and surgical scars were healing, what she liked to eat, what made her nervous. A growing library on Fly was being built daily for her rescuers and, eventually, her new owner.

Fly was being reborn, the reports said. "She has risen," one volunteer gleefully emailed me. She cowered less, and seemed less submissive. She seemed almost to be socializing herself, learning to trust all these nice people. Little remained of her former life; soon she would even acquire a new name.

As she moved about, fosterers evaluated her, checked to

make sure she had no behavioral problems—like aggression, or noise phobias—that would affect where she went. Re-homers and screeners had already begun to grill potential adopters, looking for just the right home. Fly had never lived in a house, apparently, but she liked people. Almost everyone who met her remarked on her sweet, gentle nature. I'm sure many thought of keeping her themselves.

SHE WAS SCHEDULED to arrive at my farm in early spring. My mission was either to integrate her into the existing menagerie here or to find a good home nearby where I could monitor her care.

I met her two hours south of my farm, near the Massa-chusetts border. The call had come from someone describing himself as a musician who traveled to gigs up and down the East Coast. To help pay for his gas and motel bills—and to do something useful and have company—he also transported rescued dogs, for twenty cents a mile. Whenever he headed to an engagement, there was usually a dog or two crated in the back of his Subaru, bound for a new home.

We'd agreed to meet at a restaurant off the Mass Pike. When I found the place, I saw Stan sitting at the wheel, a beautiful gray-and-white border collie in his lap, staring out the window.

We talked for a few minutes, but Stan was eager to be on his way to New Hampshire. So I shook his hand, gave him $50 for his expenses, hooked a leash onto Fly, and coaxed her into my truck. I wanted to get to know this mysterious crea-ture who'd suddenly surfaced in so many people's lives.

I could see she was bright and beautiful, but skittish—common border collie traits. She permitted my pats, then curled up on the floor of the front seat and didn't move until we got back to Bedlam Farm.

Occasionally I offered my hand, and she licked it. I dropped a tiny biscuit every so often; she gobbled them gratefully. But I knew it would be days before I had a clue as to what this dog was like. I could also already see—and hear—that Fly was in trouble.

We went straight to my vet in Salem. The sores around her neck had largely healed; so had the surgical incisions. She was still coughing persistently from the heartworms, however, and her breathing was labored. The vet took blood tests and X-rays and promised to call the next day.

At home, Fly crawled into a crate and didn't come out until the next morning.

Meanwhile, I placed one more call to the farmer from whom Fly had been taken; it seemed the right thing to do.

I told the guy who answered that I now had the dog the rescue group had taken. He said he'd gotten their messages but had no desire to get involved.

"She cost me two hundred dollars," he said, adding that he wouldn't mind being paid.

"You understand why they took the dog?" I asked.

"I guess. I don't mind her being gone, having a better life. I didn't take such good care of her." He sounded a bit embarrassed.

Living upstate these past few years, getting to know neighboring farmers, I had a better sense of how rough his life likely was, how physically taxing his work was, how pressed he might be for time and money. It's easy to be self-righteous about rescuing animals. I told him I'd mail him a check for $200.

NEXT DAY, the vet called with disheartening news: "Fly is a very sick girl. She has category-three heartworm, which is extremely serious."

Because of the anesthesia administered before her spaying, Mary explained, the worms had clustered around her heart. Now she was in real peril; a cluster that broke loose could cause a blockage, even cardiac arrest. Injecting medications to kill the worms would be dangerous, too, with the blood vessels around the heart so swollen. I told Mary I understood the risks and asked her to do the best she could for the dog.

And I began to question whether I could devote the time necessary to nurse Fly back to health and help teach her all the things—from not peeing indoors to walking on a leash—she'd never learned. My schedule on the farm was crazy: lambs coming, the house under repair, my next book due, and a tour looming. Plus, I had my own dogs to worry about.

But I had a friend down the road who kept sheep, goats, and chickens. Sarah had been looking for a dog, and she was the kind of owner rescue groups fantasize about. She was at home every day, spinning and knitting, selling yarn and garments, taking care of her animals.

Nothing made Sarah happier than sitting with an ailing goat all night in the barn; any lamb who even blinked oddly wound up in her kitchen, sucking on a bottle. This could be Fly's happy ending.

But I had to move quickly. Fly was attaching herself to me minute by minute, and vice versa. She'd begun staring at me with her deep, gray-blue eyes, working to figure me out; I was stroking her forty minutes out of every hour. I called Sarah and explained the situation. Sarah had little spare money, I knew, and Fly's treatment would be expensive. I could manage the bills but couldn't spare the time; Sarah had the opposite problems. So I proposed that I see Fly through her medical problems; then, once Fly was healthy, Sarah would take over.

"Bring the dog over," she said. "Let's have a look."

I've been writing for some years now about human-animal attachment, yet I'm often still surprised at the ways in which people and dogs bond.

At Sarah's place, Fly ignored the goats and sheep watching her nervously from behind the pasture fence. Instead, still weak and coughing, she walked slowly into Sarah's living room and curled up at her feet.

Though I know better, it was hard not to believe they'd been waiting for each other. Sarah had left a rugged life back in New England, and like many refugees from urban life, she'd found here a way to reconnect with nature. Fly, a creature who'd never had love or attention, could soak up all that Sarah could provide.

Fly didn't appear to care about sheep or chickens or work at all. After all she'd endured, it was enough for her to find one caring human.

Who knows what's in a dog's mind? But I felt I was seeing this sweet, battered little dog find peace. Perhaps sensing in Sarah a kindred spirit who needed love and was willing to give it.

"You're home now, girl," Sarah told her. I hated letting Fly go, but I knew that Sarah was right.

A few days later, I got this email from her:

"Fly is really adjusting well. We are still thinking we should keep things quiet and make certain that she gets plenty of rest, but it has been nice to see her actually play.

"She has touched us in a way that does not seem possible in such a short time. There is something magical about her. I am charged with providing her with warmth, safety, stability, and love. However, I feel that her presence in our lives has given us a far greater gift than we can ever give her. Can that be possible in such a short time? She is a tiny dog with a huge spirit. We love her. And we love you."

FLY'S SALVATION WAS NOT to be so simple, however. She was still very sick.

She slept almost all day, ate little, coughed whenever she moved quickly. She preferred to stay in her crate, or in Sarah's lap. I've had border collies for years, and it was striking how little this one moved, how indifferent she was to the livestock all around her, how little attention she paid to anything but Sarah.

She began regular blood testing at the vet's. Two weeks after I'd brought her to Sarah, she got a shot of Immiticide— a very strong, and occasionally lethal, drug that kills heartworms and other parasites.

The protocol called for Fly to remain in the veterinary hospital for twenty-four hours, monitored closely to see if she was responding to the treatment. A vet tech agreed to take her home, IV and all, and keep an eye on her through the night.

I dropped Fly off at the clinic that morning. The vets would administer the shot shortly after eight a.m.; I was to call an hour or two later for an update.

Fly pressed her nose against mine. "Be strong, girl," I urged her. "You've come such a long way."

But when I called to see how Fly was doing, the vet told me she was "struggling." I rushed back to the hospital, worrying about Fly, and now also about Sarah, who already loved the dog so dearly that her loss would be extraordinarily painful. I would feel awful about bringing these two together, over such a long distance at such great expense and trouble, only to make them both suffer so.

Fly did look dreadful, drooling and writhing in her crate, clearly in pain. One of the vets told me to call Sarah and prepare her.

I could tell Sarah sensed the pessimism in my voice; she began to cry. "She's struggling, Sarah," I said. "The vets still think she might pull through, but you need to be ready." I almost couldn't bear it. After all this dog had been through, how could she die in a crate at a vet's office?

I knew this vet well; she was competent, compassionate, and direct. When she asked if I knew whether Sarah would want Fly's body buried or cremated, she was telling me something.

At such moments the extraordinary relationship between humans and dogs comes to life. It has created a new ethical consciousness. The idea that animals should not ever be killed, and that we ought to prolong their lives at great expense for long periods of time, is as new as it is startling, even profound.

Our love of animals like dogs is causing us to redefine our relationship with another species.

It is a social and cultural phenomenon, a mirror of our society. We have to consider how much we love them. What is their place in our lives? How much do they mean to us? How much can we afford to spend on their care? Is there a point where we should let them go? How much grieving will we do, should we do, and why?

The bond between people and their animals is no longer simple, if it ever was. It reflects a growing view of dogs and cats and other animals as being like us—better, even, than us. For some, it defines how good we are, how loving and faithful.

People say, more and more, that their dogs and cats are members of the family, not really pets. If they say it, it becomes true, and if it is true, it raises all sorts of new challenges for us. If our dogs have souls, deciding their fates is not as easy as it used to be. Putting an animal down is one thing. Killing a member of the family is quite another.

I know a farmer who lives near me who had a border collie he loved and who served him faithfully for fourteen years. One morning the dog came up lame and hobbled into the kitchen. The farmer turned to his wife and said, "Honey, say goodbye to Demon."

"Why?" she asked.

"Because I'm going to take him out into the barn and shoot him."

The farmer's wife, recounting the story later, said she was very sad, because she loved Demon a great deal. But there was no questioning the decision, she added quickly. You don't keep a lame dog on a farm.

This new relationship explains the intensity of the rescue culture, the deep feelings these powerless animals spark in us. "C'mon, girl," I pleaded with Fly, who lay near death in the surgical suite. "You didn't come all this way to die here. You can get through."

I opened her crate and Fly crawled over toward me, pulling her IV tube along with her. I suddenly wished I had kept her myself, so that if she died I could have spared Sarah this blow. But losing Fly would be a blow for me, too. I'd identified with this dog months ago, when I first heard about her.

Fly's condition seesawed through the day, her fever soaring, then abating. I stayed nearby and phoned Sarah with updates, mostly grim. Then in late afternoon, as I was trying to catch a bit of sleep in my truck, a tech came and tapped on the window. Fly's fever had finally ebbed. She was looking more alert. The vets said her heart and other vital signs seemed normal.

Kris, one of the staff, took Fly home with her that night. Like all of us, she'd come to dote on this gentle creature, and she slept with Fly next to her, her hand on the dog's heart to be sure it kept beating. Late that night, as I'd asked, Kris called me.

"She's doing great," she said. "Amazing turnaround. She's alert, drinking, licking me." In turn, I called Sarah, who burst into tears at this surprising news. I was relieved, but still cautious; the dog I'd spent the day with was anything but healthy.

Fly went home to Sarah's the next day. She needed crate rest and leash walking for weeks, and her treatments would continue for months: more injections, a steady diet of steroids and anti-inflammatories and antibiotics. The shots themselves caused pain and soreness, chronic diarrhea, fatigue, and nausea. The bills climbed past $1,300, which is where the rescue culture meets the real world. How many dogs, however poignant their stories, can be saved at such steep price tags?

She never fully recovered her strength. She still tired easily, especially for a border collie, although over the next few months, her stamina increased. She did develop some of the strange and obsessive habits of the breed, staring for hours at

Sarah's guinea hens. As her appetite returned, she figured out how to open kitchen cabinets.

She's never learned herding, though, or showed much interest in sheep. Sarah loves nurturing wounded things, but she's not drawn to training. So while Fly will happily stare at beavers in the creek or chickens in the yard, she seems afraid of larger animals and backs away from them.

Hers is a happy human–meets–dog story, nonetheless. Fly attaches herself to Sarah's ankle much of the day. When Sarah does her barn chores, Fly follows along. When she sits out in her studio, spinning yarn, knitting hats and sweaters, Fly curls up between her and the woodstove.

FLY IS NOTHING if not innocent, responsible neither for her troubles nor for her subsequent good fortune. Her life is as good as human beings decide to make it; she can only go along for the ride. She can never be truly aware of the good done on her behalf, though I know many animal lovers would disagree.

The day may come, philosopher Jeremy Bentham wrote two centuries ago, when animals acquire those rights that should never have been withheld from them, except for humans' arrogance and tyranny. I don't know if he's right, or if that would be an unqualified good thing.

Bentham rejected a number of Aristotelian notions about human superiority. A full-grown horse or dog is decidedly more rational than any infant, he believed. And he wrote about our obligations to treat animals morally.

"The question," he wrote of animals, "is not, Can they *reason*? Nor Can they *talk*? But, Can they *suffer*?"

They can, of course, and I don't doubt that Fly had. Taking her in, loving her, was a moral opportunity, a way for me to perform an act of compassion.

When people meet Fly, or when I tell them about her, I see the warmth in their faces, and hear their words of praise (for me) and sympathy (for her). I feel approved of. "Thank you for the wonderful work that you do," one vet tech told me during my many visits to check on Fly.

But the praise, generously intended, makes me uncomfortable, too. I remember leaving the clinic thinking that the tech had spoken to me the same way someone might have spoken to Mother Teresa or some other humanitarian, and as I climbed into my truck, I remember thinking, Katz, you are no Mother Teresa. The "wonderful work" involved mostly making phone calls, writing checks, and driving a dog around.

This is part of what made me uneasy about rescue.

Bentham is right to see the treatment of animals as a moral issue, a matter of ethics, not just laws.

But the rescue and treatment of animals, in our time, are seen so *much* as moral issues that stories like Fly's raise real questions. I meet people almost daily who tell me their dogs or other animals were abused, and many who feel strongly that rescuing a dog is the only morally acceptable way to acquire one.

While many animals *are* severely abused, a number of studies have found that animal abuse tends to be overdiagnosed and overreported, and occurs less frequently than many animals lovers believe, notes Steven R. Lindsay in his comprehensive *Handbook of Applied Dog Behavior and Training.* Shelter and rescue workers know that "abused" dogs are much more likely to be adopted than those merely lost or abandoned. Often adopters—people like me—seem to feel that kind treatment of needy animals makes them righteous people.

Fly unlocked a response in me, something I'd been circumspect of, something that I now consciously seek to limit. It felt good to rescue her, pleasurable. But I don't feel entirely at ease about the status animals have in my life, or in our society.

So many animals are in need, and there are no clear boundaries on how many are too many for one person to manage, or how much effort animals should command compared to the efforts we make to help human beings.

The "rescue" element of acquiring animals can be psychologically and emotionally challenging, sometimes intense, especially if the people engaged in it are unaware of their own psychological backstories and motivations.

I'm leery of a life with animals in which the rescue becomes an end in itself, more important than the dog or cat or cow; in which I have more animals than I can know and understand and care for well. It's easy to spend all day running to vets, preparing special diets, cleaning up messes, dispensing pills, and applying bandages. The need is infinite, the boundaries fuzzy.

I don't want to rescue animals primarily because I want to feel better about myself, or better than some other people, or morally superior to anyone. The best part of my life with animals is the humility they teach, the humanity they foster.

I've seen that some people deeply involved in animal rescue can be self-righteous, with harsher views of their fellow humans than of dogs. It's easy to feel virtuous, harder to be aware of one's own self-interest.

So I try to limit the number of animals I bring onto the

farm and into my life. And I try hard to be aware of my own motives.

I've even grown wary of the word "rescue." It can signal a glib, self-serving perspective. I not only "rescued" Fly but, after her, Izzy and Emma, more border collies from a local abandoned farm. And Elvis the steer, in a way, and then Harold and Luna. I could call Winston a rescued rooster, I suppose. I've been directly or indirectly involved in the re-homing of scores of dogs, cats, and farm animals in recent years.

It's become too charged a word.

Izzy is not a rescued animal, in my eyes, not a piteous creature whose presence ennobles me. Like many animals (and people), he had difficult times and deserved better. He used to live there, and now he lives here. His past no longer really matters, surely not to him; the only reason for invoking it is to serve myself.

Izzy, like so many animals, is unscathed and happy to move on, with no reason or capacity to see himself as having been saved. It's a good lesson: Doing better for animals is satisfying and meaningful, but so is doing better for people.

Bringing animals to my farm or to other good homes makes me someone who wants to do good, but also someone who was wounded, in some ways broken, and who now seeks to salve his wounds through the involuntary use of unknowing animals who have no choice in the matter, no ability to elect to be elsewhere. As Aristotle pointed out so long ago, animals have no free will.

Fly benefited from my need to rescue her, as did other dogs. I know that Fly can suffer, and so can I; there, perhaps, is where animal and human meet.

But truth matters, too.

It's a lovely thing to take in an animal, but it does not make me moral. It's merciful to give a dog who needs one a home, but it's hardly a selfless act.

To treat animals well and ease their suffering, to see animals as being in need of protection and as having some elemental rights makes moral sense to me. But it's at least as ethical to ease the suffering of our own species.

I'm pleased to have transported Fly to a new home, to have treated her illness. Was I doing good for a dog, or doing good for me? I think I know the answer: for both of us, always for both.

Chapter Nine

ROSE AND MY SOUL

There is no faith which has never yet been broken,
except that of a truly faithful dog.

—KONRAD LORENZ

KEN NORMAN, THE FARRIER, WAS COMING TO TRIM THE donkeys, and as usual he didn't give me much notice. It doesn't matter. Farriers are important, and there aren't too many of them.

I had to scramble to separate the sheep from the donkeys, get the donkeys into a small room in the big barn where they couldn't fight too hard, keep them inside, get hay to them to keep them still, and keep the sheep out.

Sheep and donkeys do not understand the notion of separate tasks and individual food, and wild brawls can break out when grain is used to entice animals like donkeys inside a barn—the only way I can get them there. The sheep want the grain, and will battle for it, and they, too, will want to come into the barn. And then one of the sheep was coughing badly and I had called the Granville Large Animal Veterinary Service, and they also were on the way.

That meant I had to isolate the ewe, get her into her own stall in the barn, and keep her there. Sheep do not like to be alone, and I couldn't give this one any company, as she was sick. It was going to be one of those continuing dramas that some farm people call chores. They are all unnerving, even a bit frightening, but they usually seem to work out. You have to stay calm.

There was a time in my life, and it is fairly recent, when I had as much to do with a farrier as with a Russian cosmonaut circling the moon, and I could not imagine moving sheep and donkeys in and out of barns, nor had I a clue as to how to do it.

These days, after some years on the farm, I know how to do it. "Rosie, let's get to work," I yelled.

If Bedlam Farm had a theme song, that would be it. I "sang" it the first night we arrived, when the animals broke through the fence and ran out into a blizzard, and Rose got them back, and I have been singing it ever since.

I have all sorts of commands I give to the dogs every day—Let's take a walk, Let's go to the woods, Let's go take photos, Let's take a ride—but there is one particular command that is only for Rosie, and she absolutely lives to hear it: "Rosie, let's go to work."

It's like a bugler sounding the charge for the cavalry. Wherever Rose is, she materializes at the nearest door, head low, eyes intense, all business. Usually, it's at the back door, the one nearest the animal pastures.

Rose waits, nose to the door, while I put on my boots and then open the door. She shoots into the back of the house, down to the pasture gate, and is waiting for me impatiently by the time I lumber up. She never knows exactly what the task is on a given day.

She is not a herding dog per se, the kind you see in trials or on TV, but a working farm dog, and she constantly watches me for cues and clues about her mission. When there is work with Rose, there is no messing around. She gets it done. The rest of the world—people, food, other dogs— recedes, vanishes. She concentrates, focuses, pays attention. She is bright. She is brave. She is tireless. She is wired into me, fused almost, and knows what I want her to do, and means to do it. She hears my voice, watches my eyes, senses my mood, reads my mind.

Today, it is a bit more complicated than usual, but it never takes her too long to figure it out. And I never doubt that she will get it, and do it, because she always does and has. Sometimes I feel that we are not two things, man and dog, but one.

Rose rushes up to the pasture, then turns to me, awaiting instructions. "Get the donkeys," I say. Rose and the donkeys are not crazy about each other. The donkeys, ever protective of the sheep, often challenge Rose when she goes to herd them, and Lulu and Fanny have each kicked her once or twice. She responds by nipping both of them on the butt from time to time to keep them in line. Rose will not be deterred.

They have an uneasy truce, but when she needs to get them to do something, they usually end up doing it.

She rushes up behind Jeannette, the donkey leader, and lunges at her leg, causing Jeannette to turn and move toward me. Jeannette is a wise old girl, and she never wants to tangle with this crazy and relentless dog. As she moves down to me, Jesus and Fanny follow, as donkeys don't like to be alone any more than sheep do, especially with Rose. Lulu, ever independent, hangs back. "Look back," I yell to Rose, a command to round up stragglers, and she charges up behind Lulu, and nips at her tail.

Donkeys are willful and independent, but they don't much like trouble, and Lulu comes skittering down to join the rest of us. I go into the barn, get some grain, shake it into a cup. That's all the donkeys need to hear. I slide open the barn door, walk with the cup into the room where the trimming will be done, and the donkeys follow. I will toss some hay in to keep the donkeys occupied.

As I expected, the sheep have heard the grain in the cup and are making a lot of noise, gathering and heading for the barn. I tell Rose to lie down, permitting the sheep to charge down toward me.

Normally, she would not permit this, but in a lie-down, they will move past her, and when they do, I point to the sick ewe and tap it on the head, and Rose charges in, isolating the ewe and two others and backing them away from the flock, which takes off up the hill, and holding them near me. I slide open the barn door and, with Rose on the other side of the three sheep, they rush into the barn.

With the crook, I drag the sick ewe into the holding pen next to the donkeys, whose gate has been left open. The donkeys are ready for the farrier, the ewe is ready for the vet. I call Rose—I always have to call her several times, as she hates to leave work—and we go back into the house. I turn on the computer and go to work. I can imagine getting through a day without Rose—I just can't imagine how I would survive.

EVERYONE I ASK who loves a dog tells me their dog has a soul, and they haven't much doubt about it. I think they are really telling me something about their own souls. The dogs are never participating. They don't really need to talk about souls, and neither do the donkeys, cows, or sheep.

My animals, especially the dogs, live in the now. Their lives are elemental. They worry about food, and the life and smells around them. They worry about me, and I think perhaps they worry about each other. I do not believe they worry about their spirits or afterlives. Right after I got Rose I began to live my life. I moved upstate, bought this farm, confronted some personal issues, began taking photographs, made amazing friends, found my sister, discovered the meaning of love, got help.

Rose helped make that life possible and, in some ways, came to define it. She gave me strength. She provided support. We stood side by side through blizzards, animal dramas, lambings, quarrelsome rams, renegade donkeys, feral rabid cats, wild pigs, lonely days and nights.

I don't honestly know if I could have made it without her, but I don't believe that I could have, which is what is perhaps most important.

I need Rose to be Rose. I could not have survived that first awful winter on the farm, a winter of storms, ice, and bitter cold, and the strange and demanding life of a farm without Rose, or without the idea of her.

When I had to charge outside at three a.m. and saw the thermometer at minus 20, it was the idea of Rose charging ahead of me, leading the way, finding the sheep, getting to the lambs, that gave me the heart to do it. I knew that whatever happened to these animals—breaking through the fence, fighting over grain, bumping into me, needing medical care—Rose would help me figure it out, help me do it. And she did.

I don't believe that on some of those winter nights when I fell down on the hard ice, and knocked myself out and she nipped on my ear and barked until I stood up, that I would have always gotten up otherwise.

I don't know whether I would have had the strength or the courage to live on this remote hill, beset by coyotes, falling wires, broken water pipes, rotting fences, collapsing barns, lightning strikes and storms, and the relentless responsibilities of running a farm, caring for animals, and staying strong. When I couldn't see, Rose was always watching.

When I couldn't run fast enough, Rose got there.

When I was afraid, Rose was determined.

When I was confused, she was sure.

I didn't know what to do about a charging ram, but Rose did. I didn't know how to get a runaway donkey back into the fence. Rose always knew. I couldn't fathom how to keep the donkeys and sheep from fighting over grain, and knocking me down, but Rose always kept order.

I was worried about getting sick sheep into the barn until the vet arrived, but Rose wasn't worried, and got them there. She always seemed to know what to do.

I couldn't imagine moving sheep through the woods to find a new pasture, but Rose always got them there. For six years, day and night, hot and cold, sun or storm, Rose has watched over me and this farm, and the animals in it, and never once failed to do what she needed to do, or know what she needed to do, giving me the strength and confidence, and eventually the experience, to be here and live my life.

Her soul and mine are not really separate, one completes the other, and it isn't just about love, either—although that is a perfectly good bond. I came to the farm to live, to free my soul—to have a soul—and I believe in my heart that I could not have done this without that humorless and purposeful creature.

That's my story, and I've been telling it for some time now. It's a good story.

I suppose it's not entirely true, although I still believe it and tell it in good faith. The story of Rose gives me the strength to live my life, and that counts for something. A lot. Looking back on it, it isn't that I think it's false, but that I understand better why I came up with it. I am much too fearful a person to have come up to the farm by myself.

As I look around me, I see that people survive without Rose; in fact, most farms don't have Rose. They manage. I suppose I could manage.

I have come to see that Rose does not need to have a soul, or need to think about one. I need for her to have one.

IN THE AUTUMN of my life, I am fighting for my life, still and forever, and at each struggle, each turning point, a dog has appeared to take me where I needed to go, and to keep my spirits strong.

A dog guided me to the farm. A dog helped me live here. A dog connected me to the lives and spirits of human beings around me. A dog helped me learn to love.

Does this mean that dogs have souls, or does it mean we create the dogs we need, seek them out, reinforce them, and project our needs onto them? I think I am coming to see it, at last. It is not a cynical idea, this idea of mine, but a loving one. Dogs are very important to me.

Izzy has the soul I want him to have, give him the opportunity to have. He enriches me. At a time when I was still learning how to love, Lenore helped show me how to love.

Rose, of all my dogs, fulfills the glorious history of dogs

in service to human beings, completing them, helping them lead the lives they want and need to live.

Dogs and humans have an elaborate way of communicating with one another, and one of the things that makes it so complex is its inequality. We have narrative, language, and history. They have instincts and senses beyond our imagination. They are aware of our emotions, moods, smells, impulses; and their ability to thrive and survive is based partly on their canny skills at reading and manipulating us.

If we are happy, they know it, and respond to it. If we are angry, they grow anxious. They have no direct language with which to talk to us, yet their ability to know what we like and want is hardwired and finely and richly honed.

I can't honestly separate what people need of dogs from the souls of dogs. My instincts are just not strong enough. I am not sure enough. I have learned that there are many things I just don't know and will never know. Much of the interaction between dogs and people is a mystery to me, beyond me. I know that dogs are not inferior to us; their instincts far surpass any of ours.

One of the most compelling theories about dogs and their consciousness comes from psychologist David Premack of the University of Pennsylvania and is called the "theory of mind." It says that we are self-aware and conscious, and that other creatures are also self-aware and self-conscious; also, we must recognize that these other creatures may have their own points of view and mental processes, and that these might be the same or different from our own.

When Rose looks to see which shoes I put on so that she can know if we are going to work, she is showing an awareness of me, beyond her own reality. When Lenore goes up and hops into bed at night, anticipating that I will soon join her, she is stepping out of herself, and is aware of my behavior. When Izzy goes into a bedroom and finds a dying patient and comforts him, he is showing awareness of another being.

These examples abound in my life. When Elvis comes to the gate and bellows when I go upstairs into my study; when the donkeys bray greetings when I get up in the morning and put my feet on the floor; when the sheep head for the pasture gate when they see Rose and me come out the back door. All of these things tell me that as I am aware of them, animals are aware of me. But this does not mean we are the same thing, with the same aspirations. I worry about my soul, but there is no reason to suppose Rose worries about hers, surely not in the same language and context that I might.

In *How Dogs Think,* the famed behaviorist Stanley Coren writes that "dogs seem to be very aware of the fact that other individuals have a particular point of view that must be taken into account." I have found this to be true. They are keenly aware of us, in ways few of us really grasp or appreciate.

I have always found it a little demeaning to put our words into the minds of animals. I don't need or want them to be like me. They are better than that. They have their own kind of language, their own consciousness.

I find questions concerning loyalty, empathy, and intuitiveness closer to getting at what animals might really be feeling, or sensing. I see those traits all the time. When I am sick, Rose will not leave my side voluntarily, not to eat, go out, eliminate. What is she sensing? What is she doing?

I don't know. I know that I will never know.

Mostly, what my dogs need is me. My love, direction, and commitment, which give them the opportunity to live their lives to the fullest extent possible, as I wish to live mine. In this way, we complement one another.

AS I WRITE THIS, Rose is sitting in my study, moving from one window to another, checking to see where the donkeys are, where the sheep are, if any coyotes or stray dogs have turned up, if there is trouble, if alarms should be sounded, work should be done.

She doesn't offer me a lot of love in the traditional sense. She doesn't want to cuddle or sleep in bed with me, or need a lot of treats or fussing. She lives in service to me, gives herself over to the life I want and need to have.

In that way, she is a critical part of my soul, and I cannot really find the difference between hers and mine.

And it doesn't really matter to me. My dogs are well beyond the spiritual fussing of humans. I think sometimes that they can see us but we can't really see them beyond our own needs and projections. For sure, we are needier than they are.

Chapter Ten

LULU GOES TO HELL

God made the wild animals according to their kinds, the livestock according to their kinds, and all the creatures that move along the ground according to their kinds. And God saw that it was good.

Then God said, "Let us make man in our image, in our likeness, and let him rule over the fish of the sea and the birds of the air, over the livestock, over all the earth, and over all the creatures that move along the ground."

—Genesis 1:25–26

HENRY WHITFIELD CLIMBED OUT OF THE AGING IMPALA, offered me his hand, patted my shoulder, and handed me a jug of cider as a gift.

He always looked out of place anywhere but in church. He wore a blue parka over black slacks and a white dress shirt, with a fur hat. I suspected there was a black suit jacket in his car, plus a sober tie. He carried a pair of rubber boots in a brown paper bag, in case we ventured into the barn or pasture.

We'd first gotten to know each other, via email, a few years ago when I wrote about Thomas Merton, the late author and well-known Trappist monk. I'd visited Henry's church in central New York State once or twice, too, heard him preach and conduct services, and we'd become friendly. I invited him to come by when he was passing through, heading to Lake George on vacation or to visit friends in Canada. I'd made several friends who were deeply religious since moving upstate, and I'd come to value their perspective. It was pleasant, when Henry came by, to trade some spiritual chatter and stories about our lives, and to stroll around the farm.

"The new barn looks beautiful," said Henry on this brisk afternoon, taking in the changes since his last visit. He had the air, today, of someone with business to conduct, more like an insurance adjuster than a pal who'd come to hang around. "You look well, and I hope you are well. Let's talk about this animals and souls business."

I'd called to ask for his counsel. I was exploring the idea of the souls and spirits of animals, I explained, and even though my inquiry wasn't religious, exactly, religious questions came up from time to time. As I talked more about what I'd been reading and puzzling over, he nodded. He got it.

I always found him to be a clear thinker, with enormous conviction, yet eager to absorb other points of view. He seemed willing to hear me out, even when he didn't agree.

I saw no evidence that Henry was crazy about animals; tending to people was his passion, and he seemed quite good at it. I could use his clarity, I thought, on a subject so clouded by emotion.

Henry had a funeral to preside over that evening, he said, explaining the shirt and dress slacks. He'd put 150,000 miles on his noisy, rusting car, driving to baptisms and weddings, calling on the ill, lonely, or spiritually adrift members of his congregation.

Izzy, always hoping to charm fresh admirers, came over as we spoke and put his head in Henry's hand. Henry patted him politely, in the way of people who want to be gracious but aren't really enthusiastic.

"New dog?" he asked. "He's cute." But he didn't seem to want to hear Izzy's story, all the details of how he'd come to me.

"He's going to heaven, isn't he?" I asked jokingly as we walked toward the big dairy barn I'd just restored.

Henry shook his head. So we were into it already.

"Really?" I said sadly. "But he's such a good guy."

"He's very nice," Henry agreed, striding purposefully toward the donkeys. "But there is only one way to get to heaven, one ticket in, and that's accepting Jesus Christ as Lord and Savior. If you accept Christ, you go to heaven. If you don't, I'm afraid, you don't."

Henry, it turned out, wasn't terribly interested in hearing what Aristotle had to say about animals, nor the ideas of the minister down the hill from me who assured me that God made and loved all his creatures and would surely not exclude our pets from heaven.

The Bible, Henry said, was quite clear. "Lots of ministers want their congregants to be happy," he said. "And so do I. But wanting something to be true doesn't make it so. Animals cannot, so far as I know, accept Jesus. They are not like us." And he quoted the passage from Genesis I've partly reprinted here.

This passage is important; it established the notion, widely held in the Western world, that humans have dominion over animals, that God created animals to serve us, and clearly intended for us to rule over them.

It's shaped much of the relationship between so-called civilized people and animals, determined the fates of countless creatures. Animals are clearly not our equals, according to Genesis; they are something less, something apart.

Certainly that's how Henry read it. "The Scriptures are clear," he said. "We have dominion over the animals, over all the creatures that move along the ground.

"One woman in my congregation said to me, 'But Reverend Henry, I love my cat more than my husband. Surely you are not telling me that he won't have eternal life, that he doesn't have a soul.' "

Henry paused to look around, and noticed Elvis gazing hopefully at him over the pasture gate. Where there was a paper bag, there might be apples or carrots or a Snickers bar.

"Well," Henry said, "that is a large cow."

What about the woman who worried about her cat's soul?

"I said, 'Sorry, Charlene, I wish I had better news for you, but there are no shortcuts to heaven, no exceptions, I'm afraid, not even for your cat.' "

Henry pulled his rubber boots from his bag and, leaning against a fencepost, exchanged them for his dress shoes. Even in the boots, he looked a bit odd. "You look all shiny and pressed, like an undertaker," I kidded him. "Not like us rumpled and disheveled farm types."

He laughed. "You look appropriately rumpled and disheveled," he said. "You look the part now, limp and all. You've grown into yourself."

We opened the gate, and entered the pasture. I thought Lulu might soften the Reverend Whitfield up a bit.

LULU IS MY MOST CALM and affectionate donkey, with irresistible wide brown eyes, long lashes, and a soft warm nose. She likes contact with people, and is so gentle that newcomers quickly overcome any nervousness. If you sit down near her, she comes over and places her head on your shoulder, or nuzzles you with her cheek. She's probably the farm's most soothing presence, who's never harmed anyone or anything.

When people tell me they can't imagine how their animals could be excluded from heaven, I think of Lulu, the way she radiates gentleness. Her eyes seem to contain the wisdom and understanding that donkeys have amassed from their thousands of years serving humanity.

I handed Henry a cookie and suggested he give it to Lulu. He held it out in the palm of his hand as if it were radioactive, and Lulu slowly drifted over, carefully took the cookie, enjoyed it, and pressed her head against his shoulder. She was waiting for a scratch.

Henry patted the top of her fuzzy head a few times, while I pointed out the cross emblazoned on her back, the rich history of donkeys, the many references to them in both Jewish and Christian theology. He smiled a bit.

Then he leaned forward and looked her in the eyes. "Lulu," Henry said softly, "do you accept Jesus Christ as your Lord and Savior?"

Lulu snorted, rubbed her nose against Henry's hat.

He turned to me. "She is not going to heaven," he said. "Sorry."

She seemed to take the news with the equanimity for

which donkeys are justly famous, and edged closer to me. Perhaps I had a cookie, or better news.

Henry laughed. He enjoyed being a messenger of God, a teller of the truth—the truth as he understood it, rather than the truth people might prefer to hear. His was a fixed creed in a world where people tried on beliefs like sweaters. He knew who he was, what he was supposed to do, what his job was. It was not to cater to the animal adoration he saw around him.

Not that he didn't love animals, Henry explained. Not that they weren't important. God had made it clear that they were. He quoted from Job 12:10: " 'In his hand is the life of every creature and the breath of all mankind.' " It called on humans to love and respect all creatures.

"Think of it, 'the breath of all mankind,' " Henry said. "That's an important message, because it says to me that the breath of all mankind is in every living thing and that *his hand* is in the life of every creature. So the animals are sacred, and we should treat them with love and mercy and respect. Your animals are sacred to me because *his hand* is in them all."

Nevertheless, he went on, the Lord gave us dominion over them, and he gave us the means to choose between good and evil, and thus to have souls, which ascend to heaven—or not.

"Are you telling me that Lulu is going to hell?" I asked, now a bit concerned.

Henry smiled. "I don't know. Maybe. I think not. She can't accept Christ, so she can't be punished for not accepting him," he said. "I don't believe God would punish animals for acting in the very way he intended when he created them. But we ought not to judge animals the way we judge ourselves. They cannot do good or bad."

Wasn't it possible, I asked, as we left my possibly doomed donkeys and headed over to see Elvis and Harold and Luna, that because God and Jesus both loved and appreciated animals, they would allow them to join people in heaven? If they are sacred, aren't they too precious to be left behind?

"Anything is possible," said Henry. "And I don't mean to be arrogant. But I believe the Bible is the Word, and it is unambiguous: We have dominion over them. There's nothing in the Bible about animals having souls, being rewarded, or having eternal life." However precious or beloved animals are, he maintained, humans can't alter God's word simply because they love their pets.

I appreciated what Henry was saying, and admired his consistency and integrity. It was a relief, though, that I wasn't especially religious, not as scripturally bound as he was, and therefore freer to consider other possibilities. Not that I had any answers either.

Henry wasn't bending with the prevailing winds, swaying along with modern theologians, or comforting fervent animal lovers who find it incomprehensible that their pets won't enjoy life beyond their physical beings.

"I don't mean to upset people who love animals, but faith is faith," Henry says. "And belief is not always convenient to the tides of the moment."

He and I usually skirted questions about my own faith. I was raised a Jew, became a Quaker, have flirted with some early versions of Christianity, and am now a strange blend of all three, plus a healthy dose of secularity. One day, I hope to get these matters sorted out, but that hasn't happened yet.

Henry has made it clear that if I don't accept Jesus as the son of God, then I'm destined for hell, whether Lulu is there or not. He said—only once—"The door is always open to you, you know." And I do.

But though we have differing views on souls, faith, and animals, I can't fault him—quite the opposite—for staying true to his beliefs, reminding me that with faith comes sacrifice, and that faith shouldn't be subject to the latest public-opinion poll.

Still, dogma can be rigid, even cold, and people who study the Bible can find support for a hundred different points of view. Many theologians believe that there's plenty of room in the Gospels for animals.

A friend had given me *The Bible Promise Book,* a volume full of uplifting quotations. I'd found a reading from the Gospel of John (10:27–28) that seemed apropos, and I'd copied it down and pulled it out of my pocket to show Henry: "My sheep listen to my voice; I know them, and they follow me. I give them eternal life, and they shall never perish; no one can snatch them out of my hand."

I don't love sheep as much as John does, nor do I think mine are headed for eternal life. But if John is promising his flock eternal life, then there's hope for Lulu, right? Perhaps Henry was drawing the requirements too narrowly.

I don't know; I'm not a theologian. One of the things I love most about animals is that they're *not* dogmatic or litigious. Staking out positions about their capacities and their care, on the other hand, often triggers anger, self-righteousness, and moral superiority, traits animals themselves clearly don't possess.

I read the passage proudly, but of course I had underestimated Henry and wandered in well over my head.

The author of the passage, Henry pointed out patiently,

was the fisherman John, Jesus' most beloved disciple, and was quoting Jesus at the temple when he said that his sheep (meaning his human followers, not literal animals) know him and follow him, as a flock follows its shepherd. Henry smiled, and put one arm around my shoulder. He was expressing his love of people, not sheep.

So my sheep aren't bound for heaven, either, it seems.

Although I was joking, sort of, the idea of the shepherd has particular relevance for me. Herding sheep with Rose is probably one of the most spiritual things I do, partly because it's such a time-honored practice, partly because the figure of the protective, watchful shepherd is so deeply embedded in religious lore.

Acceptance of Jesus was the only way to eternal life, in his book and in his Book, but Henry understood the impulse to think otherwise. "People love animals so much that they want to give them this gift, which is a beautiful thing," he said.

And he countered with a quote from Matthew (10:29–31): " 'Are not two sparrows sold for a penny? Yet not one of them will fall to the ground apart from the will of your Father. And even the very hairs of your head are all numbered. So don't be afraid: you are worth more than many sparrows.' "

Lots of people in this country, I told Henry, seem to believe that animals are equal or superior to humans. That dogs are more pure and loving, and far less destructive. It makes sense to them that animals actually *deserve* to go to heaven more than many people do.

We were in the cow pasture now, where Elvis was eyeing Henry expectantly, hoping more for a Snickers than eternal life.

"Well, this is the heart of it, isn't it?" asked Henry, wrapping his scarf tightly around his neck and taking out his gloves. "God loves the people he created, and he loves them above all things. God loves animals, too, and the flowers and the mosquitoes and flies, but he loves his children the most. He gave only them the gift of good and the challenge of evil, and the most precious part of the soul—the choice between the two."

It demeans both people and animals, he said, to equate them and say that both have immortal souls. It borders on blasphemy. It is simply not so, however disappointed we are in ourselves, or smitten with the animals in our lives.

We opened the pasture gate and I went in to offer Elvis a potato, which he began to crunch on, still eyeing Henry.

"That is a large animal," Henry said again, wading over gingerly in his boots to scratch the side of Elvis's nose. Elvis appreciated the scratching, and drooled on Henry's glove.

The Bible was full of references to huge beasts of burden, Henry said, and there was definitely something biblical about Elvis.

"Elvis, you are a gentle creature and a dumb beast," he announced. "Jon wants you to go to heaven, but I can't give you that. I can bless you, though, and all of the animals here."

It was a lovely thought. I didn't remind Henry that I was not certain there was a heaven at all, for humans or for Elvis. My interest in animals and souls was more secular than religious.

BUT WHEN HENRY CLOSED HIS EYES and bowed his head, I followed suit, feeling a surge of affection for this conscientious man who'd taken the trouble to drive out to my farm on a freezing day on a somewhat hopeless mission to set us all straight.

A cold wind whistled down the pasture hill, but the sky was bright, almost painfully blue. I saw that the donkeys had come over to their side of the fence and were watching with interest. Rose was up in the far pasture, moving the sheep here and there, and Izzy was following us around, observing.

Henry raised his arm, as if to embrace my farm: "Which of all of these does not know that the hand of the Lord has done this? In his hand is the life of every creature, and the breath of all mankind. Amen." He held his hand up, signaling me not to interrupt.

" 'Open your mouth for the dumb, for the rights of all that are left desolate,' " he added. "Proverbs 31:8. I thought I might need it."

We had some tea together inside the farmhouse and talked of other things. I thanked him for coming, and he invited me to services at his church. I said I would drop by.

HENRY'S MESSAGE, which I mulled for a few hours before I got it, wasn't intended to dismiss the animal world. Though his beliefs weren't open to debate, he thought the real question wasn't whether animals could enter heaven; it was whether we loved them and treated them well. Here he and I could find comfortable common ground.

"Animals are especially deserving," he had said as we warmed up indoors, "because they cannot ask for mercy."

I worried a bit for him, envying his great clarity about his faith, yet feeling he was also somewhat out of sync with the times and with many of his own congregants.

Still, his talk reminded me of something Andrew Linzey had said in *Animal Gospels.* Even though his view of animals and souls was different from Henry's, there was common ground there, too. The Gospels, Linzey writes, have always urged us to listen to the voiceless, and he quotes biblical scholar Richard Bauckham on the special duty the powerful have to protect those who can't secure rights for themselves.

We need to feel sorrow for the cruelties we inflict on animals; indeed, we need not only to feel that sorrow but also to express it publicly, thereby helping us to change our behavior, to feel greater compassion for all species, including our own.

The issue isn't whether animals go to heaven, therefore, but whether we can give voice to the voiceless.

Animals are the "dumb" innocents "par excellence," wrote Linzey, the ones who cannot speak for themselves, who can suffer horribly at human hands and yet rely totally on humans in order to have any advocates at all. The Gospels, he explained, preach that the "dumb" must be heard, that no matter how deaf humans may be, God "hears the cries of the creatures."

I mentioned to Henry once that as a lifelong urbanite, my new life with animals felt something like a mystery, not because I was saving them, but because they were changing me and teaching me so much, and because I felt so responsible for their welfare.

He said he completely understood.

The power of animals, their animating spirits, the thing that most separates them from us, is this voicelessness. They aren't stupid but mute. We are their spokesmen, their interpreters, their advocates, and their caretakers.

An old tradition holds that at the Last Judgment, the non-human creatures of the earth will be called by God to "give evidence" against each human being. The idea pops up in books and stories about the Creation, deemed a myth, but a persistent, imposing, even haunting one: We will be judged by the very creatures so dependent on us.

So I treat, and will continue to treat, my animals—the dogs, cats, sheep, donkeys, chickens, and cows—with that in mind.

They will give evidence. What would I want them to say?

Chapter Eleven

CHASING SUNSETS

By ethical conduct toward all creatures, we enter into
a spiritual relationship with the universe.

—ALBERT SCHWEITZER

THERE IS BOTH AN EERIE BEAUTY AND AN AWFUL BLEAK-
ness to winter in upstate New York, especially after the
holiday brightness. Canadian air piles in; the temperature
plunges; the blackness and cold seem to suck the very life
from the earth.

Everything—everything—is gray, brown, black, or over-
whelmingly white. Sunlight seems to rush past, barely warming the ground.

The animals burrow into barns and corners and hardly
move. The dogs hole up in corners and under beds. The days
are short and utterly bone-chilling.

I'm close to all my dogs, but Izzy is unique. He has a soul
I've never encountered in an animal before. It comes, I think,

from his capacity to see into people, to feel their need, to open deep channels within them.

I don't know if he means to, or how he manages it, but I know that he does it. I've seen him do it time and time again, especially among the dying, people living on the edge of life, people who are suffering.

I'VE NEVER CONSIDERED MYSELF an artist, yet I've always encouraged other people to be artists, sometimes offering valuable encouragement, sometimes pushing them further than they wished to go. That winter, with the help of a smart therapist, I realized that the artist I was urging into the open was me. A creative self seemed to erupt from the photos I'd started taking. And alongside that unfamiliar new self was Izzy, riding with me in the car, lying beside me on the road, my fellow sojourner.

For as long as I can remember, I've been interested in and admired photography—other people's. I doubt I'd taken two dozen pictures of my own to that point, mostly of my daughter's birthday parties or on family vacations, none of them particularly compelling.

But I came across a small digital camera I'd bought on a book tour and stuck in a closet. I began shooting photos of a friend, and one or two of the animals. I'd launched a website by then, so I posted a few.

They were simple, obvious attempts, limited to what was right in front of me—close-ups of faces, snow scenes, the dogs. But these weren't just snapshots.

I'd begun to see the world differently, to experience rebirth, to encounter illumination and to record it, furiously and frantically. I started to notice the beautiful clarity of winter light, the way it outlined barns, bare trees, sheep.

I'd passed dead leaves thousands of times as the dogs and I walked down our woodland path; now I saw how animate they were, rich in emotion, color, and sense of place. I grew conscious of the light dancing everywhere, peeking around corners, framing life. I wanted to capture it, share it.

The stirrings I felt as I noticed this light, the waves of joy and loss, surprised me. I wondered where they were coming from, thinking for a while that it must be something like God whispering to me. Or maybe it was just me, coming alive.

As always, Izzy seemed to sense this stirring and to become part of it. He was wherever I was. I didn't need to ask or train him to do that; he was simply there, almost as much a part of the picture-taking as the camera. I talked to him about light, about what I was seeing, what I hoped to show. He listened, made me feel safe and supported.

I bought a superior (but expensive) camera, a Canon, and then an even better one. I bought a tripod, cleaning kits, lenses. Before long, I was on the phone weekly with B&H Photo in New York, asking about settings, techniques, equipment. I trawled through bookstores for works on photography, for styles I wanted to study, masters to inspire me.

All the while, I took pictures constantly, obsessively, dragging my camera, tripods, and bags everywhere I went. I haunted farms, my own and others, at sunrise, at night, shooting into the sun, around it, behind it, experimenting with focal points, thinking about composition.

This, I knew, was the way I tended to do things— impulsively, obsessively, expensively. But I also knew that I was changing, understanding stuff I hadn't understood before, using abilities I hadn't known how to use. And there, always, was Izzy, observing, standing by, part of the experience.

In the afternoon, when I was finished writing, I would

call Izzy: "Hey, Izzy, boy, let's go chase a sunset." (Rose some-how knew this wasn't her mission, so she went back to the window to watch her sheep.) Izzy dashed out the door and hopped into the backseat of the truck. I loaded up my cam-era, tripod, and lenses, brought a thermos of hot coffee or tea, turned up the car heater and defrosted the windshield, shivering in the biting cold.

We often drove over the hill to Argyle, around sharp and slick turns, through the bare woods, past staring dairy cows, watching the pale afternoon glow silhouette the old farm-houses. By midafternoon, the sun was dropping fast over the mountains, and I was rushing to catch up with it, chasing a sunset.

Izzy was present in every moment, sitting in the backseat, sitting alongside me, hopping out of the car and along the road.

You wouldn't bring Rose along on a drive like this; she would feel edgy and restless, too confined. Lenore might be too curious and friendly, apt to wander over to visit some creature. Izzy, though, could be with you without ever in-truding. He never disturbed a photo, or even moved while I was shooting one; he concentrated on me as intently as I was focused on the camera.

Kinney Road in Argyle, a sloping two-lane blacktop that ran past several dairy farms, was one of the few places nearby with a big, open sky. You could pull over at the bottom of the hill, look up, and see the sun setting against a farmhouse, barns, and silos.

Most days, my teeth were chattering and my fingers—frostbitten several times in winters past—ached and my nose ran. I could feel the wind extracting the heat from my body.

Yet the cold and wet and blasting wind didn't really bother me; I hardly noticed them. Izzy sat watching, his dark eyes fixed on me and what I was photographing. I imagined him saying something like "It's okay, do what you need to do. Take your photos. I'll be here."

By the time we got to Kinney Road and I'd pulled over and climbed out of the car with my new 14mm landscape lens and set up the tripod and mounted the camera, it was growing dark. As is often the case, I had left the house dressed inappropriately for the circumstances, in jeans and walking shoes and a tattered Old Navy sweatshirt.

Cars whizzed by in the dark, sometimes honking because they could barely see me in my dark clothes in the twilight. It *was* unwise to be standing by the roadside that way, but I lost myself, occasionally even wandering out onto the asphalt with my camera, mesmerized by the sinking sun, the farmhouses and silos framed against it. One shouldn't permit most dogs to lie by the road in the gloaming, but I never had to worry about Izzy, who always hopped out with me, found a spot in the shadows far from the passing cars, and never moved.

It was as if some other presence had taken over the process, and I was simply whirling the controls, angling the camera, releasing the shutter. I put the camera up in front of my eyes and walked forward, into the shot. Once, a truck grazed my tripod; another skidded to a screeching halt a few feet from me. I was more lucky than smart, swallowed up by this awakening, these sunsets.

All through the long and bitter winter, Izzy and I chased sunsets through New York State and Vermont, over winding roads and hills, in good weather and bad.

When I was done, the light gone, I looked around, clapped my hand or whistled, called, "Hey, Iz, truck up!" He came around to the passenger side and leaped lightly onto the front seat. I never had to call him twice, nor was he ever distracted by headlights, honks, or the many animals we encountered—deer, coyotes, cows, field mice.

I would turn up the heater, give Izzy a biscuit, sip a bit of tea, head home.

Back on the farm, Rose and Lenore greeted us. We all ventured out for a quick walk, then I fired up the woodstove, took the memory card out of my camera, and put it into my card reader. I watched in the dark, the only light coming from the big computer screen, to see what I had snared and brought home. I was always anxious, sure I had missed the shot, messed up the setting, let in too much light or too little. Sometimes I was right. But I cherished the surge of excitement and satisfaction when even one picture seemed halfway as good as I wanted it to be.

One twilight, when the wind was whipping fiercely and the car's external temperature gauge showed 5 degrees, I looked up Kinney Road and saw a blue and yellow and red sky exploding above the farmhouse—and to my great joy I got the shot. I took, by actual count, more than ten thousand photos that winter, and Izzy was with me for nearly every one.

I never tallied how many miles I logged driving back and forth to Kinney Road, how much gas I used, how many hours I spent there. Izzy never minded. But two or three times a week, Izzy and I climb into the truck and stare up at the barns on Kinney Road, watching the light play across the sky.

IZZY BROADENED HIS WORK with people beyond me, especially in our hospice work, which included regular visits to an
Alzheimer's/dementia unit in a local nursing home.

In short order, we met Jo, who thought Izzy was her poodle, and Min, who wanted to take him home, and Jen, who
asked him to love her, please. Izzy reminded everyone of
something—a beloved dog or a cat, a cow or a husband or
child. His gentle approach was the key that seemed to unlock
parts of people that might otherwise have been impossible to
see. He made people smile, laugh, remember.

In subsequent weeks, we entered the building in the same
way, punching in codes that unlocked the doors, walking
down long hallways, washing hands, wandering into common rooms and gathering places. We encountered people
walking quietly, sitting in wheelchairs, gathered around tables
or TVs, sometimes sitting alone in their rooms. We made the
circuit.

Some people didn't seem to see him, or me, so we passed
them by. But others were somehow transformed, as if Izzy
had special powers, which to my mind, he did.

The nurses and aides were shocked at first. Then they
simply watched as Izzy wafted through Pleasant Valley like a
quiet sailboat, spreading good feelings. After a while, staff
members started directing Izzy and me to people they
thought needed or wanted us. We made many friends, got
marriage proposals, danced a few times, joked and flirted.

It was a weekend, always a quieter time, the day we
walked past a beautiful woman sitting in a wheelchair, looking somewhat forlornly at a picture hanging on the wall.

I was startled by her beauty. Her white hair was pulled
back into a long braid down her back. She couldn't walk by
herself. She was distracted, confused, forgetful, yet her blue

eyes were radiant, filled with emotion. She was uncomfort-able at first, unable to grasp why we were there, what a dog was doing in her room. We must have seemed completely out of context.

But I introduced Izzy to her, and then myself, and she in-vited us to come sit with her, so we went in. The room was sparsely furnished. A bed, a night table, a dresser.

"Oh, my, what a beautiful dog," she breathed, and you could see her come to life, see how much she loved dogs. She was eager for visitors, it seemed.

She rolled her wheelchair alongside her bed, patted the mattress, and told Izzy to come on up, and he hopped up and curled up next to her, as if he'd been waiting all this time to meet her.

I looked up at the nameplate outside her room. She was Marion and, I learned before long, she was ninety-six, a wid-owed farm wife. She had an amazing face, very wrinkled but fully alive.

She had to struggle to remember things, and she was los-ing her sight and her hearing. But Izzy, of course, cared noth-ing about her deficits. He was happy just to lie calmly on Marion's bed while she stroked his paws and smiled and told him that she loved him and would never hurt him.

A friendship was born. We began visiting her two or three times a week, and the aides told us she would wait by the door, hoping Izzy would be coming. She loved to see him, to touch him, to talk to him about her farm, her children, the other dogs she had known. "But they weren't like you, Izzy," she assured him. "You are the most wonderful dog I ever met."

Marion reached into the deep well of her long life to tell

Izzy what had mattered to her, what she'd loved about her life, even as she sometimes lost track of it. She told him that she forgot things, and couldn't always see, but she never forgot him.

"You will meet my children, Izzy, because they want to meet you," she said to him one afternoon. "Except there is one of my children you will not meet. Hallys. God took her in a hurry, Izzy." She recounted how it was late at night when the state troopers came down the road. She sat up in bed, asking herself, "Who's home?"—because whoever wasn't at home, she realized with awful clarity, was dead.

"And Hallys wasn't home, Izzy. It was Hallys. The troopers said two drunken boys drove across the road in a truck, and she did everything she could to get out of the way, but she couldn't, and she was killed right away, Izzy. She was gone."

There was a long silence in Marion's room. The afternoon light was streaming through the window-blind slats. Outside the door, I could hear the confused cries of some of the patients, the chatter of the staff.

Inside the room, it remained quiet. Izzy lay still, Marion's hands kneading his fur, rubbing his head, holding his paws.

Then I remembered my hospice volunteer training and I leaned forward and said, "Marion, that is so very sad." And she nodded and said, yes, it was, it surely was.

Then she smiled, and told me that her husband's name was Horace, and her blue eyes twinkled. He was "a better man than his name," and so was his father, who was called Eustace. And she turned back to Izzy and promised that she would take care of him and love him forever.

This is what Izzy does. I began bringing cookies and

flowers along on our visits, a quilt my friend Maria made for her, a couple of photos I thought Marion might like. But it was really Izzy that was the best present.

She was confused sometimes, working so hard to remember, to see and hear. Yet she politely asked me questions about my life and my farm. She loved hearing the story of how Izzy had come to me; I told it many times.

She saved bits of doughnuts for him, ignoring my explanation that he didn't need food, wasn't hungry. You don't want a hospice dog to get into the habit of begging for food. But there was no stopping her. She loved Izzy, so she was going to give him something.

At one point, she held out her hand and said, "Here, here is a twenty-dollar bill. Buy Izzy something, please. I just can't get to the store this week." I looked down at her hand, and there was, of course, nothing in it. But I thanked her, and next time I brought her a bag of dog biscuits, so that she could give them to Izzy.

Over time, I learned how to talk with Marion, the angle at which she could best hear and see, the rhythm of my speech that she could most easily follow. I saw that I didn't need to speak so loudly, just clearly.

Hospice advocates "active listening," and I actively listened to Marion. How much of what she told me—about her family, her animals, her life—was accurate I never ascertained. And what did it matter, really? I liked hearing her stories, just as she loved hearing about Izzy, how he ran wild, how untrainable he was at first, how much I treasured him.

We came to know each other. I don't know, perhaps it was a maternal or grandmotherly feeling that she exuded, but I don't think so. It felt more like a friendship, a strong one.

Marion was easy to befriend, uncomplaining and quick to

smile. She spoke in the simple, rich dialect of a farm wife whose life had centered on family, friends, farm chores—and God. "I do believe in Jesus," she told me, matter-of-factly. "Yes, of course."

All the while we spoke, she was stroking Izzy, assuring him that she loved him and would protect him. He was a conduit for all the love in her big heart, and a means by which she was struggling to come to terms with her situation. This is what Izzy does; he's a touchstone for people on passages. This is his soul.

After we spent time with Marion we would make our rounds, see Evelyn cursing at us; Sam calling for his wife, Margaret; Jen asking if we could marry her; Jo asking if Izzy was her dog, the one she lost so many years ago. He could not soothe every resident, but he left a trail of smiles as we walked along.

In late August, the heat and sun abated a bit upstate and when we came to the nursing home, I asked if we could take Marion outside for a wheelchair ride and some time in the open air. She was eager, and the aides helped ready her, got her into her wheelchair with her slippers, a blanket in her lap.

Outside, we sat under a canopy, protected from the sun. Marion was—she told Izzy—having a tough day, a tough time. "I'm just a sick old lady, Izzy. Not good for much. But I won't forget you. I'll never forget you." We talked for a long while about our lives, our farms, our disappointments. She looked at me with her ear cocked forward, so she could hear. She nodded and smiled, seemed to understand.

Then she looked me squarely in the eye, and lowered her voice. "I have to be honest with you, I can't always remember your name," she said. "But I know you and like you. Will you promise me something?"

Yes, I said, if I can.

"Will you promise to take care of Izzy if anything happens to me? If I am gone? Will you promise that he'll never be mistreated or left to run in the wild? Promise that he will be loved?"

I looked into those fierce blue eyes, and I answered clearly and slowly, "I promise, Marion. Izzy will be loved, all the days of his life."

And she smiled and nodded, relieved.

Chapter Twelve

RUTH AND MAGNUS

A faithful friend is the medicine of life.

—Ecclesiasticus 6:16

IT'S BEEN NEARLY A DECADE SINCE ORSON, A BELOVED, NOW deceased, border collie entered my life, sparked my interest in writing about dogs, and inspired me to buy my own farm. It was also the first time that I gave much thought to dogs and souls.

Early one morning—it seems a long time ago—Orson and I were on the road. He'd seemed restless, circling near the door, a behavior that gets most dog owners moving quickly, even at four a.m. I pulled on my jeans, boots, and a shirt and went outside. That summer night in western Connecticut had been sticky, the cicadas shrill and rhythmic. I moved quietly, not wanting to wake the other participants at this sheepherding weekend. We veered away from the big house, down a path toward the woods.

In a minute or two, Orson's ruff went up and he began growling; up ahead in the dark I heard a low growl in return. Standing in the woods, half-dressed and tired, I thought none of the possibilities seemed good.

In the moonlight, I could make out a remnant of stone wall along the path, and a red glow from a cigarette, held by a thin, middle-aged woman sitting on the wall. Next to her were a pair of large, glowing yellow eyes, eerie and wolflike.

"Hey," I called, leashing Orson.

"Hello," a voice answered. "Shhh, Magnus."

I put Orson, who was not always delighted to meet strange dogs, in a lie-down.

"Don't worry about Magnus," the woman said. "As long as he can see me, he doesn't much care about anything else." Her voice was striking, deep and sexy, a cross between Garbo and Crawford. She invited me to sit down.

Orson, a wary eye on Magnus, lay down a few feet away. He clearly wanted no trouble.

Nor did Magnus, a large German shepherd, hypnotic in his beauty and stillness. One of those grounded dogs who live quietly and deeply within themselves, he was mostly brown, with streaks of black across his big head. He had presence and power; he was serious, and was to be taken seriously.

This was a one-human dog. He rarely took his eyes off Ruth, except to lie down and doze briefly once in a while. He had no interest in me or Orson or, I came to learn, anyone else.

Ruth also had a quiet dignity; a halo of sadness as well, a sense of being apart. She asked about me, my work, and Orson, but offered very little about herself. Still, she was droll, perceptive, a good listener; the two of us were soon making fun of our herding instructor and some of the other grimly intense students who pursued dog training with the zeal of Crusaders bound for the Holy Land.

"I thought it would be fun," Ruth said. "But I don't see anybody having much fun."

I agreed. Unlike Magnus, Orson was not much of a herding dog—almost three years old when I got him, he had various behavioral troubles. But the truth was, neither of us was taking well to this herding weekend, where people seemed to be queuing up to say that Orson (or I) was facing the wrong way, moving in the wrong direction, doing the wrong thing. I've never taken well to being told what to do, even when my advisers are right; Orson was not much different.

So I was glad to run into Ruth, who had the same authority issues, and Magnus. We quickly became coconspirators and fellow travelers. We abandoned most of the next day's classes and lessons, pleading illness or injury, and took long walks in the woods with our dogs.

It wasn't so easy to talk to Ruth, however comfortable we felt with each other: She went to bed at dusk and got up at two or three a.m. She'd bartered for the herding-camp fee; in exchange for her lessons, she took the sheep out to graze, mucked out the barns, and checked on the water tanks. She didn't seem to take regular meals with the other students; she grabbed vegetables, fruit, or soup on the fly.

The day after that, the session ended. We went our separate ways, but not before exchanging phone numbers and email addresses.

I VISITED RUTH at her farm in western New York State a few months later. Hers was a classically decaying dairy farm—the sprawling old white farmhouse with peeling paint, the giant faded-red barns for cows and hay, the moldering piles of hay and manure.

We'd communicated regularly since our first meeting, and she'd suggested that I bring Orson and come to see her.

I wasn't sure what, or whom, I'd find there. Ruth had mentioned a husband in one of her emails—the first I had heard of one—but I gathered that he was not living on the farm. I wasn't sure I'd ever exactly find out; Ruth didn't like saying too much about herself.

I pulled into the big drive around her farm in late afternoon. She was sitting on the front porch, waiting for me, Magnus stretched out by her feet.

She was probably in her late fifties, a wiry woman with deep eyes in a lined face, a chain-smoker who consumed each cigarette to the nub and almost immediately lit another.

She brought out a pitcher of iced tea; we sat in Adirondack chairs and watched the sun lower and a few deer emerge from the dusk.

I tossed Magnus a biscuit, but he ignored it, until Ruth nodded; then he scarfed it down. I had more in my pocket, but he just put his big beautiful head down on his paws and closed his eyes.

I could see why Ruth and her mysteriously absent husband had picked this spot. I didn't have my own farm yet; perhaps the idea grew on me during visits to Ruth's.

She had an unusual story: She'd grown up on a Nebraska farm, moved to New York for college, then went on to do graduate study in philosophy at Columbia in the early 1970s. She had hoped to teach and write.

But during an affair with another grad student, she became pregnant and, though single, decided to have the child.

Desperate for tuition money, working several jobs, she signed up for a campus job fair. A Justice Department recruiter was interested in her; the DEA, it turned out, was looking for agents, especially those who could work undercover. Pregnant women were effective and much in demand, the recruiter explained, because they aroused little suspicion among drug dealers.

Ruth took to this strange new career more than she might have imagined. She liked the challenging, high-risk nature of the job; she liked the security of a regular paycheck.

It had its less pleasant moments, too. Since I knew her only in the context of dogs, sheepherding, and our soon to be parallel experience of owning a farm and living with animals, it was easy to forget how dramatic her previous life had been. She'd been chased, beaten, shot at twice, stabbed, and "scared out of my wits" a dozen times.

Even after her son, Raphael, was born, she sometimes stuffed a pillow under her sweater so that she could keep working undercover as a pregnant woman. She perfected various other disguises, too—a homeless person, a bus driver, a junkie.

But once she had tasted that life, she told me on the single occasion she discussed her career in law enforcement, she couldn't go back to academia or business. "Life would have seemed too dull."

Somewhere during these years, she married John, a U.S. customs agent. In twenty-five years together, they lived up and down the East Coast, working hard, raising Rafe, buoyed by the same dream: One day they'd own a farm.

In the late nineties, after distinguished careers, they both retired. Along with her trophies and citations, Ruth kept her badge and her 9mm pistol; she was still called in for undercover jobs from time to time. She and John found their farm, this 140-acre haven a couple of hours south and west of Buffalo, with a pre–Civil War farmhouse, plenty of pasture, rolling hills, a stream, and patches of dense woods.

They acquired sheep, goats, and a couple of horses. They built gardens and fences, painted buildings and barns, found a tenant farmer to plant corn and alfalfa, and spent a fortune on new and improved water systems.

"We were insanely happy," she said. "This was our lifelong dream, and we'd done it." The work was brutal, the hours long, and they had a lot to learn, much of it from their mistakes. But they loved rural life, even the chores and challenges. They sold livestock and cheese.

Both of their work lives had been tense and harried—lots of time away from home, lots of stress—so it was especially sweet for John and Ruth to finally have a peaceful place, common interests, and the time to share them. They'd never had the luxury of that kind of time before.

She was driving to town one afternoon when she saw a big brown-and-black dog lying by the roadside, his legs splayed and bloodied, but his chest still rising and falling. The nearest vet's office was nearly thirty miles away, but she managed to get the dog into the truck and drive there, exceeding the speed limit the entire way. Magnus had been hit and left to die, the vet said. It cost a thousand dollars or more and took months of rehab, but Magnus recovered, thanks to good work by the vet and loving care from Ruth. By the time we met, apart from a barely noticeable limp, the dog showed no outward signs of his trauma.

"Looking back," Ruth told me now as we sat on the porch and she filled in some of the blanks, "I see that Magnus came to be with me, to prepare me for what would happen. I helped him recover, and he understood that one day he'd do the same for me."

Ruth never struck me as religious, but she had a mystical streak, one Magnus somehow triggered. And who could say—perhaps she was right.

What happened was that her son, Raphael, by then a college student in Philadelphia, sustained grave injuries in a car crash on his way back to school after winter break. He spent weeks in a hospital on life support before Ruth could agree to let him die.

John, always a heavy drinker, sank into alcoholism, and his physical and mental condition deteriorated so rapidly that a year later he needed a nursing home. Ruth found a good facility a half day's drive from their farm. He spent a year there, and then John, too, was dead.

The medical bills from Raphael's, and then John's, deaths were staggering, and Ruth's losses paralyzing. The farm, so energizing just a short time earlier, began to collapse. Fences broke, water froze, the barn roof collapsed, animals got sick, the fields flooded. A foal died. Coyotes killed four of her sheep.

"If I were religious," Ruth told me, "I would've thought that God was punishing me, striking me down. But I couldn't say for what."

The farm, first a fantasy, then a reality, then a grim burden, was consuming her, she said. It helped that she could barter services with other women living nearby. "There were a lot of single women with a lot of land around," she found. They painted one another's houses, fixed fences, helped with animal care, borrowed tractors for mowing and brush-hogging.

They helped Ruth keep her farm going, but they couldn't

do much for her mental health. "I completely lost the ability to socialize, to make small talk and chitchat," she told me. "I couldn't bear the news, or politics, or TV. I shed my friends. I couldn't handle everybody asking me how I was all the time."

Probably the only thing that helped her endure was Magnus, by her side in the fields, on walks, during chores, in the truck, alongside the sofa, at the foot of the bed. He went to the cemetery with her. "He was more than my shadow," Ruth said. "He fused with me. He was there for everything, every part of it."

Sitting on the porch, I felt honored that she'd asked me and Orson to visit, and afraid for her, too. How long could she keep this longed-for enterprise going by herself? And how much could she rely on a dog, even one this faithful, for sustenance?

Loneliness is so painful a condition that it's used as torture. They call it solitary confinement, and its purpose is to break people. Humans are innately social, and our social systems are constructed so that we can do few things without interacting with others. Life on my farm is quiet, with few people around much of the time, but to do almost anything—buy hay, get animals inoculated, shop for groceries, fill a gas tank—I have to encounter other people. This is probably fortunate.

Because however much I love the farm and my life here, sometimes, when it's dark or cold or the wind is howling outside, when it's so still that I suddenly can detect the beating of my own heart, I miss my wife and my daughter. I remember times in life when I've been even more alone, and not by choice. The pain and sadness can feel overwhelming. How much harder, unimaginably harder, to be unable to pick up a phone and hear their voices.

At these times, I look around me, and always—always—see a dog nearby. Rose is watching from across the room, or Izzy is looking into my eyes, or Lenore has curled up next to me. They are offering themselves to me, and the communication between us becomes almost palpable. *You are not alone,* they seem to be saying. And I think, Well, I'm *not* alone, at least not as alone as I felt.

Having Izzy's head on my knee is not the same as sharing the daily news of life with someone I love, not as meaningful as taking care of a young child. Those things can't be replaced. Maybe, in a more perfect world, time could stop, there would be no more pain, and the things I cherish would always be there. But time moves forward, we grow older, lives take unpredictable turns. Still, better Izzy than no one. Much better. And better Magnus than the blackness of Ruth's memories. No wonder we love our animals so much, owe them so much, and wish so fervently that they will be with us always. The soul of a dog is its faithfulness, its friendship, its comfort.

THE SUN WAS COMING UP, and Ruth and I were walking in the pasture behind her farmhouse. She'd made a wonderful breakfast of fresh coffee and home-baked corn muffins and local eggs. Magnus loped around her flock of sheep and gathered them into the barn, where Ruth was distributing grain in feed troughs to pregnant ewes.

Orson walked happily alongside us, mostly ignoring the sheep, staying out of Magnus's way. We had slept well in a guest cabin by the side of house, and it was pleasant to keep

Ruth company as she fed the horses and goats and checked the fences.

Then we headed back into her roomy old kitchen, circa 1956, complete with fluorescent lighting and linoleum floors, for more coffee. In Ruth's house, comfortable and unpretentious, you could almost see generations of farm families chowing down at the kitchen table before hitting the tractors and the fields. That sense of hard work spanning a century or two was what she loved about the farm. That and her nearly silent, but indispensable, companion.

"What can I say?" she said later, taking a drag on her Camel. "Magnus was all I could really count on, and he came through. I'm probably out of my mind, but I believe he was guiding me."

After the weekend I'd met her, she'd dropped the herding lessons. She just went out with the dog every day, and the two of them had figured out how to operate. I'd soon take the same approach with Rose when I bought my own farm, not caring precisely which way her butt was pointing, only that she brought the sheep when I asked her to, the way Magnus did. There was something beautiful, I told Ruth, about just working it out on your own farm with your own dog, even if that sort of home-schooling drove some purists crazy.

Ruth wasn't only talking about herding, though. She was used to being alone, she said, and had never needed a lot of people, yet she'd never been this alone. The shock, the loss, the grief, it was hard even for a strong person to bear. But she'd be out walking in the fields sometimes, she confided, and she'd hear a message. "Hang on," someone or something would tell her. "Hang on." And there was nobody there but Magnus.

She hung on. When loneliness got unbearable, she said,

Magnus came over to lick her hand, hop up on the sofa, lie next to her in bed. His constancy never wavered. "You couldn't distract him away from me," Ruth said. Aside from the sheep, "he didn't care about other dogs or animals or people. He has a mission, and his mission is my survival."

We spoke once or twice a week, recommended books we thought the other would like, sent email. She couldn't come to visit me—couldn't handle the drive, she said. So, I visited her on her farm, perhaps twice a year, and we would talk through the afternoon, then resume early in the morning. We herded sheep together, took walks, shared chores. I loved visiting her peaceful retreat, learned skills I would soon come to need, admired the life she'd struggled to build and was fighting to keep. There was beauty and freedom in her loneliness.

Ruth eventually came to Bedlam Farm a couple of times. She couldn't leave her place for long, since she had to ask neighbors to watch the animals, so she stayed for only a night.

She would arrive in the afternoon. We would walk around the farm or through the woods, herd the sheep together, have something to eat. Then she would disappear into the guest room, slipping out every half hour or so to smoke. I told her she was welcome to smoke indoors; she said thanks and ignored me. All during her visits, I was conscious of red lights glowing here and there around the farm at night, with Magnus's eyes often glowing alongside. Then, without a word, she would vanish, out of sight for the night.

In the morning, no matter how early I got up, she and Magnus were already out. Ruth had ferocious feelings about paying her own way, carrying her own freight, so by dawn any dishes left in the sink were done and there was a pot of fresh coffee and muffins just out of the oven. When I walked outside, I found the animals already fed, the water troughs filled, the chickens happily picking at muffin crumbs.

Magnus was as happy to herd my sheep as his own, but apart from that, he paid scant attention to my animals, or to the other dogs. He watched Ruth, his eyes following her as she worked. Orson he ignored, as usual.

People gave him a wide berth, not because he behaved aggressively but because they found him intimidating. People are afraid of big dogs with big teeth. And he certainly did give the impression—though I don't know if it was true—that anyone who tried to mess with Ruth would get torn to pieces.

It didn't really matter what he would do so much as what people thought he might, Ruth pointed out. Even on her isolated farm, she felt safe with Magnus.

While I worked, Ruth and Magnus disappeared, out with the sheep, walking in the woods, sitting in the meadow. When I'd had enough time staring at the computer, they materialized. We sat by the woodstove with mugs of coffee in the winter, Magnus at her feet, Orson or Rose at mine; if it was summer, we were all out on the front porch.

Because Ruth kept such odd hours, and because she was so extraordinarily independent and helpful, her visits always felt too short.

You could get only so close to Ruth, anyway. Though we talked frequently, the shroud of aloneness that enveloped her never fully dissipated. I couldn't claim to know what she was thinking or feeling, not because she was devious or dishonest, but because her feelings ran so deep. I suppose she confined them to the journal she kept. She wrote poetry, too, but I never saw it.

When we first met, Ruth seemed very grounded to me,

strong and clear-headed. As time went on, she seemed less so. She sounded more uncertain.

She looked different, too.

When she visited one fall, I noticed that a couple of teeth were missing from the side of her mouth. They'd had to be removed, she explained, but she didn't have the money to replace them yet. Her skin looked sallow, the lines in her face deeper. She reeked of tobacco.

The farm was overwhelming her, she said; so were her debts. She was running out of ideas. She and her neighbor women were wearing one another out, trying to keep their farms going, and Ruth didn't want to be taking advantage of them. "I've tried everything," she said as we walked with our dogs. "Different crops, different sheep. I don't have the money. I don't have the strength." She was thinking of trading the farm she and John had bought for a much smaller one, just thirty acres, one town over.

By now, Ruth was coughing a lot. She'd given up drinking when John died—she used to love whiskey—but I doubted she'd ever stop smoking. She'd lost weight. I could almost imagine her vanishing into the darkness.

She'd become just about entirely nocturnal, I told her, like a vampire. She smiled. "I think I might like living like a vampire," she said.

This was a different friend. Perhaps she'd been forced to absorb too many blows. "I'm grateful Magnus came to me," she said on our walk. By now, Orson was gone; we were walking with Izzy, Rose, and Pearl. "Magnus is my dark-time dog. That's why he's here, to see me to the other side."

I was alarmed. Did Ruth mean that Magnus was going to guide her out of this world? That she was going to die? Or wanted to? No, she said, she meant that the dog was guiding her as she shifted from one sort of life to another, "from a place of expectations, to none." She wanted to let go of grief. She'd accepted that she'd never have a child again. She'd given up on the notion of finding another partner; she was preparing to let go of her farm. The "other side" was a place where she didn't feel the lack of such things.

I sputtered about hope, about still being young enough for change, about the unpredictable nature of life.

She just sounded tired. "You're still on this side," she said, "so you can't understand. You have your wife, your daughter, your friends, your work. I'm losing all of that, and I don't know if I'll ever get them back, or if I even want to. Magnus will help me across to a different part of life. I do expect him to be there; he's always there."

I wasn't sure what to make of it, to be honest. The attachment between the two of them was indeed profound. Always the faithful friend, Magnus wasn't anxious, distracted, needy, or even playful. For years, he'd simply lived to be with Ruth, to accompany her through her increasingly traumatic life. But the way she spoke of him now, like Charon on the river Styx, was disturbing.

Ruth became difficult to reach after that autumn visit. Her emails and phone calls came less regularly. When we finally connected, she reported that she had in fact swapped properties with a farmer a few miles away, which made things easier, although she missed her old place. In the process, she'd sold off the horses and goats and most of the sheep, keeping just a few for Magnus's sake. She could no longer afford to care for many animals, she said, "and if I can't care for them well, I shouldn't have them."

Then, for a couple of months, nothing.

ONE DAY a card arrived: "Dearest Jon, I'm writing to say goodbye. I can't make it on a farm, and my sister in Oregon is dying of cancer. I am going out to help her. She doesn't have long, and I can be of some use there for the time she does have. I've put the farm up for sale and left things to a broker.

"I'm sorry not to be more in touch, but I value you very much, treasure our times together and love you and wish you well."

When I tried to call I found that the number had been disconnected. My emails started bouncing back, too.

I eventually discovered the number of her sister, outside Portland. A man answered when I called—Ruth's uncle, he said—and told me the sister had died two weeks earlier. Ruth's presence had been "a great blessing" at the end. After the memorial service—more loss—she'd left, saying she was going to travel for a bit, and that she'd let the family know when she landed. She hadn't left any address, no way to stay in touch.

Was there a dog with her? I asked.

Oh yes, said the man. Big and somewhat intimidating, but very devoted. "I don't think I ever saw him leave her side."

I missed Ruth, our herding together, our talks and walks. I could never reconcile her love of rural life with her gun-toting undercover past, another reminder not to make assumptions about people. And I couldn't imagine how she'd kept going as long as she did, given all that had befallen her. A good friend—attentive, sympathetic, funny—she'd handled the tragedy and disappointment that engulfed her bravely, without complaint or self-pity. But the demands of even a stripped-down life had become too much.

In the realm of different expectations where she and Magnus were headed she might feel freer. I hoped so. I believed Ruth wanted to be alone with her grief, to live simply and peacefully with Magnus, her companion and guardian.

It wasn't what she'd wanted when she and John dreamed about their farm, or when she and Rafe had talked about his future. But maybe it was what made sense to her now.

I thought about what James Serpell, who writes about the human-animal bond and the role animals play in our lives, said in his book *In the Company of Animals.*

"Pets complement and augment human relationships," he wrote. "They add a new and unique dimension to human social life and, thereby, help to buffer effects of loneliness and social isolation. Perhaps, in the best of all possible worlds, it would be preferable if humans satisfied all their social and affiliative needs with each other. The world would no doubt be a happier and saner place as a result."

But, he added, until that happier day comes, "we can do a great deal worse than seek the partial fulfillment of these needs in the company of animals."

Often, as I walk in the woods with my dogs, I wonder where Ruth has settled, how she is faring, whether she is peaceful, or even happy. It hurts a bit that she left me behind, that our friendship has become one of those expectations she felt she had to jettison.

We'd shared some powerful things—a love of dogs and farms, a mutual sense of growing together, along with a mutual sense of outsiderness. We'd decided to live outside the mainstream. We both found ourselves a little ridiculous, and enjoyed noticing how.

Now, thinking of animals and souls, it was impossible not to picture Magnus, whose fidelity had shored Ruth up, who'd stepped in to provide what humans couldn't give her any longer.

It's possible for people who suffer such losses to recover, to find new people to love. But Ruth seemed to have decided that this was never going to happen. Perhaps she couldn't bear to try, to risk it all over again. Perhaps she was simply too weary, after seeing so much of her life collapse so quickly and tragically.

It's in the nature of friendship, I guess, to never give up on one's friends, to offer sympathy and encouragement and concern—perhaps things Ruth didn't need or want. It's in human nature to try to lift each other up, even those who don't wish to be lifted.

Magnus would never push Ruth to hang on to her farm, as I had, or reassure her that she could meet other people, as I did, or tell her how sorry he was about what she'd suffered. He wouldn't crack jokes to make her laugh, or ship books to distract her.

I *meant well,* as friends do. But dogs *do good,* letting their humans live, rather than telling them how. I think I understand better what Ruth meant when she talked about Magnus's guiding her to another sphere—not death, but a different kind of life, where she could find peace by ceasing to have to strive.

As Serpell has written, she could do a great deal worse than seeking out the company of her remarkable dog. I know he's sitting by her side somewhere, offering himself to her as a companion on her haunting journey.

I don't see how she could have done better.

THE MYSTERY OF THINGS

Perhaps that is part of the animals' role among us,
to awaken humility, to turn our minds back
to the mystery of things, and open our hearts
to that most impractical of hopes in which
all creation speaks as one.

—MATTHEW SCULLY, *Dominion: The Power of Man,
the Suffering of Animals, and the Call to Mercy*

THE WEATHER STATION ON MY KITCHEN RADIO IS FILLED
with apocalyptic warnings: frigid cold descending from
Canada tonight, heavy sleet, shrieking winds, a windchill of
25 below zero.

This news grabs my attention, transforms the day. I confer
hurriedly with Annie. I call the large-animal vet, the local farm
supply store, and several neighboring farmers to see if they've
heard the forecast, to plot strategy, and make sure the animals
are cared for. I call a friend to see what he's heard (his source in
the town's highway department says it's going to be bad).

I start hauling firewood indoors, near the stoves. The furnace won't keep this drafty old farmhouse warm in bitter cold and high winds, so I need to keep the wood dry.

I pull my car and truck into the barn, make sure there's enough sand for the driveways and walkways. I rush to the Bedlam Corners Variety Store for milk and bread. Annie and I haul pots and buckets of hot water out to the barnyard water valves, which are already frozen.

I push back the mild panic I feel. There's often trouble in extreme weather, but we always get through it. There is help if I need it.

The necessities for people are simple, cheap, and readily available. But the animals are another story. When I hear dire weather reports, I become tense, anxious, distracted. I can't relax until I've prepared for their care, and even then I'm likely to have a long, restless night thinking of them out in the bitter winds, listening for cries of distress, going out to check on them.

I know they are hardy and resilient, but they can suffer in this kind of weather, even die. And that's not acceptable. I can't let an animal of mine freeze in a winter storm.

This is a weight that people with animals bear. I know what locals mean when they say they get tired of the responsibilities and look forward to being free of the worry. It would be nice, I think, to just see a movie tonight and get some good pizza, things abundant in New Jersey but not in my little upstate hamlet.

By nightfall, which comes awfully early this time of year, I'd better have what I need, and the animals had better have what they need.

I've been at this for more than five years now, and I've learned a lot, but it never seems easy. I always feel vulnerable to that one stiff gust of wind, one night of bitter cold, one short-circuited wire corroded by ice and water.

Car batteries die in this kind of cold; driveways and roads can become impassable; windshield wipers stick, and windshield-washer fluid freezes. It's no fun having a farm on such a night.

Annie and I ponder once more whether to bring the cows into the barn to spare them from the punishing winds, or to leave them to huddle against a big round hay bale. It's healthier for them outside, I know, if they can be protected from the wind. Elvis doesn't fit easily into a barn: He's likely to butt out windows with his head or bang into beams. Bringing him inside, I've come to see, is something *I* need, not something *he* needs.

Still, uneasy, I call the large-animal vet. Sarah laughs at me. I call her nearly every time there's a blizzard or a torrential downpour. She always tells me the same thing, and I always need to hear it. As long as they have some shelter, keep the cows outside, she says. Concrete-floored barns are not warm. If they can get out of the wind—and they can—they will do fine.

Still, Annie and I tote out grain, to give them energy, and second-cut hay, which is more nutritious (and expensive) than the first-cut they usually get. We make sure the water troughs are full and the deicers working. We know from past experience that this kind of cold alters matter. Valves freeze, hoses crack, pipes burst.

We plug in the heated water bucket for the chickens, and put out three days' worth of feed. We turn on a heatlamp so that aging Winston and his hens will have extra warmth. We fill the bird feeders, too.

We build a hay igloo in the loft for Mother and put out a tin of dried cat food, which won't freeze.

We prepare to bring the donkeys inside for the night, though. They're hardy, but might be tempted to stay out to guard the sheep and could stumble on an icy hillside. Just a few weeks earlier, Jeannette slipped and fell; struggling to right herself, she clambered to her feet only when Rose nipped her in the butt, urging her up.

So we clean out the barn's middle room, spread straw for bedding, tape up any wires and remove sharp objects (donkeys chew things). We put out grain and hay, get another huge heated water bucket and plug it in.

Next, we haul out the sand, scattering it inside the pasture gate and around the water feeder for the animals, and the salt for the places where people walk.

The sheep will be fine in the pole barn, we figure, protected on three sides from the wind and cold, or up in the pasture, where they usually clump. But they'll need energy, so Annie hauls extra hay into the pole-barn feeders so the sheep won't have to brave an icy slope down to the big feeder by the barn. And she strews straw for warmer bedding. We worry about the five-month-old lambs; they have fleece, but not as much as their mothers.

I take the three dogs down to the meadow across the road and toss slingshot rubber balls for them. They need this exercise now, since they won't be going out much for the next day or so. They tear back and forth across the big, windswept field, happy even though the thermometer says 2 degrees. Rose chases the ball; Izzy chases Rose; Lenore tries unsuccessfully to keep up with both of them. Border collie and Lab fun. After twenty minutes, by which point my fingers will barely move, the dogs' tongues are out, a signal that we can stop.

Human bodies are vulnerable, too: I've had two bouts of frostbite, and now, my circulation impaired, I can't stay outside long in such temperatures; my fingers will ache painfully even after I'm inside. Back in the farmhouse, I lay out extra sweaters, wool caps, thermal boots. In winter, I make frequent use of a paraffin-bath gizmo, dipping my hands in melted wax to keep them warm and keep the blood moving. Otherwise I hurt and, worse, I can't work.

By noon, we're all already exhausted, but we're ready. We've thawed out the valves, dragged out the hay, filled the grain buckets, stacked the firewood, laid out the straw bedding. The water troughs are full. I've checked the furnace to be sure there's oil enough in the tank, and carried in two nights' firewood.

In strong winds, with so many trees and limbs still ice-covered from the previous storm a few days ago, the likelihood of losing power is high, so I place candles and flashlights at strategic points around the house.

In late afternoon, Annie and I make a final check. The chickens have instinctively retreated early to their roosts, warmed by the heatlamp. I worry about Winston, who clearly is slowing down.

No one can tell me that animals don't have their own brand of weather forecasting. Never is it more evident than before a storm, as the chickens, slipping into their vegetative state, remind me. It's not supposed to get brutal for hours yet, but they're already hunkered down, still and waiting.

The others have their own specific rituals. When the weather gets ugly, my sheep usually climb to the highest point in the pasture, for reasons unclear to me or anyone else.

They have other options. They can go into the big barn— I usually leave the sliding door ajar on nasty nights. They could easily gather in the pole barn, the most logical place for shelter and food. But they almost always head for the top of the hill.

I've watched as they walk up slowly, almost solemnly, a trek that can take nearly an hour, with its own eerie rhythms. Two or three ewes move forward, then stop; three or four more amble a few steps farther, then stop. Eventually, they circle tightly, the lambs in the middle, each sheep tucked against two or three others, with virtually no space between them. Then they don't move, sometimes for hours, sometimes for a day or two.

In winter, I often look up to see the whole clump blanketed with snow, waiting out the storm. And as the uphill migration begins, that's what seems likely tonight.

The donkeys have commandeered the pole barn, peering out. They're almost always ready to skitter over to the gate for a cookie, but this afternoon, as the temperature drops and the skies turn a dark metal gray, they stare as I wave carrots and cookies, and refuse to come out.

The cows are perhaps the most indifferent. You get the sense that as long as they have hay and water, nothing much can trouble them, certainly not something as fleeting as snow. I've never seen them visibly uncomfortable, except when the vicious flies of summer descend.

On the eve of this storm, they mostly follow their normal routines, except that Elvis and Luna are under the feeder roof, nestled against round bales of hay. Harold is nearby, gnawing on a tree.

Rose is very busy, rushing up to the pole barn to bark at Lulu, taking a run at Mother, the barn cat, when she ventures out (Mother gives her a contemptuous stare from atop a fencepost), dashing up to check on sheep, then back to me.

Perhaps she's picked up a sense of urgency from Annie and me, but she keeps repeating this ritual, running from one spot to the next. Izzy plops down next to me wherever I am.

So does Lenore. Her work is love—loving me, loving every-body, and I like it; it nourishes me.

As prepared as we can be, I take the dogs inside and they begin to settle, finding their own quiet corners in advance of the storm.

The fired-up stoves are already roaring.

THERE'S A PART of each animal on my farm that I don't un-derstand, another dimension.

I can't fathom how Rose grasps the life of the farm so intuitively, seeming to recognize what needs to be done; I puzzle over whether the judgments she makes are based on instinct or reason.

Does Elvis actually understand how humans work, or is he just so appealing and good-natured a creature that we see in him what we wish?

I can't figure out how Mother can be purring softly in my lap one minute, and pulling the head off a songbird the next. Which is her real soul?

Why does Lenore hang out with sheep? Was she born with this capacity for affection? Did her mother lavish more attention on her than on her littermates? Or did I need her to be this way, and encourage her to make this her work?

I can't say that Izzy chose to be my dog, as my vet thinks. Maybe he was simply waiting to be anybody's dog, and I just happened along. Either way, it's hard to express just how in-stinctively and completely he's entered my life.

I can't say why Winston appeared to like Orson, or at least sought out his company, when he's shown no interest in any other dog since. Or why Henrietta the hen had so much per-sonality, while the other hens seem so generic.

And that spirituality the donkeys exude—is it real? Does it

come from thousands of years of standing by to serve, and observe, humans? If they were as small as dogs, I think they'd probably end up sleeping in our beds, too.

I can attempt explanations, but in the end I have to admit how much of their behavior and motives is unknowable. Perhaps that's part of their appeal.

I HAVE DINNER, listen to my kitchen weather radio, try to read, call friends while I still have phone service. By ten p.m. the storm is in full swing. The ice and sleet spatter audibly against the living room's tall old windows, and the winds shriek around the corners. The outside thermometer that hangs by the kitchen window says minus 18. How many storms, I wonder, has this house seen since the Civil War?

I always make a final check on the animals in weather like this, and this time, I feel an acute sense of being very alone. Annie can no longer get her truck out of her driveway, she calls to tell me. If I had some crisis, my farmer friends would come, even if it meant riding over on their John Deeres, but they will have their own problems. And any official emergency crew—sheriff's department, ambulance corps, volunteer firefighters—will have more critical tasks.

So I need to take care. It's easy to slip, fall, be butted or kicked, and in such weather it could be a while before anybody noticed I was outside on my ass, risking hypothermia. I usually call somebody when I go out on a tough night, with a request to send help if I don't call again in an hour. Tonight, I call two.

I bundle up with thermal gloves, winter boots, a heavy parka with a horse comb in one pocket. I take a cell phone, even though it probably won't work up in the pasture, and a huge flashlight, and tuck a towel into the waistband of my jeans. Instead of walking through the pasture gate, Rose and I use a smaller gate behind the house.

It's as brutal as expected: the wind blowing in great gusts, driving needles of ice and snow horizontally into my face. Rose is instantly covered, and I see ice balls beginning to collect on her feet, though she's gone just a short distance. My eyes tear, my toes and fingers and ears hurt.

Out in the pasture, Rose pauses, nearly blown backward by the wind. I shine my light, barely able to see fifty feet ahead. But when the winds shifts, or there's a small break in the snow, I can see pairs of eyes up the hill, illuminated by the beam. That would be the sheep in their tight, snowy cluster. Rose looks up at the flock, but she doesn't run up to bother them. She always knows when to work and when to leave things alone.

We trundle about a hundred yards to the pole barn, where the donkeys are huddled in a corner. Their eyelids and nostrils are ringed with icicles. We seem all alone up here, as if the rest of the world has receded, preoccupied with its own troubles.

The donkeys and I have been through this before. I take out the comb and remove the frozen ice from their ears and manes, wipe the mucus from their nostrils. Very carefully, with a gloved hand, I push the ice from their eyelashes. They hold up their heads for me, somehow (but how?) understanding that I won't hurt them, that this is not medicine or a shot. It almost seems as if they like it. I do.

Carefully inching back down the hill, I look around for Mother, but there's no sign of her. In storms, she disappears, into some secret spot. Any of my dogs, except perhaps for Rose, would be yowling to come inside the house on a night like this, but Mother won't come in, not even if I leave the cellar door open a crack.

I walk over to the paddock to look down at the cows, all gathered around the feeder, eating hay. Cows have their priorities in order.

It takes us a good while to get back to the house. The ground is terribly slippery, the ice being covered by a thickening layer of blowing snow, so even walking is tricky.

Inside, I unwrap myself, greet Izzy and Lenore, take out a towel for the intrepid Rose, covered in ice, with snowballs clinging to her fur. I put on some water for tea, pour a shot of scotch from my bottle of Glenlivet, collapse into a chair by the big woodstove. I rarely drink alcohol these days, but in a storm, with a fire going, it's nice to take a sip.

I put my feet up on the table, sit on one hand, then the other to thaw my fingers, and call my friends to give the all clear.

Thawing on the rug beside me, Rose looks tired and drifts off to sleep. Izzy hops up onto the sofa next to me; Lenore lumbers over, licks my hand furiously, then plops back onto her dog bed.

I'm enveloped by loving dogs on this awful night. They're fortunate to be inside, curled up around the stove. My animals outside are in for a long and different kind of night.

This night, I think, has presented a chance to be compassionate and responsible, to be humbled both by animals' stamina and the ferocity, sometimes, of their environment.

I'm satisfied that I've done everything I can do—until Rose growls and rushes to the window, apparently alarmed. So I suit up again, more wearily, and as we head out I grab a Snickers bar; a treat can't hurt Elvis on a night like this. This time the thermometer reads minus 20.

What's triggered Rose's protectiveness?

Rose has a map in her head of how the farm ought to

be—I have no such internal guide—and when something is amiss, a sound, a cry, a strange movement, she reacts, and thus alerts me. This has happened so often that I almost take it for granted. It is simply what she does, and when I go to sleep, I am relatively secure in the knowledge that if something is wrong, Rose will sense it and sound the alarm.

Half-afraid of what I'll find—and forgetting to let anyone know I've ventured outside again in frostbite weather—I climb up to the gate and sweep the pasture with my torchlight. I see movement, and peer through the snow. Jesus and Fanny are playing, chasing each other around and around the pole barn as the wind whips past them and blasts drifts of snow across the pasture.

Jesus tears across the field and vanishes behind a pine tree. Jeannette peers out of the pole barn, disapprovingly, but doesn't intervene as Fanny goes tearing after him. The two often play this game, but why are they feeling playful on a night this miserable? It's yet another tutorial in things I don't know.

Rose and I make our way into the big barn, where the chickens are asleep. Mother pops up on a gate to say a purring hello; she's quite dry, so she's probably stayed nestled upstairs in the hayloft.

Opening the gate to the paddock, admitting an inferno of wind-driven ice, I see Elvis, still chowing down at the feeder. He spots me and, with a strange sound of greeting, comes ambling over, perhaps to see if I've brought anything tasty.

Between Elvis and me lies my fancy new grain feeder, a three-by-six contraption of heavy steel that set me back $500. Its several compartments allow each animal to eat without butting heads with the others, or strewing the grain all over the ground.

Elvis, breaking into a trot, sails right into the new feeder, and it crumples like a sheet of paper. He keeps walking and mashes the rest of it into scrap metal without even seeming to notice that it's there.

He comes up to the fence, and I give him his Snickers and brush a cap of snow off the top of his head. I pat him, tell him I'm sorry for the long, cold night he will endure, contemplate the mangled cow feeder—so much for that agricultural innovation. Then I leave Godzilla and go back with Rose through the barn and into the house.

I have to remember, I tell myself, that this night is not the same for them as it is for me. They need food and water and the option of shelter, but they live in the now. They may feel some discomfort, but weather is part of their lives, another cycle in their own rituals, instincts, and traditions.

These nights remind me of the mystery of things. The Trappist monk and author Thomas Merton, of whom I'm a faithful reader, called these moments "journeys of the soul." I've come to believe that our encounters with certain animals can, at times, mark journeys of the soul; they may even accompany us on them.

On such nights, I often feel that my animals reveal their souls. The storm, which has us humans running around like panicked mice, means little to them. They may respond with calm acceptance, with playfulness, with a chocolate craving. It's never more clear that they're not like us, hunkering down in our heated houses, watching the weather nervously to try to anticipate what the animals seem to already know. Only the dogs, those adept social parasites, will spend the night as I do, indoors, dry and warm.

What animals know or think or want falls into that gray zone amid what religion preaches, what science shows, and what we see with our own eyes and believe. Mystery may be the greatest gift my animals provide: It keeps me humble; it evokes the potential of life. It's enthralling sometimes to wonder and not to know, to be reminded of the profoundly limited knowledge of arrogant and destructive human beings.

THE STORM LINGERED for most of two days, shifting from snow and gusting winds to freezing rain. Power outages struck all around me, but to my surprise the farm was spared, even as tree limbs were coated with ice and the roads grew treacherous.

The dogs—Izzy and Rose in particular—cut their pads running on the ice, leading to some bleeding. At one time this would have seemed a veterinary medical crisis; now it merely precipitated a two-minute drill. I already had the antibiotic cream, the gauze, the self-adhesive bandages it took Rose a good half hour to unravel.

The animals did seem a bit happier than usual to see Annie and me the third morning. The donkeys brayed more insistently than they typically do, waiting at the gate for their cookies; the chickens came rushing over for the Cheerios and birdseed I scattered as a restorative.

Elvis looked positively ebullient when I came out with my Snickers, lumbering over for his daily treat, then lingering, head down, for some neck scratching.

But the sheep were their normal selves; though swathed in ice and snow, they were fully focused on hay. Number 57 came up to me for a scratch on the nose.

Perhaps it was my imagination, but we all seemed a bit more aware of one another, more appreciative of the warmth and comfort we provided. I felt a rush of relief that we'd weathered the storm and everyone was fine.

Annie and I had much fiddling to do with frozen valves, hauling buckets of water back to the cows as we tried to figure out why the heat tape wasn't working.

Carr, a grumpy farmer, neighbor, and friend from Cossayuna, stopped by to check on me, as he often does, and to offer tips and critiques, many of them quite useful.

"Don't worry about the animals," he declared. "Do you think donkeys and sheep had people like you to bring them cookies and buckets of water five hundred years ago? A storm is nothing to them, just another day."

Maybe so.

Carr figured out the winter water problem years ago, he added. His secret? "I take the hose to bed with me," he said. "I sleep with it. Wrap it around myself and leave one end hanging off the side of the bed, dripping into a bucket. In the morning, I just get up, haul the warm hose outside and screw it in, and the water flows. Never had a problem. My animals always have water, even when it's twenty below."

I silently pondered this approach. The donkeys had gathered around, like spectators at a match, and were listening with intent.

"What does your wife think of your sleeping with a hose?" I asked.

"Don't know," he said, looking surprised. "She never said a thing about it." I chuckled about the hose all day.

As the wind picked up in late afternoon and the temperature began to plunge once again, I walked through the barn, wondering where I had tucked away the summer's hoses, and just how long they were.

Acknowledgments

Acknowledgments can be rote, even ritualistic sometimes, because there are only so many people you can thank, and sometimes you end up thanking the same ones every time.

This book is different.

I really appreciate, and truly need to acknowledge, the people who helped me get it done.

I thank Paula Span. And my daughter, Emma Span, and my sister, Jane Richter.

I appreciate Peggy Trounstine, and the wise counsel, love, and abiding friendship of Steve Draisin and Maria Heinrich. I acknowledge Steve McLean.

I am grateful for Bruce Tracy and Brian McLendon. And for Becky MacLachlan and Mary Kellogg, Ray and Joanne Smith, Annie DiLeo, Melissa Batalin, and Kurtis Albright.

ABOUT THE AUTHOR

JON KATZ has written eighteen books—six novels and twelve works of nonfiction—including *Izzy & Lenore, Dog Days, A Good Dog, A Dog Year, The Dogs of Bedlam Farm, The New Work of Dogs,* and *Katz on Dogs.* A two-time finalist for the National Magazine Award, he writes columns about dogs and rural life for the online magazine *Slate,* and has written for *The New York Times, The Wall Street Journal, Rolling Stone, GQ,* and the *AKC Gazette.* Katz is also a photographer, a member of the Association of Pet Dog Trainers, and cohost of the award-winning radio show *Dog Talk* on Northeast Public Radio. He lives on Bedlam Farm in upstate New York with his dogs, sheep, steers and cow, donkeys, barn cat, irritable rooster Winston, and three hens.

www.bedlamfarm.com
www.photosbyjonkatz.com

ABOUT THE TYPE

This book was set in Bembo, a typeface based on an old-style Roman face that was used for Cardinal Bembo's tract *De Aetna* in 1495. Bembo was cut by Francisco Griffo in the early sixteenth century. The Lanston Monotype Company of Philadelphia brought the well-proportioned letterforms of Bembo to the United States in the 1930s.

P9-CDV-462

Canine Confidential

Canine
Confidential

Why Dogs Do What They Do

LUDINGTON
PUBLIC LIBRARY & INFORMATION CENTER
5 S. BRYN MAWR AVENUE
BRYN MAWR, PA 19010-3406

MARC BEKOFF

THE UNIVERSITY OF CHICAGO PRESS | CHICAGO AND LONDON

The University of Chicago Press, Chicago 60637

The University of Chicago Press, Ltd., London

© 2018 by Marc Bekoff

All rights reserved. No part of this book may be used or reproduced
in any manner whatsoever without written permission, except in
the case of brief quotations in critical articles and reviews. For more
information, contat the University of Chicago Press, 1427 E. 60th St.,
Chicago, IL 60637.

Published 2018

Printed in the United States of America

27 26 25 24 23 22 21 20 19 18   1 2 3 4 5

ISBN-13: 978-0-226-43303-5 (cloth)

ISBN-13: 978-0-226-43317-2 (e-book)

DOI: https://doi.org/10.7208/chicago/9780226433172.001.0001

Library of Congress Cataloging-in-Publication Data

Names: Bekoff, Marc, author.

Title: Canine confidential : why dogs do what they do / Marc Bekoff.

Description: Chicago ; London : The University of Chicago Press, 2018.
Includes bibliographical references and index.

Identifiers: LCCN 2017039489 | ISBN 9780226433035 (cloth : alk.
   paper) | ISBN

9780226433172 (e-book)

Subjects: LCSH: Dogs—Behavior.

Classification: LCC SF433 .B345 2018 | DDC 636.7/0887—dc23

LC record available at https://lccn.loc.gov/2017039489

♾ This paper meets the requirements of ANSI/NISO Z39.48–1992
(Permanence of Paper).

For all of the wonderful dogs of all different colors, shapes, sizes, and personalities who have blessed my life over the years and who have constantly challenged me to continue to learn more about them—what's happening in their heads and hearts—and to use this information to provide them, all other dogs, and all nonhuman animals the very best lives possible—thank you and blessings to a fine crew of beings

CONTENTS

A Naturalist in a Dog Park

||||||||||||||||||||||||||||||||||||||||||||||||||||||||||||||||||||||||||||||||||||||||||||||||||||||||||||

One afternoon, I walk through Central Park in New York City. I stop to watch some squirrels playing, and two young boys and their mother stroll by. One of the young-sters asks me what I am doing, and I tell him I am watching the squirrels play. He gets really interested and soon his brother joins us. Within five minutes, I've trained them to become ethologists. I explain to them that squirrels are mammals, just like the dog with whom they share their home, and they can learn a lot about their dog by watching him play and interact with his human and dog friends. They get really excited, and as they walk away, I hear one of them say to his mother, "Can we please come back and watch squirrels tomorrow?" I am pleased and amazed at how incredibly easy it is to pique their interests and curiosity. I hope that they do come back to watch the squirrels and, also, that they begin watching their dog. Not only is connecting with animals and nature good for us, but also the closer we pay attention to the dogs who share our homes, the better their lives will be.

||||||||||||||||||||||||||||||||||||||||||||||||||||||||||||||||||||||||||||||||||||||||||||||||||||||||||||

Over the past forty years, as both an ethologist and a dog lover, I have experienced many encounters like this one: observing animals, an-swering questions about animals, and encouraging others to observe animals more closely. In particular, I've spent many hours—some would surely say far too many—at various dog parks, just hanging out watching dogs do whatever they choose to do. It's been part of my job for decades, for which I have been forever grateful.

Dogs, whose preferred scientific name is *Canis lupus familiaris* (according to many of the experts with whom I've consulted), are fascinating animals, and one thing I discovered long ago is that dog parks are wonderfully educational experiences.[1] They're gold mines for learning about both dogs and people. Visits can serve as myth breakers and icebreakers. For hours on end, the interactions never stop: dogs are watching dogs, people are watching dogs, dogs are watching people, and people are watching one another as they care for, play with, and try to manage their dogs. I'm always amazed and pleased about how much I learn when I just hang out and watch dog-dog, dog-human, and human-human interactions.

Dog parks never lack for an extremely interesting cast of characters on either end of the leash or on either side of the fence. Discussions and debates always arise about what humans want and what dogs want, why dogs behave the way they do and what they understand, how to care for dogs and how to train them. People are always asking questions and offering advice, proposing theories and judging the behavior of others. They want to know how to treat various problems, such as shyness or aggressiveness, and why dogs sometimes ignore what their human asks them to do. They want to know why dogs roll in disgusting things and hump with impunity. They want to become dog literate.

In fact, I've probably heard every question there is about dogs. Such as, how do you measure a dog's quality of life? How do you know if a dog is in pain? Should you just say "good dog" for "nothing"? Why do dogs bow, bark, mark, snort, and shed? Why do dogs bury bones and other objects and immediately dig them up? Why do dogs try to bury bones on the carpet and act as if the bones are invisible? Do dogs get headaches? Do dogs have a sense of self? Do dogs grieve? Do dogs suffer from posttraumatic stress disorder (PTSD) and other psychological disorders? Do some dogs have a "little dog" complex? Why do dogs eat grass? Why do dogs circle before lying down or pooping? How do dogs sniff out human diseases? How does a dog's nose work? How smart are dogs? Are dogs just using us to get them food? Do dogs understand language? Do dogs like music?[2] Do dogs like television?[3]

Over the years, I've realized I've become something of a canine and dog park "confidentialist." From time to time, people say to me, "Please don't tell anyone but . . ." Then they confide in me, telling me intimate stories about their dogs, other dogs, or other people at the dog park. I try merely to listen, since I don't want to get involved in gossip. And just when I think I've heard it all, someone tells me something I've never heard before. Surprises always abound at the dog park.

In fact, I also sometimes feel like the dogs confide in me as well. I try as hard as possible to take the dog's point of view when I visit dog parks because, obviously, they're called dog parks, not human parks. On occasion, dogs approach me as if to say, "Would you please tell my human that I simply have to roll in stinky stuff or pee all over the place or that rough play is okay? Remind them I can take care of myself."

Many people are keenly interested in all aspects of dog behavior, and my trips to the dog park often become a sort of extension class on dogs: I recommend articles and books for people to read, and I pepper our conversations with general principles of animal behavior, evolutionary biology, and conservation. One guy jokingly (I think) told me he learned more about biology and behavior on his visits to dog parks than he did in class. On a few occasions, groups of five or ten people have stood for hours discussing dogs, coyotes, and wolves from many different points of view.

Based on these encounters, I've noted that there is a need for a simple and straightforward book about dogs: one that explains their behavior; their cognitive, emotional, and moral lives; their inter-actions with other dogs and with humans; and how best to care for dogs in our homes and in our society. This book is written to fulfill that purpose. In it, I try to answer the questions I list above, but in some cases, we really don't know the answer. Ultimately, my hope is that this book will help you to develop and maintain enduring, positive, and compassionate relationships between dogs and dogs and between dogs and humans. Peaceful coexistence is a blessing for all involved, and we need to be sure we're doing all we can so that dogs can live in peace and safety.

I've studied dogs and their wild relatives for over four decades, but in a way I've been writing this book since I was around three years old. When I was a youngster, my parents always told me that I connected better with nonhumans than with humans. I was always asking them what other animals were thinking and feeling. I'd talk with the goldfish who lived in a small tank and wonder what was going on his small head. How did he feel about swimming in endless circles in a water cage? My parents told me that I "minded animals," in that I was always concerned about caring for them and never, ever thought they didn't have active minds. I knew that they did and that I could feel their feelings.[4]

Since then, I've studied dogs in a wide variety of circumstances and habitats, including at dog parks, and I've learned a lot about the behavior of these fascinating animal beings. I've studied dogs who are familiar because they've shared my home and dogs I didn't know at all, including feral dogs, in nearly every setting. I have also studied coyotes and wolves and other members of the genus *Canis*, and I feel comfortable discussing similarities and differences among species. Indeed, let me say right off, dogs are not wolves and neither are dogs coyotes or dingoes. Dogs are dogs, and they must be appreciated for who they are, not who or what we want them to be.

Naturally, dogs at dog parks are not free simply to be themselves, even when they are off leash. The humans who brought them are always watching and commenting; they are directing, correcting, and trying to control their dogs. At the dog park, you learn as much about dog-human relations, and about people, as about dogs as a species. As I watch people walk and care for their dogs—sometimes yanking their dogs here and there, and hurrying them along to do their business after being cooped up inside all day—I sometimes feel that the humans don't have any idea about who they brought into their lives. Or, in some cases, that they don't have the first clue what a dog wants and needs, at a minimum, to have a good life.

This is why, like the story of the boys and the squirrels, I always encourage people to watch their animals and to wonder and learn and act like ethologists. As I will discuss, it's wrong to talk about "the dog" as if all dogs were the same. They're not. Dogs are as individual as people, and learning to care for your dog means paying attention to your dog, discovering his or her likes and dislikes, and so on. So, another purpose for this book is to encourage readers to become ethologists or "citizen scientists," and I have included lots of stories by everyday people describing their dogs in action. In other words, this book blends stories with science. I love both, and they can inform each other. Everyday questions and observations can often inspire rigorous, important scientific research, since we need answers to the problems that have an impact on our lives. When it comes to our life with dogs, citizen science can indeed, at times, improve our knowledge of the species, but it will always improve the person's life with their own companion animal.

For instance, while we know a lot about dogs, readers will discover that what we often take to be the gospel about dog behavior isn't all that well supported by empirical research. Dogs don't always circle before they lie down, they don't always eat grass to barf, peeing isn't always marking, humping isn't always an attempt to make babies (females do it), playing tug-of-war isn't always about aggression or dominance, though dominance is alive and well, it's okay to hug a dog on *their* terms, dogs don't sleep all day (only twelve to fourteen hours a day), and while we know dogs feel joy and grief, we don't really know if they experience emotions such as shame or guilt.[5] It's also a myth that using food to train or teach a dog means that they're using you and won't love you.[6]

What I find incredibly exciting is how much there still is to learn about these wonderful beings. While many of the questions I consider raise larger principles about the evolution of canine behavior, they also highlight just how variable dog behavior can be. We are still

Me, watching Zeke. I spent countless hours watching Zeke and his buddies frolicking
and hanging out at my home in the mountains outside of Boulder, Colorado.
(Credit: R. J. Sangosti/*Denver Post*/Getty Images)

figuring out why dogs stick their noses where they do, and why they
play, bark, howl, pee, and eat turds. Not to mention the more lofty
questions about whether dogs have a theory of mind, whether they
feel jealousy, and whether they know who they are and have the capacity for self-awareness.

People with all sorts of different backgrounds are interested
in and fascinated by dogs, so I wrote this book to be accessible to a
broad audience. In essence, for all the people I meet at dog parks and
on trails: academics, other professionals, devoted dog lovers, and
everyday folks taking care of their family companion. The common
denominator for them all is that they are trying hard to give their dog
the best life possible, and many of them really want to learn about
dog behavior. Further, I hope this book mirrors the conversations
we have: personal and often light-hearted, and yet as detailed, critical, and evidence-based as I can possibly make them. It's important
to highlight when we don't have enough data to support certain
claims and where we need further study. We should use what we

know about dog behavior to care for them better, which includes dog training, or what I prefer to call dog "teaching." There is no need for the use of cruel and violent methods to get dogs to do what we want them to do in our human-dominated world.

Ultimately, I feel incredibly lucky to be "a naturalist in a dog park," and I hope I can inspire others to become one, too. I spend a lot of time reading and writing about dogs and in their company. While there always will be mysteries about what goes on in the heads and hearts of other animals, including dogs, we also know a lot about what they're thinking and feeling, and caring for them is often a matter of common sense.

Now, if you're ready, let's meet the dogs.

ONE

The Many Joys of Watching and Living with Dogs

||||||||||||||||||||||||||||||||||||||||||||||||||||||||||||||||||||||||||||||||||||||||||||||||||||||||||||||||||||||||||||||||

Bernie and Beatrice are well known as "the butters" at a local dog park in Boulder, and it's easy to understand why. On their first approach to both unfamiliar and familiar dogs and humans alike, they go right for the butt. Gus and Greta, "the groiners," love to run up to dogs and humans and shove their noses into groins and unabashedly sniff and snort. I admit on more than one occasion I have been hit so hard by an inquisitive nose I thought my voice would change.

Sassy, the "poop eater," has a seemingly unquenchable taste for poop, according to her human, and Tammy "the tongue" and Louie "the licker" run up to people with their long tongues protruding and leave a trail of saliva.

Harry and Helen are happy humpers and unhesitatingly jump on other dogs, from all different orientations, some rather acrobatic, and hump away as if it were nothing. On more than one occasion, they have chosen one of my legs for their maniacal humping and misdirected thrusting. Helen's human often exclaims, "Oh my god, my dog was fixed to stop this stuff." Helen is a good example of what I fondly call an "ADD dog"—an attention-deficit disorder dog.

I met Peter, the "pecker pecker," some years ago. No need to tell you what he loved to do, all with the blessings of the human who accompanied him. When I told Peter's human I preferred not to be peckered, the guy answered, "Well, he likes to do it to us, so what the hell . . ." Of course, all this barreling into groins, humping indiscriminately, and pecker pecking results in a lot of questions and useful conver-

sations about why dogs do these things without a care in the world and about what humans should or shouldn't do about it.

||||||||||||||||||||||||||||||||||||||||||||||||||||||||||||||||||||||||||||||||||||||||||||||||||||||||||||

When I'm at the dog park, I enjoy nicknaming the dogs I meet (as well as the dogs I live with), and I often take an anatomical approach. Dog behavior often revolves around body parts: butts and noses, mouths, tongues and legs and groins. When dogs meet one another, or greet humans, they employ every form of address: they use eye-to-eye contact as well as nose-to-nose, nose-to-butt, and nose-to-groin. In fact, as we all know, dog noses roam widely, sniffing and snorting with abandon and joy. For dogs, following their noses around a dog park leads to a rich source of great stories and data.

This canine zest for what humans might avoid, consider inappropriate, or find disgusting rarely diminishes our fondness for dogs. For instance, "flatulent" Freddy and Abe, "the anal gland expresser," think nothing is more pleasant than sharing gases and pungent odors, Freddy farting and Abe blowing out globs from his anal gland, sometimes on a person's leg. When people laugh, the dogs take this as an invitation to do more of what they love to do, nose butting as many people as possible, trying to stimulate a gag response by shoving their tongue into people's mouths, passing wind here and there, and breathing right into someone's face.[1] I well remember a guy at a dog park who pulled me aside and quietly explained what was happening with a dog, Lucifer, who was notorious for his bad breath. Lucifer's human, he said, "just doesn't get it. Her dog has the 'zactly' disease, cause her breath smells 'zactly' like her butt. Everyone here will be better off when she realizes this."

Concerning bad breath in dogs, my friend Kimberly Nuffer shared this story with me about what she calls "stinky tongue syndrome," or STS:

Zelda (Zipper, ZDog) came into our lives from the Aurora Animal Shelter. When I met her at the shelter, she climbed right into my lap in the visitation room and cried once back in her shelter cage. When we brought her home, she couldn't have a bath for a week so that her spaying incision could heal, and it was clear the shelter hadn't bathed her since finding her roaming the streets of Aurora. The homeless, dumpster-diving dog smell did not deter my need to bond with my new pup, so she slept on our bed and I snuggled her endlessly. Finally, incisions from her spaying healed, and I gave her a much-needed bath. More snuggling ensued as I was bonding well with my new family member.

Yet a significant odor lingered despite the lavender dog wash and the eventual trim of her curly gray poodle fur. It was coming from her mouth! It smelled like a dead animal; there is really no other way to describe it. Inspection of her teeth showed pearly whites, not yellow, rotting, mildewed pickets. Inspection of her tongue revealed a supple and soft pink plank ready to kiss anyone nearby. To the vet she went for a teeth cleaning. No extractions needed. Everything was in good shape. Her breath improved . . . for a day.

Fast-forward ten years. The dead animal breath remains. It persists despite teeth brushing, weekly baths, fancy organic food, and doggie breath mints. Sometimes it's a little better, sometimes a lot worse, but generally, it is always there. The mystery remains unsolved. To help alleviate the shame she must feel when we recoil in disgust as she gives kisses, we named her disorder Stinky Tongue Syndrome or STS.

We could not ask for a more loyal, loving dog. People who spend time with her want to take her home as she snuggles up in a lap as soon as one is available. The reality is we are all flawed in some way, and these flaws make us unique and lovable. We often strive to fix those flaws, and sometimes the only fix is acceptance, not change. Thank you for this life lesson, Zelda and your STS.[2]

Ken Rodriguez, Kimberly's husband, sent me a follow-up email that he claimed Zelda dictated to him:

Every year, thousands if not millions of dogs contract STS. Some are shamed by their people. Some are subjected to quack treatments. And some, lacking any sort of treatment, feel forced to run away and live a dangerous life on their own just to feel better about themselves as a person. But compassion is right now the best treatment for STS, and we all must be aware of the silent suffering of those who, like me [Zelda, that is], live with this condition.[3]

Sometimes, our "problems" with dogs are really *our* problems. There's no solution but acceptance, as Kimberly and Ken put it so compassionately. At times, I certainly have wished that dogs would turn their heads away when they breathe or burp. I've had a few dogs whose breath floored me—literally and metaphorically—and yet other dogs don't feel that way. From a dog's perspective, they can't wait to sniff around another dog's mouth and savor the odor, and on occasion the saliva, that spews out. While we don't know precisely why dogs do this, it's a safe bet that they're gathering information, and being that close to another individual could also be a social or potentially bonding event. Smelly places and private parts play a huge role in a dog's world, which can make us humans uneasy.

People are always asking me why dogs put their noses in such places, as if understanding might help us figure out how to get them to stop it. Dogs put their noses in places where people can't imagine there is anything of interest. We don't greet friends or strangers by immediately licking their mouths or with a nasal snort or genital sniff or slurp. What's perfectly normal dog-appropriate behavior might not be even marginally acceptable dog-human behavior, but dogs aren't especially interested in our social norms. One woman who was pretty open to a dog's investigative ways once said to me, "If you got it, use it," and dogs do just that.

Thus, if we want to learn about dogs, and we want to live with and love dogs, we must make our peace with an anatomical, body-parts approach to life. That's the only way to journey into the minds, sense organs, and hearts of dogs. Not everything about a dog's cognitive, emotional, and moral life is anatomically based, but little happens that doesn't involve a body part.

In many ways, I think of myself not only as a canine confidentialist but also as a myth buster. I feel strongly that both first-time and lifelong dog people can benefit from what my friend and dog trainer Kimberly Beck calls "the beginner's mind." Kimberly founded an organization called the Canine Effect, which stresses the importance of looking at the relationship between dogs and humans.[4] To hold a beginner's mind means to make no assumptions and to take the time to relate to, and learn about, *this individual dog, here and now*. It's essential to recognize that myths harm dogs and dog-human interrelationships. When we pay close attention to what we know about dogs and dog-human relationships, it's beneficial for everyone concerned.

Choosing to share your life with a dog should be fun. Of course, because dogs, like so many other nonhuman animals, experience rich and deep emotions and are witty, wise, and temperamental, they can be a challenge. But the bottom line is that living with a dog should be enjoyable, if, on occasion, noisy, smelly, and frustrating. The challenges remind us that dogs are individuals. And judging from the number of books and scientific and popular essays focused on defining who dogs are and explaining why they do the things they do, there is a good deal of interest worldwide in understanding these fascinating beings.

The Big Question: Who Are Dogs?

Domesticated dogs are fascinating mammals. We created them in our own image, favoring the traits we liked or considered useful, even though at times these have compromised the health and longevity of dogs themselves. Perhaps it's stating the obvious, but dogs vary greatly in size, shape, mass, color, coat, behavior, and personality.[5] Because dogs are so variable and so common in our lives, they make wonderful subjects for evolutionary, biological, and etholog-

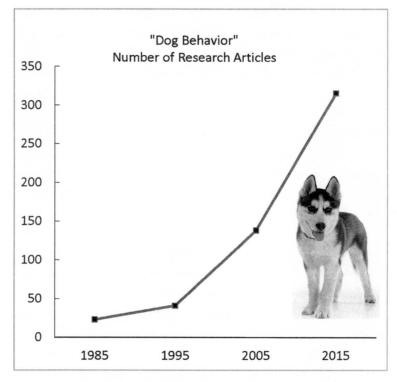

Graph showing a steady increase in studies of dog behavior over the past thirty years. Source: Hal Herzog, "25 Things You Probably Didn't Know about Dogs"; Used with permission. Dog photo courtesy flickr user alan schoolar, Creative Commons license CC BY 2.0.

ical studies, especially concerning social behaviors related to play, dominance, different types of communication, and social organization.

That said, it's interesting to note that for years "serious scientists" thought dogs weren't worth studying at all, precisely because they were considered "artifacts," products of human genetic engineering. Rather than naturally evolved beings, dogs are animals who were made to be what they are by humans, based on what we wanted or imagined. Veterinarians and geneticists could study dogs, but not serious researchers interested in behavior. Now things have really changed, and numerous renowned universities focus on dogs in a range of incredibly interesting studies. The graph here shows a steady increase in studies of dog behavior over the last thirty years, with an especially sharp increase beginning around 1995.

Among regulars at the dog park, I often hear an enduring confusion about the difference between domestication and socialization. Dogs evolved from wolves to become a new domesticated species, which means that every dog is born a dog. But occasionally, people who share their home with a wolf who is friendly toward them will say, "I have a domesticated wolf." They really don't; if this "friendly wolf" gives birth, that child will be a wolf, a wild animal. Their friendly wolf is actually a *socialized* individual. Simply put, a "domesticated wolf" is a dog.[6]

As the section title above states, this book seeks to answer the question of *who* dogs are, not *what* dogs are. Dogs continually thwart attempts to characterize them as predictable stimulus-response machines. While the well-known Nobel Prize–winning Russian physiologist Ivan Pavlov surely made significant contributions to learning theory by studying dogs, what he did not prove is that dogs are automatons. It's clear from evolutionary theory, detailed scientific data, and common sense that dogs are *neither* merely mindless machines nor simply "bundles of instincts" who mainly rely on using hardwired behavior patterns. Rather, dogs are smart, thinking (sapient), and feeling (sentient) beings who assess different situations and experience a wide range of emotions similar to our own.[7] Dogs routinely make decisions about what they do, and they don't do things "for no reason at all."[8] Indeed, many current successful training (or teaching) methods are based on the rich and deep minds and hearts of dogs. They are mammals, just like us, and we can learn a lot about them by recognizing this fact.

Scientific research has shown us that numerous animals are intelligent and emotional beings, including dogs, fishes, and insects.[9] Throughout this book, but especially in chapters 6 and 7, we will consider the heads and hearts of dogs, and the secrets and mysteries they contain, but there is no question that they think and feel. This is well supported by scientific research, and we need to let this knowledge influence how we care for dogs. Of course, this doesn't mean we need to embellish the mental life of dogs, or of other animals, to make them appear smarter than they really are.[10] But it isn't putting the cart before the horse, or the leash before the dog, to let the data drive our concern and compassion for dogs and other animals and to give them the best lives possible.

Some people—thankfully, not many anymore—still claim we really don't know what dogs want and need, but I always say, "Yes, we do." They want and need what we want and need, namely, to live in peace and safety and to coexist harmoniously with others.

Thus, throughout, I consider each aspect of what we know about dogs based on current research, and I note where we really need more information, which is just about everywhere. However, to make the book more readable, I cite most of this research in the notes; please turn to these if you want to know more. It's essential to use available evidence to understand and appreciate dogs, and I provide a fair representation, citing scientific studies, essays, and books, as appropriate.

That said, I also include numerous stories, both by scientists and everyday people.[11] Science writer Fred Pearce has written: "To change the world, scientists need to become storytellers."[12] I totally agree. Nonresearchers find it much easier to appreciate what researchers are doing when it's presented in accessible ways. Stories that "hit home" are very effective.

As importantly, good stories can point out all we don't yet know and lead us to question received wisdom, misplaced assumptions, and dogmatic certainty. It might surprise you that, while we know quite a lot about the behavior of dogs, about what they're thinking and feeling and what they want and need, much remains about which we don't have much of a clue. There are many holes in the database, despite claims to the contrary by many popular dog books that purport to tell it like it is.

The challenge at hand is to come to an appreciation and understanding of these fascinating individuals on their own terms and to use what we know on their behalf. What works for Fido might not work for Annie, and what works for Annie might not work for Pluto. Among the many dogs with whom I have shared my home, I can name few generalities other than that they all had one tail, two ears, two eyes, one nose, one mouth, and voracious appetites.

As I like to say, beware "the mythical dog."

My Dog and Your Dog, Not "the Dog"

This is a major message I'll repeat throughout, namely, talking about "the dog" can be extremely misleading because of the incredible amount of variability among dogs, even among littermates and members of the same breed. I also avoid distinguishing "good dogs" from "bad dogs" because so much of how we label a dog (or a human, for that matter) depends on context. Most of all, good and bad are human judgments, and every person's criteria is different. I've seen dogs doing what dogs typically do being called both "good" and "bad." These judgments often make no sense to the dog or to me.

Individual dogs also vary in how much they are attracted to us. It might shock some people when I say this, but dogs aren't necessarily our best friends, nor do they give love unconditionally. Sure, dogs can love and play with and entertain us until we're laughing in tears, but they have needs and "conditions" that can be a huge challenge for us, hence the burgeoning dog training or teaching industry.

Furthermore, an individual dog can have a bad day, just like we can, and his or her behavior will reflect this. I remember a dog named Cheghi who I knew well who wasn't acting like himself. Rather than being a ball of high energy, he was laid-back and seemed out if it. I later discovered that an iron had fallen on his head. His human believed Cheghi had a headache or perhaps a minor concussion. Only after a few days did he return to himself, an effusive and high-energy guy. Once, one of the dogs with whom I shared my home rapidly gulped down a lot of icy cold water after a run, and I'm sure he got a cold headache. He squinted his eyes and shook his head from side to side as if he was trying to get rid of something. He also got grouchy and seemed on edge for a while. The exact same thing has happened to me after I've gulped down some iced tea too fast after a long bike ride.

Over the years I've had numerous emails and calls from researchers and nonresearchers alike who want reliable summary statements about what we know and don't know about the cognitive capacities of dogs. For example, do they follow human pointing? Do they follow human gazing? Are there breed differences? How do dogs compare with wolves? And so on.

I try to answer these question based on current research, but it's just not possible to do accurately without some strong qualifying statements about the variables of each study, including how many dogs were studied, their genders, their ages, their backgrounds, and the exact sorts of experiments that were conducted and where they were done. Emily Bray and her colleagues have discovered that temperament, in the form of increased arousal, can influence a dog's problem-solving cognitive performance.[13] They discovered differences between pet dogs and service dogs and, also, that experimenters could manipulate a dog's level of arousal. In the problem-solving tests that were used, highly aroused pet dogs showed a decline in performance, whereas highly aroused service dogs showed enhanced performance. Clearly, we must be careful of oversimplifying what we actually know about "the dog." And, of course, this isn't a criticism of the researchers or the work they do. Rather, it's a fascinating fact that makes the science of dog cognition, emotions, and behavior all the more interesting and captivating.

One dog expert wrote to me in October 2016 and asked, "Who are these dogs in all of these tests?" He was referring to the fact that studies frequently treat all dogs as equivalent, but they are not. It's just not possible to say all or even most or many dogs do this, or that all or even most or many dogs do that, or even that dogs and wolves are similar in this way and different in that way. If many of the people I meet at dog parks know this already, that's because their dogs already act like they're one of a kind!

Therefore, when people ask me about "the dog," I often say there's no such being. Research conducted in different dog labs and in the field uniformly shows there is an incredible amount of within-species variability among dogs. Melissa Howse's master's thesis on the behavior of dogs at the Quidi Vidi Dog Park in St. John's, Newfoundland, Canada, shows this clearly when she compares her data with those of the few other studies of dogs at dog parks, including a later study in the same dog park.[14]

Clearly, more attention has to be paid to individual dogs. In a review essay that covered research on the cognitive abilities of dogs from 1911 to 2016, Rosalind Arden and her colleagues found only three studies that focused on individual differences.[15] They also found that the median sample size for studies was sixteen dogs.

Often, and understandably, people want quick fixes for this or that problem with their dog, but a rapid remedy is not always forthcoming because it depends on the individual dog. I hear the desire for a quick fix articulated over and over again at dog parks. I often feel that the quickest fix and the best take-home message I can offer is to pay close attention to the dog or dogs you care about and need to know the best. I've met a large number of dogs over the years, including a most lovely and loving pit bull. The dog's human told me he bought the pit bull to be a fighter, but the dog, turned out to be a wimp. Further, the man said he purchased the pit bull to "make some money in dog fights," but when his dog refused to fight and they were both ridiculed, he came to see his dog and others as individuals, and he vowed never again to engage in dog fighting.

I mention this story not to debate the merits of pit bulls or any breed but, rather, to make the point that rampant breedism—for example, claiming that all members of a breed are nice or all members of a breed are fighters—can be very misleading.[16] Normative thinking can be convenient, but acting on misinformed beliefs can have devastating consequences for the targets of these prejudices. As my friend Marty said to me one day at a local dog park, "Dogma about dogs don't work."

There's also an important practical side to being careful about generalizing about dog behavior. James Crosby, a certified behavior consultant and retired police lieutenant who also holds a master's degree in veterinary forensics from the University of Florida, told me that in his studies of human fatalities resulting from dog bites it is essential to evaluate each case and each dog individually. There are no quick answers concerning the causes of these tragic events.[17]

I also don't like to talk about "the coyote" or "the wolf" or "the robin" or "the goldfish." Research has clearly shown that within-species variation—what scientists call intraspecific variation—is rampant among a wide variety of animals, including fish, insects, and spiders. After eight and a half years of studying wild coyotes in Grand Teton National Park just north of Jackson, Wyoming, my students and I continued to learn that general comments about coyote behavior had limited applicability, especially in the arena of social behavior and social interactions. Even three-week-old coyotes show distinct temperaments when they first emerge from the safety of their common den, some shy and some bold. Wild animals, like domestic dogs, also defy being tightly pigeonholed by overarching species-wide explanations of who they are and why they do the things they do.

Ultimately, we'll come to a deeper understanding and appreciation of the *individuals* we call dogs if we focus on the reciprocal relationships we form. We need to understand who they are as well as how they come to understand who we are. As you'll see, when we study dogs, including at dog parks, we form relationships with those dogs, as well as with other people, and these relationships influence what dogs do as well as what we understand about what they are doing. Getting into this mindset means leaving all expectations behind. I've always tried to place myself in the paws, heads, and hearts of *individuals*, to experience their highs and lows, ranging from exuberant joy to stifling grief, and to empathize with them as deeply as I can. Dogs openly share with us a lot about what they're thinking and feeling, and we just have to be keen enough to figure it all out.

Not surprisingly, I'm always wondering what is going on in the heads and hearts of dogs and thinking about the topics about which I write here. One morning, as I was riding my bike through Boulder, I spotted Vivienne Palmer and her companions Bartleby, a tiny dog, and Blue, a huge dog who towers over his little friend, walking down the

Vivienne Palmer and her dogs Bartleby (a four-year-old rescued Chiweenie, *at left*) and Blue (a six-and-a-half-year-old rescued Great Dane).

street. I smiled as I reflected on the fact that Bartleby and Blue are the same species, and I decided to do a U-turn and asked Vivienne if I could take their picture. She happily agreed. These companions are clear reminders that speaking about "the dog" can be extremely misleading.

Citizen Science in the Dog Park

What if giving voice to the voiceless meant listening to them before pretending to know what they would say?

Matt Margini[18]

"Lots of people talk to animals," said Pooh.

"Maybe, but . . ."

"Not that many *listen* though" he said.

"That's the problem," he added.

Benjamin Hoff, *The Tao of Pooh*[19]

Clearly, when you go to a dog park—or any other place where dogs and people visit, from backyards to hiking trails to bike paths—many different sorts of encounters, exchanges, and meetings are possible. Dogs tend to introduce themselves to anyone and everyone, which can lead to everyone becoming introduced to everyone else, and for this reason, dogs are often called "social catalysts" by researchers. [20] They grease the way for people to open up to one another, and this seems particularly true at dog parks. Most people go to dog parks to let their dogs have fun and meet other dogs, but people wind up meeting one another, too.

And, what do people talk about the most? Their dogs, of course. Most of the chatter is pretty routine. It centers on dog behavior, breeds, where the dogs came from before they wound up in this or that home, how to handle problems, and the relationship of each dog to his or her human friend. However, if we pay attention, our observations at the dog park can yield valuable data about our own canine companion, about dog-human relationships, about human-human relationships, and even about the capacities and proclivities of all the dogs who are lucky enough to romp here and there with friends.

I always encourage people to act like citizen scientists and to increase their knowledge, if nothing else, to improve their relationship with their own animal companion. Yet these casual observations can also inspire scientists and become the catalyst for systematic study, which I'll explore in chapter 8. Dog parks are wonderful places for studies in cognitive ethology, or the study of animal minds, and anthrozoology, or the study of human-animal interactions.

Citizen science in the dog park and at home can also inspire the creation of scientists. Consider the world-renowned primatologist and conservationist Jane Goodall, who was strongly influenced by her dog, Rusty. Rusty was instrumental in getting Dr. Goodall interested in animals when she was young. [21] Dr. Goodall once wrote, "I had had a marvelous teacher in animal behavior throughout my childhood—my dog, Rusty." [22] Elizabeth Abbott, author of *Dogs and Underdogs*, elaborates on how Dr. Goodall's dog helped shape her as a scientist:

Rusty taught young Jane that dogs remember and think about absent objects, for instance a ball tossed from an upstairs window that he could not see and could fetch only by figuring out a series of strategic moves inside the house and then outdoors. Rusty had a sense of justice that drove him to acknowledge his own bad behavior but not to accept Jane's occasional lapses into irritation or unfairness. He was clever at performing tricks and enjoyed being togged out in pajamas. But if anyone laughed at his attire, Rusty stalked off, trailing his garments behind him.

The most important lesson Rusty taught Jane was to ignore contemporary scientists, who denied that animals had individual characters, emotions and brainpower. Instead, she named her chimpanzee subjects—Fifi, Flo, Figan, David Greybeard—and documented and interpreted their behavior and activities in ways that ultimately changed the way science would come to understand animals. Her vision and her methods, once denounced as the scientific sin of anthropomorphism, were gradually accepted into the canons of scientific research and ultimately, adopted as the gold standard.[23]

Way back in 1928, Columbia University psychologists C. J. Warden and L. H. Warner wrote, "Much of what the average man 'knows' about his own dog, and about dogs in general is, of course, quite unknown to the animal psychologist."[24] This quotation shows how much we can learn about dogs from citizen scientists. We now realize how much the observations of people who share their lives with dogs can support and supplement rigorous data from detailed scientific studies. In 2015, an international group of researchers concluded that, "in the future, citizen scientists will generate useful datasets that test hypotheses and answer questions as a complement to conventional laboratory techniques used to study dog psychology."[25]

Years ago, a woman told me that her male dog would often look around, lift one of his rear legs, and act as if he was peeing, but without actually peeing at all. Then, a few seconds later, he'd pee out a bucket's worth. The woman also thought he only did this when other dogs were around. I'd seen this same pattern of behavior from time to time in dogs and coyotes but never paid much attention to it. Afterward, my students and I began a study of this phenomenon, which we called "dry marking," during which a dog, usually a male, lifts a leg but doesn't pee. As I explain in chapter 5, this woman was right on the mark, so to speak, about her observations of her dog.

This interest in and even devotion to dogs takes many forms. For instance, once during a bike ride with world-class racer Rohan Dennis, I learned he had a tattoo of a dog, a pit bull/staffy mix, which he got after seeing the dog being walked by an "evil clown."[26] When I asked Rohan if he knew the dog or loved that mix of breeds, he said, "Nope." But somehow that dog touched him, and he just wanted to get a tattoo. He later wrote to me, "I really didn't want anything meaningful to me at the time either because I was only eighteen, and we are all pretty naive about life at that age." I love this story because of how Rohan chose to keep the dog in mind with a tattoo that is permanently displayed on his right bicep. Dogs inspire us and really bring feelings out of us, and sometimes we don't even know why.

Other people have also shown me tattoos of their dogs, and from time to time, people also share tables and graphs charting their dog's behavior in vastly different situations. They love what they do, and I'm sure their dogs have benefited from their keen observations. Whether you go as far as Rohan or these budding ethologists, I encourage you to spend a good deal of time with dogs, yours and others. We need to watch them and learn to read them, as they watch us and learn to read us. For anyone interested in what it means to observe like an ethologist, I've included a brief primer in the appendix.

In short, in order to discover what I call the essential ethology of dogs, we must focus on what dogs know, feel, and do, and to do this we must become dog literate and also "become a dog" as much as possible. I don't mean that we have to act like a dog; we don't need to sniff where they sniff or try to engage in dog behaviors. What I mean is, by carefully watching dogs, we learn to read them and recognize their perspective. We merge what research tells us about dog behavior with what we see actual dogs doing in specific contexts, and then we add in our own common sense. To understand what a certain dog feels, and why they do what they do, the challenge is to blend all these perspectives, and all the relevant data, and make sure that together they match the dog in question. There is always more to learn.

I'll be upfront here and tell you that I'm always surprised at how few people actually watch their dogs carefully. I'm also frequently shocked to learn how few dog trainers—I like to call them teachers—have spent time studying dogs independently of their work environments. Of course, this doesn't mean they're bad at their jobs, but I can't help but think this limits their understanding of dogs, dog-human relationships, and how to solve problems. If we live with or work with dogs, it's essential to watch dogs in all sorts of situations. Not only is it fun, but this is also how we learn what makes dogs tick, by observing them both in the situations they savor and in the instances when problems arise.

This knowledge isn't esoteric or academic. We use it to do our job better, the job of caring for our companion animals. As Q. Sonntag and K. Overall write, "A better understanding of animal behaviour by both pet owners and professionals, to more effectively meet the needs of dogs and cats and recognise their problems, should inform the formulation of objective welfare assessments to ensure a better quality of life for the animals. Responsible breeding practices that increase genetic diversity and select for traits that help dogs and cats fill their niche in a changing world should be based on evidence to minimise welfare risk."[27]

Minding Dogs: A Dog Companion's Guide

In the same way that, when I was a child, my parents said I "minded animals," I always encourage people to "mind dogs," along with all the animal companions who share our homes. As I've said, this means seeking a thorough understanding of their cognitive and emotional lives—what they know and what they feel—and appreciating that they also mind us. Yet this attitude also means appreciating that we are totally responsible for the well-being of dogs. We are their lifelines, and along with this power comes incredible responsibility, for this power is not a license to do whatever we like to suit ourselves. We must respect and love dogs for *who* they are, not for *what* we want them to be.

Minding animals starts with the language we use. I prefer to use the terms "companion animals" and "guardians" to refer to dogs, cats, and the other nonhuman animals who live with us. Often, people use the word "animals" to refer to all living beings except us, but of course, humans are animals too, and we should be proud of our membership in the animal kingdom.[28] When I use the word "animals," I usually intend to include humans, and when I don't, I prefer the term "nonhuman animals." When discussing any animal, I prefer to use subjective pronouns—"he," "she," and "they," "who" or "whom"—rather than objective pronouns like "it," "that," or "which."[29] In this book, I haven't changed direct quotes to reflect these preferences, and occasionally I use the words "pet" and "owner" myself, when these are appropriate or clearer. Yet I have long spoken out about how the media, journalists, and scientists should pay more attention to how language can reflect an unspoken bias, one that treats nonhuman animals like objects, and I'm pleased that there is a trend away from this.

To put this another way, in this book, when I discuss dog behavior, I often focus on the "practical turn," or using what we know to give dogs the best lives we can, while factoring in who they are as *individuals* and what they need and want as unique beings. If we choose to bring a dog into our homes and hearts, we are obligated to do all we can to give them the best life possible; this, to me, is nonnegotiable. Being too busy or assuming our lives are more important than theirs doesn't cut it when we can easily make choices that offer them what they want and need. Dogs have much to teach us about life in general.

Thus, while this entire book is meant as an illuminating "field guide" to dogs, my hope is that this knowledge is put to good use. In chapter 9, "A Dog Companion's Guide," I provide specific advice concerning caring for and living with dogs, along with some thoughts on training or teaching. Some even suggested I call the entire book a "dog owner's manual," but of course, that's not quite right. From a dog's perspective, they aren't "owned," and "ownership" doesn't and shouldn't reflect the nature of the relationship. You own a couch or a stove, and if these break down, you fix them or get rid of them and buy new ones. Living with a dog is a lifelong commitment that involves countless ongoing negotiations.

In many ways this book also can be viewed as a field guide to freedom, for when we learn more about what it is like to be a dog in a human-dominated world and that living with a dog requires trade-offs by all involved, with that understanding, dogs and their people will enjoy more freedom. Recognizing that an enduring positive and mutually rewarding relationship requires give and take is a freedom enhancer for dogs and humans alike.

Even though I am not a professional dog trainer, I am a scientist who is committed to supporting positive training methods that don't involve domination or intimidation. However, there is no one-size-fits-all approach. Like children, some dogs need that extra bit of teaching, care, and love in order to learn how to get along with other dogs, or with their human companions, but all dogs need kindness. When I write about what dogs want and need, I focus more on what dogs *feel* as the marker for how they should be treated. Intelligence doesn't really factor into how much an individual suffers, so asking if so-called less intelligent dogs suffer less than so-called more intelligent dogs isn't a meaningful question. What about people with varying smarts? The most useful guideline is that every being's capacity for suffering is the same, and dogs don't suffer more than rats or mice, nor do they suffer less than humans.

For those who choose to share their homes with dogs or other animals, I view this book as providing what I like to call preemptive humane education. Caring for a dog (or any other animal) is not enough. It's essential to turn feelings of caring into action to make the lives of all individuals the best they can be. At the end, this book includes a call for advocacy and activism on dogs' behalf.

The decision to bring another animal into our homes and hearts is oftentimes profoundly basic: we seek a companion to love and whom we hope will love us. But this relationship and our obligations can quickly become complicated. My colleague Dr. Jessica Pierce, in her book *Run, Spot, Run: The Ethics of Keeping Pets*, boils this down to a basic question: "Are you ready to give another animal the best life possible?" For example, does your home environment suit the animal? Does your lifestyle? Have you calculated lifetime expenses? Will you be able to make end-of-life decisions? Difficult practical and ethical questions await, and sometimes people realize that perhaps they didn't think deeply enough about what it means to take total responsibility for another being's life.

As an example of all this—particularly of how citizen science and observing like an ethologist can help us ask good questions, which can then inform our caretaking and help us give dogs the best life possible—here is an email that my colleague Jessica Pierce received in 2016. She shared it with me, and now I share it with you:

> My grandson of eleven has a dog which he adopted several years ago. They live in New York City and I in New Jersey. On many occasions, I take the dog for a walk. There are two places I take him to. One is the dog run and the other is Central Park.
>
> In the dog run, he would jostle with other dogs and run around, sometimes quite wild. He sniffs at other dogs and sometimes even tries to mount them. When the latter happens, almost every dog owner would discourage that behavior.
>
> In Central Park, my dog would simply walk along with me and he would acknowledge the presence of other dogs by looking at them most of the time. Only occasionally, he would try to jostle with them.
>
> Lately, I got to thinking there may be something wrong with the way we are raising our dogs and cats, especially those who live in the city.
>
> My thinking started this way. How does a dog grow up, intellectually? Even though dogs are domesticated animals, do they learn everything from us, the human being? Even if they are not

social animals, don't they have to learn something from other dogs? The intellect and knowledge of human beings are passed down through the generations, and they are accumulated in that process. My grandson certainly is going to know a lot more things than I know now. But, my grandson's dog is isolated most of the time from other dogs, except when he was taken to the dog run.

So, my question is how could a dog grow up intellectually if he has no other dogs to learn from? Does a dog end up thinking and behaving like his constant companion, a human being? And he has only his own lifetime to learn and cannot take advantage of the learning that other dogs had acquired.

Is the deprivation of a dog from learning from other dogs the greatest tragedy of being a dog?[30]

The Big Picture: Dogs in Society and the World

Dogs are amazing beings, and I appreciate all the people who try hard to make the lives of so many dogs the best they can possibly be in a world that places a lot of demands on them. At the end of this chapter, and at the end of this book, I want to step back and consider the larger context of dogs in our world, because many discussions at dog parks come back to this essential topic.

Not only do dogs make our individual lives better, but they also inspire us to make the world better. For instance, in 1925, Heinrich Zimmermann, the German writer and publisher of the magazine *Mensch und Hund* (*Man and Dog*), conceived and organized the first World Animal Day, which is still celebrated every October 4.[31] A dog named Pepper played a huge role in fostering animal welfare legislation in the United States by motivating the passage of the federal Animal Welfare Act in 1966. Pepper, a Dalmatian, was dognapped from a Pennsylvania farm in 1965 and sold to a hospital in the Bronx, where she died in an experimental test of pacemakers. Pepper and her plight helped to bridge the empathy gap; she inspired our empathy and helped us see that all species feel and suffer.

Dogs help us span all sorts of divides, even political ones. One of the few things Democrats and Republicans in the U.S. Congress agree on is that companion dogs are welcome to join lawmakers in the Capitol, and it's been that way since the 1800s. In August 2016, the town of Cormorant, Minnesota, elected Duke, a nine-year-old Great Pyrenees, to serve a third term as its mayor.[32] Afterward, I heard from a number of people who felt that putting dogs in charge of government made a lot of sense.

Dogs are "in," as I often say. As of this writing, nearly eighty million American households, or nearly 65 percent of all U.S. households, share space and time with a pet, and about 44 percent of households have a dog.[33] In total, about seventy-eight million dogs are considered to be pets in the United States. This means dogs are also big business, and the amount of money spent in the "dog-industrial complex" is staggering. Americans alone spend almost $70 billion each year on their pets, including $30 billion on pet food and over $16 billion on veterinary care.[34] Living with dogs can be expensive, with annual costs estimated at around $1,600.[35] In fact, in the United States, spending on health care for pets is rising faster than the rate of spending on people.[36] From 1996 to 2012, spending on pet purchases, medical supplies, and veterinary services rose about 60 percent compared to 50 percent for human health care. People around the world also will take risks to save their companion animals and others when the animals' lives are endangered.[37]

Dog ownership is rising in many countries around the world. As of 2012, Brazil had thirty-five million dogs, China had twenty-seven million, and Russia had fifteen million. In India, dog ownership has increased by well over 50 percent since 2007, and in Venezuela and the Philippines it has increased by 30 percent or more.[38]

Not only do people often offer dogs special treatment when compared with their attitudes toward other animals, some people are known to take care of their dogs above other family members.[39] One study showed that children get along better with their pet dog than with their siblings.[40] Perhaps this not all that surprising, given that research shows that dogs, by providing social support when things are tough, create a greater reduction in stress in youngsters than does having a parent present.[41] Numerous people decide where they can live based on whether places are animal friendly, and there is a move for residential master plans to include accommodations for the needs of companion dogs.[42]

Unfortunately, this doesn't mean that today dogs lead pampered lives. Dogs may be "in," but like so many other animals, they are caught up in our current human-dominated epoch, which has been called the Anthropocene, or "the age of humanity." In reality, the Anthropocene could be called "the rage of inhumanity," since what it means is that there are far too many of us, and other animals all too often get the short end of the stick. Or in the case of dogs, the short end of an already short leash.

Despite all the dogs who are cared for in loving homes, it's estimated that about 75 percent of the world's dogs are on their own, often living desperately hard lives in utter squalor, gravely ill, and in deep physical and psychological pain.[43] In Yangon, Myanmar, there are around 120,000 stray dogs who carry rabies and attack children.[44] In Taiwan, around 10,900 stray dogs were euthanized in 2015, and in 2016, about 8,600 shelter dogs died due to diseases and other causes.[45]

In addition to suffering human neglect, dogs are harmed more directly. Dogs are still used in blood sports, run to death in dog races, and forced to perform in shows and movies.[46] While so-called designer dogs, such as labradoodles and goldendoodles, are very popular and trendy today, intentionally crossbreeding to produce certain traits in a dog can also produce unhealthy traits.[47] In Scotland, the demand for designer dogs has been so high that there is a good deal of unlicensed breeding. Mark Rafferty of Scotland's Society for the Prevention of Cruelty to Animals noted that they're viewed by some people as "throwaway commodities."[48]

People still breed dogs who they know will have short and likely miserable lives because of inbreeding and selecting for traits that make it difficult for them to breathe or to walk.[49] These people are essentially breeding, as one observer put it, for "beauty over health . . .

at the cost of empathy."[50] Humans spend millions of dollars to get rid of their own wrinkles, yet we intentionally produce dogs with wrinkled faces who we know will suffer and die young. But it doesn't stop there. At Texas A&M University, dogs are intentionally bred with deformities to study various forms of muscular dystrophy. Many of these experimental dogs are profoundly crippled by six months of age, and half of them don't live more than ten months.[51] This surely isn't any way to treat one's "best friend." I like to say that some people love some dogs to early deaths; for example, the median life span for French bulldogs is 2.5 years for males and 3.8 for females.[52]

So it's essential to keep in mind that if dogs don't necessarily act like our best friends all the time, neither are we theirs. Dogs do not love unconditionally, and neither do we. Sure, it often seems difficult to find a dog who isn't friendly to some extent, but dogs discriminate among humans just as we discriminate among dogs. In addition, dogs who have been severely abused sometimes never regain the trust that underlies unconditional love for humans or, in some cases, for other dogs.[53]

It also bears repeating that, on both personal and societal levels, dogs depend on us much more than we depend on them. Elise Gatti, a graduate student at the University of Utah, wrote to me with the observation that "we are our dogs' whole lives but our dogs are only part of our lives."[54] I agree, and we should never forget this. That dependence places the highest obligation on us to make the lives of dogs as good as possible.

Having said that, we must ask how well we really know what goes on in the minds, hearts, and noses of our canine companions. What does it mean to be a dog? To begin, let's consider how dogs use their five senses to understand the world. Of course, how dogs sense the world is intimately connected to their behavior and why they do what they do in various situations. To appreciate what it is like to be a dog, we need to understand how they see, hear, touch, taste, and most of all, smell. Dogs are animals for whom the nose knows everything.

TWO

The World According to Dogs

‖‖

Everyone knows dogs have noses of all different shapes and sizes, often depending on the shape and size of their heads and faces. One of my favorite dogs was Sammy "the schnozzola," a huge blended mutt who had the biggest nose I've ever seen on a dog. Sammy looked like an anteater, and he seemed to know it. His nose went everywhere, including the butt, ears, body, and face of other dogs and the groins, ears, and mouth of unsuspecting humans. People at the dog park called him Hoover because he really acted like a canine vacuum cleaner. Once, while I was deeply absorbed in watching two dogs playing, Sammy approached me from behind, and before I knew it his nose was exiting the front of my legs. I'd never been skewered by a dog's nose, and I broke up laughing, and Sammy, thinking I enjoyed it, kept on walking into me. I felt he could have lifted me off the ground with his oversized snout.

‖‖

One day a woman who had rescued her first dog learned that I studied dogs, and she asked me, "Why does she sniff everything, get confused when she can't see something that looks fine to me, and get restless and agitated when she hears noises I can't hear?" I get questions like this quite a lot, and I explain that the world according to dogs is rather different from ours.

The best way to start learning about how dogs understand their world is to imagine what it's like to be a dog and have a dog's senses. Of course, dogs have the same five senses as humans, but they are not experienced or used equivalently. I fully realize suggesting you imagine what it's like to be a dog is a big ask. Not only is it impossible for us to fully appreciate all the information that a dog's wondrous nose and eager tongue provide, but dogs routinely put them both in places we find unimaginable and utterly off-putting!

So, staying within the confines of what we might call appropriate behavior, here I offer an "ethology of the senses," or a brief picture of how dogs sense their world through smell, sight, sound, taste, and touch. Of course, like other animals, including humans, dogs often process a cocktail of stimuli coming in simultaneously and sequentially. Ethologists call these composite signals, and they usually contain more information than signals in a single sensory modality.

The emerging and changing cacophony of sensory stimuli allows dogs to gather a good deal of detailed information about what's happening in the moment. It might even tell them what happened in the past and what is likely to occur in the future. This information is vital in order for them to figure out what to do in any given situation. While dogs bark (which I discuss in chapter 7), dogs don't actually talk, as do humans, to understand others and to communicate and express their feelings. Rather, they mainly use their five senses and nonverbal communication.

A Dog's Nose Is a Work of Art

Odors are everywhere. Humans can't detect them all—and we often don't need to or want to—but dogs are different. Scents mean everything to dogs, and their noses are expert at finding them. In *Being a Dog*, Dr. Alexandra Horowitz calls dogs "nosed animals"—or "a nose with a body attached"—and researchers refer to dogs as macrosmatic mammals because smell is so important, really essential, to their way of life.[1] I always think that a dog without a working nose isn't a dog. In fact, dogs also have what's called a vomeronasal organ, also called Jacobson's organ, that functions as a second nose. This is part of a dog's accessory olfactory system, and it responds to stimuli that are liquid rather than volatile vapors.[2]

We all know dogs like to stick their noses everywhere, and they often snort when they're doing it or shortly thereafter. Their super-sensitive noses are legendary, so much so that their approach to life could be summed up as "sniff first, ask questions later." It's not clear why dogs' noses evolved to be so sensitive. When I ask researchers, some suggest that it's related to the fact that their noses are so close to the ground. Others simply say that it's evidence of evolution selecting for an adaptation that benefited the animal, and now "that's the way it is." Be that as it may, dogs put their noses to work seemingly every single second.

This is troubling to us when dogs sniff places and things we consider taboo. On my forays at dog parks, I often hear something like, "Stop it, don't put your nose there." Or, "Geez, that's disgusting. Get your nose out of his butt." Dogs also like to sniff private parts, pee, and poop in order to learn a lot of pretty exciting information for them. When it comes to smells, we should let dogs be dogs and not hold them to human standards of propriety. This means we should let them sniff one another to their nose's content and we must let their walks be *their* walks, not ours, as frustrating and challenging as this might be. Their sense organs, like their muscles, heart, and lungs, need to be exercised.

WHAT CAN DOGS SMELL?

I've already introduced you to several dogs—including Bernie and Beatrice, the butters, and Gus and Greta, the groiners, along with Sammy the schnozzola—whose noses know no bounds. These dogs can't stop shamelessly running up nose first into everyone's privates, which always ignites many questions about what dogs are smelling and why, since they clearly enjoy it.

The truth is, while we know that dogs are gathering all sorts of important information, it's not always clear what exactly that information is. It's well known that male dogs pick up information about the receptivity of females using odor, and all dogs seem to be able to identify other dogs by their smell. They can also discriminate their own scent from that of other dogs and may learn where other dogs have been, who else they've been with, and how they're feeling. Given that so many people spend a good deal of time marveling and often laughing as dogs intensely vacuum different substrates and inanimate items, along with the body parts of other dogs and humans, it's odd how little we actually know. Citizen science can surely motivate more formal research in this area.

Some have even wondered if dogs can smell time. Dogs surely have some sense of time, since most dogs know when it's dinnertime and they seem to be able to anticipate when their owners are coming home. But we don't know how they tell time or with what understanding of time. Alexandra Horowitz suggests that dogs can smell odors that are in the process of evaporating, and in this way they can track time (and perhaps that's why they have a good sense of when their human is coming home).[3] I don't know if this is so; perhaps they can do this in certain instances. Given my own and others' observations, it seems as if dogs can tell not only who peed but also how long ago with real accuracy. Still, this hasn't been proven, and so we really need more research to tackle this daunting but interesting possibility.

Whatever dogs are learning, they never don't smell, perhaps even when they sleep. Dogs often sniff their friends as vigorously as they do less familiar individuals and strangers, even if they've been apart for only a few seconds. Jessica Pierce told me that her dog Bella would sniff her housemate Maya after Maya paid a visit to the veterinarian. I remember smiling as Jethro, a dog with whom I shared my home, would vigorously sniff Zeke after Zeke was gone for less than a minute. Zeke would patiently allow Jethro to run his nose all over him, and on occasion Zeke seemed to be saying, "Hey, I just went down the road to pee and to see Lolo, our friend." Dogs don't seem to question the need to sniff, and I'm sure they know what they're doing. Perhaps it's like when people text message only seconds after leaving a party. What else is there to say? Sometimes, you just want to check in again.

Whatever dogs learn, they are compelled to investigate with their noses, and they can get so into odors that they can lose awareness of their surroundings or what they are doing. So many times I've come upon a dog who's sniffing and snorting and totally oblivious, or so it seems, that I'm right behind her or him. During the time I was writing this chapter, I watched a dog on a Boulder bike path follow his nose right into the creek! Once, as I was walking up the dirt road near my mountain home, I saw my companion Jethro follow his well-equipped nose directly into a field of cactuses. I screamed for him to stop, but it was too late. I'd like to say he learned something from this prickly encounter, but sadly he didn't. Next day, same place, nose to cactuses. I have no idea whatever or whomever Jethro was savoring, but it surely took precedence over everything else. And, none of his dog friends with whom he was hanging out paid any attention to the smelly cactuses.

The skill of a dog's nose leads us to wonder about how odors travel. As I discuss next, a dog's nose can distinguish scents with a refinement that puts humans to shame. They can discern minute differences between odors that all smell the same to us. As we know, trained dogs are employed to sniff for bombs, drugs, and banned food items—and not just any and all food, but only alerting for specific kinds. Trained dogs use their fine sense of smell to sniff out different human diseases and to help doctors diagnose them. They can follow scent trails and track smells in various situations, such as in and around crime scenes or to locate a missing person, during which they detect the direction from which an odor is coming and if it is becoming diluted.

Dogs also serve as conservation biologists. They are used to track animals without having to trap and collar the individuals of interest; to find rare species; to locate scats to learn about what animals are eating and the presence of pharmaceuticals, heavy metals, and poisons; and to stop the poaching and the trafficking of animals such as elephants and rhinos who are ruthlessly killed for their ivory or their horns. What's really interesting about conservation dogs is that many come from shelters and go on to have exciting and rich lives helping human conservationists and wildlife managers. When I lived in the mountains outside of Boulder, Colorado, the dogs with whom I shared my home and land were very good at letting me know when black bears or cougars were around. I'd follow them to where their noses were going crazy, see what a scat looked like, and head home when it was clear bears or cougars were around.[4] One of my dogs also alerted me to the presence of a bobcat who I had never seen but knew was around. Good dog!

Because of trained dogs, we also know something of what dogs learn about people using smell: dogs discern our emotions and can identify certain illnesses and diseases. In fact, most of the time, dogs showed us they could detect medical conditions on their own, and only then did we think to train them to do so. One interesting point is that human diseases are not all necessarily detected the same way.[5]

In 2016, Mathew Reichertz, a professor at the Nova Scotia College of Art & Design, created an art exhibit called *Dog Park*, which is a series of paintings that show a dog's view of how different odors move around in the atmosphere. Professor Reichertz explained, "I did research about how smells move over uneven terrain, how a dog's nose works, and how they behave when they are tracking a smell. The more I sought to understand a dog's sense of smell, the more I realized that their olfactory experience creates a kind of architecture that they inhabit and move through."[6]

I have also wondered what happens when dogs are asleep. Many times I've watched dogs snoozing—or at least it looked like they were asleep—with their noses moving slowly from side to side, often accompanied or followed by a snort, another sound, or eye movements. I've also heard loud snorts and expected to see nose goo flying across the room as a dog peacefully slept, perhaps dreaming of a previous delicious meal or a day spent with friends.

HOW DOES A DOG'S NOSE WORK?

Because we all have a pretty good idea of what humans can smell, it's helpful to compare dogs and ourselves.[7] The sense of smell is the dog's most highly evolved sense. A dog's olfactory cortex, which is part of their brain, is about forty times larger in dogs than it is in humans, and about 35 percent of a dog's brain deals with odors (while only 5 percent of a human brain is devoted to smell). Dogs can use each nostril separately to further increase their smelling abilities. Researchers studying airflow in dogs' noses have discovered that they inhale through the nostrils and exhale through slits on the side of their nose. This allows odors to remain in the back of the nose. Dogs also don't push out all the odor molecules with one snort.[8] While the human nose can sense from four to ten thousand different smells, dogs can sense from thirty to a hundred thousand different odors, which makes a dog's nose about a hundred thousand to a million times more sensitive than ours.

Alexandra Horowitz has said that if we spread out a dog's nasal epithelium (the lining of a dog's nose), it would cover their entire body, while ours would only cover a mole on our shoulder.[9] Dogs sniff about five times per second, and when allowed to pursue their fancy, they spend around a third of their time sniffing. They don't exhale when trying to sniff, so they can sniff faint odors; they can move and use their two nostrils independently; and if dogs eat less protein and more fat, their sense of smell is improved.[10]

In fact, dogs can get what's called nose fatigue from smelling too much, which makes me wonder and worry about olfactory overload. For example, how do dog perfumes, shampoos, and soaps influence a dog's perception of more biologically relevant odors, and do they even like these soaps in the first place or are these really for humans? Carefully paying attention to how a dog reacts to these human-placed odors is critical.[11]

According to Norwegian researcher and dog nose specialist Dr. Frank Rosell, a dog's nostrils also aid with tempering, filtering, and humidifying the air that is inhaled as it passes down into the lungs. Even if the nostrils of all beings function for both breathing and sniffing, a dog's nostrils are remarkably well organized and far more advanced than our own.

Dr. Rosell writes:

When the dog breathes through its nose, the air passes through the respiratory region in the dog's long snout and subsequently directly into the lungs. When a dog sniffs, the air follows a side route, entering what we call the olfactory recess. The olfactory recess is covered by an olfactory epithelium containing genes for olfactory receptors (every single one of which is a protein produced by a specific gene), and olfactory receptor cells that absorb odorants. Microsomatic mammals, such as humans and primates, have a different makeup, lacking this olfactory recess. The dog has agile nostrils that stretch when it is sniffing, and this movement opens an upper passageway that sends the air directly into the part of the olfactory recess farthest in the back. An enlarged olfactory recess very likely also increases the airstream for both inhalation and exhalation. The air is filtered slowly forward through the sensory apparatus before it finds its way into the lungs.[12]

There also are breed differences. Dr. Rosell notes that "the olfactory mucous membrane varies from one breed to the next, within each breed, and with age. The German shepherd has the largest olfactory mucous membrane area, ranging from 96 cm² to 200 cm². A cocker spaniel has an olfactory mucous membrane area of 67 cm², and a fox terrier puppy can have an area as small as 11 cm². The larger the surface area of the olfactory mucous membrane, the greater the potential for absorbing weak odor signals."[13] In addition to measuring surface area, researchers also have determined the number of olfactory receptor cells for different breeds. For the record, bloodhounds have the most olfactory receptor cells, numbering in the neighborhood of three hundred million! Thus, bloodhounds have the best nose among dogs, one that is ten to a hundred million times more sensitive than ours. Meanwhile, German shepherds have 220 million, the fox terrier 147 million, and the dachshund 125 million olfactory receptor cells.

The Best Nose: Dogs versus Humans

How much more important is a dog's nose to a dog than a human's nose to a human? Consider these comparisons:

- A dog's rhinencephalon (smell brain) is almost seven times larger than a human being's.
- Dogs have an olfactory mucous membrane measuring 67–200 square centimeters, while the olfactory mucous membrane of humans is only three to ten square centimeters.
- Dogs can have 125–300 million olfactory cells. Humans have five million olfactory cells.
- Dogs have 100–150 olfactory hairs per olfactory cell. Humans have six to eight olfactory hairs per olfactory cell.
- Dogs can smell some compounds at concentrations as low as one part per trillion. For humans, the lowest concentration detected is one part per billion.

Dr. Rosell writes:

When a dog inhales, the air close to the nostril is drawn in, and the dog knows which nostril the air enters. The dog's nostril is more sophisticated than a pair of simple openings. Dogs have a wing-like flap in each nostril that opens for and shuts off the airstream moving through the nose. This flap determines the direction of the airstream in and out of the nose. When the dog inhales, there is an opening above and beside this flap. When the dog exhales, this opening closes and the air comes out below and beside this flap through another opening, enabling the dog to increase its collection of further odors. As a result, the warm air that is exhaled flows backwards and away from the odor being sniffed and prevents the odor from being mixed into the air being breathed out. Because the air is warm, odorants are heated up and more easily converted into gas form, thereby reinforcing the gathering of odors. By keeping its nose close to the ground and sniffing in quickly, a dog can blow the heavier, non-volatile odorants up from the ground, bringing the odorants up into the air and into its nose.[14]

All in all, a dog's nose is a work of art, an exquisite adaptation, evolution at its best. And all without a plan or goal. When people tell me they wish they had a dog's nose, I hasten to add they should be careful what they wish for. I'm happy to know about this most remarkable adaptation, but even I don't have any desire to experience all of the many odors dogs take in and clearly savor.

A Dog's-Eye View of the World

Dogs clearly have a keen and highly evolved sense of smell. They also have a good set of eyes, which are also important for negotiating their social world. I'm sure I'm not alone in having been stared down by a dog who has locked eyes and won't let go. Dogs are not the only nonhumans to look people in the eye. I've also had similar stare downs with wild coyotes, black bears, and cougars around my mountain home.

John Bradshaw and Nicola Rooney note: "Dogs are visual generalists, able to operate in a range of ambient light levels. Dogs have dichromatic color vision; they cannot distinguish between green and grey, or between yellow and orange, and red likely appears as black. There is little evidence for any role of color in visual communication. The visual abilities of a dog vary by breed. Greyhounds have been touted as having the best eyesight compared to other breeds, however, it hasn't been thoroughly proven."[15]

Humans have better close-up vision than dogs, who often use a cocktail of scents and sounds to help them sort close-up stimuli. Dogs also are more sensitive to moving, as compared to stationary, stimuli. Obviously, this is important in reading social signals such as tail wagging (which I consider in chapter 7). We also know that dogs can differentiate species based on visual images of heads.

People also are constantly telling me that their dog can "read" other dogs from afar and seem to be able to make reliable, long-distance assessments about whether another dog is friendly, wants to play, or is saying back off. However, dogs have a visual acuity of around 20/75, which means that when we can see something from seventy-five feet away, a dog can only see it at twenty feet. They'd do well to wear glasses! As such, I'm always amazed at how dogs know other dogs at a long distance. C. Claiborne Ray, discussing a study done by Dominique Autier-Dérian and her colleagues, says: "Ranging in size from a tiny Maltese to a giant St. Bernard, and showing myriad differences in coats, snouts, ears, tails and bone structure, dogs might not always appear to belong to one species. Yet other dogs recognize them easily, even in the absence of clues like odor, movement and vocalizations."[16]

Many people report that, on their dogs' first encounter with other dogs, members of the same breed prefer one another and that dogs treat breed members differently than individuals of other breeds. Is this odor based, as is kin recognition in some rodents? While dogs know what they themselves smell like, they don't necessarily know what they look like—or might they? Research done on birds in the 1960s suggests that they might learn their own color from reflections in water.

We also know dogs aren't color blind, but the color range they're able to perceive is limited when compared to ours. Dogs typically can see in ranges that are similar to red-green color blindness in humans. Dogs also are able to see better at night than are humans. It's estimated that dogs can see in light around five times dimmer than humans can.

Dog Ears: Sounds Canines Can Hear

The ears of dogs come in a wide variety of shapes and sizes: from long and floppy to short and erect. But whatever the shape, they hear sounds of which humans are totally unaware. Their ears are rather mobile and capable of turret-like movements, which allow them to more precisely locate a sound. Depending on the breed and age, dogs can hear in frequencies ranging from around forty to sixty thousand hertz (one hertz equals one cycle per second). Humans can hear sounds around twelve to twenty thousand hertz. Dog whistles produce a sound that's usually in the range of twenty-three to fifty-four thousand hertz.

Dogs have more than eighteen muscles that control their flexible pinna (the external part of the ears). Overall, dogs perceive frequencies approximately twice that of humans, and it's been widely reported that they can detect and distinguish sounds about four times as far as humans. This means that what a human can hear at twenty feet a dog can hear at roughly eighty feet.[17] Of course, dogs' ears are adapted to the sounds they themselves make. John Bradshaw and Nicola Rooney report that research has shown that wild canids produce twelve sounds, and dogs produce ten of these. However, researchers still debate exactly how many sounds dogs make, since some scientists lump a variety of sounds together, whereas others split them more finely.

Taste, Touch, and the Potpourri of Sensations

This chapter focuses mainly on dogs' noses, ears, and eyes, since these are their most important senses and the ones we know the most about. We know comparatively little about a dog's sense of taste and that of touch.

Concerning taste, a dog's sense of taste, as it turns out, is far less sensitive than ours. Dogs have around seventeen hundred taste buds, whereas we have around nine thousand. When you consider what dogs lick and gobble into their mouths, perhaps this is a blessing in disguise.

Touch also is important to dogs, but more so for some than others. Some dogs like to be hugged, as long as it's done on their terms, and it seems that petting or caressing an anxious or nervous dog, one who likes to be petted or caressed, calms them down. However, some dogs don't like being hugged much at all. In these cases, a dog's aversion to being touched needs to be honored.

Between dogs, touching often accompanies close encounters, and it's possible that it can add or detract from the message that is being shared. I've seen a dog slowly walk over to a stressed dog, lie down next to them, and lay a paw over their back, as if saying something like "all's well" or "I'm here, so relax." On occasion, dogs will groom one another, and often they sleep belly to back. However, we really do not know much about canine touch, other than that some dogs like it and some don't.

The real challenge for future research with dogs is to learn not only how each sense works but also how they combine the input from the different senses—the composite signals—in order to understand the world and make decisions. For instance, one study by dog researcher Ludwig Huber discovered that captive dogs are able to integrate information from sight and sound to identify other dog breeds correctly. In the study, dogs matched a projected visual image of dogs of different sizes with the vocalization that is usually made by dogs of each size.[18]

Eventually, additional research will help us figure out more precisely how smells, sights, and sounds are important on their own and how they work together, providing us with a richer view of how dogs sense their worlds. In the meantime, what we know is this: however dogs process the constant bombardment of stimuli from different modalities, when dogs have their noses to the ground or pinned to the butt of another dog, they seem lost in a symphony of smells.

THREE

Dogs Just Want to Have Fun

||||||||||||||||||||||||||||||||||||||||||||||||||||||||||||||||||||||||||||||||||||||||||||||||||||||||||||||

Jethro bounds toward Zeke, stops immediately in front of him, crouches on his forelimbs, wags his tail, barks, and immediately lunges at him, bites his scruff and shakes his head rapidly from side to side, works his way around to his backside and mounts him, jumps off, does a rapid bow, lunges at his side and slams him with his hips, leaps up and bites his neck, and runs away. Zeke takes off in wild pursuit of Jethro and leaps on his back and bites his muzzle and then his scruff and shakes his head rapidly from side to side. Suki bounds in and chases Jethro and Zeke, and they all wrestle with one another. They part for a few minutes, sniffing here and there and resting. Then, Jethro walks slowly over to Zeke, extends his paw toward Zeke's head, and nips at his ears. Zeke gets up and jumps on Jethro's back, bites him, and grasps him around his waist. They then fall to the ground and mouth wrestle. Then they chase one another and roll over and play. Suki decides to jump in, and the three of them frolic until they're exhausted. When it's over, they all look like couldn't have been happier. And then, Lolo comes, too, and it all happens once again.

||||||||||||||||||||||||||||||||||||||||||||||||||||||||||||||||||||||||||||||||||||||||||||||||||||||||||||||

These are some of my field notes, which have been mirrored in thousands of other observations of dogs at play. I've been nose deep in dog play for decades, and I never get bored thinking about it or watching dogs romping here and there. Dogs just want to have fun. And why not?

In fact, I often go to dog parks alone and just cruise around to watch dogs play. When I hear people tell their dog to go have fun and sniff to their heart's content—just go be a dog—it warms my heart. For a dog, that's providing Freedom with a capital *F*: they can sniff, run, romp, pee, and play without constantly being stopped, called back, or corrected every thirty seconds. Of course, dogs are never entirely free, not even in dog parks, but they need their own "dog time," which isn't measured by human clocks.

I also silently chuckle whenever I hear someone give their dog a two-minute warning, as if the dog has his or her own stopwatch or mobile phone or some sort of internal clock. People will say, "You have five more minutes, so hurry up and pee or play with your friends. Then we have to go." Then, if people have to call their dog more than once, they get testy: "What took you so long? I've been calling you for ten minutes. We need to leave now." I often wonder if dogs think something like, "Huh, how long is ten minutes? How long is now?" Even if dogs actually can "smell time," tracking the faintness of odors to learn how long ago something happened, they certainly don't tell time in human terms. Play is an activity that dogs love almost above everything else, during which time rapidly melts away. For many dogs there simply isn't enough time to play.

In addition to freedom, play requires two other important ingredients: fun and friends. In itself, play is a rich area of study, since it sheds light on so much that goes on in a dog's head and heart. For instance, I know two dogs—Sadie, a small hairy mix of lots of different genes, and Roxy, a lean boxer mix—who are clearly best friends. When Sadie arrives at the dog park, she immediately sniffs and pees, checks out who's there by lifting her head and sniffing, and then almost invariably runs back to the entrance to wait for Roxy, who, if she's already at the dog park, races up to Sadie around 95 percent of the time (according to Roxy and Sadie's humans). Then they play as if they were the only two dogs in the world.

However, an interesting thing happens on the days when Roxy

doesn't show. Sadie will pace along the fence line and look around, clearly wondering where Roxy is, even as other dogs come up to say hello and ask her to play. Sadie usually paces for around twenty seconds or so, which is all the time she needs to establish that Roxy is absent. At that point, Sadie goes off and finds other dogs to play with.

How does Sadie know so quickly that Roxy isn't there? I have no idea, but when Sadie chooses to give up waiting and go find other friends to romp with, she is correct 99 percent of the time; Roxie isn't coming. Is it safe to say that Sadie and Roxy are friends, and that they prefer to hang out and play together? Yes, it is, and their humans agree. Using her senses, and perhaps even a sense of time, does Sadie display an uncanny knack for identifying Roxie's presence or absence? Surely. And if Roxie is missing, does Sadie ever let her freedom in the dog park go to waste? Never. What dog would ever do that?

Canis ludens: Play Is Universal

Dogs sometimes play just for the hell of it, just for the fun of it, having a ball as they run around frenetically as if no one and nothing else existed except themselves in the present moment. When dogs see others playing, they often want to jump right in. Play is socially contagious and can spread rapidly as a play epidemic. Watching dogs, I often want to enter the fray, but I don't, and I know I might not be welcomed. I've often seen a dog trying to join a play group by running around and barking until they're either exhausted or welcomed into the fray. Play surely is fun, but it also can be serious business.

Not surprisingly I'm often asked lots of questions about dog play: what it is, how dogs do it, and why. People want to know how dogs keep playing even when it gets rough, whether dogs can play too much, and if dogs play fair. There's also no shortage of opinions among some dog park dwellers concerning dog play. I often hear statements like, "If they keep playing like that, it's gonna escalate into a fight." "He's gonna hump her because he really wants to mate with her, not play with her." And, "They're not playing right now because he feels badly for biting so hard while they were playing, and he's ashamed."

This chapter will answer these and many other questions about play. By carefully analyzing what dogs do when they play, we can learn about their sense of empathy, cooperation, justice, fairness, and morality, among other things. In his book *The Descent of Man and Selection in Relation to Sex*, Charles Darwin wrote: "Happiness is never better exhibited than by young animals, such as puppies, kittens, lambs, etc., when playing together, like our own children."[1] In the same book Darwin also wrote: "It is a significant fact, that the more the habits of any particular animal are studied by a naturalist, the more he attributes to reason and the less to unlearned instincts."[2]

Social play is not accidental or automatic, and dogs engage in it almost universally. The desire to play seems inherent to a dog's nature, as if it were a biological drive. I often think that the scientific name of dogs should be changed from *Canis lupus familiaris* to *Canis ludens*. The Latin word *ludens* refers to sport and play, which dogs enjoy literally to the point of exhaustion. Then, after resting for a few seconds, they are up and at it for more.

In fact, many other animals play. Even rats, who laugh when they're tickled.[3] Tickling calms them down! Play releases neurochemicals in the brain, such as dopamine (and perhaps serotonin and norepinephrine), which make play desirable and also help regulate play itself. Rats show an increase in dopamine activity when anticipating the opportunity to play, and they enjoy being playfully tickled.

Indeed, dogs frequently play with such reckless abandon that I'm often asked how dogs keep play in mind as they fly around, tumble, tackle, bite, and run, often with unbelievable rapidity. How do playmates not harm one another? It's incredible to watch dogs play, yet they typically know the bounds of their own body—or where their body is in relation to other playmates, dog park traffic, and objects. Despite what it seems, dogs are mindful and "bodyful," as Naropa University psychologist Christine Caldwell calls it.[4]

As I'm about to discuss, detailed analyses of film shows that playing dogs engage in ongoing negotiations and can read others' intentions and desires. This maintains play even when things get rough. Once, when I was being filmed for a news piece on play in dogs, one of the film crew fit his dog with GoPro cameras on his head and neck. When I saw the films from the dog's point of view, it blew my mind. There's a project waiting to be done using these cameras.

DO DOGS PLAY ON THEIR OWN?

This chapter focuses mostly on social play, but it's important to acknowledge that dogs will play all by themselves. Play is its own reward and doesn't need a social context. Anyone who lives with a dog knows they sometimes play for the hell of it, just to have fun.

One of my favorite stories of self-play involves a wonderful dog who was aptly named Darwin, a.k.a. "the water fountain dog." According to his human, Sarah Bexell, Darwin, "an Australian Shepard-Catahoula Hound mix, is high energy and wickedly smart, willing to work 24/7/365 for the person with the highest treat bid."[5] I agree! I have seen Darwin in action countless times. Sarah wrote:

> Darwin has multiple fascinations, but other than for food and squirrels, water is his strongest motivator. He is well known for not being willing to come out of swimming holes; I have to bring water sandals to walk out to get him if two hours have passed. Even beyond this addiction is his fervent desire to drink fast-moving water. This was first discovered at a shooting water display in the square of Old Town in Ft. Collins, Colorado, where he would entertain passersby with his antics of chasing the shooting plumes of water, drinking them head on when he could catch them, which was more often than not. This drinking desire manifests every day at shower time, too, and the word "shower" must never be mentioned in his presence. At the slightest hint of a shower about to be taken (such as a set of clean clothes being placed in the bathroom), Darwin rushes to the tub and sticks his snout under the spout with anticipation. If said person decides to

Dr. Carl Safina's dog Chula having fun running on a beach in Amagansett on Long Island. (Courtesy of Carl Safina)

get a few more tasks done before the shower, Darwin often disappears. Where is Darwin? Fully in the tub behind the shower curtain, waiting in anguish for his shot of water. Garden time is another favorite, oh my, the hose!!!!

Darwin truly represents *Canis ludens* in all his glory. Watching Darwin, I often laughed uncontrollably, and I always thought it would be a wonderful project to study his obsession with water in more detail. Different types of play provide excellent windows into the minds, emotions, and hearts of dogs and other animals.

Of course, some dogs love to chase their own tails, to play with various objects, and to dash frantically here and there as if they're having a fit or suffering from Sydenham's chorea, otherwise known as Saint Vitus's dance. And they enjoy engaging in these "zoomies" entirely alone. A picture of Chula, one of Dr. Carl Safina's dogs, shows her clearly having fun running frenetically on a beach in Amagansett on Long Island. It's easy to feel Chula's joy. Dr. Safina, author of *Beyond Words: What Animals Think and Feel*, sent me several pictures of his dogs Chula and Jude playing, and he wrote, "I hope you enjoy their joy (and Chula's tongue) as much as we do."[6]

DO ALL DOGS PLAY?

"I want to play, play, and play some more." I have heard and seen this desire in all of the dogs with whom I have shared my home and at the vast majority of dog parks and areas where dogs are allowed to run free. Some dogs are more enthusiastic than others, and there are dogs who are more "people dogs" than "dog dogs." I must admit I was utterly shocked when I learned that an ethologist once claimed that dogs and other animals don't play. As far as I know, he was, and remains, an *n* of 1, so I immediately tossed out that claim.

Similarly, early in my career, some people, including researchers, told me that it was a waste of time to study play behavior. Some people said that "real ethologists" do not study dogs because they are artifacts—merely "creations of humans"—and we cannot really learn much about the behavior of wild animals by studying them. Some added that the study of play was a mess and that we'll never learn much about this activity because it was a wastebasket into which people tossed data that were difficult or impossible to deal with. At that time, pretty much only veterinarians and people interested in practical applications of behavioral data studied dogs. Since then, these historical mistakes have been revisited and soundly rejected. Clearly, play can be an ethologist's dream, and I have been involved studying social play in dogs and their wild relatives for more than four decades, for my entire career. Today, many other researchers have joined me in taking seriously the various aspects of play in dogs, asking why it evolved, why it's adaptive, what causes play, how it develops, and what animals are feeling when they play.

Play also is a voluntary activity, and if a dog doesn't want to play, he or she can opt out. During play, dogs can quit whenever they want to, and others often seem to know when one dog has had enough for the moment. Perhaps it could be said that all dogs play, but they

Ari, an indefatigable Frisbee player. (Courtesy of Katie Simmons)

don't play all the time. In my experience, the only exceptions to this maxim are dogs who suffered extreme trauma early in life. The vast majority of dogs I've known and watched love to play, but some dogs who suffered abuse when they were young seem not to know how to play, even if they later share homes with loving humans. This is sad. As Jessica Pierce puts it, their play lives were stolen away by early abuse, and some dogs never recover enough to feel comfortable playing with other dogs or with humans. In addition, some dogs can be extremely picky about their playmates. I lived with two dogs who loved to play, but not always and not with just any dog.

Along the way I've also met some street dogs and feral dogs who just aren't sure about how to play. They seem entirely focused on just trying to survive for their next meal. However, the norm is that most dogs I've met love to play, whether alone or with others. And, of course, we all know dogs who love playing Frisbee.

DO DOGS MAKE FRIENDS?

If there's anything that many dogs do and do well, it's playing with friends, which along with "fun," is one of the F words that is being used by more and more researchers. I have to say that when some researchers debate whether dogs and other animals form friendships or feel fun, it strikes me as one of the most absurd wastes of time I can imagine. Of course they do, and detailed comparative research confirms it in a wide variety of species. I've had a number of people, including a few dog trainers, tell me that debates like this turn them off to science. Anyone who knows a dog knows that dogs make friends.

I once asked a woman why she came to the dog park every day, and she said, "I come to the dog park every single day, regardless of how busy I am or regardless of the weather, so that Lolita and Rondo can have fun with friends. I can't give them what they need, so here I am, a regular." As the story of Roxy and Sadie shows, some dogs really do have preferred play partners. I can't count the number of times I've seen dogs searching out a specific individual with whom to hang out and play, although numerous others are readily available. I always laugh when I see a dog searching for his or her best play partner, ignoring the invitations to play coming from many other dogs as they search far and wide for that special friend.

To me, when people seriously question whether dogs can have fun or make friends, I think it says more about the humans doing the questioning. They ignore what's self-evident at any dog park. That said, there are important questions to ask about why dogs and other animals evolved to value fun and friendships. This topic is neither frivolous nor unscientific. Indeed, the journal *Current Biology* devoted an entire section of one of its issues to discussions about the biology of fun, and many of the essays by renowned scientists centered on play behavior in various animals.[7] When it comes to fun and friendships in a wide variety of nonhumans, true skeptics are in an ever-dwindling minority. Nevertheless, I hope this arena will remain a robust focus of scientific research, since it's critical for understanding dogs and learning how to give them the best lives possible.

CAN DOGS PLAY TOO MUCH?

On a few occasions people have asked me if dogs can play too much. The short, everyday answer is "not really," though it's entirely possible that dogs can get carried away and ignore that they're getting exhausted or dehydrated. Dogs sometimes do need to pay more attention to what they are doing and to what else is happening around them. I was most fortunate to be able to talk about this topic with Dr. June Gruber, an expert on the downside of being "too happy" in humans. Our discussions resulted in a research paper called "A Cross-Species Comparative Approach to Positive Emotion Disturbance."[8]

While dogs generally don't have to worry about predators or risk being beaten up by another animal when they're too wired or too fatigued, field observations of golden marmots living in Pakistan's Khunjerab National Park show that the marmots might be exposed to higher rates of predation while playing. In addition, southern fur seals are more likely to be killed by southern sea lions when they're playing in the sea than at other times because they're less vigilant. On two occasions I saw Rocky, a medium-size mutt, get so wired and "lost in play" that he wound up playing with unfamiliar dogs who made it clear that they didn't want to play as roughly as Rocky did. What fascinated me was that Rocky clearly understood what the other dogs were telling him, and it didn't take but one or two mild reprimands, one being an almost inaudible and short growl, before Rocky adjusted and they were all playing at a level that everyone enjoyed. They all were still playing when I left the dog park ten minutes later. Research shows that dogs growl what they mean to say.[9]

These observations beg the question: How did play evolve in this particular way, so that all dogs seem to know intuitively what works and what doesn't work and how to play successfully? In evolutionary terms, keeping play within certain bounds falls under the type of selection called stabilizing selection. Basically, stabilizing selection is "a type of natural selection in which genetic diversity decreases and the population mean stabilizes on a particular trait value."[10] Stabilizing works against extremes in different traits (for example, activity levels, size, and color). Thus, playing too much or too little is selected against, just as would an individual being too wimpy or too aggressive, too big or too small, or too brightly colored or too dull.[11]

Watching dogs in a dog park, I love when these sorts of conversations arise, since they lead to informal lessons about general principles of evolutionary biology, psychology, and different types of social behavior. These lessons are a plus for dogs as well, since people tell me that the more they learn about basic ethology and evolution—why and how dogs do what they do—the more they appreciate dogs in general.

Social Play in Dogs

The rest of this chapter is devoted to social play in dogs. First, we'll learn what social play is and why dogs do it. Then we'll analyze the landscape of play, if you will, and focus on how dogs tell other dogs "I want to play with you," and how they carefully negotiate play on the run so that it remains a fair game. As we'll see, play rarely escalates into serious aggression, despite the impression that it happens frequently. Most dogs are "moral mutts," and when fairness breaks down, so too does play. This is an interesting scenario to observe, especially in large groups of dogs, where the ability to read one another is compromised because there are too many social signals at once. When dogs have difficulty reading or interpreting behavior on the fly, mistakes can happen. I'll also discuss how play differs between familiar and unfamiliar dogs using new data. It may come as a surprise to many people that there haven't been any formal studies that center on this question.

Let me say right up front that, while I focus on the general principles of play, exceptions to the "rules" abound. Indeed, this is what makes studying play so much fun and so challenging. If your dog is different, or doesn't fit some or all of what's said, regard this as a challenge to figure out why. Many dogs exhibit the trends I describe when they play, but not all do, and not every dog all the time. Always be ready to tweak what you know to fit each dog's personality and biography.

WHAT IS PLAY?

To answer the question "What is play?" we must, of course, look closely at how dogs and other animals act when they play. So, when you study play, get down and dirty with your dog, and even play with them. You can learn a lot about your dog, such as what your dog considers playful, and who your dog likes to play with and who's not their favorite playmate. It's really easy, and you'll discover more about what your dog wants and needs and who they love to hang out and romp around with.

Generally speaking, though, the deceptively simple question "What is play?" has troubled researchers for many years. The following definition of social play resulted from research on play that I did with behavioral ecologist John Byers. John studied wild pigs, or peccaries, and I studied various canids, or members of the dog family, including domestic dogs, wolves, coyotes, jackals, and foxes. We (and other researchers) discovered many common features of play among these various mammals. This is the definition we came up with: social play is an activity directed toward another individual in which actions from other contexts are used in modified forms and in altered sequences. Some actions also are not performed for the same amount of time during play as they are when animals are not playing.

As you may notice, our definition centers on what animals do when they play, or the structure of play. In his book *The Genesis of Play*, University of Tennessee psychologist Gordon Burghardt characterized play activities as having five criteria: play is voluntary,

Top left: Two dogs, Molly (*left*) and Charlotte, playing tug-of-war. This game went on for more than five minutes and was interspersed with social and self-play. *Top right*: Three dogs (*left to right*), Yekeela, Charlotte, and Molly, playing, during which they rapidly changed positions and used a variety of actions including bows, biting accompanied by head shaking, and body slamming. *Bottom left*: Ruby (*left*) performing a play bow in front of Scone. *Bottom right*: Scone (*right*) mounting Ruby.

pleasurable, self-rewarding, different structurally or temporally from related serious behavior systems, and initiated in benign situations.[12]

What this all means is that when animals play, they use or mimic actions that are used in other activities, such as predation (hunting), reproduction (mating), and aggression. Full-blown threats and submission occur only rarely, if ever, during play. Behavior patterns that

Dr. Carl Safina's dogs Chula (*right*) and Jude playing on the water in Amagansett on Long Island. (Courtesy of Carl Safina)

Dr. Carl Safina's dogs Chula (*left*) and Jude playing on a beach in Amagansett on Long Island. If you didn't know they were playing, you might think they were fighting. Using actions from different contexts is one of the characteristics of social play in dogs and other animals. (Courtesy of Carl Safina)

are used in antipredatory behavior are also observed in play. This occurs especially among prey animals such as ungulates (deer, elk, moose, gazelles), who run about in unpredictable zigzag patterns during play. When animals play, these actions may be changed in their form and intensity and combined in a wide variety of unpredictable sequences. For example, in polecats, coyotes, and American black bears, biting during play fighting is inhibited when compared to biting in real fighting. Clawing in bears is also inhibited and less intense. Play in bears is also typically nonvocal, and biting and clawing during play are directed to more parts of the other individual's body than during aggression. Play sequences may also be more variable and less predictable.

I always call play a kaleidoscope, a mixed bag of actions borrowed from other contexts, and a rigorous analysis has shown this to be the case. In his book *Religious Affects: Animality, Evolution, and Power*, science and religion scholar Donovan Schaefer calls play an "affective concoction."[13] Indeed, the variability in play sequences when compared with sequences of behavior in other contexts may be one cue to dogs that play is the name of the game, rather than mating or fighting. Solid scientific research supports the claim that play is a kaleidoscope of frenetic frivolity.

We've all seen it. When dogs play, they look like they're going crazy, frenetically wrestling, mouthing, biting, chasing, and rolling over. They use actions from other contexts in random, unpredictable ways. Play sequences don't reflect the sequences of behavior seen in mating, real fighting, and predation. Years ago, play expert Robert Fagen, author of the classic book *Animal Play Behavior*, analyzed data my students and I had collected on sequences of play and aggression in young dogs, coyotes, and wolves, and he showed that play sequences were significantly more variable than sequences we recorded during aggressive encounters.

Play sequences are more variable and less predictable than sequences of actions in other contexts because individuals are mixing actions from a number of different contexts. More actions are available to playing dogs, and therefore, during any single play sequence, it is more difficult to predict which actions will follow one another. For example, during real aggression or mating, sequences of actions are more highly structured and predictable. These actions have specific end goals. A dog who's being aggressive typically exhibits a common escalating sequence, first threatening, chasing, lunging, attacking, biting, and then wrestling, until one individual submits to the other. When dogs, coyotes, or wolves play, the action sequence is significantly more variable: one sequence might be biting, chasing, wrestling, body slamming, wrestling again, mouthing, chasing, lunging, more biting, more wrestling, and so on.

Finally, people often ask me if there are gender differences in dog play. For dogs and other canids, the answer is no; they don't typically show gender differences in play. However, many other animals, including great apes and mountain sheep, do.

WHY DO DOGS PLAY?

It's important for all dogs to play but perhaps especially youngsters. Play is highly important from about three to twelve weeks of age as dogs become socialized, both to other dogs and to humans. This does not mean that dogs who don't play will never play; it simply means that during the period when they are developing social skills, it's important to play with other dogs and humans.[14] Because many dogs are taken care of by us, dog play persists into adulthood, whereas in many species in which individuals are on their own when they get older, youngsters play more than older individuals.

Of course, there is no single reason why dogs or other animals play. There are no right or wrong explanations but, rather, different reasons why play has evolved and persisted in numerous animals.

Play likely serves a number of functions simultaneously. Detailed studies show play is important in social development, physical development—the development of joints, muscles, tendons, and bones, plus aerobic and anaerobic conditioning—cognitive development, and training for the unexpected. Moreover, neurobiological research strongly suggests play can be pleasurable and fun, and animals may simply play because it feels good. One aspect of fun that is relevant is the element of surprise, and this is related to the idea that play has evolved as training for unexpected situations.[15]

This last theory of play is based on the kaleidoscopic and unpredictable nature of play sequences. Play may also be an icebreaker and have what's called an anxiolytic effect by reducing anxiety during tense situations and preventing escalation to an aggressive encounter. I've seen many encounters where a dog approaches another dog or human slowly, clearly unsure, at least to my eyes, of what to expect. Then, the approaching dog stops slinking or walking, does a bow, and play happens instantaneously. Chimpanzees, bonobos, and juvenile gorillas show an increase in social play during prefeeding periods compared to other times, and humans also use play to reduce tension.

No matter what the other functions of play may be, many researchers believe play provides important nourishment for brain growth and helps to rewire the brain, increasing the connections between neurons in the cerebral cortex.

How Dogs Play

There's great interest in how dogs play—for example, what they do to ask another dog to play, how they maintain the play mood, how they negotiate play on the run, how they manage to play fairly despite all the frenetic action, and how they resolve potential conflicts.

Dogs use a number of different actions to signal their desire to play. These include bowing, face pawing, approaching and rapidly withdrawing, faking one direction and going the other, mouthing, and running right at a potential playmate. Play signals are an example of what ethologists call honest signals. Across different and diverse species, there's little evidence that social play evolved as a manipulative activity. Play signals are rarely used to deceive others, whether in canids or other species. My own long-term studies indicate that deceptive signaling is so rare I cannot recall more than a few occurrences in observations of thousands of play sequences in dogs, captive young coyotes and wolves, and wild coyotes.

However, as before, I want to remind readers that variability exists among different studies, and this is fully expected for all sorts of reasons: different dogs are studied in different contexts; age and gender differences can lead to varying results; and each dog's biography is unique. Rather than seeing variability as a problem, it should serve as a stimulus for further studies.

HOW DO DOGS DECIDE TO PLAY?

We tend to notice and study visual signals of play, particularly the play bow, but as dog researchers John Bradshaw and Nicola Rooney point out, not all play signals are visual. Dogs do what's called the play-pant, and they bark and growl when they want to play. I often wonder if there is a play scent, as there is in bank voles who live along the banks of the Thames River, among other places. In dogs, like in other animals, play itself may be so contagious as to stimulate others to play, even dogs who were not so eager to play previously. This social contagion might be due to a strong composite signal associated with dogs having a good time with their friends. And this contagion can cross species lines, not just to include humans, but even—hmm—a cockatoo?

Jennifer Miller, a tireless animal advocate and student of cockatoo behavior, told me how Malcolm, a Goffin's cockatoo whom she rescued in January 2009, loved to mimic the behavior of her dog, Lucky. She wrote:

Malcolm and Lucky came to me as abandoned animals, passing through my home as "fosters"—in a never ending line of other animals hoping to find a forever home. They arrived at different times, Malcolm in January 2009 and Lucky in September 2012. In true foster-fail-form, both Malcolm and Lucky are still with me. I have joined the flock and I have joined the pack, my home is now their forever home. . . . Malcolm is also known to mimic dog behavior. The familiar sequence of play bow and shuffle is one Malcolm knows and loves. Somehow he can decipher this behavior as "friendly" and not "hyper aggressive." When dogs play, he lifts his wings up, stretches them out and bounces. This is his play bow.[16]

WHAT IS A PLAY BOW?

I haven't met anyone who hasn't seen a dog do a bow—crouching on forelimbs and perhaps wagging their tail and barking. Bows are easy to film and to study, and we actually know quite a bit about them.

Bows essentially are contracts to play. They are highly stereotyped and recognizable signals used to solicit and maintain play. Bows may also be calming signals.[17] While bows are used predominantly in play by young and adult dogs, different studies, not unexpectedly, have uncovered different functions. Bows can work differently during play among young dogs, among older dogs, and among young and old dogs. As Patricia McConnell rightly notes, science should generate and test hypotheses, and different results are not unexpected.[18]

When young dogs, coyotes, and wolves perform bows to ask another dog to play, they are more stereotyped (less variable) in form and duration than when they are performed during a play bout.[19] This might be because the dogs need to indicate they want to play, rather than reinforcing that they are indeed continuing to play and not changing behaviors to do something else. In a sense, bows change the meaning of the actions that follow, such as biting and mounting. Bows also allow dogs to perform a wide variety of different actions as they spring up after bowing.

In a study of pairs of adult dogs, Sarah-Elizabeth Byosiere and her colleagues discovered that play bows serve to reinitiate play after a pause rather than to mediate offensive or ambiguous actions.[20] They also reported that 409 of 415 bows were used when the dogs could see one another. These results fit in well with, and complement, what others have observed, in that bows are a sort of punctuation mark, a comma if you will, that is used strategically during ongoing play.[21] Many studies have shown that bows are not performed randomly, and this is related to how they may be used to maintain fair play.

HOW DO DOGS PLAY FAIR?

In dog parks, it's remarkable to watch dogs of vastly different shapes, sizes, speeds, and strengths playing together successfully, without conflict or injury. How do they do this? Dogs and other animals know they must play fair for play to work, so bigger, stronger, and more dominant dogs hold back through role reversing and self-handicaping. These trade-offs help to maintain fair play. Role reversing occurs when a dominant animal performs an action during play that would not normally occur during real aggression. For example, a dominant or higher-ranking dog, coyote, or wolf would not roll over on their back during fighting, but they will do so while playing. Erika Bauer and Barbara Smuts discovered that role reversals are not always necessary to maintain play, but they probably do facilitate play. They discovered that "role reversals occurred during chases and tackles, but never during mounts, muzzle bites or muzzle licks, suggesting that these latter behaviours may be invariant indicators of formal dominance during play in domestic dogs."[22]

Self-handicaping also can be used to maintain play and to keep it fair. For example, individuals of many species will inhibit the intensity of their bites during play, thus abiding by the rules and helping to maintain the play mood. Rolling over can be role reversing as well as self-handicaping, and different studies, not surprisingly, have produced different results. Rolling over is not a straightforward action, and no one should expect a simple one-to-one relationship in any behavior, especially one as variable as play. For example, Kerri Norman and her colleagues noted that supine postures, such as rolling over, could facilitate play in dogs and that none of the postures were submissive. Smaller dogs were no more likely to roll over than were larger dogs, and "most rollovers were either defensive (evading a nape bite) or offensive (launching an attack). None could be categorized as submissive."[23] In this study, supine did not mean subordinate.

In contrast to these findings, Barbara Smuts and her colleagues note that older and bigger dogs "tended to end up as top dog during rollovers" and that rollovers could be defensive.[24]

Dog researcher Julie Hecht has also weighed in on the topic of rollovers:

1) When two dogs are playing, rollovers most often *facilitate* play. For example, a dog on its back often engages in playful sparring with another dog, delivering or avoiding neck bites, or engaging in open-mouth lunges. The researchers . . . found that the majority of in-play rollovers were part of *play* fighting (meaning the "fighting" was itself playful, not *real* fighting). The important takeaway is that rolling over during play is about play, it is NOT about "aggression." . . .

2) Another way to think about rolling over in play is as a self-handicapping behavior because it helps dogs of different sizes or sociabilities play together. Self-handicapping is instrumental to play, and it implies that a dog is tempering his or her behavior in some way. For example, during play, dogs do not deliver bites at full force, and a larger dog might roll over to allow a smaller dog to jump on or mouth him. In *Inside of a Dog: What Dogs See, Smell, and Know*, Alexandra Horowitz describes the behavior: "Some of the largest dogs regularly flop themselves on the ground, revealing their bellies for their smaller playmates to maul for a while—what I called a *self-takedown*." . . . Self-takedowns can be a type of self-handicapping behavior that promote play.[25]

All in all, a lot more research has to be done on bows, role reversing, and self-handicapping. For instance, I received the following note from one early reader of this book indicating that rolling over isn't always a benign play indicator: "I once had a 35-pound dog who loved yellow Labradors to the point that she would charge across the park to greet them—she was not a Lab. She also hated Rottweilers with singular passion. She would use rollover to expose her underside and entice them—and other dogs she found unacceptable to her—but as soon as they approached to investigate, she would flip to her feet and attack without fear or doubt dogs weighing 60 pounds more than her. What was she up to? How common is such behavior?"

I honestly don't know. And this is a perfect example of one of the major messages in this book, namely, beware the mythical dog. Not every dog plays fair, or not in every situation. Dogs make messes of prescriptive theories about how and why they do the things they do.

ARE THERE WINNERS AND LOSERS IN PLAY?

In their study of third-party interventions in play between litter-mates of dogs, Camille Ward, Rebecca Trisko, and Barbara Smuts discovered that littermates "use interventions opportunistically to practice offence behaviours directed at littermates already behaving subordinately."[26] They conclude that these sorts of interventions may help structure dominance relationships among littermates.

In my own research, I did not look at play bouts as having been "won" or "lost" mainly because they were not in any obvious way related to an individual's position in the social/dominance hier-archy, to the leadership of their group, or to their social status with the individual with whom they were playing. Giada Cordoni and her colleagues agree, based on their study of dogs at an off-leash dog park in Palermo, Italy. They note that, if anything, play plays a limited role in forming dominance relationships in dogs.[27] In his book *The Genesis of Play*, Gordon Burghardt has also noted that there are no individual winners and losers in play. Likewise, in their book *The Playful Brain*, Sergio and Vivien Pellis report that play fighting (also called rough-and-tumble play) does not appear to be important in the development of motor training for fighting skills in laboratory rats. And, along these lines, John Bradshaw and Nicola Rooney have noted that when dogs play, there seems to be little desire to enhance social status.[28]

While writing this book, I wanted to know more about play and dominance, so I asked Dr. Sergio Pellis, a play expert. Along with his wife and various students, he has studied social play in a number of different species including rats, dogs, and Visayan pigs. He wrote to me in an email:

> I think that the data are there to show that an individual trying to dominate play leads to either escalation to serious fighting or to that individual being ostracized as a play partner (e.g., as shown in studies of children, rhesus monkeys, and rats). This means that there are rules the animals follow and monitor that keeps the play mood going and the play bouts relatively reciprocal. That I think is a fairly likely general principle.
>
> However, I think you are correct about the messes dogs make. It is clear that we are far from being privy to the individual dog's mind as to what is important to them in a playful contest, making any simple-minded theoretical prescription on our behalf [is] bound to be inadequate. Indeed, we have recently shown that across strains of rats there is a stable 30 percent role-reversal rate in playful contests, even though there can be marked strain differences in the combat tactics used. To me this suggests that while focusing on the actions themselves may be useful, it can also be misleading; actions can only be meaningfully interpreted when viewed from the participants' perspective. This is why I find using outcome measures to assess asymmetry as being limited in what they can tell us. *The dog has to view it as being asymmetrical, not the human observer* [my emphasis].[29]

In his email, Dr. Pellis uses the word "asymmetry" to mean that the dogs themselves have to view a social interaction as being unequal or unfair. Each participant, not the human who is watching them, would have to think their play resulted in a different outcome for each.

DO FAMILIAR DOGS PLAY DIFFERENTLY
THAN UNFAMILIAR DOGS?

A few years ago, I was thrilled when Alexandra Weber, an eighth grader at a Boulder middle school, emailed me to ask if I would help her with a science fair project on play in dogs. After enlisting her mother, Lisa, and her younger sister, Sophia, to become her field assistants, Alexandra and I decided to focus on the question of whether familiar dogs play differently than unfamiliar dogs. Alexandra thought that simple question had been studied extensively, but it hasn't been. There are tidbits of ideas scattered about in the research, but no one has really studied this question in depth. For example, Patricia McConnell notes: "My observations suggest that dogs who are less familiar tend to play bow more to each other than familiar dogs do."[30]

Alexandra studied her two dogs—Tinkerbell, a highly social dog who loves to play with any dog, and Huggins, who is more picky about his playmates—as confederates in her study, which she conducted at a local dog park in Boulder. Alexandra discovered that play was more rough-and-tumble when familiar dogs play. When they know the dog with whom they're playing, dogs aren't as worried about formalities, and they jump right into play. All dogs in the study showed similar behavior, and they treated both dogs they knew and dogs they didn't know in almost the exact same ways as the dogs with whom I personally am more familiar. Overall, dogs who know each other play rougher and don't take the time to sniff and greet each other. Dogs who don't know each other are more formal and respectful, and they take the time to get to know the dog with whom they are about to play by sniffing and lots of nose bumping.

Obviously, this question needs further research, but I'm proud that Alexandra and her family became ethologists to help answer it, and her father also became much more interested in dogs. As they all told me countless times, it was a lot of fun to do, and they learned a lot about dogs and people at dog parks. And Alexandra won a science fair award for her research.

WHAT ARE THE RULES OF FAIR PLAY?

Research with domestic dogs provides a unique approach for exploring the evolution of fairness and justice. Not only are dogs descended from highly social canids, but they have also been bred for cooperative tasks with humans. Dogs act cooperatively in social play and are skilled on other social cognitive tasks. It's reasonable to ask whether dogs behave in ways similar to primates in other social contexts. In particular, do dogs perceive and respond to unfairness or injustice, a skill potentially borne of long-term affiliation with and selection by humans?

Play only very rarely escalates into real aggression. This is so in various settings. Based on extensive research, we have discovered that there are four basic aspects of fair play in animals: ask first, be honest, follow the rules, and admit when you're wrong. Dogs and other animals share these norms of play. When the rules of play are violated and when fairness breaks down, so, too, does play. Dogs and other animals keep track of what is happening when they play, so we need to keep track also.

Of course, dogs sometimes do break the rules, and studies show that cheaters are indeed "punished" in their own way. Cheaters are less likely to be chosen as play partners in the future, since other dogs can simply refuse to play with them and choose others. Infant wild coyotes who mislead others into playing so that they can dominate their partners have difficulty getting other young coyotes to play with them. This can have real effects, since some of these "cheaters" disperse from their natal group and suffer higher mortality. So, perhaps there are reproductive fitness consequences associated with being labeled as an individual who doesn't play fairly and obey the rules of the game. There isn't much information on this, but it would be fascinating to know just how robust this relationship really is.

In addition, these four rules of fair play are one reason that dogs are believed to possess a "theory of mind," or the concept that others have separate thoughts and feelings, which I discuss in chapter 6.

HOW OFTEN DOES SOCIAL PLAY
ESCALATE INTO FIGHTING?

I'm often asked some version of the question, "How often does social play escalate into fighting?" Many people are quick to declare: "Oh whenever dogs play, it turns into aggression."

It doesn't. Play escalating to serious aggression is extremely rare, but when it does occur, it's an attention-getter, and these rare instances are often used to criticize dog parks and people whose dogs get nasty when play gets rough. People also ask how they can recognize the signs of play escalating into fighting, but it's difficult to come up with any hard-and-fast rules because so much depends on the individuals who are playing. Some variables include how well the dogs know one another, how much they've previously played, and perhaps their relative sizes. Thus, it is important to stress that it's essential to pay close attention to who the dogs are and how they typically play. Because escalation occurs so rarely, it's difficult to get enough data that can be used to make accurate predictions.

Although my students and I haven't kept detailed records on this aspect of play for dogs, we all agree that play hasn't turned into serious fighting more than around 2 percent of the time among the thousands of play bouts we've observed. Current observations at dog parks around Boulder, Colorado, support our conclusion. Additionally, my students and I observed about a thousand play bouts among wild coyotes, mainly youngsters, and on only about five occasions did we see play fighting escalate into serious fighting. Likewise, Melissa Shyan and her colleagues discovered that fewer than 0.5 percent of play fights in dogs developed into conflict, and only half of these were clearly aggressive encounters.[31]

Lindsay Mehrkam has also studied this issue in dog parks, and in an email to me, she wrote:

In our study, we saw almost no serious fighting, and we witnessed only one observable injury stemming from play out of the over seven hundred play bouts we analyzed. Interestingly, we found a significantly higher likelihood of aggression/conflict in the smaller dog park than in the larger dog park (possibly due to crowding or relative inattentiveness of the owners, but certainly there are many other variables that could be contributing to that difference). So, what I've taken from our data is that inter-dog aggression certainly does happen in the dog parks, and can be a risk (as could any scenario where two or more dogs interact), but the data do not suggest that it is quite as prevalent as many trainers, etc., make it out to be.[32]

Of course, at times, a certain dog may get highly aroused and lost in play and simply bite too hard or slam too hard into their play partners, and this can result in an aggressive moment of varying intensity. I've also seen a dog get excited and rambunctious and, as a result, "get into the face of other dogs" when his human yelled something like, "Stop playing so roughly." All was fair and well before the human got involved. But these are exceptions that prove the rule, as it were. Play is founded on fairness and involves a good deal of cooperation among the players as they negotiate the ongoing interaction so that it remains playful. So long as the rules of play are followed, play fighting only rarely escalates into real fighting.

DOES GROUP SIZE INFLUENCE PLAY?

People often ask me how well dogs read one another when large groups are running around like they're in a daze. My answer is that while no one has carefully studied this yet, it seems as if they do it pretty well. Research of dogs during play and other contexts finds low levels of escalation, and the rapid-fire exchange of signals— those cocktails of composite signals—contain a lot of information about what is happening and what is likely to happen.

In an ongoing study I'm currently involved with, our preliminary data show two somewhat different conclusions. One is that group size doesn't seem to be a factor in the extremely rare occasions when play escalates into fighting or aggression. There is no real difference comparing groups of two, three, four, and five or more dogs. Yet we've also noticed that play in large groups breaks down more rapidly than play in smaller groups. This happens not because play escalates into aggression but, rather, because the dogs can't always read one another as well in large groups, so play ends before a fight might ensue. I'm hoping that, as this study continues, more data will clarify just what is happening. Elisabetta Palagi and her colleagues have data that strongly suggest that dogs maintain a play mood based on rapid mimicry and emotional contagion, a building block of empathy.[33] Perhaps rapid mimicry and emotional contagion break down in large groups of dogs.

An interesting aspect of Dr. Palagi's study is that "the distribution of rapid mimicry was strongly affected by the familiarity linking the subjects: the stronger the social bonding, the higher the level of rapid mimicry."[34] This supports the conclusions of Alexandra Weber's science-fair project: familiar dogs play more quickly and roughly than unfamiliar dogs.

Play Means Improvising: One Size Doesn't Fit All

Play looks like a messy behavior, and it is. It's inherently variable, using a hodgepodge of actions from various other contexts. In other words, play is about improvising, and every dog improvises in his or her own way. As such, and as I've said, play makes messes of our prescriptive theories of why dogs do this or that when they romp around with their friends.

Clearly, much more research is needed on play behavior in dogs. I can tell you firsthand, studying play is fun, and I hope many other researchers will take play seriously. For example, in a fascinating research paper called "Beware, I Am Big and Non-dangerous!" Anna Bálint and her colleagues discovered that "dogs may communicate an exaggerated body size by the means of their growls during play, which may help in maintaining or enhancing the playful interaction." Since the growls of genuinely aggressive dogs "were proven to be honest regarding their referential and size-related information content, our results gave evidence that exaggeration may work as a play signal in the case of animal vocalizations."[35]

Dogma about play doesn't work. Varying results are to be expected for a number of reasons. For instance, I recently was told that in a study of play in adult dogs that biting accompanied by head shaking was never observed. However, my students and I have seen it many times among dogs, adults as well as youngsters, and among wild coyotes, wolves, and red foxes of all ages. When I asked others about this, they, too, were surprised that it wasn't observed in the study. Why might this be so? Are we talking about the same behavior? Just recently I watched three dogs playing on campus, and they were jumping on one another's back and biting and head shaking rather vigorously. The guy who was with them told me that they play like this all of the time and never once has it escalated into an assertion of dominance. Yet to the untrained eye, it looked as if they really were beating the hell out of one another.

Comparative ethological studies on dogs and many other animals show that this variability is actually to be expected. Even ritualized signals like play bows will be used differently, depending on the individual dogs being studied, the social context, and the study conditions. The same is true for ritualized signals that are used in aggressive encounters. While they share certain features, they are used differently depending on the individuals who are quarreling and the context in which the disagreements are taking place. So perhaps some dogs simply do not bite and shake their heads from side to side.

Yet even variability has limits. One trend that emerges from all studies is that play bows are highly ritualized signals that have been shaped through evolution to be clear and unambiguous. They communicate either the intention to play or the intention to continue playing after an interruption. Dogs love to play, and so differentiating the desire to play from other intentions is extremely important to them. Thus, if we've learned just one thing from all the studies of dogs at play, it's that you don't bow if you don't want to play. *Canis ludens* also loves fairness.

FOUR

Dominance and the Society of Dogs

||||||||||||||||||||||||||||||||||||||||||||||||||||||||||||||||||||||||||||||||||||||||||||||||||||||||||||||||||||||||||||||||||||||||||

William, a seventy-five-pound mutt, arrives at the dog park each day around 7 A.M. Milly, a fifteen-pound mutt, usually arrives a few minutes before William (his human insists on calling him William rather than Willy, but that's another story). When Milly sees William, she immediately runs right at him, jumps up in an attempt to stand over him, and when she invariably falls off, she growls, runs around him, and in no uncertain way tells him that she's the boss. William, a gentle being, accepts it all as if a fly had landed on his thick fur, and he keeps on walking to meet his friends, both dogs and humans. Everyone loves him. Milly, on the other paw, continues jumping on William, circling him, growling, and running right at him and even bouncing off his side. Never has anyone seen anything more between these two dogs than these sorts of encounters. Milly never physically hurts William, and William never fights back or even seems annoyed. Milly clearly wants to control William, and she often successfully influences where he goes and with whom he interacts. It's safe to say she dominates him in her own gentle, but forceful, way.

Johnson (or Dr. J, as his human often calls him) is a petite mutt who truly defies any sort of classification as to which breeds he represents. He is a true control freak, like his human, who abashedly admits he is as well! Johnson has many friends at the dog park, and they always seem to be watching him—where he goes, what he's doing, and with whom he's interacting. Johnson, however, never seems to watch other dogs at all. He freely walks around as if he's boss, clearly controlling where some of his friends go, and in this manner he dominates their movements with great finesse and subtlety. No one has ever seen Johnson do much more than strolling around: going wherever he wants, whenever he wants, and however he wants. No one has ever heard even a mild growl. The other dogs defer as if they're thinking, "Oh, it's just Johnson doing his thing."

|||||||||||||||||||||||||||||||||||||||||||||||||||||||||||||||||||||||||||||||||||||||||||||||||||||||||||||||||||||

I remember a few years ago how surprised I was when someone asked me, "Do you think dogs display dominance?" My first response was something like, "Are you kidding?"

Then I realized the person was not, and a valuable discussion followed. These conversations continue today. Many people ask me the same question, as the issue of dominance and dogs has grown into a heated, controversial topic, one that is fiercely debated and argued over among researchers, dog trainers, and the public.

For instance, a colleague shared with me what happened at a research conference on dogs a few years ago, writing: "Ah, the *D* word. One of my grad students gave a talk about dog play, in which she mentioned the *D* word because she was asking if dominance outside of play influenced what the dogs did during play. And the instant she said the *D* word, a woman stood up and began shouting at her, 'There is no such thing as dominance in dogs!' and a number of audience members clapped."[1]

In a similar vein, I was talking with a man named John at a dog park one day. He was quite friendly with me, but he got rather upset as he discussed a certain dog, Gabrielle, who ran roughshod over just about every other dog at the dog park. He said, "Gabrielle dominates all of the dogs here, and I'm sick and tired of it. Her owner doesn't do a damned thing about it, even when other people complain. I asked a trainer about it, and they said dominance does not exist in dogs. Well, if it ain't dominance, what the hell is it?"

I honestly don't see why there is any debate about whether dogs display dominance. I can't think of any animal with whom I'm familiar, whether human or nonhuman, who doesn't display some form of dominance, including wild canids, and there is no reason whatsoever why dogs should be different from other animals. However, I've come to realize that there is a basic misunderstanding of what being "dominant" actually means among dogs and that the concept of dominance can be misused by people to justify harsh training methods and to punish unwanted behavior.

For instance, sometimes people will see "dominance" in any willful, excited, or aggressive act by a dog, such as if dogs hump, or jump on people, or pull on a leash, or growl over a toy. As dog trainer and journalist Tracy Krulik has written: "With this one word, we get a descriptor for pretty much every behavior dogs do that we would rather they didn't, and because of it, people stop investigating and ultimately have no clue why their dog does any of that stuff. What's worse is that because people use this word—which means to them that the dog is trying to show them up or is in some kind of power struggle with them—they punish the dog."[2]

In reality, some people acknowledge that dominance exists, but they argue that it's best to ignore this fact because it's misunderstood and misused by people, who then think that if dominance exists it's just fine to dominate dogs when they're training them. Meanwhile, some people genuinely believe dominance is a myth. Some claim that dogs are unique among mammals in not displaying dominance, while others claim that *no* animals display dominance. But these beliefs, for that's surely what they are, ignore detailed comparative data on the evolution of dominance in a wide variety of animals, spanning numerous and diverse vertebrates and invertebrates.

I don't see any reason to ignore facts. Rather, we should acknowledge what we know, and yet carefully distinguish how dogs relate with one another from how we relate with and treat them. Just because dogs (and other animals) form dominance relationships doesn't mean we should dominate dogs. So, let's begin by looking at the social hierarchy of dogs, and how dominance fits within it, and by defining what dominance is and what it isn't among dogs. This will allow us to explore how people misunderstand dominance in relationship with their dogs and why it has no place in dog training.

Let me stress that just because dogs and other nonhuman animals display dominance, this does not mean we should dominate dogs when we are trying to teach them to live in harmony with us and other dogs. We should always work in partnership with dogs with whom we share our homes and hearts. Taking this as one's mantra will serve well everyone involved.

Social Hierarchies of Dogs

Let's get right to the point: based on the large and growing amount of detailed comparative data from a wide range of species I mentioned above, I can assert that dominance is alive and well, so let's understand what it's all about. Dr. John Bradshaw and his colleagues correctly point out, dominance is all about relationships.[3] This is a major point I stress in this book about all sorts of social interactions.

In particular, dogs and their wild relatives display social dominance hierarchies, which includes dominance-submission relationships. In ethology, this fact is so well known and accepted it's like saying, "If I jump off my roof, I'll hit the ground." While I'm at it, let me dispel a few other myths. One is that dominant individuals always produce more offspring than subordinate animals. They don't. Another is that dogs don't form packs. They do. I've seen them, and dog packs are well documented in the detailed research by Roberto Bonanni and his colleagues on free-ranging dogs living outside of Rome, Italy, and by other researchers.[4]

Social dominance hierarchies are often called "pecking orders," a term that stems from the classic research conducted by Norwegian zoologist and comparative psychologist Thorleif Schjelderup-Ebbe on chickens. He was keenly interested in chickens and published his PhD dissertation on this work in 1921.

The renowned zoologist Edward O. Wilson, in his classic book *Sociobiology: The New Synthesis*, identified three different types of hierarchies: despotism, linear hierarchies, and nonlinear hierarchies. In despotism, one individual dominates all other members of his or her social group, and there is no rank differentiation among other members. This can be expressed as A > B = C = D = E. Linear hierarchies are just what they sound like: each individual is submissive to the individual above and dominant of the individual below, like rungs on a ladder. This can be expressed as A > B > C > D > E, in which B > D and C > E, and so on. Finally, nonlinear hierarchies don't have a single individual who is above all others, and relationships among individuals don't follow a linear order. This can be expressed as A > B, B > C, C > D, D > E, and also E > A and D > B. There might also be "subordinate hierarchies," similar to dominance hierarchies.

Detailed research has shown that dogs form linear relationships. In "Understanding Canine Social Hierarchies," Dr. Jessica Hekman, referring to a study of a group of dogs in the Netherlands, reports that "this group was not particularly egalitarian. Division between ranks was nearly always strict, requiring a dog to greet his superior, even one just a single rank above him, with deferential behavior such as lowered body posture."[5] And, in agreement with the study I mention above by Roberto Bonanni, Dr. Hekman writes, "Indeed, the social hierarchy in this group did look ladder-like. Some species have a dizzying hierarchical structure, in which rank order may loop in an entirely nonlinear fashion. In this dog group, however, the hierarchy was strictly linear: if dog A was higher ranking than dog B, and dog B was higher ranking than dog C, then dog A would always be higher ranking than dog C. No weird circular messes—occasions, for example, when dog C was surprisingly dominant over dog A—were observed."

I've seen all types of dominance relationships in captive and free-ranging dogs, as have many other researchers. While these relationships can be stable, they can also rearrange themselves, though over time they almost always restore a linear order. Two dogs with whom I shared my mountain home clearly liked to boss around other dogs who lived up the road. They'd growl at them and try to get them to leave the area around my/our land. These confrontations never escalated into an all-out fight (though one time I thought they might), and there was no indication that any of the dogs was afraid of any of the others. Neighbors confirmed this. Yet when all five dogs were around, it was easy to see a linear hierarchy. As in other animals, the formation of this hierarchy regulated the behavior of the individual dogs so they could play and cruise around without having to continually reassert their position in the group. Over time, the ranking order changed, but for the most part each individual simply accepted his or her place, and the group got on royally. Why waste time bickering when they could sniff to their nose's content and play until they were too exhausted to walk home?

A dog trainer once asked me how many animals it takes to form a linear hierarchy, since she had heard it takes a minimum of six individuals. This is not so, although I've heard this myth a number of times. Three animals can easily form a stable linear hierarchy. Over the course of three months at one dog park, Maude, Malcolm, and Maddie formed what others and I saw as a linear hierarchy, with only one altercation during the whole period of time: Maude, the leader, once growled and snapped at Maddie. My take on the situation was that they formed this linear relationship without fighting, and all three were quite content. They played roughly and excessively with never a hint that Maude was boss, and the relationship broke up when Maddie's human moved to another city. Maude and Malcolm continued on as if nothing had changed.

On many occasions I've seen two dogs growl at one another, accept where they fall in some sort of hierarchy, and play fairly with absolutely no indication at all that either was nervous about what was happening. I well remember a woman asking me, "How come Jessie always growls at Matilda, baring his teeth and all, and then flops into a play bow, and they play fairly to their heart's content?" I explained to her how bows and other play signals initiate and maintain play. As a voluntary activity, play requires cooperation and agreement, and it allows actions and behaviors that, in other contexts, might be perceived as threatening. Simply put, Jessie and Matilda both wanted to play, so they did, and when they played fair, nothing they did during play threatened their established relationship.

One possible reason that people misunderstand dominance among dogs, or claim that it doesn't exist, might be because dominant dogs so rarely act in overtly aggressive, threatening, or domineering ways. Dominance displays are usually subtle, rather than combative and injurious. Further, as the stories of William and Milly, Johnson, and Jessie and Matilda show, dogs are comfortable within a linear hierarchy. It helps them get along.

Do Wolves Display Dominance?

Among scientists and the public, there's just as much confusion and conflict over whether wolves display dominance and over what social dominance means for wolves. Simply put, wolves do display dominance. Both wolves and dogs establish dominance-submission relationships, but they don't necessarily establish social relationships or form hierarchies for the same reasons or in the same ways. And there is no reason to think they would. Wolves are wild animals, and dogs are domestic animals whose welfare often depends on the humans they live with.

Wolf expert L. David Mech has been routinely misquoted about his views on dominance, for instance, with some believing that he claims dominance in wolves does not exist. But as he wrote to me in an email: "This misinterpretation and total misinformation has plagued me for years now. I do not in any way reject the notion of dominance."[6]

It's essential to correct the myths that are flying around, in part because some people claim that if wolves don't display dominance relationships, neither should dogs. Rather, Dr. Mech argues, as do others, that the notion of social dominance in wolves is not as ubiquitous as some claim it to be, but he doesn't reject it across the board. As Dr. Mech writes elsewhere: "Similarly, pups are subordinate to both parents and to older siblings, yet they are fed preferentially by the parents, and even by their older (dominant) siblings. On the other hand, parents both dominate older offspring and restrict their food intake when food is scarce, feeding pups instead. Thus, the most practical effect of social dominance is to allow the dominant individual the choice of to whom to allot food."[7]

Dog expert James Serpell also describes dominance among dogs and wolves as much less antagonistic than the public imagines. He writes: "When left to their own devices, free-living dogs and wolves do form and maintain social hierarchies, even though rank order within such groups seems to be maintained primarily by younger individuals deferring to their elders rather than by top-down physical enforcement by 'alpha' animals."[8]

To summarize, dogs and numerous other animals display dominance. Comparative data from detailed studies on a wide range of animals inarguably support this claim. Ideology and politics must be trumped with facts from rigorous research.

The *D* Word: What Dominance Is and What It Isn't

Some people like to dance around the *D* word because of a lack of understanding of what dominance or being dominant really mean to scientists when they discuss dogs. Synonyms include "controlling," "influencing," "managing," and "paying attention to others". In the most basic sense, researchers use the term "dominant" to refer to the relative position in a linear social hierarchy of certain dogs in relationship to others.

The term "dominance" does not necessarily define or refer to a specific behavior by dogs. A dominant dog may not engage in any injurious fighting or harm. Many animals have evolved behavior patterns and strategies to reduce the likelihood of injurious fighting, and all one has to do is go to a dog park and watch dogs to see that they can dominate one another without any physical interactions at all. A dog can control or influence the behavior of another dog in many ways, some very subtle, without any physical contact or harm. Nor do subordinate or submissive dogs necessarily suffer discomfort, isolation, deprivation, or abuse from other dogs because of their "lower" position in a social hierarchy.

Ethologists identify a "dominant" dog as one who controls or influences the behavior of another individual. How that influence is exerted is as various as dogs themselves. A dog may influence the behavior of another individual by staring at them, moving toward them, vocalizing, displaying specific facial expressions and body postures, and so on, without any physical contact. Whether dogs are aware of the concept of dominance itself, they surely know when they are in control of a social interaction and where they fit in the social hierarchy of a group of dogs.

An important corollary is this: since there is no single behavior that defines dominance among dogs, behaviors only become dominant from the way they are used or the context in which they're used. A dog can do something in one context and it won't be an expression of dominance, but in another context, it could be. It is essential to look at the *relationship* between and among the individuals involved because dominance reflects relationships. It is contextual.

Having said that, what's the purpose of dominance among dogs? Dogs and other nonhuman animals dominate one another for a number of reasons. Individuals may dominate or control access to various resources, including food, potential and actual mates, territory, and resting and sleeping areas. They may seek the location within a group that's most protected from predators. They may want to influence the movements of others or get the attention of others. In fact, dominance interactions can be rare, though they do occur; that is why it's important to log many hours carefully observing known individuals. As researchers get to know individuals in a group, they also learn more and more about the subtle ways in which a wide variety of social messages are communicated, including those used in interactions in which one individual controls another.

Complicating the picture is the phenomenon of situational dominance. For example, a low-ranking individual may be able to keep possession of food even when challenged by another individual who actively dominates him or her in other contexts. I've seen this in wild coyotes, dogs, other mammals, and various birds. In these cases, possession is what counts. Indeed, instances of situational dominance, in which the established order is overturned in a specific way and for a limited time, might make a human observer wonder: What's the point of being "top dog" if you can't get what you want all the time, or at least whenever you want it?

In essence, that presumption—that what dominance actually means is winning at the expense of others—is where some people make their first mistake about dogs.

When Dogs Play Tug-of-War, Are They Competing?

While I'm attempting to bust myths about dominance, let me consider a game in which many dogs partake, namely tug-of-war. Some claim tug-of-war is all about competition or dominance. However, when dogs play tug-of-war, they are not always trying to compete with or dominate one another.[9]

When dogs play tug-of-war, it's actually more complex and interesting than just being competitive. I've watched numerous tugs-of-war among dogs and wild coyotes. For example, when Molly played tug-of-war with her friend Charlotta, they'd run frantically about, each holding tightly onto the rope. Then one would let go and tease the other, and they'd run around some more, each holding the rope in her mouth. The game went on and on, with no obvious competition, end goal, or winner. Molly and Charlotta freely exchanged possession of the rope for minutes on end. They were friends, and clearly they enjoyed what they were doing.

Then again, on some occasions, dogs may actually be competing when they play tug-of-war. I once recruited some regulars at the dog park to help me collect data and analyze a hundred random tugs-of-war (out of the many I'd observed during different visits to dog parks). We came up with what can only be called preliminary data, but the evidence we found showed clearly that competition is one, but only one, explanation for what's happening when dogs play tug-of-war. For each example, I always had another person observing with me, to be sure both of us were on the same page about what was happening. Most of the people really enjoyed doing this, since it was part of an informal course on dog ethology, and they were eager to learn more about their dogs. On only four occasions did my partner and I disagree as to what was taking place.

We were in agreement, though, that only seven times out of a hundred tugs-of-war was there a competitive element, and of these, there were six cases in which there were some growls and a clear indication that one dog wanted the rope all for her- or himself. But nothing came of these vocalizations. We only saw one instance where there was a strong likelihood that, if one of the dogs didn't give up the rope, there might have been a fight. None of the people who saw this considered anything close to what people call resource guarding. The rope was a good catalyst for play, and dogs used it to their heart's delight.

How did we go about performing this pilot study? First, a number of variables needed to be considered, including the relative size of the dogs, their social relationship and familiarity with one another, gender, context—what they were doing right before they began playing tug-of-war—age, and perhaps breed. We had information on all of these variables. We didn't observe any gender differences or breed differences, and many of the dogs were mixes.

We discovered that when dogs of different sizes played tug-of-war, they engaged in self-handicapping, which I describe in chapter 3. If the game was to continue, the larger dog had to restrain how hard she or he pulled on the rope. When a large dog pulled so hard so that the smaller dog couldn't play, the game usually ended. On one occasion, a large mutt pulled so hard he almost lifted his small friend off the ground. When the large dog saw what was happening, he dropped the rope, ran right at the smaller dog, skidded to a stop, and did a play bow. He wanted to play, and they did. Clearly, tug-of-war wasn't going to work with dogs who were radically different in size and strength unless there were compromises.

Familiarity also was important. When dogs such as Molly and Charlotta played tug-of-war, there were more exchanges and a willingness to let the other dog have the rope. When I asked people who saw these interactions, no one thought they indicated competition. More difficult to assess was how previous events—whether the dogs had been playing, just walking about, or were wired from other dog encounters—influenced the outcome of tugs-of-war. However, once again, the impression we got was that if a rope was picked up during an ongoing play interaction, or right after one of the dogs had been playing, the play continued as the dogs yanked on the rope and exchanged it on the run.

In addition, tug-of-war between humans and dogs is also not necessarily about dominance. Not only can it be fun, but it also can be important in bonding and maintaining a positive and friendly relationship and training experience with your dog. In her book *Play With Your Dog*, dog trainer Pat Miller offers, "Tug to your hearts' content," and don't worry if your dog growls. It's all "part of the game," and if the dog's other behaviors are appropriate, "let him growl his heart out!"[10] It's perfectly okay to get down and dirty with your dog. Do some play bows, play tug-of-war, and keep your special relationship alive and growing.

To me, this tug-of-war study is a great example of how we need to observe dogs closely before assuming we know what their intentions are. Tug-of-war looks like a familiar human game, but dogs don't play by our rules, and we can get into trouble when we presume that they do.

Misunderstanding Dominance: People, Power Trips, and "Bad Dogs"

As I hope I've made clear, animal researchers and ethologists define "dominance" in dogs in a very specific, almost technical way, one that means something different than our casual understanding of the word. In everyday life, when people talk about "dominating the competition," they usually mean they seek a significant advantage over everyone else. The one who dominates "wins," and everyone else loses. Meanwhile, occupying a submissive or subordinate position is to "be a loser," to be hurt or weakened, and it can be a source of shame.

Is it any wonder, then, that people can fear being "dominated" by their dog? When they confuse these two meanings of dominance, people get into mistaken power struggles with their dog, thinking they must act dominant in order to control their companion animal. Some dog trainers teach this explicitly, coaching their clients to impose their will on misbehaving dogs by force, if necessary.

For instance, let me share an email that Tracy Krulik wrote to me in response to an essay I wrote called "Dogs, Dominance, Breeding, and Legislation: A Mixed Bag."[11] Krulik wrote:

> As I continue to ponder the *D* word in relation to dogs, I realize that this goes beyond "training." The people who tell me their dog "is being dominant" are involved in a battle for power with the dog. They aren't thinking, "I'm going to dominate my dog to teach him." They're thinking, "My dog is so stubborn and is doing this bad behavior to show me," so I'll show him! So, in my mind, "dominance" has become a catch-all term for "my dog is doing something I don't want him to do, and he knows better!" And because people don't understand their dogs as "dogs"—meaning they don't know that dogs chew because they enjoy it or dig because it's a fun thing to do—they jump to the conclusion that the dog chewed their pillow because "he's mad at me for leaving him alone and he needs to be taught a lesson."[12]

In addition, a dog walking through a door first is not necessarily dominance. And neither are sitting on the couch, mounting, separation anxiety, or a dog getting you to rub her or his belly when you'd rather be doing something else.[13] People often conflate dominance with fighting, but there is no reason to do so. Numerous animals have evolved fairly unambiguous threat signals that say something like, "If you approach me or annoy me, I'll fight with you." Different actions are used to tell other individuals, "I accept that you're above me and that's just fine." Indeed, in some species, subordinate individuals benefit from just being part of the gang, and they accept their position willingly. Higher-ranking animals know that the integrity of the group depends on everyone getting along. Also, in a case like Johnson, he does what he wants to do and "controls" other dogs because they eye him carefully. He dominates their attention but not to any specific goal. Primatologists have noted that some nonhuman primates also dominate others' attention, and they aptly call this the attention structure theory of dominance.

Another email I received perceptively shows how focusing on dominance can be misleading and can actually cause problems rather than lead to solutions. Any person who chooses to share their life with a dog needs to pay close attention to the context and social situations in which a dog behavior occurs, especially an unwanted one. I wish I could say that the situation described here is rare or unusual, but unfortunately, I've received a number of similar notes over the years, and this seems quite common:

> Had an interesting (and disturbing) encounter with an acquaintance on Friday. I walk into her shop and her German Shepherd is behind a barrier barking and jumping up. Friend walks back and shoos her away yelling, "Bad! Bad! Bad!" After the pup has quieted down, I ask Friend how old the dog is. "Oh, she's about eight, we think. She's the most nervous of all of the rescues I've ever had."
>
> I look at pup and see the prong collar around her neck.
>
> "She's terrible around people," Friend says. "Like when you came in and she was barking. She's just so dominant."
>
> I inquire about the prong collar, wondering how that might affect the dog if she is already "nervous."
>
> "We have no other choice," Friend says. "And even with it, I have to hold on tight and close in to me. She jumps on people, lunges at other dogs . . ."
>
> Friend then tells me that the pup was saved from a hoarding situation. "We're pretty sure that the reason she's so dominant all the time is that she must have been the most dominant at the hoarding house. That has to be how she survived and got food."[14]
>
> Here's my take on the situation:

> The dog wants to say hi when people come in. Her body was loose and relaxed, her tail was wagging, and she was jumping up—all prosocial behaviors. She's not jumping because she's

"dominant." She wants to greet people! And she's probably really frustrated that this barrier keeps her from doing so, hence all the barking.

We could very easily teach her to sit instead of jumping up on people, and even get her to where a person approaching is the cue for her to sit.

I haven't seen her on leash or around other dogs, but I would not be surprised if the prongs digging into her neck have created a negative association with other dogs. She's walking along, another dog walks by, she is eager to say hi and sniff, and so she pulls. The collar tightens on her neck, and OUCH! If that happens over and over, she eventually learns that "other dog" equals "OUCH!" So she sees other dogs as threats and responds accordingly.

If we add in the fact that the pup has underlying anxiety already, this leash reactivity/barrier frustration explanation becomes even more likely.

Dominant. Friend said this word five or six times in our five-minute conversation. She is located in a town where easily 90 percent of the dogs are trained by one school that employs pain and fear to teach dogs. Dominance is the root cause for every "bad" behavior, and dogs are punished because of it. I had forgotten how bad it really was there until I had this encounter.

For those readers who want to learn more about this issue, the *Journal of Veterinary Behavior* devoted a special issue in 2016 to the dominance debate, with a lead essay by Dr. Karen Overall.[15] I couldn't agree more with Dr. Overall's conclusion that "there is no justification for the most devastating advice given to people with dogs with behavioral pathology: that they 'dominate' their dogs and show the 'problem' dogs 'who is boss.'" Dr. Overall writes, "The concept of a 'dominant dog' is simply neither valid nor useful in our relationship with our companion dogs, and its application encourages behaviors that can cause morbidity and mortality for dogs and humans."[16]

Swedish dog trainer Anders Hallgren agrees with Dr. Overall and others about the lack of need to be bossy. He notes that people shouldn't worry about their dog taking charge and that there's no reason to show her or him that you're the boss. Being kind and loving work just fine. In her discussion of the hierarchy of dog needs adapted from Abraham Maslow's hierarchy of human needs, dog trainer Linda Michaels emphasizes the importance of force-free training, gentle care, and being nice to your dog as the most effective way to teach them what they need to learn to coexist peacefully with other dogs and with humans.[17]

When I'm at dog parks I hear "helicopter humans" saying—or yelling—"don't do that" or "stop that" or screaming "no!" far more frequently than I hear people simply saying something like "you're a good dog" or "thanks for being so well-behaved." People often wonder why I sometimes go up to a dog and say "you're a good dog" or, simply, "good dog" when they haven't done anything other than be who they are. Dogs, like people, like to be treated kindly and respectfully, and there's nothing wrong with some out-of-the-blue positive interactions to reinforce the friendship.

Teaching Dominance Is Bad Training

The main reason that dominance is such a controversial topic is how the concept is applied in dog training. With dog training, people aren't really arguing over science but over ideology, politics, and animal welfare. In other words, some trainers will say that, since dogs display dominance, people must learn to dominate dogs, even though this misunderstands the term. Meanwhile, others claim the opposite—that dominance does not exist in dogs (even though we know it does)—as a way to legitimize force-free training methods and to criticize aversive methods based on dominance.

To me, both sides get it wrong. Ethology makes clear that dogs display dominance, but that doesn't mean that dominance by humans has any place in dog training or teaching.

Let me repeat: training a companion dog lays the groundwork for a lifelong relationship, and it should not be based on dominance but rather on mutual tolerance, understanding, and respect.

The misinterpretation of what dominance means for dogs results in dogs being abused by us, since people think that, if dogs dominate one another, it's perfectly okay for us to do it, too. This leads to what Jennifer Arnold calls the "because I said so" technique of training, which so often fails and doesn't result in "a fair and mutually beneficial relationship."[18]

Personally, I don't see how the "I'll show him who's boss" approach would ever improve a human-dog relationship. There's *no* reason that domination ever *has* to be part of any training program at all. Dogs also exhibit behavior patterns that indicate submission, appeasement, and uncertainty, and we must pay attention to, and respect, an individual's reluctance to do something, not force them to do it or regard them as intentionally "misbehaving" or self-consciously defying us. Tony Milligan provides an excellent discussion of these issues in an essay called "The Ethics of Animal Training."

Along these lines, Ilana Reisner writes, "The misinterpretation of 'dominance theory' as a basis for human-dog interactions thus led to its being accepted, absorbed and widely practiced among dog trainers and behaviorists justifying the need for discipline and often harsh methods in training and handling dogs."[19] When we understand and correctly interpret what dominance really is, there's no reason to use choke chains, prong collars, or shock collars.

Likewise, John Bradshaw and Nicola Rooney note that "there is a growing consensus that the concept of dog-human relationships being based on continually enforcing dominance status, for example during training, is not only ill founded, but also potentially detrimental to both owner safety and dog welfare."[20]

Dr. John Bradshaw has written powerfully on this issue, and in an email message to me, he raised the critical issues of misunderstanding, ethics, and the imperative of scientists to speak out:

For me, the real issue is an ethical one, how concepts of "dominance" impact on the treatment of dogs by dog trainers and the

owners they advise. . . . Many trainers use "dominance reduction" to justify the routine infliction of pain on dogs. For this
reason, I believe that all responsible ethologists should take great
pains to distinguish between their technical (and, of course, well-
established) concept of dominance, as one method for describing
social interactions, and the everyday use of the word "dominant,"
which denotes a tendency to be aggressive, threatening, and/or
controlling. Many dog trainers use the two interchangeably, and
some take great delight when academics appear to do the same.
As a direct consequence, dogs suffer.[21]

If all of that isn't convincing enough, please consider the position
statement put out by the American Veterinary Society of Animal
Behavior (AVSAB) titled "The Use of Dominance Theory in Behavior
Modification of Animals," which reads, in part: "The AVSAB emphasizes that the standard of care for veterinarians specializing in behavior is that dominance theory should not be used as a general guide for
behavior modification. Instead, the AVSAB emphasizes that behavior
modification and training should focus on reinforcing desirable behaviors, avoiding the reinforcement of undesirable behaviors, and
striving to address the underlying emotional state and motivations,
including medical and genetic factors, that are driving the undesirable behavior." This organization also is "concerned with the recent
re-emergence of dominance theory and forcing dogs and other animals into submission as a means of preventing and correcting behavior problems."[22]

Is It Better for Dogs If We Pretend
Dominance Doesn't Exist?

I fully understand the concerns of people who *know* that dogs and
numerous other animals display dominance, and that there are dominant individuals, but who also are concerned about the use of dominance in training. Some well-intentioned people, including some
trainers, argue that we should be careful about what is written about

dominance in dogs because the data might compromise dogs' well-being. They truly want to protect dogs.

For instance, psychologist James O'Heare presents a valuable detailed analysis of dominance in his book *Dominance Theory and Dogs*. He dedicates his book "to all dogs who have been mistreated as a result of the ideas of social dominance," and he concludes his book by writing, "In the end, in applied settings, I suggest dropping social dominance all together."[23]

While I strongly agree that the notion of social dominance has been, and is being, misused, and that dogs are suffering, I don't agree that the way to go forward is to pretend that social dominance among dogs doesn't exist. Instead, we need to accept social dominance for what it is and understand that it doesn't apply to training or teaching dogs.

Ethologists and other researchers will continue to study dominance in dogs, and this begs the question: What should we do with data stemming from scientific studies that show that dogs do form dominance relationships? The question of what we should do with the data can be answered in several ways. As with any legitimate, well-researched data, we should acknowledge the information. We should embrace the increase in our knowledge. This is the essence of science.

Yet there are also ethical questions. Namely, what do we do if the data are used to harm dogs? And if it is, is it acceptable to twist the truth to avoid that harmful use? These are moral and political concerns. They raise the issue of human actions and of our obligations to the well-being of dogs.

And that, I think, is the way forward, namely, to embrace both knowledge and our moral obligation to the well-being of dogs and of all nonhuman animals. If we do both, we will act in humane ways and slowly change the debate. Aversive, dominance-focused training methods are not based on science; they misuse science. Yes, dogs form dominance relationships, and individual dogs can be called dominant, but for dogs, dominance does not necessarily involve aggression. Further, the human understanding of dominance—which can be applied in hurtful, manipulative, and punishing ways—is self-evidently harmful to dogs and other animals. We can respect science while also respecting dogs. There is *no* reason at all for us to dominate dogs in any injurious ways, especially not when our goal is to create a harmonious, healthy, loving relationship.

FIVE

Who's Walking Whom?

IIIIIIIIIIIIIIIIIIIIIIIIIIIIIIIIIIIIIIIIIIIIIIIIIIIIIIIIIIIIIIIIIIIIIIIIIIIIIIIIIIIIIIIIIIIIIIIIIIIIIIIIIIIIIIIIIIIIIIIIIIIIII

"Okay, Harry, I've got a meeting soon, so go pee and poop."

"Esmeralda, you have five minutes to play and do your thing before we leave."

"Come on, Ted, just pee and be done. Stop dribbling a little every ten feet."

"Sarah, stop spinning in circles and poop!"

"Oh, here we go. What's so special about this fence that you always pee on it?"

"Stop pulling, Stanford! You know I can't keep up if you run."

"You've sniffed that spot long enough. Let's go."

"Geez, can you please stop sniffing everything and just pee?"

"Why do you always have to have a pissing match before we leave?"

"We're going home and you'll just have to hold it."

IIIIIIIIIIIIIIIIIIIIIIIIIIIIIIIIIIIIIIIIIIIIIIIIIIIIIIIIIIIIIIIIIIIIIIIIIIIIIIIIIIIIIIIIIIIIIIIIIIIIIIIIIIIIIIIIIIIIIIIIIIIIII

Walking a dog is a daily, if not an hourly, job. It's a time for exercise, bonding, and fun—a boon for all. Or at least it should be. Swedish dog trainer Anders Hallgren emphasizes that dogs should get a good mental workout when they're walking. I like to flesh this out as saying that a dog's senses need to be exercised just as their lungs and muscles need to be simulated. If you choose to bring a dog into your life, you accept that every day, several times a day, you will tether your companion to a leash and head outside, even when you'd rather be doing something else. I've always been amazed at how synchronous dogs and humans seem to be when they're walking either tethered or unattached, and it would be good to know if this is in fact the case. Perhaps there is more coordination than meets the eye, and dogs and their humans are learning one another's patterns of movement. This would be a very fruitful area of research.

But the real question is, who's walking whom? Or even better, who is the walk really for? It's obviously for the dog, but it's also for the person, who doesn't want their dog to pee and poop in the house, and who knows that a dog who doesn't exercise will become one high-strung pup and no fun to live with. The walk is for both of you. It helps maintain a harmonious household. Further, what happens during the walk reflects the personalities of the human and the dog, and how the walk is handled can strengthen or weaken that bond.[1]

It's important to keep this in mind because we live in a high-strung world. People often rush their dog along because they're in a hurry. Some days are more leisurely than others, but I have never in all my thousands of trips to dog parks, and in all my walks along dog paths, ever not heard a chorus of complaints like the ones that opens this chapter. People want their dog to take care of their business fast. They have other things to do. And they can't understand what takes their dog so long. What in the world are dogs doing, sniffing everything in sight?

So, this chapter asks: What are dogs doing on a walk? What do they need when they finally get outside? Elimination is just one item on *their* to-do list.

In chapter 2, I discussed a dog's most amazing organ and adaptation: their nose. Here, I will consider how dogs use their amazing noses to explore the world and negotiate their social milieu. It's a scent-filled journey, providing lots to ponder about how dogs sense and interact in their odor-rich world. It's also important to appreciate how important walking and exercising off leash is to a dog. Dogs spend a lot of time tethered to a human, and to keep the leash from feeling like a form of bondage and a tug-of-war, it's helpful to consider the walk from a dog's perspective.

Relax the Leash: Dogs Need to Sniff

We've all seen dogs being dragged along by their human, who is saying something like, "Let's go, I've gotta go to work," or "Come on, there's nothing there." Well, the human might not smell anything, but I bet if they put their nose where their dog's nose is probing, they'd discover something: pungent odors that often indicate the passage of other dogs and perhaps how they were feeling. Humans often don't care about these other dogs, and they find the odors themselves disgusting, but dogs find them most lovely and extremely interesting. I've seen dogs literally using their legs to brake so they can continue taking in a most odiferous scent.

It's no news flash to say a dog's nose leads the way on many, if not most, forays. Many dogs spend an incredible amount of time at the end of a leash, and their nose sets the pace. I estimate that my dog Jethro, who was the main character in my "yellow snow" study, was off leash 99.9 percent of the time, and he sniffed and often peed around 25–30 percent of the time. This is in the range of the 33 percent the late Sophia Yin estimated for dogs on leash. This, then, is the major source of tension or conflict on most walks: people in a hurry pull their dog along whenever their dog's nose goes down to the ground, but taking in odors, and leaving their own scent, constitutes fully a third of a dog's agenda.

You might compare it to text messaging. By sniffing, dogs are getting the previous messages left by others, and peeing is, perhaps, a way of replying. Forcing dogs to walk when they are "texting" is like pulling a smartphone from a teenager's hand. I'm sure the dogs living along the mountain road where I lived were sharing messages throughout the day.

In a succinct summary of sniffing, John Bradshaw and Nicola Rooney write: "Dogs' great interest in sniffing urine-marks presumably stems from a motivation to gain information about other dogs within their home range. In addition to information about the sex and reproductive status of the producer of the urine-mark, dogs are also likely to be comparing the odor of scent-marks with the odor of dogs that they have sniffed during encounters—a form of scent-matching—thereby assessing the home ranges of those dogs."[2]

As with many other aspects of dog behavior, we still have much to learn about why dogs do what they do when they pee and what they learn as they sniff the pee of other dogs. But clearly, dogs want and need to sniff, so we should *let them sniff to their noses' content!* It's essential to let dogs use their noses, and if peeing follows, then so be it. Dog researcher and author Alexandra Horowitz warns that pulling dogs away from smell-rich environments, such as fire hydrants and tree trunks, can cause them to lose their predisposition to smell. When dogs are living in "our visual world," she says, "they start attending to our pointing and our gestures and our facial expressions more, and less to smells."[3]

On a visit to a dog park one day, a woman told me, rather seriously, that she thought that not allowing dogs to use their noses the way they want could cause serious psychological problems. I've thought about this a lot since then. We really don't know if dogs suffer psychologically when they're deprived and can't fulfill their need to sniff and pee if they choose to do so. Surely, when dogs are rushed along, they don't get to savor and properly assess and process various odors, and who knows what this does to them. This form of sensory deprivation might be devastating, since they lose detailed information about their social and nonsocial worlds.

Scent Marking: Canine Conversation

Of course, dogs often pee simply because they have to go, but peeing is also used for what ethologists call scent marking. When scent marking, dogs intentionally direct a stream or two of urine at a particular object or area, and this practice is widespread among numerous animals. It's possible that pooping is also a form of marking, but if so, then it's less directed or controlled. After all, dogs (and most animals) tend to poop less often and all at once; in contrast, leaving a shot of pee can be easy.

Marking is a form of communication, and the presence of multiple marks by multiple animals may amount to a type of conversation. By marking, individual dogs are saying things like, "This is my place and you better stay out." Or, "I'm in heat," or "I was here," or perhaps even, "I smell that you were here, and this is my way of saying I'm still around, too." I discuss some of this below, but we really don't know the extent of what dogs can communicate and understand through marking. My bet is that it's far more than we think.

Another puzzling behavior is when dogs and other animals on occasion scratch the ground after peeing or pooping. This might be done to spread the scent or to leave a visual mark on the ground, or an individual might scratch simply because he or she is wired. I've seen dogs pee or poop and scratch the ground with wild abandon, as people get covered by urine-soaked sand and grass, and on occasion splattered with fragments of poop. It would be good to know when and why dogs do this, since it might help us get out of the way.

While I was pondering all these questions about peeing, I wrote to Anneke Lisberg, who works out of the University of Wisconsin–Whitewater. She is an expert on canine peeing, and Dr. Lisberg kindly summarized some of the results of her recent studies, which I share below.[4]

WHAT DO DOGS LEARN BY SNIFFING PEE?

I've never met a dog who doesn't sniff and pee. Both genders, all ages save for newborns, every breed, and dogs of every social status will stop to check out the pee of other dogs. The reasons dogs stop and what they learn probably differs, and how long individual dogs investigate another dog's pee varies tremendously. Not all pee is equal. Or, as we might expect, the messages or information pee conveys will be more or less important depending on the dog sniffing and who peed.

In summarizing her research, Dr. Lisberg wrote to me that "urine is used in part to advertise/detect the female reproductive state (especially of interest to intact males) but is also clearly used outside of this context. For example, intact males and females showed the same high interest in urine from unfamiliar dogs, and investigated male and female urine equally. Neutered males had little interest in the urine of intact female[s], but maintained their high interest in intact male urine."

Overall, this suggests that dogs smell urine to learn generally about unfamiliar dogs. While we don't yet know most of what they are likely able to detect, this appears to be an important part of how they get to know each other. Allowing dogs to take their time getting to know each other's marks (prior to face-to-face interactions) might therefore help dogs have smoother introductions, giving them more social cues to guide their behaviors. This applies to dog parks (can we build them with secluded entryways that let them sniff in private before joining the mob?) and introducing new dogs to homes.

Another interesting idea was put forth by Anneke Lisberg and Charles Snowdon when they reported that "gonadal hormones may affect urine investigation patterns both by increasing sexually motivated urine investigation in males and by creating signals in urine that allow assessment of potentially risky conspecifics."[5]

WHAT ARE DOGS DOING BY SCENT MARKING?

It's harder to say for certain the exact messages that dogs intend to leave when they mark. That is, pee may say a lot about the dog who left it, but is there sometimes a deliberate message that one dog means to send to other dogs? Research suggests yes. Dogs advertise their own social status, females advertise their reproductive status, and dogs may be defining their territory. Dogs don't advertise casually or randomly, either. Marking varies depending on who's doing the marking and on who marked before.

As Dr. Lisberg says: "High-status free ranging dogs and high tail-base-position companion dogs show similar patterns—high-status males and females mark, countermark, and males in particular overmark unfamiliar urine more than low-status/low-tail dogs. This basic pattern is seen in many other mammals as well."

If marking behaviors change over time, might this be an indicator of relationship changes? If we let dogs work out their relationships with marking before they meet face to face, can we decrease the occurrence of aggressive encounters? Too soon to tell, but there is potential here!

Dr. Lisberg went on to write:

A urine mark has more to it than smell! High-status dogs also mark more frequently, so just encountering a signal more often (or first) could help enforce the validity of the status, since a low-status dog might be less successful at defending a space or covering/displacing other marks. My unpublished data suggest that this (mark frequency or order) may be an important part of the signal itself. Similarly, being the "top mark" (urine placed as an overmark) might enhance the validity of a high-status signal (again, high-status males in particular seem to use overmarks). The effect of mark location ("over" vs. "under") on response to the mark has been studied beautifully in several rodent species, and I am finishing data collection now on a habituation test that should determine whether overmarks a) hide the previous signal, b) blend with the previous signal, c) create a "bulletin board" in which each mark is considered similarly but distinctly, or d) be given preferential or more significant attention than the previous signal.

Dr. Lisberg's takeaway message also is rather important: "Urine marks are really complex signals, and dogs seem to be far savvier than most owners seem to think when it comes to deciding what to sniff (and for how long) and what to countermark (adjacent or overmark). When we walk our dogs, all we notice are the big responses, but we don't see the likely *many* signals that they are ignoring or avoiding. For the most part, dogs are not wantonly running around and sniffing and urinating on everything (despite appearances to the contrary), but rather appear to be making decisions about what marks are important to pay attention to and whether and how to respond."

In a study of scent marking in a pack of free-ranging dogs outside of Rome, Italy, Simona Cafazzo and her colleagues report that "both males and females utilized scent marking to assert dominance and probably to relocate food or maintain possession over it. Raised-leg urination and ground scratching probably play a role in olfactory and visual communication in both males and females. Urinations released by females, especially through flexed-leg posture, may also convey information about their reproductive state."[6]

There is so much still to learn about marking among dogs. It's more complex and common than we might guess, yet as with the study of play, "simple" ethological approaches to urination patterns can produce extremely interesting and useful results. As the story below makes clear, we can sometimes start with the dogs in our own house.

ARE COUNTERMARKING PISSING MATCHES ABOUT TERRITORY?

People often ask me if dogs mark territorial borders as do their wild relatives. They wonder if canine pissing matches, or as Tracy Krulik calls them "sniffaris," mean something like, "This is my place!" While some people claim dogs don't mark territorially, it's premature to say they never do. In fact, I've seen free-ranging dogs on my mountain road behave just like wild coyotes and wolves when they mark territorial boundaries. These dogs will pee, scratch the ground, look around to see if others are around, and then pee some more. On occasion, they'll lift a leg and not urinate, and then they walk a few feet and immediately lift a leg and pee. The same thing was observed among free-ranging dogs in Italy by Simona Cafazzo and her colleagues. John Bradshaw and Nicola Rooney note: "Among free-roaming dogs, males may urine-mark as a component of territorial behavior, while females mark most frequently around their den sites."[7]

Dr. Lisberg writes: "Location of urine marks on territory boundary as indicating 'territory boundary marking' or 'territory defense' is always an interesting measure to me—most studies can't/don't differentiate between 'first' marks placed on boundary vs. marks that might be countermarks. Territory boundaries are also places where encountering a mark from a member of a different social group is also more likely, so are they marking their territory boundary because they are making a 'fence' or 'signpost' showing where their territory boundary is, or are they just countermarking unfamiliar urine that they encounter on their territory? Of course, these are certainly not mutually exclusive in function, but it's a factor I think that is worthwhile to tease out in future studies."

I agree. There still is so much to learn about peeing and pooping by dogs, and dog parks are great places in which to do these studies.

Pissing matches don't always take place outdoors, however. My cycling teammate John Talley and his wife, Tyla, were understandably quite concerned about a continual pissing match between their two dogs, Rigby and Bodie. Bodie is Rigby's father, but Rigby joined the Talley household first. Once Rigby was nicely settled in, Bodie arrived, and soon after, Bodie started peeing in the house. Even though Rigby was already house trained, once Bodie started peeing inside, Rigby did, too. Plus, it turns out that Rigby always has to have the last pee, and he will pee right in front of Tyla, she told me. No shame there!

In addition, Bodie will ground scratch after peeing, and this has become part of their ongoing pissing contest. Tyla told me that Rigby never ground scratched before Bodie came along, and now Rigby does it regularly, even if Bodie isn't around.

Is this a territorial battle? Is Bodie just doing what dogs do in a new habitat, and is Rigby, into whose home Bodie intruded, just "defending" his place? I honestly don't know. I've seen hundreds if not thousands of pissing matches over the years, but all of them were outdoors. Dr. Lisberg notes, and I agree, that it's a testament to dogs' social skills that so many dogs are thrown together at our whim, and they are able to work out sharing space in a home without resorting to pissing matches or duking it out.

What the Talleys observed is often called overmarking or countermarking, and we don't know all the reasons for it. I'm often asked if males overmark or countermark more than females. As I tell people, according to one study that focused on these behavior patterns, it's not as straightforward as it may seem. In their study, Dr. Lisberg and Charles Snowdon reported that "males and females were equally likely to countermark and investigate urine and countermarks made up a similarly large portion of countermarking for males and females."[8] Dr. Lisberg told me that

males accounted for more marks and countermarks at the dog park than females—marking males were more like energizer bunnies who just kept marking. While a typical marking female might urinate once or maybe twice and be done, a typical male marker might urinate two to three times or more. So total percent of urine marks would have been strongly male biased, as seen in other studies. Within each sex, again, higher-tailed females marked more times per dog than low-tailed females, and higher-tailed males marked more times than low-tailed males. The lowest-tailed males and females didn't countermark at all, and the lowest-tailed females didn't urinate at all in the entryway.

Once again, if you don an ethologist's hat at the dog park, you can learn a lot about dog behavior and conduct "citizen science" along the way.

DO DOGS PREFER TO LIFT ONE LEG
MORE THAN THE OTHER?

If you've ever walked a dog, then you know your life would be made much easier if you knew which leg your dog was most likely to raise in order to pee. People ask me this question often, and it really depends on your dog. The bottom line is that it's impossible to say there are population differences in leg preference. Dogs are ambilateral (they are able to lift both legs), as shown in an experiment by William Gough and Betty McGuire. However, an individual dog might show a preference for lifting one leg rather than the other, and you could factor this in when deciding on which side of the street to walk your dog. Gough and McGuire concluded: "Assessing motor laterality for a natural hindlimb behavior in dogs during walks has both advantages and disadvantages, which include ease of observation during a positive experience for the dog and the challenge of obtaining sufficient scores for each dog."[9]

WHY DO DOGS SOMETIMES LIFT THEIR LEGS WITHOUT PEEING?

This is a question that comes up a good deal. It's usually males who do this. Simona Cafazzo and her colleagues suggested that raising a leg to urinate, with or without urinating, could indicate that a dog is ready to engage in a conflict if need be.[10]

To learn more about this behavior, often called dry marking, my students and I studied urination patterns in two populations of free-running dogs, one on the campus of Washington University in St. Louis, Missouri, and the other in and around Nederland, Colorado, a small mountain town about seventeen miles west of Boulder. Twenty-seven males and twenty-four females who were not in heat, all individually identified, were observed. Marking was distinguished from merely urinating in two main ways: the urine was aimed at a specific object or area (it had what ethologists call directional quality) and generally less urine was expelled during marking. We also scored the frequency of occurrence of what we called the raised leg display that occurred when a dog raised his leg but did not deposit any obvious urine.

The results can be summarized as follows:

males marked more than females and at a higher rate (for males, 71.1 percent of urinations qualified as marking; females, 18 percent);

males ground scratched significantly more than females after marking
and males did it significantly more when other dogs could see them
do it;

both males and females marked at the lowest rate in areas in which they
spent the greatest amount of time;

seeing another male dog mark was a strong visual releaser for urine
marking by males;

sniffing did not invariably precede marking by either males or females;

the raised leg display appeared to function as a visual display;

and males performed the raised leg display significantly more frequently
when other males were in sight.

We concluded that the raised leg display might be a ploy by which
one male gets another male to use his urine, since it was a strong
visual releaser or trigger for urination by other males. We also concluded that we need to pay more attention to the visual aspects of the
postures and behavior patterns involved in the deposition of scent, in
this case urine. What has been accomplished by observing dogs can
serve as a model for studying other species.

DOES THE SIZE OF THE DOG MATTER?

You might not think that size matters, but it's possible that it might
be in relation to peeing, at least in shelter dogs. In a study called
"Scent Marking in Shelter Dogs: Effects of Body Size," Betty McGuire
and Katherine Bernis found that "small dogs urinated at higher
rates and directed more urinations than did large dogs." They hy-
pothesized that "small dogs favor urine marking over direct social
interactions because direct interactions may be particularly risky for
them."[11]

I never really thought about this possibility. As noted above,
Dr. Lisberg thinks that dogs might be avoiding conflict through sniff-

ing and marking, and here is another wonderful and important topic that can be studied in nonshelter dogs at the dog park to learn just how robust these results are. I've often wondered if dogs who have to lift their heads to get a good or better whiff of pee know that a larger dog left it. Perhaps size does matter, after all.

WHY DO DOGS ROLL IN STINKY STUFF?

At the dog park, every now and again someone shouts a warning to others, like, "Oh my, Brutus just rolled on another dog's turd. Watch it! He's pretty proud and is trying to let everyone know what he just did." Dogs roll in poop and all sorts of "disgustingly awful" stuff, as one person put it. If I'm there when this happens, someone usually turns to me and almost pleads, "Why do dogs do this?"

Unfortunately, we really don't know why dogs roll on stinky stuff. Some dive in like it's their dream come true. Some people say it's because dogs want to mask their own odor by taking on a more pungent odor or one that's more prevalent where they are, whereas others say they're trying to spread their own odor around. Judging from what I've seen, dogs usually roll in things that are far smellier than they are, and like Brutus, they often want everyone to know what they just did. Lending credence to the theory that they're trying to mask their own odor, research suggests that red foxes appear to roll on scent left by pumas (mountain lions) to mask their own scent so as not to call attention to themselves and confuse predators.[12]

Some people really get into analyzing this issue. For example, Greg Coffin, who lives in Northern California, came up with a rolling rating system for his dog, Sophia, about whom there is an interesting and popular video.[13] As Coffin wrote to me: "On our walks on and around the beach, there are many delightful things my Rhodesian Ridgeback enjoys rolling in. She does it frequently enough that I have developed a simple rating system, classifying the nicest to the nastiest. Dead birds are the best you can hope for. A little musty, but nothing too gag-worthy. Fish, just really fishy. Land mammals are next. A special kind of vulgarity. Yes, it escalates quickly. But the crème de la crème are dead sea mammals. They're full of all that rotting blubber, slathered in delicious fatty oils."[14]

What can I tell you? This probably isn't related to scent marking, but it definitely satisfies some important need in dogs to smell, in every sense of the word.

Sometimes You Just Have to Go

Dogs like to pee and poop, and people like to talk about their dog's pee and poop, as if they're freer to discuss these usually off-limits topics so long as it's about their dog. If you visit a dog park, expect to hear a lot about elimination. In his book *Off the Leash: A Year at the Dog Park*, Matthew Gilbert notes that "poop was more of a thing at the park than I had expected."[15] Gilbert himself gets into the spirit of all the poop, describing a "stray bowel movement" as a "voluminous and frozen still life."[16] Alexandra Horowitz writes about pee as graffiti, and one can say the same about poop, which is messier and more obvious to human eyes and noses.[17]

A few people have asked me if dogs really do like to poop. I don't really know. One woman told me that she was sure Ishmael, her dog, enjoyed pooping, and that's why he was always asking to be let out. Certainly, people sometimes enjoy pooping, so it is possible that dogs enjoy it, too! Some dogs also like to sniff poop and then share the scent and perhaps saliva with their human as if it's simply business as usual. Stephanie Miller, one of my friends in Boulder, lets her and her mother's dog, Smoochie, clearly know that "if you sniff poop, you kiss me later." I don't blame her for taking this point of view, having lived with a dog who thought it was great to sniff and share in rapid succession.

Unlike pee, however, there is less evidence that dogs use poop to deliberately mark. In a study of scent marking in a pack of free-ranging dogs outside of Rome, Italy, Simona Cafazzo and her colleagues report: "Our observations suggest that defecation does not play an essential role in olfactory communication among free-ranging dogs and that standing and squat postures are associated with normal excretion."[18]

One of the most interesting and unexpected poop question I've been asked is: "Why don't animals need toilet paper?" The simple answer is an anatomical one: they don't need it because they can poop without soiling themselves.[19]

Finally, here's another fascinating tidbit. Did you know that many dogs line up with the earth's magnetic field to poop and pee? I surely didn't! However, I'm certain that many people have seen dogs work hard to orient themselves before they do their business. More to the point, an analysis of more than seventy dogs representing thirty-seven breeds showed that dogs "preferred to excrete with the body being aligned along the North-South axis under calm MF [magnetic field] conditions." When the magnetic field was thrown out of whack, the dogs were "less picky about their crapping preferences."[20] However, we really don't know why many animals show a preference for this orientation in different situations, including defecating, sleeping, and hunting.[21]

After I read this phenomenon, I tried to confirm its validity, as did a few people at a local dog park. The data we collected were ambiguous. We observed three dogs who would pace here and there before peeing or pooping, and they wound up pretty much aligned to the north-south axis. One woman asked me if I knew if this is why so many dogs move around or circle when getting ready to pee or poop, but I really don't know. When nature calls, it calls and dogs don't always have to time to assume the position. I suggested that the woman study it, but she never did.

Off leash: Walking, Running, and Playing

For a good number of reasons, people most often walk their dogs on leash. Dogs need to be protected from cars, for example, and from animals who might harm them, and they also need to be kept from jumping on people or harassing other dogs. There really are a lot of demands imposed on dogs, day in and day out. What we ask or demand of them can be quite stressful. It might sound odd, but many dogs who are fortunate enough to share their life with a human are stressed, a point highlighted in Jessica Pierce's book *Run, Spot, Run* and in Jennifer Arnold's *Love Is All You Need*.

Most dogs love exercise, and this is the other main reason we take dogs for a walk. This is also a main reason for dog parks. They provide a protected space where we can let dogs run off leash, rather than having them pull our arms out of our sockets if we don't keep up.

The lack of suitable exercise can be a stressor. Exercise is how dogs relieve that stress and stay physically healthy. However, not all dogs love exercise, or not all the time. How much exercise is enough, what kinds, and whether being off leash makes a difference varies among dogs. You must get to know your dog and what she or he needs to be happy and healthy. As you learn more about your dog as an individual, you can tailor their exercise regime to what they indicate they need. The dogs with whom I shared my home varied in how much running here and there was necessary to keep them content. Mishka, a rather large malamute, was happy with a half-hour romp in the early morning and a shorter one in the evening. Jethro, a wired mutt, loved it when I would walk or jog the four miles down to town with him around six in the morning, and this eight-mile round-trip journey satisfied him until late in the afternoon, when, once again, we'd head out for a couple of miles.

Even when the dogs with whom I have shared my mountain home became elders, they'd love to take strolls in the mountains, on their own terms, and when they just didn't feel like it, they clearly let me know what they wanted. For example, when Jethro became a senior dog, he would walk up the road, sniff here and there, say hello to dog and human friends, and come home. Sometimes he'd just go outside, eat, and go to sleep. Whatever he wanted he got, and believe me, I know I was incredibly lucky to live in a place where dogs could freely roam.

In the end, we humans have to pay attention to what each individual dog needs when we tether and walk them. At a minimum, we should let their noses lead the way. Like it or not, dogs are captive to our every wish, and we need to be sure we're not depriving them of vital activities, sensory stimulation, and communication. When it's dog-walk time, let your dog set the pace.

SIX

Minding Dogs

||||||||||||||||||||||||||||||||||||||||||||||||||||||||||||||||||||||||||||||||||||||||||||||||||||||||||||||||||||||||||||||||

In August 2016, Mary Devine shared with me this lovely story about her dog Meeka, which is an excellent example of citizen science and some of what goes on in a dog's mind:

My husband and I "adopted" a puppy from a shelter. We named her Meeka and brought her home when she was about three months old. Meeka was a Doberman, shep, lab, chow mix: the vet called her a "Heinz 57" dog. She weighed fifty pounds as an adult dog.

Meeka was a highly intelligent and "territorial" dog. She had a tremendous receptive vocabulary (somewhere in my journals I wrote down the hundreds of words she understood). She learned and could follow multistep commands: it was second nature to me to say, "Meeka, you need to pick up your toys." She, in turn, would pick up her toys, one by one, depositing them in her toy box until the floor was cleared. Although I understand dogs don't see color (at least as we do), she could be told to "pick up your blue ball" because she had learned other differentiating traits of the "blue ball."

Meeka was extremely territorial. She would walk the perimeter of our yard and, with limited instruction from us, NEVER leave the yard: not to follow an errant ball, not to chase a much-hated cat, etc. It wasn't uncommon to have cars screech to a stop if a ball rolled onto our street with her in pursuit—only to have Meeka screech to a halt at the edge of the yard.

Once, when we visited my parents' house in another state, we put Meeka in the backyard and headed out for lunch. When we got home, Meeka was sitting on the front step of my parents' house. A neighbor immediately came over and described the scene: He was so nervous because he saw that Meeka had gotten out of the backyard. He watched her walk the limits of the front yard, then she sat at the front doorstep, waiting for us. Needless to say, he was amazed!

After all these tales, though, Meeka's most wondrous gift was her acceptance of our daughter. When Meeka was three years old we had our daughter. Friends of ours said things such as, "That dog is going to eat your child." This was based on the ferocity of Meeka's bark and her protectiveness and attachment to me and my husband.

My husband became a little worried, so as a freelance writer, he managed to wrangle an assignment with (I think it was) Better Homes & Gardens about how to prepare the dog for the homecoming of a baby.

The most significant points we learned (through him talking to dog experts) was: 1. We brought home our daughter's smell to Meeka before we brought home our daughter; and 2. We ignored Meeka when Sarah was asleep, but gave Meeka all sorts of attention when Sarah awakened (and throughout her being awake). Within ONE DAY, every time Sarah cried from her crib, Meeka's tail would wag and she would wait at Sarah's door (we taught Meeka to stay out of Sarah's room) until we got Sarah up. It was the beginning of a magical relationship.

Finally, one of Meeka's favorite pastimes was to tug at a "sockie" with us; she was really strong and could practically yank our arms out of the socket! When Sarah was ten months old, and was just beginning to stand independently, we could be playing the most vicious sockie tug game with Meeka, then hand the sockie to Sarah. Immediately Meeka would hold the sock in her front nibbler teeth, very gently. NEVER ONCE IN SARAH'S LIFE DID MEEKA KNOCK SARAH OVER OR PULL HER DOWN. Seriously, for the time they spent together and the seriousness of their play, it was miraculous. Back to the sock: it was amazing that Meeka didn't overdo the sock tugging, but what was more amazing is, Meeka increased her "tugging" as Sarah was able to handle it. As a five-year-old child, Sarah was overjoyed to hold the sock and have Meeka drag her across the kitchen floor![1]

IIIIIIIIIIIIIIIIIIIIIIIIIIIIIIIIIIIIIIIIIIIIIIIIIIIIIIIIIIIIIIIIIIIIIIIIIIIIIIIIIIIIIIIIIIIIIIIIIIIIIIIIIIIIIIIIIIIIIIIII

The phrase "minding dogs" means attributing active minds to these amazing beings and fully recognizing that they are not robotic machines. It also means that we must take care of them and give them the best lives possible, a point I stress in my book *Minding Animals*, which concerns all types of animals. There's a lot of interest in the emotional lives of dogs from a wide array of people, including young students, because an understanding of what dogs feel is central to giving them the best lives we can.

For various reasons we often "unmind" nonhuman animals—we make them out to be less intelligent and less emotional than detailed research in cognitive ethology shows them to be. However, we rarely do this with dogs.[2] Indeed, we often embellish dogs' abilities by attributing special powers of knowing and feeling to them, but there's no reason to do this because, as detailed empirical research has shown quite clearly, they are, in fact, smart and deeply emotional beings.[3] All animals are smart in their own ways, to serve their own needs, and they demonstrate this intelligence all the time, if we only mind them enough to see it.

Fred Jungclaus, writing about his dog, Smokey, captures this well: "I used to look at Smokey and think, 'If you were a little smarter, you could tell me what you were thinking,' and he'd look at me like he was saying, 'If you were a little smarter, I wouldn't have to.'"[4]

Canine Intelligence: "Smart" Dogs versus "Dumb" Dogs

In a 2013 interview in *Scientific American*, Dr. Brian Hare, coauthor, with Vanessa Woods, of *The Genius of Dogs* and founder of the Duke Canine Cognition Center, was asked, "What is the biggest misconception people have about the dog mind?"

"That there are 'smart' dogs and 'dumb' dogs," replied Dr. Hare. "There's still this throwback to a unidimensional version of intelligence, as though there is only one type of intelligence that you either have more or less of."[5]

Dr. Hare is right on the mark. There are multiple intelligences in dogs and other animals, and individual differences are to be expected. Differences are the rule rather than the exception. Research has shown that many different variables can influence a dog's performance in laboratory settings, and I often wonder how the data collected in controlled experiments transfer to dogs in real life, as dogs run around at dog parks and other venues and cope with changing social contexts and physical environs.

The word "intelligence" generally refers to the ability of an individual to acquire knowledge and to use it to adapt to different situations and do what's needed to accomplish various tasks and to survive. A friend of mine once told me about the free-running dogs she knew in a small town in Mexico who were cleverly street-smart and could survive in difficult conditions, but they didn't listen to humans all that well. Some were skilled at finding and snatching food and avoiding dogcatchers, unfriendly dogs, and people. Some were good at "playing" humans for food, whereas others weren't. Conversely, I've known some intelligent, crafty, and adaptable dogs who weren't street-smart and likely couldn't make it in such an environment. However, a few with whom I shared my home could easily steal my food and that of the other resident dog in a heartbeat, without either of us knowing what was happening.

Which dogs were "smarter" and which "dumber"? Neither, of course. Relatively speaking, these dogs were equally intelligent, but they adapted their smarts to different circumstances. Outside those contexts, they might appear quite "dumb" to us. I've lived with and met enough dogs to know that saying one is smarter than another is usually a mischaracterization of who, as individuals, they truly are.

In January 2017, Jan Hoffman wrote an essay in the *New York Times* called "To Rate How Smart Dogs Are, Humans Learn New

Tricks."[6] Two quotes there by Dr. Clive Wynne, an Arizona State University dog researcher, caught my eye: "Smart dogs are often a nuisance. . . . They get restless, bored and create trouble" and "I think 'smarts' is a red herring. . . . What we really need in our dogs is affection. My own dog is an idiot, but she's a lovable idiot." Sure, smart dogs can be a nuisance, but so too can dogs whom we believe are not all that clever. I've seen this over and over again. All sorts of dogs become a nuisance to us for all sorts of reasons, but it's not because of their levels of intelligence. The same is true regarding affection: all dogs, relatively speaking, can be equally affectionate, and this has nothing to do with smarts. These value judgments reflect us, who we are, and what we want from our dog. They arise from the particular success or frustrations that humans encounter as they interact with particular dogs, but they don't reflect a common truth about who dogs really are. When dogs are experienced as a "nuisance," it's usually because their human simply doesn't understand what their dog is doing or trying to tell them. Because there are different types of canine intelligence, I'm not sure what it means to talk about smart and not-so-smart dogs.

But people still ask me, What about dogs who truly act like idiots? Aren't there really dunce dogs? Once again, we need to be careful about characterizing dogs in this way. One of my favorite quotes about how we refer to other animals comes from the Hungarian anatomist János Szentágothai, who famously remarked, "There are no 'unintelligent' animals; only careless observations and poorly designed experiments."[7] We've known for a long time that dogs aren't brain-dead beings.[8]

In this and the next chapter, I review some of what we know from detailed cognitive ethological research (the study of animal minds) about just how smart and emotional dogs are. It's impossible to review all of it, but I'll try to answer the common questions I often get asked as I stand with people at a dog park, when I meet people walking dogs on the street, and even when I sit with folks over meals, and we stop to watch dogs doing their thing.

DO DOGS HAVE A THEORY OF MIND?

One of the hot topics in ethology and animal research today is try-ing to figure out if nonhuman animals have what is called a theory of mind. That is, do nonhuman animals know that other animals have their own thoughts and feelings, ones that may be different than their own and that they can anticipate and account for? A good deal of "higher" thinking and more complex emotions depend on having a theory of mind, so confirming this could open the door to confirm-ing much else.

With dogs, evidence is increasingly showing that they probably do have a theory of mind, and one of the main ways we've discerned this is through research on dog play. When dogs (and other animals) play, there is a good deal of mind reading going on. Dogs note where others dog are looking—they confirm whether other dogs are paying attention to them—and they have to make careful and rapid assess-ments and predictions of what their play partner is likely to do.

Consider two dogs, Harry and Mary. Each needs to pay close at-tention to what the other dog has done and is doing, and each uses this to predict what the other is likely to do next. Alexandra Horowitz has studied how dogs pay attention to attention itself during play. She discovered that

> play signals were sent nearly exclusively to forward-facing con-specifics [members of the same species, in this case other dogs]; attention-getting behaviors were used most often when a play-mate was facing away, and before signaling an interest to play. In addition, the mode of attention-getter matched the degree of inattentiveness of the playmate: stronger attention-getters were used when a playmate was looking away or distracted, less forceful ones when the partner was facing forward or laterally. In other words, these dogs showed attention to, and acted to ma-nipulate, a feature of other dogs that mediates their ability to re-spond: which feature in human interaction is called "attention."[9]

Psychologist Cindy Harmon-Hill and ethologist Simon Gadbois at Dalhousie University in Halifax, Nova Scotia, agree that play is a good place to look for theory of mind in nonhuman animals, and they offer a neurobiological account of why it's likely that dogs have a theory of mind.[10] As animals play, they reappraise what their partner is doing—what I call fine-tuning on the run. In addition, play requires that the players cooperate, it emerges without training, and even adults engage in it. As a result, Harmon-Hill and Gadbois suggest that play is modulated by subcortical processes into a three-part motivational system: animals *like* to play and gain pleasure from doing it (1), and so they *want* to play (2), which leads them to *learn* how to play (3). The variability of play indicates that players have to assess what's happening and change their behavior according to their beliefs about what their play partner wants and plans to do. This takes a theory of mind.

Clearly, we need significantly more comparative data before we even begin to make reliable assessments of the taxonomic distribution of theory of mind—that is, determining which species have it and which don't. However, watching dogs negotiating play on the run strongly suggests they know that other dogs are also thinking and feeling.

DO DOGS FOLLOW THE GAZE OF OTHERS?

Following another dog's gaze is something that some dogs do quite well. Dogs can learn a good deal about what another dog is thinking when they do this, and this simple act may help demonstrate that dogs have a theory of mind. Dogs also can follow human gazes, but results differ from study to study, which as I've said is not surprising because different dogs are studied by different researchers in various contexts using different methods.[11]

When it comes to dogs following a person's gaze, we need to pay close attention to the relationship between the dog and the human. In an interesting paper called "DogTube: An Examination of Dogmanship Online," the researchers suggest that "reciprocal attention in the dog-human dyad" is important in gaining a dog's attention and in handling and training them. Further, they write that dogs who "are perceived as difficult to train may be in the hands of people who lack the timing and awareness that characterize good dogmanship." The researchers state that "dogmanship is reflected in the timeliness of rewards and the ability to acquire and retain a dog's attention when handling or training them."[12]

From my everyday observations at dog parks, I've seen enough of these encounters to feel safe saying that dogs are able to follow dog and human gazes. They don't always do this, surely, but they are capable of it. And, of course, dogs may be picking up information but not showing us that they have in ways we can detect.

DO DOGS HAVE A SENSE OF HUMOR?

People often ask me if dogs and other animals have a sense of humor. I go back and forth on which animals may or may not have this, but I'm pretty certain that dogs do. So, too, thinks Dr. Stanley Coren, who also notes there are likely breed differences in addition to individual differences among dogs.[13] Pondering a dog's sense of humor can uncover a lot about what they know. In his classic book *The Descent of Man and Selection in Relation to Sex*, Charles Darwin wrote: "Dogs show what may be fairly called a sense of humor, as distinct from mere play; if a bit of stick or other such object be thrown to one, he will often carry it away for a short distance; and then squatting down with it on the ground close before him, will wait until his master comes quite close to take it away. The dog will then seize it and rush away in triumph, repeating the same maneuver, and evidently enjoying the practical joke."

Having a sense of humor means that an individual knows whatever they're doing has an effect on others, and although they themselves might enjoy doing whatever they're doing, the reaction of human (and perhaps nonhuman) observers keeps them doing what they're doing. Having a sense of humor might also confirm that animals have a theory of mind.

While I'm always careful to say that I don't really know if dogs and other animals have a sense of humor and enjoy comedy, since there are few formal, ethological studies on this, the anecdotal evidence is pretty overwhelming. For example, my companion Jethro not only was a savvy food thief but also quite a jokester. He'd run around with his favorite stuffed animal, a rabbit, in his mouth, shaking it from side to side and often looking at the people who were around to see what effect this had on them. When they laughed while he was doing this, he seemed to do it more and more. When they weren't paying attention to him, he would stop running around or he would bark, look to see if they were watching him, and continue running here and there with his stuffed toy.

Or consider Benson the burper. My friend Marije terEllen tells me that Benson, a five-year-old Bernese mountain dog, likes to come up to her, face to face, look her in the eyes, and burp. He seems to get a kick out of doing it and doesn't burp at other times. Is this his way of saying "hello" or "I love you"? Or is he just having a good old time doing it to his human? Marije also insists that Benson is not mimicking her or her daughter Arianne.

I've also come across numerous examples of other species who act like stand-up comedians and jokesters, including horses, moon bears (a.k.a. Asian black bears), a scarlet macaw, and more.[14] In fact, humor may be more widespread among nonhuman animals than we think.

ARE DOGS DELIBERATELY DECEITFUL
WHEN THEY STEAL FOOD?

Most people have witnessed dogs acting like thieves, especially to get food, and trickery can be art of humor. But when dogs steal food, are they being knowingly deceitful or just hungry and greedy? In fact, we can learn a good deal about the cognitive skills of dogs by watching them strategize how to steal food. I've been told many stories about dogs pilfering food over the years, and I've witnessed many crafty dogs doing just that. Jethro, a mutt whom I rescued when he was about nine months old, was "food smart." When he and his house-mate Sasha were offered food, Jethro would always run to the front door as if someone was there. When Sasha meandered over to the door to see what was going on, Jethro beelined back to her dish and vacuumed up whatever he could. That always looked like deliberate trickery to me.

That said, I should add that while some dogs are good at stealing another dog's food, it's also known that dogs will share food, espe-cially with friends (as opposed to strangers). The simple presence of another dog actually makes them more generous than when another dog wasn't present.[15]

I think Jethro's being smart about food was related to his street-smarts. Before I met him, Jethro had spent his life on the streets hon-ing his food-stealing skills to great success. When I brought Jethro home, he met Sasha, and the two dogs got along famously. For one thing, even though Jethro took advantage of Sasha and her food, he only did so up to a point. He knew that Sasha was possessive of her food and that he could fool her into going to the front door, but he was careful not to rile her. He'd eye her carefully, watching for her to make the slightest move away from her bowl, and then he'd quietly and quickly slink in, grab a few morsels, and gulp them. After which he would lick her muzzle, then stroll away as if nothing had hap-pened. Sasha seemed to have no clue. Jethro was, in fact, quite savvy at stealing my own food as well.

Along these lines, I once watched an amazing scene at a local dog park. Henrietta and Rosie were deeply engaged in play. Henrietta's human needed to go home, so he offered Henrietta a treat. Rosie, of course, followed closely. When Henrietta's human started to put the treat in front of Henrietta's nose, Rosie turned her head to the left and bowed as if another dog was approaching to play, but there was no other dog! Henrietta followed Rosie's gaze, and in that instant, Rosie snatched the treat and ran off, and without a blink, Henrietta and Rosie were at it, deep in play, oblivious to everything else. Need-less to say, Henrietta's human was upset. Not for the thievery, but because he had to leave!

DO DOGS USE US TO GET FOOD?

Food also can be used as a powerful training or teaching reward, and people often ask if getting food is the only reason dogs seem to "love" us. In short, no. Dogs are more complicated than that. In her essay "Eager to Please?" dog trainer and journalist Tracy Krulik shows that giving food to a dog as a reward does not mean she or he will love you less or that the dog is using you absent any positive emotion.

I have lived in the mountains outside of Boulder, Colorado, with a number of dogs who were able to run free when I was home, and I have watched countless dogs at dog parks and on various trails where they could run free. In all these settings, I've seen food used to keep off-leash dogs under control with absolutely no indication that the dogs didn't feel extremely closely attached to—and, I feel comfortable saying, loving toward—their humans.

My dog Jethro knew that when my hand went into my right pocket there was a treat for him, and when he saw the slightest move in this direction, he came to me. I created this association deliberately. When I talk with people about how to call their dog using gestures, I refer to this practice simply as the hand-to-pocket method of teaching. And it works rather well. Some of my neighbors in the mountains were cougars, black bears, and coyotes—which meant that sometimes I couldn't use a word or a sound to cue Jethro to come to me immediately without the other animals coming to him and/or me, too! Did Jethro love me? I'm sure he did. Did he want the food treat? Of course. Was he pretending to like me just for food? Not at all. When it was okay for me to call him by saying something like "Come" or simply "J," Jethro responded without any treat.

I once had a neighbor who questioned my use of food to train the dogs I lived with. She'd say, "Jethro is using you and doesn't really love you." In contrast, Maya, my neighbor's dog, was the proverbial loose cannon, who rarely listened to her human. However, Maya came to me when I offered food and a hug. Maya knew what my right hand going into my pocket meant. We lived in risky environs, their safety came first, and food worked just fine as a motivational tool.

Like Jethro, Maya would also come when she was called, and she was wonderful and loving even when there were no treats to hand out. Dogs don't need food to be inspired to express affection, and using food as a teaching tool doesn't change that at all.

Neuroimaging studies seem to confirm this. Peter Cook and his colleagues have shown that dogs prefer praise over food, and their data "may help to explain the apparent efficacy of social interaction in dog training."[16] However, food also can be very important, and one study seemed, in fact, to show that dogs preferred food to petting. Yet there was a good deal of variability in the results the researchers of the latter study got, depending on the familiarity of the person who was doing the petting and how deprived the dogs were of social interaction.[17]

As Tracy Krulik notes, this issue with food is more of a people problem than a dog problem. It's time to get over the view that dogs are always using us for food and don't really give a hoot about us. In training, food should be used when it works, and when it does, we shouldn't then doubt a dog's love for us.[18]

STILL, CAN'T WE TEST A DOG'S IQ?

As I say, not every dog is as savvy as others, and people always wonder, since we measure intelligence in people, can't we do it with dogs? Yes, or so we hope: researchers are trying to figure out how. As I've mentioned, very few studies of dog cognition focus on individual differences; a 2016 article that reviewed recent research found only three studies to review. Thus, in order to get more of a handle on the intelligence of dogs, in February 2016 Rosalind Arden and Mark Adams published a research paper called "A General Intelligence Factor in Dogs," which was well-summarized in the article "Mensa Mutts? Dog IQ Tests Reveal Canine 'General Intelligence.'"[19]

First, the researchers created a prototype IQ test for dogs that included navigation tests, timed puzzle or barrier tests, tests of following gaze, and tests for assessing food quantities. Then they gave the test to sixty-eight border collies. Ultimately, dogs who did better on one test also did better on other tests, and dogs who completed tests faster were also more accurate than dogs who worked more slowly.

Thus, the dogs varied in similar ways to how people vary in IQ tests. (An interesting side note is that, in people, these differences may correlate to longevity: smarter people tend to be somewhat healthier and live longer.) Yet the purpose of the study wasn't simply to compare individual dogs, but to quantify a "general intelligence" level among all dogs in an effort to help understand the evolution of intelligence itself.

Some key highlights of the study include:

- The structure of cognitive abilities in dogs is *similar* to that found in people.
- Dogs who solved problems more *quickly* were also more *accurate*.
- Dogs' cognitive abilities can be tested quickly, like those of people.
- Bigger individual differences studies on dog cognition will contribute to cognitive epidemiology.

As the researchers concluded: "Learning about individual differences in animal intelligence is a first step in understanding how cognitive abilities fit into the fitness landscape. It will provide crucial information on the relationship between intelligence and health, aging, and mortality. Data from nonhuman animals are essential if we are to develop a complete understanding of intelligence, one of the most important traits in the entire animal kingdom."

Stanley Coren summarized the results of this study noting, "This provides strong evidence for the idea of a general factor in intelligence, with smart dogs being generally proficient at everything and not-so-smart dogs doing generally more poorly on most other measures.[20]

ARE DOGS SMARTER THAN CATS?

It's always tempting to think about cross-species comparisons and ask questions such as, "Are dogs really smarter than cats?" People ask me this sort of question quite a bit, and I always explain that these sorts of comparisons aren't really meaningful. They are fraught with error because individuals do what they need to do to be card-carrying members of their species. Dogs do what they need to do to be dogs, and cats do what they need to do to be cats.[21] Mice can do things that dogs can't do, as can ants, and all these species can do things that people can't do, so it's like comparing apples and acorns to start ranking one species as smarter than others.

It really doesn't get us anywhere to ask if dogs are smarter than cats or if cats are smarter than dogs. Intelligence can be viewed as an evolutionary adaptation whose expression differs for each species. Yes, individuals within species vary, so it's possible to ask if one dog is smarter or more adaptable than another, but this also must be done with care. Dogs, like other animals, display multiple intelligences; street-smart dogs might be better at stealing food and living independently while human-smart dogs might be better at understanding people and adapting to human homes.

Even among dogs from similar backgrounds and breeds, the variations in relative intelligence may not teach us much. For example, border collies are regarded as a very intelligent breed, but as in the study above, not all are equally intelligent. In some contexts, it might be accurate to say that one dog, Herman, is smarter than another dog, Brutus, but it's just as likely that Brutus will outsmart Herman in other contexts. I also avoid comparing or ranking dog breeds in terms of intelligence because, once again, individuals from each breed do what they need to do to fulfill the needs of that breed.

Canine Awareness: Memory and Decision Making

It's hard to get inside the head of another animal. For instance, how much do dogs and other animals learn from just hanging out and observing their surroundings? We don't really know. Many animals spend a lot of time resting, often peering around and taking in the landscape's sights, sounds, and smells. Dogs surely do this. I have often smiled as I have watched the dogs with whom I share my home just hanging out and looking around at their dog and human friends and their environs.

When I've done fieldwork on a number of different animals, including wild coyotes, I have always noted that they spend a lot of time not doing much of anything but looking around as they rest. I am convinced that they pick up a lot of information this way and that what they learn can be used in their social encounters with others. Indeed, we know that dogs aren't passive observers. They are able to make what are called third-party evaluations of humans, and they avoid people who don't support their own human. Researcher James Anderson and his colleagues argue that dogs and other animals display a core morality that doesn't depend on language or teaching—individuals learn who's helpful or not and base their future interactions on what they've determined.[22] Clearly, dogs are not automatons who are programmed to act in specific ways with little or no thought. They remember and make decisions.

In discussions with people at dog parks and on trails, I've heard many similar stories centering on how smart and how emotional dogs are and what impressive memories they have. I recall being shocked when I once read an essay by a psychologist claiming dogs don't remember yesterday and are stuck in "an eternal present."[23] This ludicrous claim ignores tons of research showing that dogs and many other animals have great memories and use this information in social and nonsocial contexts. Not only do past events influence dogs, but dogs also plan for the future. Anyone who's rescued a dog who's been abused knows how their past influences their behavior. Many detailed studies show that mental "time travel"—imagining the past and looking ahead to the future—is not uniquely human. Dogs also are able to infer the physical properties of an object by watching a human manipulate it and then recall the information thus gained for later use. In one study, after dogs were allowed to watch two swinging doors of different weights being opened, they were able to open the doors themselves, but only after first experiencing opening both doors themselves could they infer which door was lighter and act on that information.[24]

The other dogs with whom I have happily shared my home were not as savvy as Jethro. A few rapidly learned about the black bears and cougars who visited our home and surrounding land, whereas a few didn't and rather brazenly took forays beyond my property. None ever had a problem with our wild neighbors, so clearly each figured out their own way to coexist with these predators. Each dog was an individual, with her or his own "belief system" or conception of how the world works and the best choices to make. Dogs and many other animals can adapt to a wide range of varying situations, and there is no reason at all to think that their differing responses are merely hard-wired stimulus-response reactions. I fully realize how tempting and easy it can be to reduce behavior to automatic reflexive reactions, but these sorts of explanations can't fully explain the variability with which animals respond to different situations. The late Donald Griffin, an award-winning scientist who is often called the father of cognitive ethology, argued forcefully that flexibility in behavior, as a response to varying social and nonsocial conditions, is a marker of consciousness in nonhuman animals. Many other researchers and I agree.

People often wonder how much information a dog can remember. A 2016 study by Claudia Fugazza, Ákos Pogány, and Ádám Miklósi from Eötvös Loránd University in Budapest, called "Recall of Others' Actions after Incidental Encoding Reveals Episodic-Like Memory in Dogs," showed just how much dogs remember, which is often more than we realize.[25] I asked Dr. Miklósi how his study extends what we know from other formal studies and from what people learn from watching their dog at home or at dog parks, to which he replied:

As usual this is something that dog people may have assumed the dog is capable of doing. But most of them did not think about the possibility that dogs remember specific events happening around them. This study shows now that dogs (and probably many other animals) are able to do this. So they not only remember (spontaneously) what they have done (there are studies on chimps, rats, dolphins along these lines), but also what their owner did. For example, they may watch the owner cut the roses in the garden one day, and then when they see those flowers again, this memory could pop up in their mind. This could happen without showing any change in behaviour because this is just a spontaneous "thought," although in some other cases such thoughts may actually become causes of (spontaneous) behaviour.[26]

This research reminded me of the many dogs I've known who acted like know-it-alls. They seemed to sense or know what I was going to do or what I wanted them to do, although I'd never explicitly taught them to make certain associations. They gleaned my intentions and figured out the way their world worked without any formal teaching. I felt the same about some of the wild coyotes I studied for years. They just seemed to know what others were thinking, feeling, and wanting them to do. This is yet one more reason why I'm pretty certain dogs, coyotes, and many other animals have some sort of theory of mind.[27]

DO DOGS MAKE AND USE TOOLS?

People interested in "dog smarts" often wonder if dogs make and use tools. Years ago I also was told about a dog named Grendel who made a back scratcher, and I once saw a video of a dog moving and then using a chair to get onto a counter to get food.[28] Dingoes also use tools.

Grendel's human friend, Lenny Frieling, told me the following story:

> It would have been about 1973 that Grendel made her first tool. Because of her short legs and long torso, she could not reach the center of her back to scratch. One day we gave her a bone which was likely sawn from a large leg bone, perhaps lamb, because it was quite hard. It was cylindrical, with parallel flat sides. About a week (at most) after we gave her the bone, we noticed that she had chewed it so that one side was still flat, and the other side

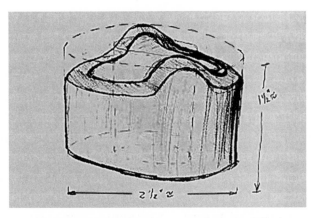

Grendel's back scratcher. (Courtesy of Lenny Frieling)

had two raised ridges (shaped like a sine wave going around the outer rim of the bone). She would place the bone, flat side down, on the floor, and roll over onto the two raised ridges using the protrusions to scratch the center of her back. I was convinced that she had made a tool, but in my mind I thought that behavior had to be repeated to be scientifically significant. She had that first bone, as I recall it, for quite a while, maybe a year. It disappeared. We gave her another bone and within days, or a week, she had carved the second bone into a very similar shape, and used it for the same purpose. She had repeated the making of the tool.

DO DOGS UNDERSTAND WHAT WE SAY?

There's a lot of interest in whether dogs understand human communication better than other animals because of their close relationship with people. We all know many dogs are able to learn the meaning of words such as "sit," "stay," and "come," and the story of Meeka at the start of this chapter is another vivid example of how well dogs can understand what we mean quite specifically. Research shows that dogs have the ability to learn the meaning of hundreds or even as many as a thousand words.[29]

In a paper called "Do Dogs Get the Point? A Review of Dog-Human Communication Ability," researchers Juliane Kaminski and Marie

Nitzschner noted that dogs use human communication more flexibly than either chimpanzees or wolves. "One hypothesis, the so-called by-product hypothesis," they write, "suggests that dogs have been selected against fear and aggression and as a by-product this paved the way for the evolution of generally more flexible social cognitive skills, which surpassed those of their ancestor, the wolf." They also remark that "another hypothesis, the adaptation hypothesis, has claimed that dogs may have been specifically selected for certain tasks for which using human forms of communication was necessary" and conclude that the "evidence to date suggests that dogs' understanding of human forms of communication may be more specialized than was predicted by some and may be best explained as the result of a special adaptation of dogs to the specific activities humans have used them for."[30]

We also know that dogs can read our facial expressions.[31] Dogs can recognize emotional states using mental representations, and they snub people who are mean to their owners and even reject their treats.[32] Dogs can tell differences between happy and angry faces and recognize human emotions.[33] We also know that, when a person is angry, dogs don't trust that individual and won't follow their pointing.[34] So, even though dogs don't speak human languages, they've learned to read us pretty well.

Social Dynamics in Groups of Dogs

As we've seen, dogs can be both cooperative and competitive with other dogs, and dogs will trick and cheat other dogs. What's interesting is that dogs may adjust what they do based on group size. Italian researcher and dog expert Roberto Bonanni and his colleagues studied the variables that influenced whether free-ranging dogs outside of Rome, Italy, would participate in intergroup conflicts. They discovered that "dogs belonging to the smallest pack tended to be more cooperative than those belonging to larger groups." Also, young and high-ranking dogs cooperated more when their group confronted larger groups, but they remained behind other dogs during actual conflict.[35] Dogs in larger groups also had a greater opportunity to cheat. The researchers stressed that the behavior of dogs is complex, and individuals may take advantage of who's there and doing the work for them. They can assess group size, displaying what the researchers call numerical cognition.

Dr. Bonanni and his colleagues also provided another example of numerical cognition. They observed that free-ranging dogs living in a suburban environment are able to assess the number of opponents during intergroup conflicts. They concluded:

> The overall probability of at least one pack member approaching opponents aggressively increased with a decreasing ratio of the number of rivals to that of companions. Moreover, the probability that more than half of the pack members withdrew from a conflict increased when this ratio increased. The skill of dogs in correctly assessing relative group size appeared to improve with increasing the asymmetry in size when at least one pack comprised more than four individuals, and appeared affected to a lesser extent by group size asymmetries when dogs had to compare only small numbers. These results provide the first indications that a representation of quantity based on noisy mental magnitudes may be involved in the assessment of opponents in intergroup conflicts and leave open the possibility that an additional, more precise mechanism may operate with small numbers.[36]

In other words, maybe dogs can't do math, but when it matters, they can discriminate quantity, or as academics like to put it, they have numerosity, or some sort of numerical sense.

Self-Awareness in Dogs

The short and correct answer to the question of whether dogs are self-aware is that *we just really don't know*. I conducted what has come to be called "the yellow snow study" when I walked my dog companion Jethro along the Boulder Creek trail, just outside city limits. To study the role of urine in eliciting urinating and marking, I moved urine-saturated snow ("yellow snow") from place to place during five winters, and I compared the responses of Jethro to his own and others' urine. When people saw me do this, they tended to avoid me and shake their head, clearly questioning my sanity. But the experiment was easy to conduct. You can easily don an ethologist's hat and repeat this experiment and risk being called weird.[37]

I learned that Jethro spent less time sniffing his own urine than that of other males or females and that, while his interest in his own urine waned with time, it remained relatively constant for other individuals' urine. Jethro infrequently urinated over or sniffed and then immediately urinated over his own urine, and he marked over the urine of other males more frequently than he marked over the urine of females. I concluded from this that Jethro clearly had some sense of "self." He displayed a sense of "mine-ness," if not necessarily of "I-ness." Biologist Roberto Cazzola Gatti confirmed my findings using what he called the "Sniff Test of Self-Recognition" on four dogs.[38] In her book *Being a Dog: Following the Dog into a World of Smell*, Dr. Horowitz wrote about the results of a more systematic study of self-recognition with dogs in her cognition laboratory. She observes that the dogs "peed only on other dogs' containers, not their own. They saw themselves."[39]

While neither Dr. Horowitz nor I are sure that these studies confirm the presence of self-awareness, they do indicate an awareness of identity.[40]

Do Dogs Recognize Themselves in a Mirror?

Many people have watched their dogs watching themselves in a mirror, and this provides another great opportunity for citizen science, which can help us identify and understand self-awareness in dogs. In January 2017, Arianna Schlumbohm, who partook in a class discussion with me and my colleague Jessica Pierce, wrote me this story about her dog, Honey:

One day a few years ago, Honey had been lying with me on my bed. I was wearing these truly awful purple fuzzy socks, and she got some fuzz on her forehead at some point. It was adorable. After a little bit of this, she caught a glance of herself in my mirror and almost immediately reacted. She batted at the fuzz with her front paws until it caught, then sat on my stomach until I pulled the fuzz off her paw. Then she went back to the foot of the bed for a few more hours. Honey was really upset, but calmed down as soon as she saw the purple was off. I always just thought of it as a cute, dopey dog story, but I really hope that it will help out your research!![41]

Arianna's story is the best I've heard about a dog paying attention to something on their forehead after seeing it in a mirror. Honey hadn't been observed paying any attention to herself in the mirror previously. This observation reminds me of the more formal "red dot" studies that have been done on nonhuman primates, dolphins, orcas, elephants, and birds, in which a red dot is placed, without the animal knowing it, on their forehead or on an area of their body that they cannot see without using the mirror. Then a mirror is placed in front of the animal, and any self-directed movements responding to the red dot are interpreted as indicating some form of self-recognition. This procedure is called the mirror test, and it depends on the animals using visual rather than olfactory or auditory cues to make assessments of who's in the mirror.

All in all, the results of studies of self-recognition are a mixed bag. While some individuals, and often only one, will touch the dot, not all individuals in a study show these self-directed movements. However, just because some animals don't, this does not mean that they don't have some sense of self. For example, decades ago, Michael Fox and I tried to do the mirror test on dogs and wolves, and none showed any interest in the spot on their forehead. Yet my yellow snow test with Jethro shows that a dog's sense of self may be primarily related to olfactory rather than visual cues. There still is a lot of work to be done, but there is no reason at all to think that dogs do not have some sense of self.[42]

Dogs surely can figure out how mirrors work. I once received an interesting email from Zeno Zimmerman about a dog using a mirror to recognize different people:

> I have a German Pinscher who is incredibly smart and aware of way too much. In fact, she is so intelligent she has been difficult to train this past decade. However, from sheer love and training she has developed exceptional skills.
>
> Both my roommate and I were shocked to realize she clearly is able to recognize herself in our wall-length mirror at the top of the stairs. But what is most revealing to us is she is able to recognize different people in the mirror with herself.
>
> For instance, we will often find her looking into the mirror at the top of the stairs and waiting for our reflections perceived behind her in the mirror to tell her it is ok to run down the stairs, someone is coming behind her to open the door. If she does start down the steps after seeing our reflections moving behind her in the mirror, and we stop, she will often notice it in the mirror and stop herself or turn around and give us signals to continue walking down the steps behind her.
>
> I was shocked to read most people believe dogs do not have this ability. Of course every dog owner thinks their "Fee-fee" is the smartest, best thing on the planet . . . and prefer to believe their dog is incredible beyond belief. . . .
>
> If there are two people behind her in the mirror, she will turn and respond to the person who makes the gesture in the mirror while she can only see the person by watching the mirror. . . . From what I am reading on the net, this awareness is rare?[43]

Along these lines, in a study by Megumi Fukuzawa and Ayano Hashi called "Can We Estimate Dogs' Recognition of Objects in Mirrors from Their Behavior and Response Time?" the researchers show that dogs can learn to use mirrors to locate food without humans helping them.

In May 2016, I received an email from Rebecca Savage about her dog Sammy that exemplifies much of what this chapter discusses—that we should never presume what dogs know or how smart our own dog may, or may not, be:

> Growing up, I had a very sweet all-black cocker spaniel, Sammy. While he was very sweet, he wasn't the smartest dog I've met, but there was one day where Sammy became markedly self-aware.
>
> Sammy never watched TV, as some dogs do. But, one day, my parents and I were watching a Discovery Channel show on dogs and Sammy came over to the TV, sat down, and intently watched the show. He paid attention for a time and then got up and went to the back of the TV to look for the dogs, finding nothing, he came back to the screen, watched, looked behind the TV again, and repeated this process a number of times.
>
> There also happened to be a full-length mirror that was set on the floor and stored in the same corner the TV was backed into. After a time going back and forth between the screen and the back of the TV, Sammy went over to the mirror and regarded himself, came closer, moved back, poked his nose to the mirror and was trying to figure out who the dog in the mirror was. He went over to the TV and then back to the mirror and did this a number of times. He was undeniably becoming self-aware and recognizing himself as a dog. We were awestruck.[44]

It's difficult for me to imagine that dogs don't have some sense of self, but right now we don't know much at all about this cognitive capacity. Indeed, when we look at all the data that are available for other animals, it's still not clear who has it and who doesn't. This is a wonderful area of research for those who want to know more. And it's surely an area that's ripe for citizen science.

SEVEN

Emotions and Heart

||||||||||||||||||||||||||||||||||||||||||||||||||||||||||||||||||||||||||||||||||||||||||||||||||||||||||||||

A few years ago, Rebecca Johnson shared with me this story of her dog Cash, which is another great example of citizen science:

I know animals are capable of joy, but do you think they feel pride? Are they aware when they have accomplished something difficult or something they didn't know they were capable of?

I ask because of a moment with Cash. We went on an eleven-mile hike into Tolovana hot springs. After a lovely two days there, it was time to hike out. The first two miles out are a very steep switchback. One of my friends had a snow mobile and offered to run me to the top of the hill. I knew Cash would not let me hold him on the snow machine, so this would only work if Cash would follow us up the trail. We started slowly. I sat backward and called to Cash.

Understandably, he was at first nervous due to the noise, but he saw me leaving and trotted after us. Then he became excited to be running, so we went a bit faster. Cash also picked up his pace. We continued to increase our speed till Cash was running at top speed, faster than he'd ever run before. When we arrived at the top I got off the snow machine, and Cash came bounding up to me. He was so excited. He ran around me in huge circles, very fast, and then would stop near me and bounce in a play bow before taking off again at top speed. It seemed like he was saying, "Did you see me? Did you see how fast I was? WOW!!" This single event was a big boost to his confidence.[1]

||||||||||||||||||||||||||||||||||||||||||||||||||||||||||||||||||||||||||||||||||||||||||||||||||||||||||||||||||

One does not have to be a rocket scientist to know that dogs are conscious, smart, and emotional individuals. They show their deep and varied emotions clearly and openly. No one watching dogs even casually could doubt that they are deeply emotional beings, right? It's obvious from Rebecca's story that, whether Cash felt pride or not, he was clearly experiencing strong emotions that resembled joy. And what is pride if not a particular kind of joy?

Well, a dwindling few people and researchers do still try to argue today that we don't really know if dogs feel joy or grief, but thankfully, these doubters are rapidly and rightly evaporating like ice on a hot stove. At a class I was teaching, a student once asked, "Why don't people blink when a dog displays grief over losing a human friend, but some people wonder if they truly feel grief when a dog friend leaves or dies?" This is a great question, and many animal welfare and other organizations have pamphlets about how to deal with a dog who's grieving the loss of a human or nonhuman friend.

If we could confirm that Cash's joy was a direct response to doing something he'd never done before, then we might be able to label it pride—or a canine version of pride. The study of animal emotions is not science fiction, and there is a large and rapidly growing database on the cognitive and emotional lives of dogs. Recognizing rich and deep emotions in other animals is good biology. They publicize their emotional lives, and it's clear from all sides—evolutionary theory, detailed scientific data, and common sense—that dogs are not mindless machines but, rather, smart, thinking, and feeling beings who experience a wide range of emotions similar to our own. This is not to say they feel exactly what we feel. Just as my joy and grief are not the same as another person's, so a dog's emotions aren't the same as human ones. But acknowledging difference also does not mean that humans have emotions and dogs don't. Rather, one basic truth about evolution is that all species retain certain similarities and develop certain differences, and we should be careful not to fall into the trap of regarding humans as the sole template for comparisons and for understanding other species.

Dealing with Doubt and the Limits of Knowing

Ample research shows that dogs and numerous other nonhuman animals are conscious and experience deep and meaningful feelings. I agree wholeheartedly with Patricia McConnell when she writes in *For the Love of a Dog*: "It's time to stop apologizing for the belief that animals, like our dogs, have emotions. *Of course*, our dogs can experience emotions like fear, anger, happiness, and jealousy. And yes, as far as we can tell, their experience of those emotions is comparable in many ways to ours. People who argue otherwise might as well argue that the earth is flat."[2]

At the same time, that doesn't mean that we understand everything that exists in the minds and hearts of another animal, including humans. There are limits to what we can know. We will always encounter uncertainty about what nonhuman animals actually think and feel, and comparisons to our own thoughts and feelings will only take us so far. In this chapter, I try to distinguish what we know with virtual certainty from what is less likely and what we can still only guess, but to a degree, discussions of animal minds and emotions will always include some room for doubt, differences, and the limits of knowing others.

I emphasize this because people and researchers still sometimes regard the presence of doubt as a reason to deny animal emotions altogether, even when this flies in the face of their own experience. This has always been exemplified to me by a scientist I once knew named Bill, about whom I've written before. In casual conversations, Bill loved to tell stories about his companion dog Reno, who was so smart he could beat Bill at chess (!) and who openly resented the attention that Bill gave to his daughter and who got angry when Bill left him alone. Yet when Bill went to work and put on his white laboratory coat, he was reluctant to admit to Reno's emotions and smarts. Bill, like many scientists, lived a split life concerning animal cognition and animal emotions. He regarded and treated his dog at home differently than he treated the dogs in his laboratory, but aren't they essentially the same dog? Along these lines, when people tell me they love animals but then abuse them or allow abuse to happen, I tell them that I'm glad that they don't love me.

Why do some people maintain these contradictory views? Because acknowledging animal minds and emotions would require them to change or give up other ideas that they are more attached to. As I like to say, I think that *Homo sapiens* could easily be reclassified as *Homo denialus* because we are so good at denying what is right in front of our senses when it suits our purposes.

HOW DOES EVOLUTION HELP US UNDERSTAND ANIMAL EMOTIONS?

The real question at hand is *why* emotions and consciousness have evolved, not *if* other animals are emotional, conscious beings. Our doubt and uncertainty relate to what purpose these attributes serve and what shape they take in other species, not if other species have them. This is made abundantly clear in the 2012 Cambridge Declaration on Consciousness, in which a consortium of scientists declared that "all mammals and birds" and most other creatures display consciousness and emotions. Meanwhile, *Animal Sentience: An International Journal on Animal Feeling* is dedicated to studies of animal hearts and minds; one recent essay focused on primitive organisms and the likelihood that they, too, have conscious experiences.[3]

Charles Darwin's idea about evolutionary continuity provides a good way to understand the evolution of emotions. Darwin argued that differences among species are differences in *degree* rather than *kind*. What this means is that differences among species are shades of gray, rather than black and white. In other words, if humans experience joy and grief, for example, so too do other animals. This does not mean that human joy and grief are the same as dog joy and grief, nor will these be the same as cat, mouse, or chimpanzee joy and grief, nor does it mean that the inner lives of individuals of the same species are necessarily the same. What it does mean is that if humans evolved to possess some capacity, this must have previously existed in some form in other animals. Particularly when it comes to useful adaptations, evolution isn't stingy; helpful traits get passed along and appear in many different species.

Consider, for instance, the discussion of self-awareness in chapter 6. Humans are highly visual mammals, and we have no problem recognizing ourselves in a mirror. Dogs may or may not be able to do this, but they live by smell, and so their preferred method of identifying others and themselves probably uses their noses. How might dogs experience self-awareness through smell? We probably will never really know, which is why humans often aren't the most useful template against which to compare other animals.[4]

ISN'T ATTRIBUTING EMOTIONS TO ANIMALS BEING ANTHROPOMORPHIC?

For a long time, whenever a scientist attributed emotions and intentions to animals, they were accused of being anthropomorphic. Still today, a few people come up to me and say, "Oh, you're being anthropomorphic." This charge is an easy way to dismiss all claims about the emotional lives of nonhuman animals. However, there really is no worry at all. Simply put, it's okay to be anthropomorphic. It's natural to do so, and critics are wrong to say we must never do it.

Nonhuman animals and human animals share many traits, including emotions. Thus, when we recognize and name emotions in other animals, we're not inserting something human into them. We are merely using human language to communicate what we observe and understand. Neurobiological studies support this point of view. It's certainly possible to project false understandings onto animals, but we cannot avoid using anthropomorphic or human language to describe other animals. What alternatives do critics suggest that might really help us come to a further understanding of animal cognition and animal emotions? As with my scientist colleague Bill, what I find is that there is often a double standard at work. Some critics will say, for example, that an elephant in a tiny cage in a zoo is happy, but when I, or others, say that she is unhappy, this is dismissed as anthropomorphism. It's self-serving double-talk to claim that animals can be happy but not unhappy.[5]

Along these lines, I have written about what I call *biocentric* anthropomorphism, and Gordon Burghardt has written about what he calls *critical* anthropomorphism.[6] What both of these ideas emphasize is that, when we use human language to describe what other animals are feeling, we need to do it carefully and take into account who the animals are. There is no substitute for using emotional language, unless we restrict ourselves to describing muscle contractions and neurons firing, descriptions that say nothing about what is actually happening or being felt. As Alexandra Horowitz and I have argued, it's possible to be "anthropomorphic" and still easily stay within the bounds of science.

ARE ANIMAL EMOTIONS "QUASI-EMOTIONS"?

The idea that dog joy or jealousy are "primordial forms" of emotion doesn't sit well with me. I know of no careful discussion of what a "primordial" emotion would look like, and the word usually is used to refer to something ancient, existing from the beginning of time. The implication is that the emotions of nonhuman animals are not as developed as those of humans. Similarly, some people use the prefixes "quasi-" or "proto-" to indicate some early or lesser form of an emotion, without providing a detailed account of what they mean, other than to imply that the animals aren't feeling something as deeply or richly as we do.

Some people also like to put quotation marks or scare quotes around such words as "love," "grief," "sadness," and "guilt" when they talk about the emotional lives of animals, or skeptics will use qualifiers like "sort of," as if these emotions are not real—as if only we have true emotions and other animals don't. There's simply no reason to use scare quotes or make these qualifications when talking or writing about animal emotions. There's no reason to assume that the emotions of animals aren't experienced as profoundly or as deeply as we experience our own emotions.

A personal example shows why it's so difficult to make comparisons, even among humans. My sisters and I grieved rather differently after my mother passed away, but the grief we each felt was profound. *Different from* does not mean *less than*. The use of words like "primordial" and the use of scare quotes cheapens what other animals are feeling—as if they're only acting "as if" they truly feel something. This is speciesist, since it elevates humans above other animals and presumes that, because animals experience emotions differently, those emotions must be less than ours.

All in all, based on detailed scientific research, there's no doubt that many animals experience rich and deep emotions. We must never forget that our emotions are the gifts of our ancestors, our nonhuman animal kin. We have feelings and so, too, do other animals.

In this book I frequently acknowledge what we don't know, but these reminders are intended to keep the door open on the cognitive, emotional, and moral capacities of other animals. We are constantly discovering "surprises," such as fish using gestural or referential communication to indicate the location of food to other fish, prairie dogs having communication systems that rival those of great apes, rats displaying regret, and mice, rats, and chickens displaying empathy. In fact, when we call these and other discoveries surprises, we are admitting that we didn't think fish or other animals could do these things in the first place. We reveal our negative assumptions, which were made before the necessary research had been conducted.

I suspect that many more surprises await us, as studies focus on identifying such emotions as jealousy, guilt, shame, envy, embarrassment, and so on in dogs and other nonhuman animals. The many good stories and anecdotes from both citizen scientists and renowned researchers indicate we still have much to learn.

The Basics: Dogs Feel Joy, Anger, Grief, Fear, and Pain

Most people accept that domestic dogs and other nonhuman animals experience a handful of basic emotions. These include joy, pleasure, happiness, love, anger, fear, grief, sadness, pain, suffering, anxiety, and depression. These emotions don't require self-awareness or a theory of mind in order to be felt.

As we've seen, many dogs love to play—it's a voluntary activity, they seek it out, and they play to exhaustion. It's highly likely that dogs and other mammals share the same neural circuits that underlie play in rats, who also laugh and like to be tickled. Recent research has also shown that mice can sense and feel the pain of other mice via olfactory cues.[7] We don't know yet if dogs can do this, but I hear many stories that strongly suggest that they can. My discussion of how play can break down in larger groups of dogs, perhaps because rapid mimicry and emotional contagion break down, might have something to say about empathy in dogs.

This discussion about empathy reminds me of a wonderful story by renowned author Elizabeth Marshall Thomas titled "A Friend in Need," which appeared in a book I edited called *The Smile of a Dolphin: Remarkable Accounts of Animal Emotions*, about a dog named Ruby who helped another dog, Wicket, cross a partly frozen stream. Wicket was afraid to cross on her own, and Ruby, who had already crossed the stream, went back to Wicket, greeted her, and after around ten unsuccessful attempts, convinced Wicket to follow her across the ice. Psychologist Stanley Coren remarks that it's hard to imagine that animals as social and intelligent as dogs would not show empathy.[8] I agree. Nevertheless, there is really still so much to learn.

Finally, on the subject of basic emotions, dogs also suffer from a wide variety of psychological disorders, including posttraumatic stress disorder, anxiety, and obsessive-compulsive disorder. There's a large literature on this aspect of dog emotions. Nicholas Dodman's book *Pets on the Couch: Neurotic Dogs, Compulsive Cats, Anxious Birds, and the New Science of Animal Psychiatry* is an excellent review of this field of study. In a world in which humans are getting busier and busier by the second, it seems we must pay careful attention to how dogs (and other animals) respond to the stress that their human companions are experiencing.

More Complex Emotions: Jealousy, Guilt, Shame, Embarrassment, Pride, and Compassion

Beyond the "basic emotions" described above, we simply don't know yet whether dogs are cognitively sophisticated enough to experience all of the so-called higher or more complex emotions, like jealousy, guilt, shame, embarrassment, pride, and empathy. Based on existing data, it's likely that dogs do experience some of these emotions. However, while I have discussed empathy (just above) and the presence of some type of moral awareness—of fairness, justice, and right/wrong (in chapter 3)—and will discuss guilt shortly, it nevertheless may be that dogs don't experience some of these complex emotions or that they don't experience certain other feelings that humans do, such as spirituality. At the same time, no evidence yet confirms that dogs don't or can't experience these more complex emotions. Any claims that dogs don't experience one of these is premature at best and may turn out to be flat-out wrong.[9]

So-called higher emotions are usually distinguished by requiring self-awareness and/or a theory of mind in order to be experienced. As it's not possible to look closely at all of these emotions, in the spirit of myth busting, let's consider jealousy and guilt, since arguing that dogs have the capacity to experience these two emotions seems problematic for some people. In some cases, for instance, people deny dogs feel guilt because, as with considerations of dominance, they fear it'll be used against dogs.

As I've said, I'm all for keeping to the data, but I don't accept using lack of data on a specific topic as an excuse for bad treatment. People with an agenda will often claim that dogs don't experience jealousy or guilt or make some other strong statement about the absence of certain emotions in dogs and other animals. If I respond that we really don't know, I mean we can't make categorical claims one way or the other. I don't know anyone who would say that dogs don't experience a wide range of emotions. How wide remains to be seen. This is why I always find it alarming when people are so certain dogs do *not* feel particular emotions, absent any data to support this contention.

DO DOGS FEEL JEALOUSY?

A story my friend Christy Orris told me about her dog, Anna, and her neighbor's dog, Daisy, is one of many I've heard on the topic of jealousy:

> Anna and Daisy have been best friends since they were crazy puppies running wild all over our neighborhood. Anna is our good-natured golden retriever—aren't they all?—and Daisy lives next door. Daisy is a cheerful medium-sized dog with a huge personality. I love her! She makes me smile whenever I see her. This should not cause a problem, but it has. Anna has become aggressively jealous with Daisy when I am around. Instead of the playful greeting they usually give each other, Anna exhibits domineering behavior and makes Daisy roll over on her back while she stands above her. I now try to ignore Daisy when I see her so Anna does not get jealous and behave meanly to her best friend. I have asked Daisy's owners if they see Anna's aggressive behavior when I am not around. They say they have never seen it.[10]

It often seems that not a day goes by at a dog park without someone telling me how jealous their dog is when they give attention to another dog or to another human. I often hear something like, "Josie always pushes herself between Jack and me"; "Whenever I give Mervin attention, Pluto pushes him aside and leans into me"; and "If I rub Smoochie's belly, Diablo sidles in for a rub." Pretty much anyone who's lived with a dog has seen what we'd call jealousy.

I know that these anecdotes aren't hard scientific data, but we need to pay careful attention when different people tell the same story over and over again. These stories can and should motivate systematic research. As Stanley Coren writes: "It is strange that behavioral scientists often ignore such common observations. It is well accepted that dogs have a broad range of emotions. Dogs are certainly social animals, and jealousy and envy are triggered by social interactions. Dogs also have the same hormone, oxytocin, which has been shown to be involved in both expressions of love and jealousy in experiments involving humans."[11]

In her book *The Secret Language of Dogs*, Victoria Stilwell observes that "the canine expression of jealousy mirrors that of a human. This seems to explain canine behavior that is pushy."[12] And dog expert Patricia McConnell, as quoted earlier in this chapter, also claims dogs do, indeed, feel jealousy.

As it turns out, an important and carefully done formal scientific study directly supports this claim. We now have data showing that dogs know when they've been dissed and they don't like it one bit.[13] The 2014 study "Jealousy in Dogs," by Christine Harris and Caroline Prouvost of the University of California, San Diego, shows that dogs do experience jealousy in the way humans define it, namely, resentment of another individual's success, advantage, or something another individual does or possesses. As it says in the abstract for this study:

It is commonly assumed that jealousy is unique to humans, partially because of the complex cognitions often involved in this emotion. However, from a functional perspective, one might expect that an emotion that evolved to protect social bonds from interlopers might exist in other social species, particularly one as cognitively sophisticated as the dog. The current experiment adapted a paradigm from human infant studies to examine jealousy in domestic dogs. We found that dogs exhibited significantly more jealous behaviors (e.g., snapping, getting between the owner and object, pushing/touching the object/owner) when their owners displayed affectionate behaviors towards what appeared to be another dog as compared to nonsocial objects.[14]

Harris and Prouvost studied jealousy in thirty-six dogs using a test similar to one used to study jealousy in human infants. The dogs were videotaped while their owners ignored them and did something else: either interacting with a stuffed dog that could bark and wag its tail, interacting with a novel object (a jack-o'-lantern pail), or reading a children's book aloud. The dogs' owners were unaware of the goal of the study.

As the abstract describes, dogs displayed plenty of jealous-seeming behaviors when owners showed affection to the stuffed dog, but far fewer when they showed attention to inanimate objects. And, as the authors conclude, we might expect that jealousy occurs in social species other than humans—so it shouldn't surprise us to be able to find it and recognize it in dogs. I'm sure I'm not alone in having seen similar behavior patterns among wild coyotes and wolves, and I feel certain that other researchers have seen similar behavior patterns in other wild animals. Furthermore, I like that this team adopted an experimental design that is used on prelinguistic humans, since we must also infer what human babies are feeling. By observing behaviors, we can draw inferences about what nonhuman animals and prelinguistic youngsters are feeling, and when we see similar patterns of behavior, we can infer a common underlying emotion.

Of course, much more comparative research is needed to confirm this beyond doubt, but there is no reason to think we won't be able to do so.

DO DOGS FEEL GUILT?

When it comes to dogs, if dominance is the D word, then guilt is the G word: it inspires lots of denials and controversy. On the one hand, some people make misleading claims that dogs cannot feel guilt, but, on the other hand, as far as I can determine, and I've asked other researchers, there are no studies that show that "dogs don't feel or display guilt" (as a veterinary scientist once claimed). Nothing has disproven this possibility, so the worst we can say is that we don't know.

Then again, when I insist that we really *don't* know if dogs feel guilt, other people get frustrated with me.[15] They think it sounds like a cop out, and they accuse me of being "too scientific." They say things like, "You know dogs feel guilt, but you're too uptight as a scientist to say they do. Come on, get out of the stifling ivory tower. I appreciate your scientific caution, but there is no way dogs, like other mammals, including us, don't feel guilt."

Many people clearly believe dogs are capable of feeling a sense of guilt. Research by Dr. Paul Morris and his colleagues shows that more than 75 percent of dog owners believe their dogs feel guilty, and 81 percent think that their dogs experience jealousy.[16] And maybe dogs do feel guilt, but there is evidence that people may also sometimes misread their dogs and assume guilt when it doesn't exist.

In 2009, Dr. Alexandra Horowitz published a study called "Disambiguating the 'Guilty Look': Salient Prompts to a Familiar Dog Behaviour" that looked at whether humans are being anthropomorphic when they believe they are detecting guilt in dogs. This study has since been misrepresented and misunderstood as a study of whether dogs actually feel guilt.[17] Rather, Dr. Horowitz was studying us and how dogs react to our cues, and she discovered that *we are not very good at detecting guilt*. In the study, dogs tended to act guilty if their human accused them of misbehaving for having eaten a forbidden treat, even if the dog hadn't actually eaten the treat or misbehaved. Meanwhile, dogs who ate the treat and weren't scolded didn't act guilty at all. A dog's "guilty look" seemed to correspond to how we treated them, not to their self-perception of doing something wrong. In response to an essay of mine about the misrepresentations of this study, Dr. Horowitz wrote to me, saying:

> Thanks so much for correcting the ubiquitous error about my study, some years back, which found that dogs showed a more "guilty look" when a person scolded or was about to scold them, not when the dog actually disobeyed the person's request not to eat a treat. Clearly, what the results indicated was that the "guilty look" did not most often arise when a dog was actually "guilty."

My study was decidedly NOT about whether dogs "feel guilt" or not. (Indeed, I'd love to know . . . but this behavior didn't turn out to indicate yay or nay.)[18]

That said, the fact that dogs have a recognizable guilty look might be partial evidence that they are in fact capable of feeling genuine guilt, but since their canine moral compass is different than ours, they may not feel guilty about the things we do or about the things we think they should (like stealing a treat).

Indeed, this is why some people wish that, like dominance, we could simply deny that dogs feel guilt, since they fear it is sometimes used against them. In 2016, John Bradshaw wrote to me:

> Regarding Alexandra [Horowitz]'s "guilt" study, I guess I'm mainly coming from a welfare perspective. She showed that many owners routinely punish their dogs based on a misinterpretation of their dog's body language. More generally, I'm concerned that overestimation of dogs' cognitive capacities—i.e., always giving them the benefit of the doubt—plays straight into the hands of those who preach that dogs are conniving little so-and-so's who are constantly trying to "dominate" their owners and can only be dissuaded from doing so by inflicting pain. So while attributing rich cognitive and emotional lives to elephants (for example) may make people more inclined to donate to conservation charities, doing the same to dogs may provide the very same people with an excuse to hurt them.[19]

It's essential not to let the science or a lack thereof become a justification for abuse or neglect. There's absolutely no reason to embellish the abilities of dogs or other animals by ascribing to them more capacity for feeling more than they actually have. Meanwhile, researchers and others are responsible for presenting data accurately and for being clear when they're representing beliefs rather than facts. Of course, as research continues, it's highly likely that yesterday's facts will have to be fine-tuned because dogs and other animals are such highly variable individuals. But isn't this why science is so exciting? Isn't this why we love to learn about dogs? Just when we think we know it all, it's clear we don't.

The Grammar of Tail Wagging

How do dogs communicate or express their rich and deep emotional lives? One obvious way is with their tails. Dog tails are amazing appendages. They come in all shapes, girths, and lengths. Like the nose, tails are fascinating pieces of work—wonderful, beautiful adaptations—and they can be a source of both whimsy (dogs love to chase their tails) and destruction: I've had many occasions when my dog's tail knocked over some good wine or single-malt scotch. Tails can also disperse a lovely anal gland scent. In 1947, Swiss ethologist Rudolph Schenkel published an extremely important study called "Expression Studies on Wolves," in which he discussed how wolves express their emotions, including how they use their tails.[20] This study provides an interesting perspective on the latest dog research because, not surprisingly, there are many similarities between the way wolves and dogs use their tails.

A tail can be an excellent barometer of what a dog is feeling, and they are often used in combination with a whole host of other signals—gait, ear position, body posture, facial expressions, vocalizations, and odors, for example. Taken together, these form composite signals that carry a lot of information about what a dog is thinking and feeling.

I never thought much about what would happen if a dog lost his or her tail due to an accident. My friend Marisa Ware told me her dog Echo had this happen to her. As a result, Echo changed the way she communicated with dogs and people by using her body and ears to compensate for the loss of her tail: "Mainly I notice that Echo relies more on her ears to express her feelings—particularly if she is excited to see someone, instead of wagging her tail, she puts her ears very far back and will almost wiggle them. She also has developed this move where she gives a little hop and wiggles her butt very quickly if she is excited to see someone. It's not a typical butt wiggle that I've seen border collies or other dogs with docked tails do—it's quite different, and she never did it before losing her tail."[21]

Stanley Coren tells a similar story about a dog who lost her tail after a collision with a motorcycle. He notes that other dogs seemed unable to understand what she was trying to communicate after her tail had to be amputated.[22]

The stories of Echo and the other dog made me think that we really don't know if dogs with no tails use different ways to communicate than dogs with tails. I also wonder about the effects of tail docking and how it might deprive a dog of her or his ability to effectively communicate with other dogs and with humans. Docking takes away a significant mode of communication. We already know from research, for instance, that a longer tail is more effective at sending a message than a shorter tail.[23]

So what messages are dogs sending with their tails? Can we learn to "read" this emotional grammar? A classic 2011 research paper called "Behavioural Responses of Dogs to Asymmetrical Tail Wagging of a Robotic Dog" discovered what has become something of a truism: when a dog's tail wags to the right, it's a sign of positive emotions, while a left-wagging tail is expressing negative emotion.[24]

This discovery begs another question concerning a dog's telltale tail that needs more detailed study: What do dogs understand when they see another dog wag his or her tail? Do they know that a dog wagging their tail to the right is feeling good and a dog wagging their tail to the left is feeling a negative emotion? Some of the same researchers in the tail-wagging study have recently discovered that dogs do, in fact, draw such conclusions. A *New York Times* story about this research, called "A Dog's Tail Wag Says a Lot, to Other Dogs," reported that, "when watching a tail wag to the left, the dogs showed signs of anxiety, like a higher heart rate. When the tail went in the opposite direction, they remained calm."[25]

Are dogs really talking to one another with their tails? According to the same account in the *New York Times*, "It is unlikely that dogs are wagging their tails to communicate with one another. 'This is something that could be explained in quite a mechanistic way,'" said researcher Giorgio Vallortigara, a neuroscientist at the University of Trento in Italy. "'It's simply a byproduct of the asymmetry of the brain,' and dogs learn to recognize the pattern over time."

Perhaps that's true. Perhaps a tail doesn't wag to convey an intentional message, but it simply expresses whatever is being felt. As I say, tails are fascinating appendages, and there still is much to learn about how dogs use them in different contexts, how dogs read the movements of other dogs' tails, and how they use the information they glean. Dr. Stanley Coren provides a useful guide about what we know about tail wagging.

> A slight wag, with each swing of only small breadth, is usually seen during greetings as a tentative "Hello there," or a hopeful "I'm here."
>
> A broad wag is friendly: "I am not challenging or threatening you." This can also mean: "I'm pleased." This is the closest to the popular concept of the happiness wag, especially if the tail seems to drag the hips with it.
>
> A slow wag with the tail at *half-mast* is less social than most other tail signals. Generally speaking, slow wags with the tail in neither a particularly dominant (high) nor a submissive (low) position are signs of insecurity.
>
> Tiny, high-speed movements that give the impression of the tail vibrating are signs the dog is about to do something, usually run or fight. If the tail is held high while vibrating, it is most likely an active threat.[26]

Barking and Growling: Something to Talk About

Dogs obviously express their emotions, motivations, and intentions through a variety of vocalizations. What kinds of sounds do dogs produce and how many? We've all heard barking, howling, growling, yelping, whimpering, whining, and creative combinations thereof. Because researchers categorize sounds and other behavior patterns differently, it's impossible to say whether dogs produce ten, twelve, or even more different sounds. The facial structure of a dog might also influence what vocalizations sound like, and dogs often mix different sounds together. These distinctions obviously make a difference in what a dog is trying to communicate, and this makes studying vocalizations more difficult because of the complexity of sounds and the variety of combinations.[27]

I'm always surprised that we don't know more about the different common sounds dogs make and why they make them. Some dogs are barkers, whereas others don't bark much at all. And we really don't know if dogs *always* bark for a reason or if sometimes they do it just for the hell of it because it feels good.[28]

That said, dogs seem to understand what other dogs are saying, and humans are quite adept at understanding the emotional content of dog barks. This might be important for effective communication between dogs and humans.[29] Dog researcher Julie Hecht says: "The takeaway message is that barking is a nuanced and flexible behavior, and relationships can grow by paying attention to what your dog's vocalizations mean."[30]

According to Stanley Coren, pitch, duration, and frequency (how often the vocalization occurs) are important to consider when we're trying to figure out what a dog is saying.[31] Low-pitched growls may say the dog is angry; they may signal a threat, declaring that if you come closer, I could get rather nasty. High-pitched sounds such as whimpering may be saying it's safe to approach. Dr. Coren also notes that the longer a sound, the more likely the dog has made a conscious decision to vocalize. A shorter vocalization such as a growl, for example, may indicate fear. Sounds that are uttered frequently in succession may indicate excitement and a sense of urgency, whereas sounds that are spaced out may mean that the dog is less excited.

All in all, it's essential to respect what a dog is saying, or trying to say, and punishing a dog for growling is ill-advised. It's essential to know what is stressing the dog and come up with solutions to remove the stressors.[32] Growling can also occur when dogs are playing and having a good old time. As with so many dog behaviors, one sound probably doesn't mean the same thing all the time; always consider the context.

The bottom line is that lots more research needs to be done to come to a fuller understanding of the sounds dogs make and why they utter them, and it's exciting to think that, with more detailed studies, we'll come to better understand what dogs are trying to tell us.

Measuring Emotions: The Human-Dog Bond

We all know that dogs and humans form close and enduring bonds. These relationships are extremely special to many of us, and they often seem important to dogs, but how can we really know? In fact, we can learn about the nature of these bonds not only by observing dogs but also by studying how their brains work. This is useful information. According to one study, "Indicators of mutual physiological changes during positive interaction between dog lovers and dogs may contribute to a better understanding of the human-animal bond in veterinary practice."[33]

For instance, in a study called "Dogs Show Left Facial Lateralization upon Reunion with Their Owners," Miho Nagasawa and his colleagues found that a dog's left eyebrow moved more when the owner was present, but there was no difference in how eyebrows moved when the dogs saw attractive toys.[34] The researchers suggest that this reflects the dog's attachment to their human.

We also can learn a lot about dog brains by using neuroimaging.[35] For example, researchers Gregory Berns and his colleagues at Emory University in Atlanta, Georgia, studied twelve awake and unrestrained dogs who were trained to cooperate with these studies and voluntarily enter a functional magnetic resonance imaging (fMRI) machine. Berns discovered that the dogs responded more strongly to scents of familiar humans, even to those who were not their primary caregivers, compared to the scents of other dogs, even familiar dogs. Conversely, dogs responded more strongly to the sounds of other dogs than to the sounds made by humans.[36] However, human sounds are important to dogs, and we also know that when people use baby talk with dogs, and they do this very often, puppies are much more responsive than older dogs.[37]

In addition, Berns and his colleagues discovered that, when dogs respond to people they know, they use the caudate nucleus, the part of the brain that humans likewise use when they anticipate things they enjoy, such as food, love, and money.[38]

These results, when taken together, highlight the incredible importance of humans in the social lives of dogs, a fact we've known for a long, long time. Indeed, Duke University dog researchers Evan MacLean and Brian Hare claim that dogs hijacked the human bonding pathway as they became "embedded in human societies."[39] However, no matter how tight the bonds between humans and dogs can be, Yale University's Laurie Santos discovered that dogs ignore bad advice that human children will follow.[40] In a study conducted by Santos and fellow researchers, for instance, dogs who were shown that in order to open a puzzle box to get a treat it was necessary to move a lever and then lift the box top off were able to ignore the lever once they discovered it was actually irrelevant—unlike young children, who, in a related study, continued to use the lever even after it was obvious it served no function.

Researchers are increasingly using fMRI, also called awake imaging, to study animal emotions, and these studies reveal a lot about what dogs think and feel. In addition to the pioneering research by Gregory Berns and his colleagues in this area, a group of researchers at Eötvös Loránd University in Budapest have also published fascinating studies using this kind of imaging.

One study published by Attila Andics and his colleagues titled "Neural Mechanisms for Lexical Processing in Dogs" looked at how dogs process speech.[41] I've often wondered if dogs understand the conflicting or contradictory messages they frequently hear. When humans rub their heads or bellies, they say things like, "I love my dog but she's too fat," and "You're so beautiful, but you're so dumb."

To perform this study, thirteen dogs of four breeds were trained to lie still in an fMRI brain scanner. Then they listened to a series of words that were previously recorded by their trainers, so they were listening to a familiar voice. The words were a mix of praise and neutral phrases, and they were spoken with a mix of positive and negative intonations, which sometimes didn't match the meaning of the words themselves.[42] What the researchers found was that canines used their left hemisphere to process words and the right hemisphere to process intonation, just like humans do, and then they combined them to understand what was said. The reward centers of the dogs' brains only lit up when both the spoken tone and the meaning of the words reflected praise.

In other words, dogs notice both what we say and how we say it. As we know, dogs learn many human words, but even when dogs don't understand language, our meaning comes through in our voices. While it remains an open question about what dogs understand of our conflicting messages, my guess is that they understand us better than we think. And they often pick up on our personal quirks.

For instance, it's a cliché that the personalities of dogs and humans often come to mirror one another, and yet there may be some truth to this. When I've been able to spend a good deal of time around a particular dog and their human, I'm often struck by how similar they are. I've casually noticed that anxious and pessimistic people seem to have anxious and pessimistic dogs, while calm people seem to have calm dogs. People are often surprised when they notice this themselves, saying something like, "Gosh, my dog is just like me!" While it's not that surprising to me, given how sensitive dogs are to us, there hasn't been much research exploring this phenomenon. However, in a 2017 study, a team of researchers discovered that, by measuring levels of the stress hormone cortisol, "dogs are not only able to recognize human emotion but also adopt certain personality traits of their owners. . . . Pet owners who are pessimistic and prone to anxiety have dogs who also exhibit these qualities."[43] For instance, the study found that dogs of anxiety-prone owners don't cope well with threats and stressful situations. Perhaps obviously, they also found that humans have more of an influence on their dog's personality than dogs do on their human's.

There's much more I could talk about on the topic of dogs and emotions, which clearly shows that current research—including noninvasive neuroimaging studies where dogs can choose to partake—supports a lot of what many of us already believe about the cognitive, emotional, and moral lives of dogs. Certainly, we know enough right now, today, to know that dogs are smart and sentient beings and should be treated with respect and dignity. They should not be dominated nor shamed into serving us with no regard for who they truly are. Dog trainers need to stay abreast of the latest research, and many do. They, too, are a dog's guardian, just like the human or humans with whom a dog lives. Of course, there's still a lot to learn, and sometimes the best place to learn it is at the dog park.

EIGHT

Dog Park Confidential

||||||||||||||||||||||||||||||||||||||||||||||||||||||||||||||||||||||||||||||||||||||||||||||||||||||||||||||||||||||||||||

Early one gorgeous morning at the dog park, a woman sipping coffee and fiddling with her mobile phone came up to me and said, "Oh lord, my best friend has no idea how she has revealed who she truly is by adopting Miranda. I, I . . . just can't take her anymore, and I wish the best for Miranda. How could she have kept her secrets so hidden? How could I have been her friend for so long?"

As the woman explained, she felt she could no longer be friends with her friend because of how she was treating a dog she'd just adopted. I said something like, "Oh, that's very interesting," hoping to wiggle out of that one-sided conversation—it was TMI! (too much information)—but my strategy didn't work. After about five minutes, I was at my wit's end with the amount of personal detail she was spewing forth, when someone who had been watching came up to me and asked a question about dog play. Thank goodness! I used this polite excuse to smoothly slide away.

I've experienced every imaginable variation on this scene during my many years visiting dog parks. People freely talk about other people, especially the regulars, who take ownership of particular parking spaces and chairs, and some of whom get upset when other visitors have the gall to occupy their chosen places.

Sometimes within a few seconds of people having met me, they talk to me as if I'm their best friend, and they occasionally open up to me about deeply personal laments, as if I'm their confidant or even their counselor. I just listen and never say anything. Personally, I come for the dogs, but I've learned that, especially at dog parks, a dog's human companion always comes along. Maybe that's for the best. As I've said, dogs play an integral role in human interactions. Dogs are social catalysts who make connections and stimulate conversations among people who were, moments before, strangers. I think of dogs as a social lubricant who seem to be able to absorb negative energy when it arises between humans. They foster cooperation and trust in people. Dog parks are never just about the dogs. Many people freely offer advice to others, solicited or not, and make assumptions about who people are based on who their dog is and how they treat them.

There's no predicting what people will say. Within seconds of meeting someone she didn't know, one of my friends was told that she had severe psychological problems and that she and her dog needed to use flower essences to fix the situation. Another person told me his life story and how he met his wife when he helped her bag some poop, a gesture for which she remains ever grateful. People often debate good training versus bad training and discuss end-of-life decisions for older, sickly dogs. People support one another and learn a lot about how to make these incredibly difficult choices. The stories go on and on, and I've learned a lot from carefully listening, such as how much kindness and compassion people feel. I often feel that if people spent more time at dog parks, the world would be a better and more peaceful place.

|||||||||||||||||||||||||||||||||||||||||||||||||||||||||||||||||||||||||||||||||||||||||||||||||||||||||||

Dog parks can play a surprisingly important role in our lives, in addition to all the benefits they provide for dogs. Much as in the story I tell in the preface, about the two boys I met watching squirrels in Central Park, people can easily rewild at dog parks and reconnect with nature and other animals, including a myriad of dogs and the small mammals, birds, and others who live there.[1] University of Pennsylvania professor and dog expert James Serpell sees dogs as mediators in three principle areas, namely, as social lubricants (catalysts of social relationships between people), social ambassadors (a moral link with other animals and nature in general), and the animal within (a sort of unconscious connection with other animals and nature).[2]

For some people, their visit to a dog park, I'm told, comprises a large percentage of their interactions with other humans. Some people spend upward of one to two hours at dog parks each and every day—drinking coffee, texting, chatting on the phone, hanging out with friends, meeting new people and dogs, and having a good old time with everyone, dog and human. In many instances, when I see the care and attention people lavish on their companions, I wish I were one of their dogs—though surely not always. Dog parks are not perfect places, and people are not perfect, either. At times, I wish people spent more time watching their dogs and were more focused on their canine friend's needs. Some people visit a dog park more for themselves than for their dog, and it shows. Neglectful people and frustrated, unmanaged dogs tend to be at the center of dog park conflicts and troubles when they arise.

Nevertheless, I love going to dog parks, even when I don't have a dog with me. Dog parks are a fascinating, recent, and growing cultural phenomenon. I go rather often to what I call my field sites, for that's what they are, to study play behavior and other aspects of dog behavior, such as urination and marking patterns, greeting patterns, and social interactions, including how and why dogs enter, become part of, and leave short-term and long-term groups and social relationships.

I also study human-dog interactions, which often reveals a lot about humans. For example, people often express to me how happy they are to let their dogs run free and be with other dogs at the dog park. People assume that dog parks visits are all good for their companion. But dog parks aren't always as free and relaxing for dogs as people think, and sometimes without realizing it, people themselves can undermine their dog's freedom: constantly calling them back, telling them not to sniff this or that, and interrupting interactions and play when it seems too rough. You call this free?

So in addition to exploring dog park ethology, I also want to ask readers to examine whether their dog park experiences are fulfilling their good intentions.

Dog Parks: The Good, the Bad, and the Ugly

Dog parks are the fastest-growing part of city parks.[3] There were 569 off-leash dog parks in the hundred largest U.S. cities in 2010, a 34 percent jump in five years, while overall parks increased only 3 percent.[4] Some dog parks also are making accommodations for special-needs individuals, and some cities are offering places for dogs and humans to interact that are in between homes and dog parks.[5]

You might say that dog parks have never been more popular, and they are becoming better and better places to be. A quick ask of people at dogs parks around Boulder showed that more than 95 percent of people loved them for the obvious reasons: they are safe places for dogs to run off leash and play with friends, and people can chat as their dogs have fun. Most people find dog parks a relaxing experience.[6] In addition, I love when I see local trainers at dog parks, since they get to see dogs outside of the context of training. As I mentioned earlier, dog parks can be great classrooms for learning about basic principles of animal behavior and evolutionary biology. These Cliff Notes–like discussions benefit people as well as their dogs.

Still, I want to consider some of the negative aspects of dog parks. First, while most of the dogs I've known love to go to dog parks, some dogs do not enjoy them, and it is essential to respect a dog's decision if he or she would rather not join in the fun. The dog park environment is not fun for them. A young man once told me, "I know my dog doesn't like dog parks. She gets all sorts of nervous and resists leaving the car, but she just has to get used to it because I like going." This is a classic example of undermining otherwise good intentions: Why go to a dog park if it doesn't benefit the dog?

I have to admit, I was extremely surprised to discover that a good number of people don't like dog parks at all. Sometimes this is a safety concern, since conflicts among dogs can occasionally— though very rarely—escalate into fighting, which can lead to injury for dogs and people.[7] Personally, I don't find dog parks to be unsafe environments, but we don't have any empirical studies that focus on this question. More often, though, it's more a matter of dog park etiquette and of the social environment that turns some people off to dog parks.[8] Many people simply don't like the way other people and their dogs behave at dog parks.[9] I don't want to belabor dog park courtesy here, since there's a good deal of information about this online.[10] However, I do want to note that often these issues are a people problem for which the dog can get blamed. When people complain about a dog, it's really their human companion who's at fault, leaving the dog to get the short end of the leash, so to speak.

The same sort of issue arises when dogs are walked along public trails and their people throw tennis balls and Frisbees for them to chase off trail.[11] When dogs and humans are sharing space, it's essential to remember that not all people like dogs. Years ago, I was walking a large, some might say zaftig, malamute on a loose leash. I saw a man approaching us, and when he saw us, he began crossing the street, obviously afraid of the dog. I stopped and said, "There's no problem. He doesn't bite," Unfettered, the man asked me, "Well, how does he eat?" I told him that was a good question, and we went on to have a nice conversation during which he told me that he had been nipped by a dog when he was young, and now he was afraid of them. My mother also was bitten when she was young, which is why I grew up with a goldfish with whom I had numerous conversations, rather than a dog. It's essential to respect the fact that not all people love or even like dogs.

However, in dog parks, the more common issue is frustration with how people are managing their particular dog. In an email to me, Elise Gatti noted that a good deal of conflict comes down to different forms of "dog parenting"—some humans are very controlling and protective helicopter guardians and others are more relaxed about their dog's behavior.[12] I will address this more below.

In addition, each dog park has a unique identity that reflects the culture and attitudes of the locals or regulars. Even within a small city like Boulder, there are differences among dog parks. Without mentioning names, one I go to often is open to newcomers, both dogs and humans, but another one I frequent is, as one of my friends puts it, "a bit more uppity." When my friend went to the latter park for the first time, people became concerned at seeing a newcomer and asked her if she lived in Boulder! The same thing happened to another friend who went to this same park because he wanted a change of scenery for him and his dog.

Finally, I've had cause, though only rarely, to marvel at just how inconsiderate a few people can be. This is not related to dog park etiquette but rather to basic human courtesy. On a few occasions, I've been asked by someone why their own dog has bad manners when they themselves are rather inconsiderate. I'm always tempted to quip, "Have you looked in the mirror?"—as we saw last chapter, it's not an accident when people and their canine companions reflect one another—but rather than get involved, I redirect their attention to some interesting dog-dog interaction happening elsewhere.

Dog Park Ethology: Studies of Dog Parks

Not only are dogs an ethologist's dream, but so too are dog parks. As I say, I find dog parks to be a gold mine of information about all sorts of behavior. In addition, dog parks are fertile places for citizen science, such as the work that one of my students, Alexandra Weber, conducted on whether familiar and unfamiliar dogs play differently. I always encourage people to become ethologists in a dog park, and one good focus for study is what Jessica Pierce and I call "the ethology of freedom" in our book *The Animals' Agenda*. At the dog park, simply select a focal dog and see how much time they spend on their own (or with other dogs) without being interrupted by their own or another human. When I do this, I'm often pretty surprised by just how tethered some "free" dogs actually are at dog parks. (For more on becoming an ethologist, turn to the appendix.)

However, there are an increasing number of formal scientific studies set in dog parks. From a research perspective, dog parks are sometimes criticized as "too uncontrolled." With so much going on, and so many variables, some researchers question whether you can accurately study, for example, whether dogs follow human gazing or pointing and how well, or if dogs have a theory of mind. But let's face it, some laboratory studies are also rather uncontrolled, mainly because dogs are such a mixed bag of participants (as might be the researchers themselves). Watching animals in their "natural habitats"—and within certain limits, dog parks might qualify as such—has shed much light on various aspects of behavior that are difficult to study with animals in captivity or in other more controlled environs. Although many lab studies of dogs are likely more controlled than those conducted on free-running dogs, controlled studies can also limit what dogs do. Many people have seen behavior patterns that warrant reinvestigation in more ecologically relevant situations.

As a graduate student at Memorial University in St. John's, Newfoundland, Melissa Howse did an important study called "Exploring the Social Behaviour of Domestic Dogs (*Canis familiaris*) in a Public Off-leash Dog Park." Previously, she notes, there had only been six similar studies, plus one conducted later at the same place, called Quidi Vidi Dog Park, by Lydia Ottenheimer Carrier and her colleagues, "Exploring the Dog Park: Relationships between Social Behaviours, Personality and Cortisol in Companion Dogs."[13]

Using focal animal sampling and video recordings of 220 dogs, of whom sixty-nine were included in her focal sample, Howse discovered that in the first four hundred seconds following entry into the dog park, "on average, focal dogs spent 50% of their time alone, nearly 40% with other dogs and 11% in other activities; time with dogs decreased and time alone increased over the first six minutes. Some behaviours were very frequent (i.e., more than 90% of focal dogs initiated and received snout-muzzle contact to the anogenital and head areas), while others were rare (i.e., 9% and 12% of focal dogs initiated and received lunge approaches, respectively). Dog density and focal dog age, sex, neuter status, and size were found to influence some behavioural variables."[14]

All in all, Howse learned that sex and age influenced social behavior, and the dog's size was also important. She found that older dogs generally spent more time alone, and older females spent the least amount of time interacting exclusively with other dogs compared to all other sex/age combinations. There was also a good deal of mutual chasing; males eliminated (peed and pooped) more than females; and older dogs eliminated more than younger dogs. Smaller dogs were also more likely than larger dogs to receive running/leaping approaches from other dogs.

Consistent with other studies in dogs parks, Howse never observed serious aggression, observing that, "indeed, aggression in dog parks may be unlikely[,] due to the personality characteristics of dogs brought by owners to the dog park, owner intervention, and/or other factors. Thus, canine aggression may be better studied in other contexts where it is more likely to occur (i.e., multi-dog households, feral groups)."[15]

Another aspect of Howse's study is that her data differ from those of another project conducted at the same dog park after she completed her observations. For example, Howse observed that play bows were initiated by 23 percent of the focal dogs within the first four hundred seconds of entry into the dog park. In the other study conducted at the same dog park, 51 percent of focal dogs used play bows over twenty minutes, a time period three times longer. It wouldn't be surprising that the rate at which dogs use play bows changes over the course of a visit to a dog park. This would be a wonderful topic for future studies. I wonder if dogs use play bows more when they first arrive at a dog park, when they try to play with an unfamiliar dog or with a dog they don't know well, or when they first begin playing to establish a "play mood." Then, when play is in the air, they may use bows less frequently. I discovered that play bows are more stereotyped when they are first used to initiate play than when they are used after dogs, coyotes, and wolves are already playing.[16]

Once again, when we begin talking about *the* behavior of *the* dog at *the* dog park, we soon see that we can't make general statements with any reliability. Howse explained that some of the differences between her study and the other one done at the same dog park could be due to differences in observation durations, dog groupings, and definitions of dog-dog activities.

The stress a dog is experiencing may also be a factor in his or her behavior at dog parks, and this also is important to consider when comparing results among different studies. For example, in a study done at the same dog park as Howse's study, Lydia Carrier and her colleagues discovered that "cortisol was correlated with dog park visit frequency, such that dogs which visited the park least often had higher cortisol levels." Cortisol is a measure of stress levels, and these data indicate that when we study the behavior of dogs at dog parks, we need to pay attention to how frequently they visit and possibly who's already there. Of course, an individual dog's familiarity with his or her surroundings as well as with the dogs who are there can also influence their behavior, including how they play and if they try to run the show or hang out on the periphery.

Clearly, we need much more research into what dogs do at dog parks, with particular focus on *individual* differences. Howse concluded: "Given the number of questions generated by the present work, and that dog park studies remain scarce, it is obvious that observations of dogs in dog parks should be greatly increased. Dog parks hold much potential for answering questions about intraspecific sociality of companion dogs, which will help us to better understand dogs as complete and unique social beings, and possibly aid in our ability to protect or improve their welfare." I couldn't agree more.

Dog Park Managers: Of Leashes, Fences, and Freedom

Anyone who's visited a dog park knows that there's clearly a lot happening all at once, and both humans and dogs are involved. Everyone influences everyone else. Taryn Graham and Troy Glover, in a paper titled "On the Fence: Dog Parks in the (Un)Leashing of Community and Social Capital," write that "findings from this study suggest owners navigate parks through their pet. How dogs behave toward other dogs and toward people influence their owners' social networks and access to resources. Positive interactions provide opportunities for relationships and communities of interest to form, where sources of support, information sharing, collective action, and conformity can be mobilized. Negative perceptions of dogs, however, often extend towards owners, thereby leading to tension, judgment, and sometimes even exclusion from social networks or public space altogether."[17]

In other words, no one is really "in charge" at the dog park. All the relationships are negotiated on the fly, and each alignment or conflict can affect every other type of relationship, whether dog-dog, dog-human, or human-human.

In his essay titled "Situated Activities in a Dog Park: Identity and Conflict in Human-Animal Space," Sonoma State University's Patrick Jackson captures this in his discussion of how humor helps people manage potential conflict around dog behavior:

> For example, one woman yelled, "Stop that, you dirty old man" in response to an older dog mounting her companion dog. In other circumstances there is no criticism of negative commentary. Among three men:
>
> > While we were talking, the black dog mounted the golden and then the bull terrier after the golden shrugged it off. People were laughing. The terrier caretaker said, "Some people get upset by this." The golden's caretaker said that he didn't. The bull terrier caretaker added, "I don't mind watching it. It's the most exciting thing in my day. I'm not getting much at home." Everyone laughed.[18]

Dogs mounting other dogs is a common source of friction among people at dog parks, and it often raises the conundrum for dog caretakers of freedom versus control. As I say, dogs are not as free as some people claim they are at dog parks. People regularly call their dogs back or yell something like "Stop that!" over every perceived misdeed. Or people run over to their dog and leash them up to avoid annoying someone else.

Freedom clearly raises its complex head at dog parks, as well as in cars, on leashes, on walks and hikes, and at home. People often ask me when you should manage and monitor your dog closely, and risk frustrating the dog, and when should you relax and allow your dog to do whatever they like, and risk being accused of having an out-of-control dog. Honestly, I try to avoid these debates as much as possible, since everything depends on the people and the dogs involved.

However, questions about how free dogs should be, or how free they truly are, are clearly not as simple and straightforward as they seem, and many people get pretty worked up about it. People are not just managing their dogs, but their dogs' relationships to other dogs, since those dog relationships affect all the human relationships. And everyone has a different idea about what is and is not acceptable. An essay by Wes Siler in *Outside* magazine called "Why Dogs Belong Off-Leash in the Outdoors" got a lot of people thinking about these sorts of questions, and many people, including myself, weighed in on all sides of the issues.[19] Siler writes, "If the owners are responsible, the presence of off-leash dogs can actually make the outdoors a better place."

Obviously, dog parks are fenced, which allows dogs to be off leash and yet contained. This isn't the place to get into a long discussion about whether dogs should be allowed off leash in open areas.[20] Yet some studies show clearly that when dogs are allowed off leash, even in areas where this is permitted, problems arise more due to people than dogs.[21] In one study, for example, we learn that "many more people reported seeing other people disturb wildlife (92.2 percent), . . . significantly more often than dogs (49.7 percent)."

The bottom line is that enforcement of local regulations is critical for keeping dogs and humans in line. If someone chooses to let their dogs run off leash where it's assumed to be safe to do so, they need to be responsible for their dog's behavior. This is not always the case. I conducted a study of dog–prairie dog interactions with my student Robert Ickes called "Behavioral Interactions and Conflict among Domestic Dogs, Black-Tailed Prairie Dogs, and People in Boulder, Colorado."[22] To quote from our study: "People tried to stop dogs from harassing prairie dogs only 25 percent of the time. A survey showed that 58 percent of people polled at the Dry Creek dog park where we conducted our study (all dog owners) did not believe that prairie dogs should be protected even if dogs are a problem. Increased human responsibility would likely go a long way towards reducing existing conflict among people wanting to protect prairie dogs and those who do not." We also suggested that "proactive strategies grounded by empirical data can be developed and implemented so that the interests of all parties can be accommodated."

In our study, people weren't good about controlling their dogs. However, in Patrick Jackson's essay "Situated Activities in a Dog Park," he noted: "Caretakers become 'control managers' who must negotiate problems related to a variety of dog behaviors, especially mounting, aggression, and waste management. In this process, caretakers use various strategies to manage their own and others' possible perceptions and understandings of appropriate behavior for dogs in public places." Dr. Jackson kindly followed up on some of his thoughts in an email to me, in which he wrote:

> I was impressed with the high level of the disconnect that may or does exist between the humans and the nonhumans in dog parks I've been to. Perhaps we may be able to more easily get a handle on what the humans are feeling about how and why they do what they do in relation to their dogs in the park, and what I notice (and I'm thinking you would agree to some extent) is that people often have no idea what their dogs are "really" up to. But the fact that that exists—that humans in the dog park create interpretations and act on them (regardless of their "objective" accuracy or relevancy to the dogs in the way the humans intend)—can have huge implications for the dogs and their inter- and intra-species interactions in that context. Since a lot of the questions and work that you and others are doing is appropriately centered on nonhuman species, which is under/unstudied, I suppose my long-winded thought is it may be directly relevant to comprehending the implications of the species divide for interaction in the dog park.[23]

I agree with Dr. Jackson that we really don't know all that much about the dynamics of control and freedom at dog parks. At the conclusion of his thoughtful essay, he writes: "This study suggests that dog parks not only provide insight into canine behavior, but also into human-animal and human-human interaction. Thus, while dog parks may appear as urban playgrounds for dogs, the interactions that take place there have implications that extend far beyond the fence that defines their boundary."

It's clear we need a lot more research about dog parks. One early reader of this book asked, "Do people with expensive purebred dogs visit dog parks more or less frequently than people with mutts? Do dogs play more or less when meeting in the confines of the dog park than when off-leash in a larger space? What is the optimum size for a dog park—that is, the density?" These are great questions, and I know of no available data to answer them.

The list of questions that can be studied at dog parks seems almost endless. It seems as if each time I go to a dog park I come away with new questions. What happens when one dog leaves a group and another joins? Are there differences when the dogs know one another than when they don't? What's the best size for a play group? How often do dogs sniff versus sniff and pee, and how often do people interfere in what their dog is doing?

All of these questions represent research projects just waiting to be done. Perhaps you, on your next visit to the dog park, could try to tackle one of them. I love visiting dog parks, and I find it incredibly exciting how much we can learn about dogs and humans by studying what happens when we visit them.

NINE

A Dog Companion's Guide

||||||||||||||||||||||||||||||||||||||||||||||||||||||||||||||||||||||||||||||||||||||||||||||||||||||||||||||||||||||||

"I love Mervin, but I'm not sure I can give him what he wants and needs, although I'm his total slave from the time we get up until the time we go to sleep. Do you think pet keeping will end?"

"When I get up in the morning, I love spooning with Serena, my lovely beagle. I get out of bed slowly, make some coffee and some eggs, and as I sip my coffee, Serena gulps down her eggs, sometimes boiled and sometimes scrambled. If she's been good, I sometimes add some bacon."

"Molly's been rather ill—she's getting old and lame. I love her and have tried to give her all she needs, and now I'm not sure if I'm just keeping her alive to keep myself alive. What should I do?"

"What do you think about pet hospice? I like it but is it really worth it?"

"Jamie died yesterday. I feel like I made the decision to let her go at the right time. Maybe she would have had a few more weeks, but she told me 'it's time.'"

"I decided to give Patricia up and let her have the opportunity for a better life. I just can't do what I need to do and what she needs to do, and it breaks my heart."

"How many dogs should a person be allowed to adopt and return? I know someone who's done it eight times. Thank goodness, when she tried again, she was told 'no.'"

"I was essentially clinically depressed, and when Shelby came into my life, I felt better, stopped taking far too many prescription drugs, went out more and made friends, and lost fifteen pounds."

‖‖

Hardly a day or dog park visit goes by during which I don't hear stories or questions such as those above. I offer what information I can, but rarely, if ever, do I offer advice. I also try never to be judgmental because I know most people care deeply about the dog, or dogs, with whom they live. Oftentimes, these various questions lead to deep and serious conversations about the ethics of pet keeping.

That's the focus of this final chapter, in which I discuss how individuals and society can provide the best possible life for dogs. I hope, by this point, you realize that dogs are amazing and fascinating beings. So too are humans. I also hope it's clear that while we know quite a bit about dog behavior and dog-human relationships, there still is much to learn. Most of all, we need to pay attention to and respect individual differences. Not every dog, and not every person, is the same, and what works in one relationship may not in another. In a way, the messes dogs make—literal and metaphorical—can't be avoided. We have to accept that even when dogs are disruptive, we can learn from these experiences and still continue loving and caring for our dog companions, both in our homes and in our society, in our parks and ranging free.

The Ethics of Pet Keeping: Negotiating Human-Dog Relationships and Caring for Our Companions

When you offer a dog or other animal a place in your life, it's a "cradle-to-grave" commitment. The cradle, of course, is when you make the decision to share your home, and I hope your heart, with a dog. The grave, in contrast, is usually the end of the animal's life, since unless you're over seventy or so when you adopt a dog, you most likely will outlive your canine companion.

The other commitment you make is to give your dog or other animal the best life possible that you can. I was talking recently with my cycling buddy and close friend Randy Gaffney about his dog, Gracie, who has blessed his life for ten years. I asked how she was, and his response echoes what I often hear. He said: "Gracie is living the life. My primary purpose in life is to make her happy." I only wish these words applied to all dogs in the world.

People also always ask me, what does a good life for a dog mean? Questions about the ethics of pet keeping are coming more and more into public discussions, and I've noticed this when I go to dog parks or when I give talks about dog behavior. People wonder how to give their dog the best life possible, and they wonder if the best they can provide is good enough. Naturally, making someone else happy all the time is impossible. No one is happy all the time. Life can be a series of compromises, and as I say, every individual is different. Some trade-offs are harder than others, and everyone copes differently. Given how variable dogs are, and how variable humans are, we get into trouble when try to provide, or try to live by, overriding prescriptive conclusions that we insist apply to everyone.

This is why I think it's so essential that we all become naturalists in a dog park. Every human companion of a dog should dedicate themselves to becoming a student of their dog's behavior, so that they learn what their dog considers a good, satisfying life. Like good ethologists, we should talk to others, including scientists and trainers, and learn from one another as much as possible. We need to read what researchers are publishing, including in related fields of animal studies, and listen to knowledgeable friends at the dog park. Then we need to confirm what others say with what we see with our own eyes and in our own dog. (For more on how to observe like an ethologist, please turn to the appendix.)

One thing that's true, and that no individual can fix, is that human life is often stressful for dogs. Thus, it's important to manage your own human-dog relationship so that it eases this stress and so that your relationship works successfully for both of you. While people often think of training as a one-time thing, living with a dog is an ongoing negotiation of desires and needs that evolve over time.

For instance, along that spectrum of negotiations, we have to think about and prepare for end-of-life decisions. Illness can strike at any time, and what makes a good life for an old dog is as various as at any other time of life. Indeed, people often wonder about trade-offs between quality and quantity—is a shorter life that's good better than a longer life filled with pain and suffering? I'm also sometimes asked if dogs ever want to die to end the pain.[1] While such an inclination by a dog is likely unusual, I do think that this could sometimes be the case, and the only way you can ever know is if you have spent a lot of time carefully listening to your dog and coming to understand her or him as a unique individual.

Do Dogs Get Stressed Out by Human Life?

The downside of choosing to live with another animal is that many can be highly stressed because they can't do what they want and need to do in order to experience high-quality lives. This point is clearly made by Dr. Jessica Pierce in her book *Run, Spot, Run: The Ethics of Keeping Pets* and by service-dog trainer Jennifer Arnold in her book *Love Is All You Need*. Arnold notes that dogs live in an environment that "makes it impossible for them to alleviate their own stress and anxiety." Dogs, like humans and other animals, may go gray when they're anxious, prematurely growing gray hair on their muzzles.[2] Researchers have also found that females tend to show more gray than males, as do dogs who are fearful of loud noises and unfamiliar animals and people. Premature gray muzzles in young dogs might call attention to a dog who is anxious or fearful.[3]

Arnold writes: "In modern society, there is no way for our dogs to keep themselves safe, and thus we are unable to afford them the freedom to meet their own needs. Instead, they must depend on our benevolence for survival." Think about it: we teach dogs that they can't pee or poop wherever they want. To eliminate, they must get our attention and ask for permission to go outside the house. When we go outside, we often restrain dogs with a leash or fence them within yards or parks. Dogs eat what and when we feed them, and they are scolded if they eat what or when we say they shouldn't. Dogs play with the toys we give them, and they get in trouble for turning our shoes and furniture into toys. Most of the time, our schedule and relationships determine who dogs play with and who their friends will be. All things considered, it's a very asymmetric, one-sided relationship, one that many would not tolerate with another human.

Many dogs, perhaps most of them, make their peace with these compromises. Yet millions of dogs also live with stress-related disorders or are on drugs to relieve that stress and anxiety. Arnold notes that we abuse our power over dogs when we impose our will on them without considering their thoughts and feelings—because they are, in fact, thinking and feeling social beings. What Arnold calls the "because I said so (BISS) technique" of training fails and doesn't result in "a fair and mutually beneficial relationship."[4] By studying dogs carefully, we can avoid this situation. There really is no reason at all to become involved in a power struggle with a dog.

Tony Milligan, in the book *Pets and People: The Ethics of Our Relationships with Companion Animals*, notes that dogs have to do a lot. We place a good number of demands and expectations on them. He writes: "An additional wrinkle in this picture is that companion animals such as dogs of course need to learn about far more than just getting along with humans. In the case of a dog, for example, the community in which she will have an opportunity to flourish will include various different humans and nonhumans. Given this, 'She needs to be housebroken, to learn not to bite or to jump up on people, to be wary of cars, and not to chase the family cat (unless it's a play chase!).' . . . And such socialization is learned partly from the humans but also, in part, from the nonhumans."[5]

I've often been asked if free-ranging dogs are actually less stressed than dogs living with humans because of the demands placed on dogs in a human-centered relationship. Of course, it's impossible to answer this question with any certainty because individual dogs and individual humans and the nature of their relationships need to be considered. However, in Bangalore, India, in one study of street dogs—called "streeties" by the locals—Sindhoor

Pangal observes: "I found the dogs that I studied to not seem stressed at all. They showed no signs of elevated stress levels in their body language. When approached, all of them were relaxed, cautiously curious (like most street dogs) and very friendly once they realized I was no threat. When awake, they seemed to spend most of their time perched on an elevated surface if they could find one, and just watching the world go by."[6]

Norwegian dog trainer Turid Rugaas also has written a good deal on stress in dogs, and she is an expert in using what she calls "calming signals" to soothe dogs and to reduce stress. In her work, she emphasizes the importance of watching dogs carefully at home and in other venues, including when they interact with other dogs. Just how effective "calming signals" are remains to be determined.[7] My take is that calming signals do indeed work, but like many other behavior patterns, not always. People need to pay close attention to what the dogs are doing, their familiarity with one another, and watch them carefully. I'm sure that future studies will shed more light on how dogs use calming signals to tell one another what's acceptable and what's not, how effective they are, and why they work and don't work in different contexts.[8]

IS IT OKAY TO HUG YOUR DOG?

If there's one tried-and-true method for relieving stress, while also expressing our affection for our dogs, it's through physical contact. We pet our dogs all the time, and they appeal to us constantly for back scratches and belly rubs. Sometimes dogs sleep with us, and they freely jump into our laps and lounge in our arms. For some dogs, touch is important and actively sought, whereas for others it's less important and can be downright aversive.

Hugging is a form of positive touching; however, some researchers and others have questioned whether hugging your dog is okay. Not long ago, I read a rather alarmist essay that basically said, "Don't ever hug your dog." So in the spirit of myth busting, let me say that, yes, it's really okay to carefully hug your dog, so long as you do so on *their* terms. Not all dogs like to be hugged, and neither do all humans. And that goes for every other type of physical interaction. Some dogs adore roughhousing and wrestling, and other dogs definitely do not.

Concerning hugging, a topic in which numerous humans are interested, I was talking with some people about dog behavior at a party last year. This happens a lot. We had discussed various aspects of behavior, when Virginia Arnette, who had seen the article telling people not to hug a dog, asked me, "So, is it okay to hug a dog?" I could tell that she really wanted to know. After I told her it was okay to do so on their terms, she told me about her dog, Marketa, a Shiba-Inu, who was quite ill and loved to be hugged. Her friend continued to hug Marketa, and she found it hard to believe that hugging dogs could be wrong. Good for them! Please hug your dog if your dog likes to be hugged, and you might consider tickling them as well, as many dogs (and rats) like to be tickled.

In fact, dogs can be very—some might say too—open about want they want and need and how they feel. Their emotional lives are rather public. You don't need an advanced degree to understand your dog and give them what they need. We don't, and likely will never, know all there is to know about dogs, but I don't find that problem to be staggering. Filling in the blanks and connecting the dots to understand dogs better is surely important, but we know enough now to provide dogs with fulfilling and happy lives.

WHAT'S A GOOD LIFE FOR AN OLD DOG?

I often get involved in discussions about quality of life, end-of-life decisions, and hospice for old "senior" dogs.[9] I agree with Mary Gardner who observes that there is a difference between a "senior" dog and a "geriatric" dog, the former being a dog who simply has reached a certain age and the latter being a dog who has health problems.[10] Many people go out of their way to care for an elder dog. In my home-town of Boulder, Jeff Kramer, a mail carrier, built a ramp for an aging dog, Tashi, along his route.[11]

I remember a few years ago when I met an old dog who was clearly totally blind. Jack lumbered along with his nose to the ground and occasionally bumped into things. I smiled because he seemed to be having a good old time, tail wagging wildly whenever he came upon an appealing scent. I assumed Jack and his human had been together a long time, but when I talked with the woman who was with him, I learned she had adopted him when he was thirteen years old and already completely blind. Jack had been given only a month or two to live because of bone cancer, and here he was, two years later and fifteen years old, still alive and one happy dog being. His human said he had an "awesome disposition" and always seemed content; he was always "polite with other dogs and humans." I still think about Jack often, along with the woman who selflessly took him in and increased his quality of life when she thought he only had a month or two to live.[12]

What follows is a personal story that contrasts questions of quality versus quantity of life. Inuk was a dog who lived with me, and I first published this story on my *Psychology Today* site in 2016. I have to admit I have been stunned by all of the positive feedback I have received about it since then.

Inuk was a very fit dog, getting regular long runs, as he was a mountain dog, and very healthy for thirteen-plus years. But he declined fairly rapidly due to a gastrointestinal problem, so the veterinarian to whom he went and really liked prescribed a large orange pill, as I remember it, that had to be shoved down his throat. There was no guarantee that the pill would work, but it was worth a try. To say the least, Inuk hated the pills, and after having three a day for four days, he ran away when he knew the pills were coming no matter how softly I spoke to him. He'd cringe in the corner of his large outdoor run or scoot up the dirt road as best he could. No one seeing him would draw any conclusion other than he didn't want to take the pills. If Inuk were a human, and in many ways he was, there wouldn't have been a shred of doubt that the pills were not at all welcomed. Inuk also did not appear to get any better and clearly was telling me no more pills, please.

What to do? We considered different alternatives and then decided (without asking the veterinarian, but letting her know after the fact what we had decided to do) that because the pills weren't working and were causing him a good deal of unneeded and obvious emotional distress, Inuk should spend the last weeks of his life enjoying every single moment as much as possible. He loved ice cream, so that's what he got. Every day he got a frozen pint of ice cream, and he worked on it for hours on end, tail wagging, ears up, and clearly enjoying every second of this special treat. And, most remarkably, after a few days, he had more energy, took longer walks up the road, played with some with his dog friends who lived up the road, and loved to snuggle once again.

So, am I happy with how Inuk spent the last few months of life? I am, indeed, even if he might have had a few more days on earth if he'd gotten the awful pills. Would I do something similar again? Yes, I would, without a doubt. Inuk had a great life, and there was no reason he should have spent his last days agonizing over the big orange pills. That's what we decided was a good life for an old dog.

Jane Sobel Klonsky, author of *Unconditional: Older Dogs, Deeper Love,* shared a story with me that mirrored my experiences with Inuk:

I've heard over and over from people who have dogs nearing the end of their lives, and the resounding sentiment is definitely to let them spend the end of their lives enjoying every single moment. They would wholeheartedly agree with how Inuk spent the last few months of his life, relishing in his doggy life pleasures and loves. The cover girl of my book, Olivia, is almost thirteen and was diagnosed with cancer over a year ago. Annie, her human mom, opted not to do chemo, but she did try for a few months to stuff all kinds of herbal supplements down Ol-

Thirteen-year-old Ozzie enjoying a bath. (Courtesy of Jane Sobel Klonsky)

ivia's throat. Olivia HATED them. She wouldn't eat. She was depressed. Annie decided that she hated seeing Olivia like this, so she stopped all the herbs and went back to Olivia's normal diet and lifestyle. Within a week, Olivia was a happy dog again, taking long walks, frog hunting at the pond, smiling and snuggling. Annie understands that Olivia probably won't live the number of extra days she might live if she ate her supplements, but wow, is she a happy dog living life to its fullest every day, and when she does go on, she'll do it with a smile on her face.[13]

Another story about old dogs came to me via Cici Franklin:

I adopted both Buddy and Daisy from Golden Retriever Rescue of the Rockies—Daisy was four months and Buddy was ten years. He was quite sick when we got him, very overweight, oily coarse coat, on wrong meds, etc., and I thought he was coming home with us for hospice care—to have a little bit of time in a fabulous place before he left us. Well, with lots of love, constant harassment from Daisy, good food, and the right meds, he was easily hiking six to eight miles with me in no time. We had over four years of being blessed by his presence in our lives. We miss him so much but were so lucky we found each other! He was one of the most special dogs I've ever known![14]

Basically, old dogs rock. And there is so much we can learn from them.

Positive Teaching Methods: Managing the Human-Dog Relationship

As I've said many times before, I like to say that we don't train dogs, we "teach" them. The word "teach" gets us closer to the truth of what we do during dog training: we establish the do's and don'ts of our human-dog relationship, and we create a system of signals, so both we and our dogs can communicate what's wanted and needed on the run. Dogs learn our system, but that doesn't mean they will always choose to follow the rules or do what we ask. When we become fluent in dog, it's good for them and good for us.

It's really no different than raising children. Parents teach their kids what's proper behavior for their household, and until the kids leave home, those rules and expectations are a constantly evolving negotiation.

In addition, how we teach is part of what we teach. This is certainly true with children, and it's equally true with dogs. We love our children, so we teach with love, and we hope that if our teaching methods are caring and respectful, we will teach care and respect. In this way, we create an environment in which everyone feels cared for, even when they can't do everything they want.

Training, alternatively, emphasizes obedience, and when the dog or a child disobeys, they are usually punished. There is little to no negotiation, and conflict and tension are almost guaranteed, since no conscious being—and that's who dogs are—obeys every rule 100 percent of the time.

So when it comes to methods of dog training, I fully encourage and support using positive reinforcement and reward-based methods rather than punishment, aversion, and domination.[15]

Kimberly Beck, founder of the organization the Canine Effect, stresses that we must pay careful attention to the relationships that are formed among dogs and between dogs and humans.[16] In her work as a dog trainer, Kimberly is concerned with dog-human interactions, and she views training as troubleshooting, in which there is constant tweaking of the relationship between dog and human. It's also essential to recognize that we choose the dogs with whom we want to share our life, and often they didn't have any voice—or bark—in choosing us, although of course there can be a deep connection and clear reciprocity at work.

I like the way Kimberly put it when she told me that training is frequently about trying to close the gap between human expectations, which vary from person to person, and what each dog as an individual wants and needs. The gap rarely closes fully, which leads to acceptable levels of tolerance from both the human and the dog. Kimberly also emphasizes that there is constant flow in leadership, which is essential for a healthy relationship. This means that sometimes the human leads and sometimes it's the dog's turn. Also, each side of the relationship has "nonnegotiables." For example, dogs shouldn't be allowed to jump on people without the human's permission, and we are obliged to protect dogs from running into traffic and from the risk of being attacked by wild predators.

Of course, nonnegotiables vary in different dog-human relationships; some humans are looser or more permissive than others in allowing dogs to do certain things. While there are some rules of thumb, there also is a good deal of flexibility, which can try our science, minds, and patience. Mutual tolerance and trust are key. So, too, is patience. It might sound paradoxical, but it's really true that when dogs know we have their best interests in mind, and when we carefully exercise control in positive, not dominating, ways, dogs can enjoy more freedom over what they can and cannot do. Another way to put this is that the goal isn't to train the dog out of the dog, but to show the dog how to cope in a human world.[17]

Bridging the Empathy Gap: Dogs Inspire Compassion

Often, when I'm discussing some aspect of animal abuse that involves chickens, pigs, cows, or laboratory animals such as mice and rats, I get people's attention by asking whether they would do the same thing to their dog. Across the board, people are incredulous when I ask this question. Of course they wouldn't do something harmful to their dog. They love their dog without qualification—which is why the question works. Dogs aren't more sentient or emotional than food animals or animals used in other contexts, such as in research and entertainment, so why would we do things to these animals that we wouldn't dream of doing to our own dog?

In this way, dogs help us bridge the empathy gap we sometimes have with other animals, just as Jane Goodall's dog, Rusty, helped her bridge the empathy gap when she was a youngster.

In August 2016, *New York Times* columnist Nicholas Kristof published an essay called "Do You Care More about a Dog Than a Refugee?"[18] I was surprised and even more pleased by his essay, which begins as follows:

> Last Thursday, our beloved family dog, Katie, died at the age of twelve. She was a gentle giant who respectfully deferred even to any mite-size puppy with a prior claim to a bone. Katie might have won the Nobel Peace Prize if not for her weakness for squirrels.
>
> I mourned Katie's passing on social media and received a torrent of touching condolences, easing my ache at the loss of a member of the family. Yet on the same day that Katie died, I published a column calling for greater international efforts to end Syria's suffering and civil war, which has claimed perhaps 470,000 lives so far. That column led to a different torrent of comments, many laced with a harsh indifference: Why should *we* help *them?*
>
> These mingled on my Twitter feed: heartfelt sympathy for an American dog who expired of old age, and what felt to me like

callousness toward millions of Syrian children facing starvation or bombing. If only, I thought, we valued kids in Aleppo as much as we did our terriers!

Clearly, Kristof used the passing of his dog to bridge the empathy gap that people sometimes have with those from another country, race, or religion. To drive this home, Kristof ends his essay with a bit of speculation:

I wonder what would happen if Aleppo were full of golden retrievers, if we could see barrel bombs maiming helpless, innocent puppies. Would we still harden our hearts and "otherize" the victims? Would we still say "it's an Arab problem; let the Arabs solve it"?

Yes, solutions in Syria are hard and uncertain. But I think even Katie in her gentle wisdom would have agreed that not only do all human lives have value, but also that a human's life is worth every bit as much as a golden retriever's.

Historically, dogs have motivated others to try to put an end to invasive research. In Peter Singer's classic book *Animal Liberation*, he writes:

In July 1973 Congressman Les Aspin of Wisconsin learned through an advertisement in an obscure newspaper that the United States Air Force was planning to purchase two hundred beagle puppies, with vocal cords tied to prevent normal barking, for tests of poisonous gases. Shortly afterward it became known that the army was also proposing to use beagles—four hundred this time—in similar tests.

Aspin began a vigorous protest, supported by antivivisection societies. Advertisements were placed in major newspapers across the country. Letters from an outraged public began pouring in. An aide from the House of Representatives Armed Services Committee said that the committee received more mail on the beagles than it had received on any other subject since Truman sacked General MacArthur, while an internal Department of Defense memo released by Aspin said that *the volume of mail the department had received was the greatest ever for any single event, surpassing even the mail on the bombings of North Vietnam and Cambodia.* After defending the experiments initially, the Defense Department then announced that it was postponing them, and looking into the possibility of replacing the beagles with other experimental animals. [my emphasis][19]

Kristof's piece prompted me to write an essay of my own, titled "Valuing Dogs More Than War Victims: Bridging the Empathy Gap."[20] This, in turn, inspired Dr. Patty Gowaty, a world-renowned evolutionary biologist, to write to me about her dog Rocky and the effect that living with Rocky has had on her and her husband, Steve:

Rocky's empathy was the leading, determining emotion in our house during this entire year of living with him. Rocky changed us: Steve and I are both calmer and happier. We suffer when we are away from him. We are constantly impressed with Rocky's thoughtfulness, his kindness, his politeness, and his play with us, his gazing into our eyes! Our dogs do a loving number on us, which is hard for those stuck in Aleppo to do: any empathy we might feel for them is not reciprocated with the immediacy of our interactions with our dogs. Empathy is not theoretical.[21]

Are Dogs Therapeutic?

Many people say that living with a dog is comforting. While dogs do not love unconditionally, as I've mentioned, we connect with dogs in a directly emotional way that many people find healing. This is one reason dogs are so helpful in bridging the empathy gap. Dogs give us so much and improve our lives simply by being themselves.

That said, is it really true that dogs are therapeutic? In fact, the research and scientific literature on whether dogs and other animals really make a positive difference in humans' lives is not as robust as some make it out to be. They're measurably beneficial for some people and not for others. Further, the popular media likes to run with this idea a bit too indiscriminately, claiming that animals are a wonderful panacea for *everyone* who's down and out.[22]

My take on this is if a dog makes a positive difference in your life, then that's wonderful, and you should treasure that relationship. However, don't expect or hope that living with a dog will fix you. Dogs are not medicine but, rather, living beings who need love and care themselves. The dogs with whom I've shared my home, along with many other dogs, have been constant reminders that I am alive and lucky to have had them in my life. In turn, I've always done the best I could to give them a great life.

Caring for a companion animal is sometimes exactly what helps people feel better about the world and themselves. Further, dogs can and are trained to be empathetic and compassionate and to assist us emotionally, not to mention all the practical help dogs are trained to give us.

While some researchers still debate whether dogs really help people get through difficult times, if a dog helps you emotionally and you are able to give the dog what he or she needs to have a good life, that's really what counts. For more than fifteen years, I've been teaching a course on animal behavior and conservation at the Boulder County Jail as part of Jane Goodall's global Roots & Shoots Program. I've heard many stories about how, for some people, dogs were their only friends when they were young, or when they were down and out, because dogs trusted them and didn't judge them. The dogs accepted them for who they were.

In 2017, I exchanged letters with Chante Alberts, a woman incarcerated at the Denver Women's Correctional Facility, which runs a dog-training program called the Prison Trained K-9 Companion Program. In one letter, Chante described her work in this program, which takes in shelter and puppy mill rescues, as well as family-owned dogs brought there for training, and what the dogs have meant to her:

When I first came to prison, I was two months pregnant with my daughter. Once I had her, I almost immediately joined the dog team. I found so much healing from being around the dogs. I was able to "mother" them . . . in a way I was unable toward my daughter. . . .

Not only does this program save dog's lives but also ours as inmates. After I had my daughter, my postpartum really became overwhelming for me. The interactions and focus I had with my dogs literally kept me grounded and sane. Being on the team, we are held at a higher standard than the rest of the prison population.

Chante and others working with the dogs have to keep their prison records incident free and be role models for other prisoners. She also wrote: "Once a week, as a handler, I was able to actually meet with the public families who were interested in adopting my dog or had brought their dog to us to train. Once a week I wasn't looked at as a criminal or an inmate, but as a woman who was introducing them to their new family member or showing them how much more behaved and obedient their family member became. That right there is the best feeling in the entire world."

I was speechless when I received Chante's letter. Clearly, being in the company of dogs, training them, and being responsible for giving them the best life possible greatly helped her along and gave her life meaning. She has also told me that her mother has a dream of starting a program based on the idea of "pets and parolees," but geared toward anyone going through a hardship or in a "pit" in life. Her intention is for people to "find healing with the relationship with the dog."

When I think about Chante, I'm reminded of a wonderful documentary called *Dogs on the Inside*, in which I was featured, that also clearly shows how interacting with dogs can soften even the most hardened inmates and give their lives a lot of meaning.[23] According to the makers of this this landmark film, "*Dogs on the Inside* follows the relationships between abused stray dogs and prison inmates working towards a second chance at a better life. In an attempt to rebuild their confidence and prepare for a new life outside, these prisoners must first learn to handle and care for a group of neglected strays. This heart-warming story reconfirms the timeless connection between man and dog, showing the resiliency of a dog's trust and the generosity of the human spirit in the unlikeliest of places."

Dogs in Our Manic, Busy World: Protecting Dogs from Abuse

With all this in mind, I'd like to ask a pointed question: If we love dogs so much, why don't we take care of them better as a society? Dogs, like all other animals, are considered to be objects or property in our legal system and also in many others throughout the world.[24] This legal status as property does not remotely align with our feelings toward the canine companions who share our homes, which prompts another empathy gap question: Would we treat *our* dog the way society too often treats *other* dogs?

It's worth remembering that, along with us, all dogs suffer from the pollution, ecological problems, and environmental damage of our modern world. Some people have even suggested that, in a meaningful and grand way, dogs might be the proverbial canaries in the coal mine, and their health might provide useful warnings about the devastating effects of environmental contaminants. A study published in August 2016 noted a decrease in the fertility of male dogs, and researchers "were able to demonstrate that chemicals found in the sperm and testes of adult dogs—and in some commercially available pet foods—had a detrimental effect on sperm function at the concentrations detected."[25] While more research is needed, it's sobering to think that dogs and other nonhuman animals can give us advanced warnings about what is wrong in our environment, one that we are all supposed to share.

However, the point I really want to raise here is the sort of preventable abuse, and at times intentional cruelty, that dogs can still suffer in our world. It's estimated that about one million companion animals are abused each year in the United States alone, and I'm pleased to say that slowly but surely more and more people are being punished for this cruelty.[26] While there always will be ups and downs concerning the legal status of, and legal protections for, other animals, I hope the stories below show that *justice truly is a dog's best friend.*

It has become a felony, for instance, to abuse companion animals in Ohio, an Ohio hunter was fired from his job for killing two dogs, and an animal cruelty unit was established in Orange County, Florida, in July 2016.[27] In a number of states, people are rallying to have state laws changed so that charges of animal abuse are treated as felonies, rather than misdemeanors. This was movingly captured in the outstanding 2015 documentary called *A Dog Named Gucci*, which details the story of a severely abused dog named Gucci, a chow-husky mix, and his rescuer, Doug James, who worked relentlessly to get legislation passed in Alabama to make domestic animal abuse a felony.[28] In 2017, the same type of legislation was also sought in Wyoming, New Mexico, Virginia, and Mississippi.[29] In Mississippi, Senator Angela Burks Hill stressed the strong relationship between abuse to nonhumans and abuse to humans, which is often referred to as "the link."[30] Also in 2017, Alaska became the first U.S. state to take "into consideration the well-being of an animal," allowing "judges to assign joint custody of pets"; a bill called the Pet and Women Safety Act (PAWS) was reintroduced into the U.S. Congress by Massachusetts's Katherine Clark that would protect pets in homes where there is domestic violence; and a federal court in New York City upheld a ban on puppy mill sales.[31]

Promising progress to protect dogs from abuse is also occurring internationally. In November 2016, greyhound racing was banned in Argentina, and in December 2016, the mayor of London was called on to review the Dangerous Dog Act (1991) because it was ineffective in reducing dog bites and didn't protect dog welfare.[32] As of April 2017, dogfighting will be penalized as a felony in Mexico.[33] Also in Britain, the environment secretary, arguing for better welfare, announced that the sale of dogs under eight weeks old will be made illegal to stop backstreet breeders who run puppy farms. The penalty for breaking the rules could be an unlimited fine or up to six months behind bars.[34] In Wales, the Royal Society for the Prevention of Cruelty to Animals (RSPCA) had more successful animal welfare convictions in 2016 than ever before.[35] In February 2017, a new law banned euthanizing animals in Taiwan; the intent is to cut down the number of abandoned and stray dogs who uncontrollably reproduce and to make the public aware of this enormous problem. In May 2016, Taiwanese veterinarian Chien Chih-cheng, most likely suffering from deep and enduring empathy burnout and compassion fatigue, committed suicide from the stress of having to kill numerous stray dogs.[36] Of course, many people everywhere are sick and tired of organized dog fighting, and since 2006, the RSPCA in the United Kingdom reports receiving nearly five thousand calls about organized dog fighting in England and Wales.[37]

To avoid feeling demoralized, it's important to balance reports of bad news with examples of good news. And I prefer to focus on the good. Take Ohio: in 2016, Ohio lawmakers cracked down on bestiality and cockfighting, and in a separate decision, an Ohio Appeals Court ruled that "dogs are not dining chairs or television sets" and that damages for an injured pet need to be more than "simple 'market value.'"[38] And yet Ohio continued to allow pet stores to sell dogs from puppy mills because of pressure from the Ohio-based Petland franchise, which is the largest puppy-selling pet store chain in the United States.[39] Also in the bad news column, in December 2016, a federal court in Detroit, Michigan, gave police the go-ahead to shoot a dog if they move or bark when an officer enters a home, and a Canadian judge ruled that dogs are to be considered as property and have "no familial rights."[40] However, in January 2017, the premiere of the movie *A Dog's Purpose* was canceled after a video showed a stunt dog in distress.[41] As with Gucci, public opinion and concerns really can make a positive difference for the lives of dogs. And, more good news came in June 2017, when Pennsylvania's governor, Tom Wolf, signed an upgraded anticruelty bill for his state.[42] Around the same time, the city council of Vancouver, Canada, banned the sale of dogs, cats, and rabbits in pet stores; abused dogs in Connecticut got their own lawyers; and Vermont passed a new law banning the sexual abuse of animals.[43] Businesses have also gotten involved in helping dogs. For instance, in 2017 BrewDog, a craft brewery in Ohio and Scotland, started giving employees a week off when they took a new dog into their homes.[44]

The fight continues. In February 2017, animal welfare and animal abuse data were removed for unknown reasons from the website of the U.S. Department of Agriculture, a reprehensible form of censorship.[45]

ARE DOG TRAINERS REGULATED?

In the United States, anyone can call themselves a dog trainer, and there simply are no dog-training regulations of which I or the people I have spoken to are aware.

Most incidents of abuse arise from dominance-based or aversive dog training. This approach uses and encourages the harsh physical handling of dogs, which is justified by the belief that dogs need to be physically "dominated" before they will respect or listen to a person. As I've said, this idea is flat-out wrong and terribly misguided. This type of "training" traumatizes dogs and leads to injury and even death. For instance, in January 2017, I received an email that broke my heart:

> I am writing you to seek your support; I am on a team working with lawmakers in Florida to introduce legislation for dog training techniques, which Animal Legal Defense Fund worked with me to draft. ALDF surveyed the country and found that this legislation is unprecedented, so we all think it is time.
>
> My puppy, Sarge, was attending daycare, where they use dominance-based techniques. He was dead within two hours of a cruel tactic used on him.
>
> Sarge was a three-and-a-half-month-old Shih Tzu/Pekingese mix. He weighed eight pounds.

Because Sarge wasn't "heeling," the trainer grabbed Sarge and held his mouth closed with his right hand while holding his neck with his left—Sarge thrashed and collapsed. The trainer said, "That's normal. Because he's a puppy, he exerted all his energy," and "I won that battle, but you may not next time because he is strong." I said, "But his eyes are glazed over, and his tongue is hanging out." The trainer made Sarge get up. Sarge tried, but collapsed again.

I first took him to the training facility's veterinarian close by. I was then referred to the emergency clinic. I believe Sarge died in my arms as I was entering the door of the emergency vet; I could feel his heartbeat fading. He suffered terribly and had a hard time breathing his last two hours.

Sarge died in May 2015, and in March 2017, two months after I received the above email and got involved, there was some movement to regulate dog trainers in the county in which Sarge had lived.[46] In December 2016, abuse at a dog training facility in Oceanside, New York, led to a call for legislation that would create a state-issued license for dog trainers "to curb the unregulated practice of individuals claiming to be dog-training experts."[47]

These are only a few examples. In an excellent and well-researched 2016 essay, Elizabeth Foubert points out that "in the United States anyone can work as a dog trainer, regardless of the person's qualifications," and the Academy for Dog Trainers rightfully has called for transparency.[48] In a Facebook post, they wrote: "What should owners look for in a dog trainer? If you ask us, the most important thing is **transparency**. If a dog trainer is not willing to fully disclose, in clear language, exactly what will happen to your dog (in the physical world) during the training process, keep shopping. Look for verbs, not adjectives. Demand to know what specific methods will be employed in what specific situations. Don't settle for smoke and mirrors."[49]

I agree completely with this advice. Dog training can be abusive, and we must do all we can to make sure it is not. There still is a lot of work to be done, and it is essential for people to get involved at a grassroots level. Dogs need all the voices and justice they can get.

ARE ELECTIVE, COSMETIC SURGERIES ABUSIVE?

Dogs and other animals also need protection from elective "cosmetic" surgeries. These include tail docking, ear cropping, devocalization, cat declawing, and piercing and tattooing. Some dogs also are being treated with Botox for eye lifts, testicular implants to regain masculinity, and plastic surgery for nose jobs and tummy tucks.[50] I see absolutely no reason for any cosmetic or breed-specific surgeries, or those that are done to make it easier to live with a dog. I think that dogs who are born with tails look much better with them rather than having their tails cut off because some humans like them tailless. Let's work hard to let dogs keep their tails. One reason given for the use of elective cosmetic procedures is that they make dogs more attractive, sometimes so that their humans won't dump them and sometimes to make them more adoptable. Says one veterinarian, "Hangy boobs and lumps and bumps make people uncomfortable." I can see where fixing these "imperfections" might serve a dog well on certain occasions, but cosmetic surgeries to please people or to prevent human guardians from giving up their companion don't say much at all about these people. Dogs don't give a hoot or a bark about how their eyes look or if they have a big nose, even if they can look in a mirror and recognize themselves.

Spaying and neutering are also elective surgeries. These are typically done to prevent unwanted breeding (and unwanted puppies) and to reduce aggression or problem behaviors. However, only the first outcome is assured, and the topic of spaying and neutering is complex. Opinions and evidence are mixed about whether these surgeries actually result in the positive behavioral changes some claim.[51] I regularly hear from people like the woman I quote in chapter 1, whose dog, Helen, continues to hump wildly despite being "fixed." Ultimately, spaying and neutering are not panaceas for behavioral issues.

It's important to keep in mind that we can do whatever we want to dogs and other animals, whether they like it or not. While dogs may still love us regardless of what we decide to do to make them more attractive or easy to live with, it's essential to honor that this imbalance in power is not a license to do whatever we choose.[52] There's lots of money in the pet cosmetic surgery industry, and we shouldn't let money rule because of human vanity.

A variety of state laws govern elective surgical procedures on pets, and the American Veterinary Medical Association offers a useful summary, which was last updated in December 2014.[53] These laws typically restrict such surgeries unless there is a medical reason to perform them. Of course, there is always more to do to protect dogs. On the positive side of the ledger, in November 2016, Canadian veterinarians in British Columbia banned tail docking and ear cropping.[54]

Concerning the debarking of dogs—that is, performing a procedure in which dogs' vocal cords are cut to quiet them—the National Animal Interest Alliance (NAIA), which also favors the use of animals for research, dismisses debarking as "bark softening" and thinks it's just fine to do.[55] Yet we don't really know how this changes the behavior of individual dogs. Of course, many others and I take issue with their position. Dog trainer and writer Anna Jane Grossman nicely covers the pitfalls of this surgical procedure. She suggests that dog noise really is a human problem, and these surgeries have side effects that include the buildup of scar tissue (which makes breathing or swallowing difficult), chronic coughing (which can cause infection), and swelling of the throat (which can cause heatstroke).[56] She writes: "The governments of the U.K. and 18 other countries have signed the European Convention for the Protection of Pet Animals into law. This convention also prohibits ear cropping, tail docking, and declawing (in cats). In 2010, Massachusetts outlawed the procedure, following a bill filed by a teenager. New Yorkers are hoping a similar bill will be passed next year."[57]

All in all, laws on dog abuse are slowly changing for the better. There are also many organizations that work to protect dogs, too many to mention here, including the wonderful Sound of Silence

Campaign to protect dogs from being used in testing.[58] We still have a long way to go, but any progress is good. We just need to keep working for more protection for dogs and other animals in a world in which human interests typically outweigh those of nonhuman animals.

The Big Picture: What You Can Do

We need a new social contract for our relationships with all nonhuman animals.[59] There always will be mysteries about other animals, and recognizing that we don't know all there is to know should keep us on our toes. But let me stress again that we know enough right now—and we have for a long period of time—to do more for dogs and other animals in an increasingly human-dominated world. I know this seems like a big ask, but I do feel that if we always try to do more, everyone will benefit, dogs and humans.

One thing this means is making sure our big picture view always includes nonhuman animals, so that we extend our respect and compassion throughout the animal kingdom. I'm always amazed by how dogs help us bridge the empathy gap to do this. As I was writing this chapter, I discovered an essay by Andy Newman in the *New York Times* called "World (or at least Brooklyn) Stops for Lost Dog."[60] Bailey, a two-and-a-half-year-old goldendoodle, went missing in Brooklyn. Her human, Orna Le Pape, was understandably distraught, and numerous strangers got involved looking for Bailey. Why would people interrupt their busy lives to do this? One of Le Pape's friends weighed in: "At a time like this, when there's so much turmoil going on around the election, here's this story that everyone can latch on to and be on the same side. Everyone wants a lost dog found."

As William Shakespeare wrote, "All's well that ends well," and of course, Bailey's story has a happy ending. Bailey was eventually found, eight pounds lighter, starving, and dehydrated. Yet Bailey perfectly exemplifies how dogs can help us bridge the empathy gap and come together. Bailey catalyzed cooperation during a time when cooperation was severely strained by our political divisions. His story reminds me of the story I told in chapter 1 about how Pepper's dognapping from a Pennsylvania farm in 1965 lead to the passage of the federal Animal Welfare Act in 1966. With a little help from our canine friends, we can easily wrap other animals into the folds of respect and compassion, so they, too, know we're doing all we can for them.

Of course, there always is more to do.[61] Our work on behalf of dogs (and other animals) never stops. Abuse must be countered head on. Dogs need all the voices they can get. They are totally dependent on our goodwill and rely on us to work selflessly and tirelessly on their behalf. If we don't, it's a dirty double-cross. It's indisputable that we cause severe psychological and physical harm to our companions when we let them down, when we neglect them or dominate them selfishly, taking no responsibility for the deep hurt we've created. The hearts of our companion animals, like our own hearts, are fragile, so we must be mindfully gentle with them. We can never be too nice or too generous with our love for our dear and trusting companions, who are so deeply pure of heart.

When we betray our companion's trust and take advantage of their innocence, our actions are ethically indefensible. These actions make us less than human and are simply wrong. Much unadulterated joy will come our way as we clear the path for profound and rich two-way interdependent relationships based on immutable trust with our companions and all other beings.

Simply put, we must care for dogs' fears and stress as they try to live in a human-dominated and over-busy world. Dogs need to feel safe, and attachment is all about trust. They truly comprise a class of vulnerable and highly sentient beings. Of course, many people are lucky to have animals like dogs in their lives, and many dogs are lucky to have us. But we need to keep in mind that around 75 percent of dogs in the world are on their own, just trying to make it through a day. Trying to make it through another day is an issue as well, I'm afraid, for many dogs who live in ostensibly far better circumstances.

Concerning the plight of dogs who are on their own, I was thrilled to learn that, in January 2017, a mall in Istanbul, Turkey, opened its doors to stray dogs during a winter storm.[62] In the same month, an Indonesian charity helped to find new homes for unwanted dogs.[63] Pippin, a dog who was stranded at the bottom of a concrete drain in Jakarta, found a new home in Atlanta, Georgia. Small acts of kindness are important. They help specific animals, of course, and they might also inspire similar acts elsewhere.

Because I work with Jane Goodall's global Roots & Shoots Program, I interact with youngsters quite a lot.[64] If we show them how important it is to treat dogs and others well, and to respect them for who they are, there really is hope for the future. I love how humane educator Zoe Weil puts it: "The world becomes what we teach."[65]

The State and Future of Dogs

We need another and a wiser and perhaps a more mystical concept of animals. Remote from universal nature, and living by complicated artifice, man in civilization surveys the creature through the glass of his knowledge and sees thereby a feather magnified and the whole image in distortion. We patronize them for their incompleteness, for their tragic fate of having taken form so far below ourselves. And therein we err, and greatly err. For the animal shall not be measured by man. In a world older and more complete than ours they move finished and complete, gifted with extensions of the senses we have lost or never attained, living by voices we shall never hear. They are not brethren, they are not underlings; they are other nations, caught with ourselves in the net of life and time, fellow prisoners of the splendour and travail of the earth.

Henry Beston, *The Outermost House*

This quote from Beston is one of my all-time favorites. I go to it constantly because it says so much about who other animals are and about our relationships with them. First, we do indeed view others through our own senses, and as we have clearly seen, dogs don't sense the world how we do. So our views are, indeed, distorted. We also patronize them for not being like us, for what we perceive as their incompleteness, as if we are complete. This misrepresentation allows some people to place dogs and other animals below us on some mythical evolutionary scale. They're referred to as "lower" beings, a move that results in rampant mistreatment and egregious abuse. As Beston asserts, "And therein we err," for we should not be the template against which we measure other animals. I also like how he views other animals as "other nations," since this asks us to view them as the *beings* they are, not as *what* we want them to be. And surely, dogs and other animals are caught up in the "travail of the earth," captive to whatever we want them to do and whoever we want them to be. As we've seen, this makes for a good deal of stress in their lives as they try to adapt to a human-dominated world.

One aspect of the world in which dogs are captive is our busyness. I often wonder what the future is going to be like as people get even busier and more stressed. How will dogs fit into our lives in a more demanding world? How will we prioritize dogs, those companions with whom we choose to share our lives? Many people who work closely with dogs are concerned with just how stressed dogs truly are in all sorts of situations. Dog trainer Kimberly Beck suggests that we need to work toward tolerance in our relationships with dogs. She also wonders whether we love them simply because they love us. This question opens the door to discussions in all sorts of settings, ranging from cocktail parties to ivory towers.

I hope I've been successful in showing you how fascinating dogs are and why we need to let dogs be dogs. Of course, we need to be sure they learn what is and is not acceptable in the world of humans they inhabit, but we should not train the dog out of them. We can learn a lot about respect, dignity, commitment, and love from sharing our lives with dogs. Dogs can also show us that a violent world is not a natural world.

The state of dogs is slowly getting better. Dogs want to live in peace and safety just like we do. So feel free to don your ethologist's hat, take a pen and pad, have a video camera ready if possible, make it a social outing or family affair, and show the dog with whom you share your home and heart that you really care about them. These feelings of empathy and compassion can easily spread to other dogs, other animals, and other humans.

It's often claimed that humans have a natural affinity for nature, including other animals. This is called the biophilia hypothesis.[66] Let's all tap into what's in our genes, bridge the empathy gap, and do what's right. What a great example this would be for youngsters and for future generations. The more we learn about dogs and other animals, the more informed our actions and activism on their behalf should be. But as I've pointed out repeatedly, we already know enough to do more for them right now.

When we give dogs and other animals the very best lives possible, it can easily spill over into more freedom and justice for all animals, including ourselves. Wouldn't that be grand? Who could argue that more trust, empathy, compassion, freedom, and justice wouldn't be the best thing we could do for all animals and for future generations who will inherit our wondrous planet? I surely don't know anyone who would do so.

I often wonder if dogs, by bridging the empathy gap among humans, could help to heal our wounded world by bringing together people of all ages and all cultures who share an attachment and affection for these wonderful beings.

We are most fortunate to have dogs in our lives, and we must work for the day when all dogs are most fortunate to have us in their lives. In the long run, we'll all be better for it.

ACKNOWLEDGMENTS

I'm happy to thank, once again, Christie Henry, for her unwavering support and positive attitude about just about everything. She is the consummate editress. Jessica Pierce is also always there to talk about whatever comes up and provided excellent comments on an earlier draft of this book. Likewise, Mark Derr is always available as well to talk about anything "dog." Miranda Martin helped to organize the images in this book and kindly answered a number of questions that came up as I was writing, Yvonne Zipter did a fine job at copyediting, and Lybi Ma, my editor at *Psychology Today*, for whom I've written more than a thousand essays, many on dogs, has been unfailingly supportive of my attempts to communicate the latest and greatest science on animal behavior, animal cognition, and animal emotions to a broad audience.

Carl Safina kindly provided the pictures of Chula and Jude playing here and there on a beach on Long Island. I thank Chante Alberts for sharing her story of how dogs helped her through extremely difficult times. Dog trainer and journalist Tracy Krulik willingly helped me along with some extremely useful discussions, as did Kimberly Beck (founder of the Canine Effect). Kimberly went far beyond the call of duty, for which I am ever grateful. Jeff Campbell offered invaluable help in polishing up my prose, and Elise Gatti kindly provided numerous sources on human-dog relationships with which I was unfamiliar and also generously offered many useful comments on chapter 8. Ritchie Patterson and Molly got me out to the dog park on a number of occasions, and we all talked a lot about dog-dog and human-human behavior.

Ádám Miklósi, Brian Hare, Luigi Boitani, John Bradshaw, and Sergio Pellis kindly offered their views on the value of dog research. Patrick Jackson, Melissa Howse, Rita Anderson, Carolyn Walsh, Anneke Lisberg, and Simon Gadbois provided feedback on various parts of the manuscript. Two anonymous reviewers also offered many helpful suggestions as I prepared this book.

I thank, too, with all my heart, all of the fine people who helped me study dogs for decades on end, human visitors to dog parks who asked me wide-ranging questions and shared stories over the years, and people who emailed me questions and stories primarily about their dog(s). Of course, I also thank the dogs, who kept me on my toes and cautioned me that just when I thought I knew it all, I didn't. Without a good deal of dog and human help, this book would never have materialized.

So, You Want to Become an Ethologist?

||||||||||||||||||||||||||||||||||||||||||||||||||||||||||||||||||||||||||||||||||||||||||||||||||||||||

Merl arrives at the dog park, waits impatiently for his human to open the gate. He strides through the gate and immediately goes over to a rock, lifts his right leg high as if he's the "top dog," pees a steady stream, scratches the ground vigorously, walks over to the fence surrounding the park, lifts his leg again, dribbles some pee, and then looks around either to see who else is there or to see if anyone saw him do this. This is Merl's routine, and I've seen him do it many times. However, after he pees a bit the second time, if Merl sees his friend Antonio, he takes off, runs straight at him, does a few quick play bows, and the two wrestle, bite one another with abandon, chase one another all over the place, often running over other dogs and nearly taking down some people. They play as long as their humans allow them to. However, if Antonio isn't there, and Merl sees other dogs looking at him, he pees and scratches the ground again to be sure they know what he's done. And if another dog comes over and sniffs Merl's pee and pees over it, pissing matches ensue. I once watched Merl and another dog engage in five rapid exchanges of the yellow stuff.

||||||||||||||||||||||||||||||||||||||||||||||||||||||||||||||||||||||||||||||||||||||||||||||||||||||||

This description of Merl playing and peeing is an excellent example of what field notes look like, as is the story of Jethro and Zeke that opens chapter 3. Indeed, people at dog parks spend a lot of time watching and commenting on these two behaviors. At dog parks, when I teach people how to become ethologists, I usually focus on playing, peeing, ground scratching, and dogs observing one another. These behaviors are excellent teaching tools because individuals can be identified, they can be seen throughout the encounter, and the actions are clear and easy to score. When training students, I use a standard clip of these sorts of interactions, and over time students learn to become better observers. Everyone is pleased when we agree on what dogs are doing and on what behaviors mean. Instances of occasional differences in opinions are instructive as well. People can see things differently, and these differences are important to parse.

At the dog park, people are often grateful for these mini-lessons in ethology. I remember one man, Jack, whom I coached in observing his three dogs, Henry, Max, and Violet. He was pleased that I had taken the time to train him to become a citizen ethologist, which allowed him to "become" one of his three dogs whenever he chose to do so. He told me he really felt closer to his dogs, and he had begun training other humans at the dog park. I consider this outcome advantageous to everyone affected, since the dogs and the humans always benefit from these quick courses on dog behavior.

Dogs are an ethologist's dream. When we carefully observe dogs, what we learn is a never-ending story. There always is something more to the puzzle of why dogs do what they do. Further, to understand dogs, there are *no* substitutes for careful observation and description. For ethologists, watching dogs in every type of setting and situation is critical for generating experiments, models, and theories. For you, as the human companion of a dog, closely observing your own dog is the best way to improve your dog's quality of life and to relieve the stress so many dogs endure day in and day out.

This appendix is for those who want to learn how to observe like an ethologist. A good place to begin is with the realization that to learn what it is like to be a dog, we have to, in some sense, become a dog. We have to try to adopt a dog's perspective, even if this takes an imaginative leap. When we watch dogs and other animals, it's essential that we see exactly what they're doing and try to understand it from their point of view; in this way, we, the see-ers, become the seen.[1] There's a narrative to a dog's body movements, and within the larger narrative, there are micro-movements or smaller narratives. To understand what a dog thinks and feels, we must pay close attention to the subtleties in their behavior, all of which matter.

I love meeting and inspiring citizen scientists in dog parks. I love hearing what other people think about the dogs we observe together. I learn a lot from the questions people ask and the observations they make. And I feel strongly that science in general, and the ethology of dogs in particular, will only be improved and grow through the efforts of citizen scientists.

Ethology: What It's All About

Simply put, ethologists observe animals and ask questions about the evolution and ecology of different behavior patterns. In the most basic terms, ethology is all about the details of who does what to whom, how many times, and when and where. Many psychologists are also interested in the behavior of dogs, but they typically don't take such a broad evolutionary and ecological view of behavior.

Ethologists also usually focus on free-ranging rather than captive animals. And some dogs are of course free-ranging, and we can learn a lot by watching them and seeing where they go, with whom, and for what purpose when no humans interfere with their choices. We can study feral dogs just as we study other wild animals. However, we can also study companion dogs in every setting and context. In a general sense, this field of study is called the behavioral ecology of dogs because we can observe and study them in different ecological niches, if you will, including trails where they can run free, dog parks, and in our homes, on leash and off leash, and during their various interactions: with other dogs, with combinations of dogs and people, with strangers, and with their human family. One major advantage of studying companion dogs is that it's possible to identify individuals, see them interact with other identifiable dogs, and watch them over time. When studying other animals in the field, it's not always possible to identify individuals reliably or to watch them over time.

It's essential to realize that behavior is not only something an individual *does*, but it is something an individual *has*, actions that can be measured. Behavior patterns that endure over time (or across generations) are considered evolutionary adaptations. For example, the play bow is adaptive because it works to initiate and to maintain a "play mood." This gesture has been exhibited for many generations, and each new generation continues to use it. The play bow isn't performed by a few individual dogs now and then; it seems that all dogs (with the exception of New Guinea singing dogs—a type of wild dog notable for its unique vocalizations) use bows as a successful method of communicating specific intentions.[2] Remember: the play bow changes the meaning of the behaviors that follow it. In other contexts, actions that would be regarded as aggressive or mating behavior become, after the play bow, only play.

By thinking of and studying animal behavior in this way, as a structure that an individual has, ethologist Konrad Lorenz showed how evolution can influence a wide variety of behavior patterns, including the signals used to communicate threat and dominance, as well as play, among other behaviors. The author of *Man Meets Dog*, Dr. Lorenz is often called the father of ethology, and he became famous for having ducklings and young geese imprint on him and follow him around as he crawled on the grass.

The wide-ranging importance of ethological investigations was highlighted in 1973 when Konrad Lorenz—along with Niko Tinbergen, who is often called the curious naturalist, and Karl von Frisch, for his work on bee language—jointly won the Nobel Prize in Physiology or Medicine.[3] Many scientists who deemed their own work "real research" were quite irritated that this hallowed prize went to three fellows who got paid to watch animals. What, creating ingenious field experiments to study animal behavior—and having fun doing it—isn't real research? Nothing could be further from the truth. Each scientist keenly observed animals, devised novel and often incredibly simple experiments, and offered useful and enduring theories concerning the evolution of behavior. One of my favorite books about the study of ethology and the natural history of animals is poet Hoffman

Hays's easy-to-read *Birds, Beasts, and Men*.[4] I regularly recommend it to people who want to know more about these three scientists, the history of animal behavior, and what ethologists do.

NIKO TINBERGEN'S FOUR QUESTIONS

Many ethologists, myself included, follow Niko Tinbergen's integrative ideas about the questions with which ethological studies should be concerned, namely:

evolution (Why did a behavior evolve? What is it good for?);

adaptation (How does a particular behavior allow an individual to adapt to the immediate situation? How does it contribute to individual reproductive fitness?);

causation (an overt cause is like a red light that causes you to put your foot on the brake of your car; an internal cause is like a hormonal or neural reaction that causes you to startle);

and *ontogeny* (the development and the emergence of individual differences and the role of learning).[5]

Dr. Tinbergen's ideas about how to study animal behavior became well accepted. Subsequently, University of Tennessee psychologist Gordon Burghardt added the question of personal experience to Tinbergen's scheme.[6] Burghardt had worked with Donald Griffin, a world-renowned biologist who shocked many of his colleagues when, in the mid-1970s, he suggested that we needed to pay more attention to the evolution of consciousness in animals.[7] Personal experience was an important addition to Tinbergen's four questions because it stressed that animals are conscious and sentient beings who have feelings and emotional/personal lives, which are adaptations that also evolve.

In my studies, I take a strongly comparative, evolutionary, and ecological approach, which means I look for similarities and differences among different species; I try to understand why particular behavior patterns have evolved and why they are maintained in (selected for), or disappear from, a species' repertoire; and I observe how behavior changes in different ecological and other venues. Of course, it's rare that one or only a few studies can do all this, and that's why it's so important for researchers to share results and talk with one another. Surely, research on dogs has benefited from these sorts of cooperative endeavors, though some researchers are more willing than others to engage in them.

CORRELATION ≠ CAUSATION!

As we begin, it's essential to make one more comment about analyzing behavior, namely, correlation does not imply causation. Just because different events happen at the same time, or at almost the same time, that does not necessarily mean that they are *causally* related. If, on occasion, I pour myself a glass of good red wine while a police car speeds by my home, these events are correlated in time, but there's no plausible causal explanation. Likewise, if your dog gets up (and wakes you up) whenever your neighbor pours a cup of coffee in the early morning, it would be difficult to argue for a causal relationship between the two events. However, in other, less obviously unrelated scenarios, people make this mistake all the time. For instance, when training dogs, we can inadvertently reward the wrong behavior and create an accidental association that implies causation, but that doesn't solve the problem at hand. This is why I emphasize close observations over time.

Becoming a Dog, or the Practice of Ethology

As an ethologist—a biologist who studies animal behavior with an emphasis on evolution, ecology, and comparisons of closely and more distantly related species—I always want to learn more about everything dogs do and why they do it. I am also interested in comparing individuals of one species to one another and doing cross-species comparisons to try to get a handle on why there are similarities and differences.

The bottom line is that, by becoming an ethologist yourself, you can "become a dog," or at least get a good approximation of what it's like to be a dog. Those readers well versed in philosophy will see I'm teetering on writing about phenomenology, a field that stresses the importance of direct experiences. So, in some ways I'm advocating for a field some might call phenomenological ethology.

In any case, what follows is a step-by-step primer in basic ethological research.

PATTERNS OF SOCIAL INTERACTION

Throughout this book, I discuss dog → dog (cell number 1 in the matrix below), dog → human (cell number 2), human → dog (cell number 3), and human → human (cell number 4) interactions.

It's important to note that often, when watching dogs or other animals, the different sorts of interactions become blurred awfully fast. Sometimes it's simply impossible to figure out who initiated and who ended an encounter, and when there are more than two dogs, or a dog and a human, it can become a nightmare very fast. Nonetheless, we still can learn a lot from parsing out the different types of interactions using this simple matrix.

	Receiver	
Initiator	Dog	Human
Dog	1	2
Human	3	4

On your journey to becoming an ethologist, you can make your own matrix or a set of matrices and fill in the numbers for all sorts of interactions. It's a simple and fun exercise through which you'll learn a lot about your dog's personality. For example, is she or he a leader or a follower, a player or more of a loner? What types of interactions do they initiate, and what sorts of encounters don't they especially like and try to avoid? You also can discover if they prefer some dogs rather than others, if they're having a good or bad day, and how their behavior changes over time with familiar and unfamiliar dogs and humans in different social and physical contexts. The list of things you can learn is long, depending on your interests. That's what makes watching dogs so exciting!

HOW TO MEASURE BEHAVIOR

As you become an ethologist, you'll also learn that the sorts of data you collect depend on the methods you use to watch individuals or groups of animals. Ethologists try to use objective criteria and measurements when observing and analyzing behavior. Some of these measurements include:

FREQUENCY: This is simply the number of times a behavior is performed.

RATE (frequency/time): This is a refinement of frequency, in that *rate* factors in time or duration. How frequently does a dog perform a particular behavior during a specific period of time?

INTENSITY: It's difficult to measure intensity (or concentration) when observing individuals, so some researchers often use what's called the distraction index. Namely, how difficult is it to stop an animal from doing something? So, for example, when a dog is walking around with their nose pinned to the ground, sometimes it's almost impossible to get their attention. Intensity is a subjective measurement, but it can be made somewhat more objective by measuring the strength of a scent needed, the loudness of a noise required, and the length of time it takes to get the individual's attention.

SAMPLING TECHNIQUES

Another aspect of doing ethological research is to decide how to watch dogs. Researchers call these sampling techniques. Here are a few outlined by Dr. Jeanne Altmann, who did seminal studies on the behavior of nonhuman primates.[8]

AD LIB SAMPLING: This means you record everything you can. It's easier to do this when filming animals, but it's also possible to do when recording ongoing behavior into a tape recorder of a smart phone. Of course, when an individual is out of sight, you have little to no idea of what they did or what was done to them.

FOCAL ANIMAL SAMPLING: This sampling method means you observe and score everything that one member of the group does and everything that is done to that focal animal for a period of time. Then you rotate in order (or randomly) among all the members of the group. Sampling must be randomized so that all individuals are observed at different times of day (or differing periods throughout the observation time window). It is necessary to be able to identify individuals for this method to work.

1–0 SAMPLING: With this method, you choose one individual and set a time interval during which you simply score if they do something or something is done to them. This is a very crude method that doesn't generate many detailed data, but often it's all that can be done, especially when it's difficult to follow or to identify individuals.

CHOOSING A METHOD: In the best of all possible worlds, it would be great if you could record everything that an individual does as well as everything that other group members do, but this is often difficult, so you just have to go with what works and make the best of it. It's essential to know the limitations of the sampling methods you use. If you can't see a dog all of the time, or if you can't identify individuals reliably, then there are limits to what you can learn. But this is okay. Rather, do what you can do and recognize whatever limitations you face.

Of course, short-term results may vary significantly from results gained over long periods of observation. A good question that often comes my way is: "How do you know when to stop?" If no new patterns or observations are made after a period of time, it's likely you saw most of what is important. Of course, many animals breed only once a year, so if you missed this, you will have missed a very important set of events! After around three years of studying dogs, I didn't note any new behavior patterns that could be added to the catalog of actions I recorded. But in my eight-year study of wild coyotes, we were still learning new facts about these incredibly cunning and adaptable canids right up until the end.

CONSTRUCTING AN ETHOGRAM

As I say, the easiest way to become a dog or other animal is first to spend time watching them. It's incredibly instructive simply to observe them running freely, or nearly so, such as at dog parks and on trails where they're allowed to run and explore on their own. However, observing dogs as they walk tethered by a leash to a human also yields data. Of course, it's almost equally important to watch the people who are with the dogs. The outcome of these observations would be a list of behavior patterns called an ethogram. This list is just that, a descriptive menu of what the dogs and humans do with no interpretation or explanation for why they do it. Actions can be described by their physical characteristics—what they look like—such as postures, gestures, facial expressions, and gait, or by the consequence they have, such as an individual's orientation to objects or to individuals in the environment, the results of which lead to the accomplishment of a task or to some result.

When I taught courses in animal behavior, every student had to do some sort of field project. Many chose to observe dogs with whom they lived or unfamiliar dogs in and around Boulder, Colorado, and the first thing they did was simply to observe dogs and humans for fifteen to twenty hours. They could take notes or just watch all sorts of interactions to familiarize themselves with the various behavior patterns and interactions that occurred. Other students chose to watch squirrels or birds on campus, for example, and they also spent the same amount of time watching the animals to get a feel for who they are and what they do. After this time, they developed an ethogram and compared notes to be sure they had a good sampling of difference actions and encounters.

The information collected from direct observations could then be supplemented by filming the animals, but the first set of observations were through their own eyes, ears, and noses. Today, you can record the data using a tape recorder, phone, or computer, and new methods and devices are constantly being developed. Students routinely told me they were amazed by how much they learned by watching dogs with whom they were familiar, individuals whom they thought they really knew. I told them that I was always amazed as well when I simply stepped back and watched dogs with whom I lived or dogs in other venues. Having been trained in ethology, I know that all ethologists spend a lot of time "just watching" the animals in whom they are interested with no agenda other than to learn about the things they do and to get a feel for how they negotiate various social and nonsocial situations. As you know by now, I treasure the ethological approach to learning about animal behavior.

Developing an ethogram, or a menu of what animals do, is the most important part of a behavioral study. To me, it really is fun and a great experience in learning about how animals act. There are numerous dog ethograms available, and two I use are offered by ethologists Roger Abrantes (*Dog Language*) and Michael W. Fox (*Behaviour of Wolves, Dogs, and Related Canids*). Barbara Handelman's *Canine Behavior: A Photo Illustrated Handbook* is also an excellent resource, as are the numerous illustrations at "Learning to Speak Dog Part 4: Reading a Dog's Body."[9] Some behavior patterns that people score include a dog's approach to other dogs (speed and orientation); biting directed toward different parts of the body; biting intensity (inhibited and soft, or hard and accompanied by either shaking of the head or not); rolling over; standing over; chin resting, play soliciting; self-play; peeing and the posture used; pooping; growling; barking; whining; approaching and withdrawing; pawing directed toward different parts of the body; ear position; tail position; gait; and so on. Over the years, I have found that I can account for the behavior of most dogs by scoring around fifty different behavior patterns.

SPLITTERS AND LUMPERS

Depending on their focus, researchers tend to approach or organize their data in two ways: by splitting or lumping. Splitters do micro-analyses of actions, and lumpers are interested in broad categories of behavior, such as play, aggression, and mating, for example. Whether you split or lump actions depends on the questions in which you're interested. I always split because then you can lump later on if that's the best strategy. But if you lump first, it's impossible to split later on. It turns out that there is a lot of agreement among people who construct dog ethograms, so there are some basic behavior patterns that transcend dogs.

To put this all together, the simple steps in constructing an ethogram are as follows: watch animals in person or on videos; list each different behavior; compare your list with others; watch more and write down more behaviors; come up with a code for each behavior so you can "score" observations easily; and split behaviors rather than lumping two or more together. For instance, rather than write "bite," distinguish where the bite occurred: face bite, ear bite, neck bite, body bite, and so on. Or denote intensity: an intense hip slam versus a mild hip slam. You can group all bites together later, but you will lose the subtle differences if you do not record them first. Finally, you generate flow charts and matrices of interactions from the raw data.

What Good Does Ethology Do? Experts Weigh In

Let me end by considering a question that I'm often asked: "So, what the hell does all this ethological research do for me and my dog?" Some people follow up this question with something like, "You all need to get out of the ivory tower and into the field." Of course, this is something I believe myself. Too many researchers and dog trainers only observe dogs in the lab and when there's a problem, but they also need to go to places where dogs are walked and allowed to run freely. They need to observe dogs in the real world.

People want to know whether anything practical comes from all this research on dog behavior. For instance, many people who want to adopt dogs are interested in the value of assessment tests that are used to understand an individual's personality. While there are some debates about their reliability, I feel they work well enough so that they should be continued.[10] One example of practical application comes by way of Alexandra Protopopova, an assistant professor in companion animal science in the Department of Animal and Food Sciences at Texas Tech University. According to *Science Daily*, she is working "to determine what behavioral traits in dogs are most attractive to potential adopters and then working with shelters to train dogs to exhibit those traits when an adopter shows interest."[11] "We are very excited about this procedure," said Protopopova, "because this is really the first time we have experimentally and systematically demonstrated an increase in adoption rates through behavioral training." This really is good news for the millions of dogs who need homes and who spend far too long in cages at shelters or are put to sleep.

I certainly hope that this book has helped in many ways to answer the question of whether all this research into the ethology of dogs actually benefits dogs themselves. Research on dogs increases our understanding of our family pets and companions, and it helps us improve their lives so we can provide the best life for them that we can. So I thought I'd end the book by letting an international group of experts in the field of dog studies share their insights about how research benefits dogs. I asked each this question, and this is what they replied:

DR. ÁDÁM MIKLÓSI: The author of the excellent book *Dog Behaviour, Evolution, and Cognition* and numerous research essays with many colleagues at Eötvös Loránd University in Budapest, Dr. Miklósi oversees the Family Dog Project.

This is a very general question. In my experience people know very little about dogs, both about their general behavior and their problem-solving ability. In some situations they may overestimate the dogs' performance (e.g., talking about their smelling skills); at other times they underestimate it (e.g., dogs can learn by observing humans and other dogs — not just clicker training). So our research aims to provide objective knowledge about behaviors and skills of dogs.

People often make parallels between humans and dogs. Stanley Coren says that dogs are like two- to three-year-old children. We would like to be more precise and find out exactly in which case (behavior function/skill) can we say that the performance of dogs is comparable to that of a two-year-old, and when is this comparison problematic. Moreover, even if we find similarities, the underlying mental mechanisms can be still different.

I also support the notion of friendship, which means that people need to invest time and effort in their relationship with dogs, and they should allow the dog to be a dog, and should not try to turn it to a "little baby."

I hope when people read our one hundred-plus papers, then they get a good overall picture about the dog, which has made a very interesting evolutionary journey from the "wild" to become our best friend.[12]

DR. JOHN BRADSHAW: Internationally known for his research on dogs and cats, Dr. Bradshaw is the author of *Dog Sense: How the New Science of Dog Behavior Can Make You a Better Friend to Your Pet*.[13] In an email, he addressed research on feral dogs, stating: "In my view, the main contribution that studies of feral dogs have made is to confirm that dogs are not wolves." Then he pointed me to an essay he wrote with Nicola Rooney, in which they note:

The relevance of wolf social biology to furthering our comprehension of the behavior of domestic dogs has recently been cast into doubt, partly because wolves and dogs are now known to be significantly different in their cognitive abilities, and partly because studies of free-roaming dogs have revealed a preferred social structure that is pack-based but otherwise quite unlike that of the wolf. The apparent certainties of the wolf-pack model, which was still universally adopted as recently as two decades ago, have not yet been replaced by any new consensus. To explain dog behavior functionally ("what is it for?") requires an understanding of the adaptive pressures that have shaped dogs since their divergence from the wolf. It is likely that these are essentially anthropogenic, and that each dog's lifetime reproductive success is influenced more by interactions with people than by interactions with other dogs. If so, it follows that any social structure adopted by free-roaming dogs may not be fully adapted to feral life.[14]

DR. LUIGI BOITANI: Well known for his research on wolves and feral dogs, Dr. Luigi Boitani replied that

this is not a simple question! I think that studying feral dogs we have the opportunity to learn at least two orders of information:

1) How much has been lost through domestication of the dog's capacity to cope with natural environments. In other words, how much domestication has changed traits of wolf natural history (hierarchy, territoriality, social cohesion within a pack . . .). This may not be of interest to a dog owner, I agree, but it is of great interest to biologists.

2) How thin is the separation between wild and domesticated environments. In an epoch (the Anthropocene) in which human domination is extending rapidly all over the world, the maintenance of clear boundaries between what is (or should be) wild and what is a human environment becomes a crucial question that has huge ethical, biological, evolutionary, economic, and many other aspects. Feral dogs and hybrids (wolf-dog) are the perfect paradigms to explore the friction between the two realms and help us think of what owning a dog means.[15]

DR. ROBERTO BONANNI: I asked Dr. Bonanni—who is well known for the detailed research he and his colleagues do on free-ranging dog packs on the outskirts of Rome in an area called Muratella—how what we learn from feral dogs can be applied to companion dogs.

As you know, that's a very difficult question! I suspect that stray/feral dogs may be genetically different from companion dogs (and not just ontogenetically different), so for this and many other reasons every comparison should be taken with great caution. Anyway, I will try to tell you what I have learnt from my experience in the field.

In brief, dogs are emotional animals and they need to live in stable social groups, e.g., if they lose the support of their companions, for any reasons, they seek immediately to associate with someone else (dog or human); however, they are also able to maintain looser affiliative relationships with individuals (dogs and humans) who are not belonging to their stable social unit. So, for dogs going to parks, interactions with familiar individuals would be preferable, although interactions with less-familiar dogs are also possible and can be affiliative.

Dogs living with human families suffer from many limitations and constraints that are usually not experienced at all by stray/feral dogs. Although there are dominance hierarchies in dog packs, and these affect several aspects of social life, dog leaders are usually much less despotic than human leaders. For example, subordinates are sometimes allowed to lead collective movements; pack members are never forced to follow the leaders. They are completely free to go wherever they want at any time; they are free to smell everything they want without being taken on the leash; subordinates are allowed to breed at least to some extent; they are often allowed to spray their urine to mark. Importantly, our research has shown that subordinates like staying and resting close by the leaders, and this is the reason why they usually follow them! Coordination, as well as cooperation, are promoted by having developed a positive and affiliative relationship. Another point is that dominance rank in these packs is mainly affected by age, a variable that seems to be even more important than body size (unpublished information), so social status seems to be more often acquired by getting old than by aggressive challenges.

In summary, dogs are cooperative carnivores, they like doing things together especially in a coordinated fashion, aggression among pack companions is rare (especially in small groups), and severe aggression is extremely rare. Aggression tends to increase when dogs are competing for food and females, although you will often see pack members feeding close to each other without showing any tension. In practice, this may mean (for example) that since there are usually short social distances between leaders and subordinates in dog packs, allowing your dog to sleep with you in your bed or on the grass may be even a good idea, indeed! Also, doing things together (e.g., walking, running, playing, exploring a natural environment, resting together, marking) should contribute to improve the quality of dog-human relationships. Feeding before your dog, as well as forcing your dog to walk always behind you, is despotic behavior and should be avoided.[16]

DR. BRIAN HARE: Director of Duke University's Canine Cognition Center, Dr. Hare is also coauthor with Vanessa Woods of *The Genius of Dogs: How Dogs Are Smarter Than You Think*.[17] In answer to the question of how citizen science can help, Dr. Hare shared the abstract of a paper that he and his colleagues authored on this topic:

Family dogs and dog owners offer a potentially powerful way to conduct citizen science to answer questions about animal behavior that are difficult to answer with more conventional approaches. Here we evaluate the quality of the first data on dog cognition collected by citizen scientists using the Dognition.com website. We conducted analyses to understand if data generated by over five hundred citizen scientists replicates internally and in comparison to previously published findings. Half of participants participated for free while the other half paid for access. The website provided each participant a temperament questionnaire and instructions on how to conduct a series of ten cognitive tests. Participation required internet access, a dog, and some common household items. Participants could record their responses on any PC, tablet, or smartphone from anywhere in the world, and data were retained on servers.

Results from citizen scientists and their dogs replicated a number of previously described phenomena from conventional lab-based research. There was little evidence that citizen scientists manipulated their results. To illustrate the potential uses of relatively large samples of citizen science data, we then used factor analysis to examine individual differences across the cognitive tasks. The data were best explained by multiple factors in support of the hypothesis that nonhumans, including dogs, can evolve multiple cognitive domains that vary independently. This analysis suggests that in the future, citizen scientists will generate useful datasets that test hypotheses and answer questions as a complement to conventional laboratory techniques used to study dog psychology.[18]

I'm really glad these experts took the time to answer these questions. Agree or not, they offer a lot of food for thought. Ultimately, our common goal is to use what we know to make the lives of dogs, with whom we share our homes and hearts, the best they can possibly be. By following some of the material provided in this crash course on dog behavior, you can play a vital role in helping the dog or dogs with whom you live enjoy life to its fullest.

NOTES

Preface

1. There are on-going debates about how to refer to domestic dogs; some people prefer the traditional *Canis familiaris*, whereas others prefer *Canis lupus familiaris*.

2. My own experience is that some dogs like music and many are rather indifferent. A study published in March 2017 indicated that music could be used to reduce stress in some dogs when they listened to soft rock and reggae (Bowman, Dowell, and Evans, "The Effect of Different Genres of Music").

3. Hirskyj-Douglas, "Here's What Dogs See When They Watch Television."

4. Ma, "Take a Walk on the Rewild Side."

5. Bekoff, "Hugging a Dog Is Just Fine"; "Sleep Habits of the Animal Kingdom."

6. Bekoff, "Training Dogs"; also see Tracy Krulik, "Eager to Please"; and Bekoff, "If Dogs Were Humans They Would Be Jerks."

Chapter One

1. Nonhuman animals often make humans laugh, but we know little about why. In "Tails of Laughter," Robin Maria Vilari suggests that "dogs may serve as friends with whom to laugh or their behaviors may provide a greater source of laughter."

2. Kimberly Nuffer, email message to author, November 13, 2016.

3. Ken Rodriguez, email message to author, November 13, 2016.

4. For additional information on the Canine Effect's style of dog training, see https://www.facebook.com/thecanineeffect/.

5.   Researchers at the University of Lincoln in Great Britain are conducting many ongoing studies of dog personality that are providing important information about the range of personalities dogs display. These projects include detailed genetic, neurobiological, and behavior analyses (http://www.uoldogtemperament .co.uk/dogpersonality/).

6.   For more information and reviews of research papers and books on the origin of dogs, please see a series of essays by Mark Derr in *PsychologyToday* (*Dog's Best Friend* [blog]) and his book *How the Dog Became the Dog*; David Grimm's *Citizen Canine*; Ádám Miklósi's *Dog Behaviour, Evolution, and Cognition*; Pat Shipman's *The Invaders*; Jacob Mikanowski's "Wild Thing"; Morey and Jeger's "From Wolf to Dog"; and Janice Koler-Matznick's *Dawn of the Dog*.

7.   Nonhumans and humans rely on instincts or innate patterns of behavior in certain situations, especially when something has to be done "correctly" the first time. These actions include staying close to an adult for food and protection or avoiding predators. Contrary to much popular use of words such as "instinct" or "innate" that suggests that instincts are not modifiable, research shows that instincts can be modified through learning, and are not set in stone. For more on this topic please see Jack Hailman's classic essay titled "How an Instinct Is Learned"; and books, including Konrad Lorenz's *The Foundations of Ethology*; and Niko Tinbergen's *The Study of Instinct*.

8.   In response to an essay I wrote about Cesar Millan being bitten by a dog named Holly because he continually intruded into her space despite Holly giving him many warnings to leave her alone, someone suggested that Holly bit her humans and perhaps Millan "for no reason at all" ("Do Dogs Really Bite Someone for 'No Reason at All'?). Of course, Holly has plenty of good reason to bite people who don't take heed of her warnings that "enough's enough: please leave me alone."

9.   Please see Jonathan Balcombe's *What a Fish Knows*. We also know that bumblebees can use tools, count to four, and play soccer (Handwerk, "Bees Can Learn to Play 'Soccer'").

10.   Numerous essays published in *Animal Sentience: An Interdisciplinary Journal on Animal Feeling* (http://animalstudiesrepository.org/animsent/) provide excellent examples of the amount of interest and research there is on this topic; please also see material on the Cambridge Declaration on Consciousness (http:// fcmconference.org/img/CambridgeDeclarationOnConsciousness.pdf).

11.   For most personal stories in this book, I've used pseudonyms to protect the guilty and the innocent. Many quotes are just as they were spoken; others I paraphrase because I don't want to identify the humans, who, I hope, will read this book.

12.   Pearce, "Down with Data."

13. Bray, MacLean, and Hare, "Increasing Arousal Enhances Inhibitory Control in Calm but Not Excitable Dogs."

14. Howse, "Exploring the Social Behaviour of Domestic Dogs."

15. Arden, Bensky, and Adams, "A Review of Cognitive Abilities in Dogs."

16. Bekoff, "Pit Bulls"; please also see Dickey, *Pit Bull.*

17. James Crosby, email message to author, July 15, 2017; Crosby, "The Specific Use of Evidence in the Investigation of Dog Bite Related Human Fatalities." For more details about dog bites from different points of view, see Mills and Westgarth, *Dog Bites: A Multidisciplinary Perspective.*

18. Margini, "What Is It Like to Be an Elephant?"

19. Hoff, *The Tao of Pooh*, 29.

20. A touching story of how hundreds of strangers escorted a dying dog for his last walk nicely exemplifies how dogs can be social catalysts (Corbley, "Hundreds of Strangers Escort Dying Dog").

21. Abbott, "Jane Goodall, Rusty and Me."

22. Peterson, *Jane Goodall*, 277.

23. Abbott, "Dogs (and Cats) without Borders."

24. Warden and Warner, "The Sensory Capacities and Intelligence of Dogs," 2.

25. For an excellent summary of this topic, see Stewart et al., "Citizen Science as a New Tool in Dog Cognition Research." Also see Cavalier and Kennedy, *The Rightful Place of Science*; and Cooper, *Citizen Science.*

26. This story by Rohan Dennis is from a personal conversation with the author, while quotes are from an email message to author, November 11, 2016.

27. Sonntag and Overall, "Key Determinants of Cat and Dog Welfare," 213.

28. Bekoff, "We Are Animals and Therein Lies Hope for a Better Future."

29. Bekoff, "Is an Unnamed Cow Less Sentient Than a Named Cow?"

30. Jamin Chen, email message to Jessica Pierce, May 8, 2016.

31. DeKok, "The Origin of World Animal Day."

32. Pascaline, "Minnesota Town Elects Dog Mayor Named Duke for the Third Time."

33. Chan, "The Mysterious History behind Humanity's Love of Dogs."

34. Good News for Pets, "Pet Industry Spending at All-Time High."

35. Addady, "This Is How Much Americans Spend on Their Dogs."

36. Brulliard, "Americans Are Spending More on Health Care—for Their Pets."; see also Riley, "Puppy Love."

37. "People Living in Cities Will Risk Own Safety to Save Animals"; see also Irvine's *Filling the Ark.*

38. Bradley and King, "The Dog Economy Is Global."

39. For more discussion on this topic, please see Archer, "Why Do People Love Their Pets?"; and also Carr's *Dogs in the Leisure Experience* and references therein.

40. Pilgrim, "Children Are Closer to Their Pets Than Their Siblings."

41. "Pet Dogs Help Kids Feel Less Stressed."

42. Tasaki, "Trending: Dog-Friendly Housing Associations."

43. I can't find any "academic" reference for this number, but it comes up in many conversations. Even if it were 5–10 percent, it would be far too high.

44. McPherson, "'I Want to Kill These Dogs.'"

45. "The Vet Who 'Euthanised' Herself in Taiwan."

46. In January 2017, fifty-one greyhound trainers in Australia were accused of doping dogs with ketamine, amphetamines, pesticides, and cobalt (Knaus, "Greyhound Doping).

47. Designer dogs are not purebred dogs as some often refer to them. It's important to note that Wally Conron, the man who first produced labradoodles, regrets his creation. In an essay by Stanley Coren called "A Designer Dog-Maker Regrets His Creation," Conron notes, "I opened a Pandora's box, that's what I did. I released a Frankenstein. So many people are just breeding for the money. So many of these dogs have physical problems, and a lot of them are just crazy."

48. "Appetite for Designer Dogs 'Unquenchable.'"

49. Kaplan, "Dog Domestication Saddled Man's Best Friend with Defective Genes"; also see Brandow's *A Matter of Breeding*. There are, in addition, issues centering on dogs sold in pet shops that go beyond what I cover here.

    Along these lines, on a few occasions I've been asked how selecting for different traits works. A few of the people who have asked this question had degrees in biology, so I offered them a brief "lecture" on evolutionary biology. I explained to them that, when breeders select, for example, for traits such as a smushed nose or crunched-up face, I tell them that Elliott Sober, a philosopher at the University of Wisconsin in Madison, draws a distinction between the notion of "selection *for*" and "selection *of*" different traits in his book called *The Nature of Selection*.

    Basically, when a trait is selected *for* we are intentionally trying to produce it, and the other traits that accompany it are examples of by-products. What I also find very interesting is how many people, even those without any background in biology or any degree at all, are open to these sorts of discussions when they can see concrete examples of what we're talking about. Dog parks are great "classrooms" for field classes in animal behavior and biology. And this is a plus for the dogs as well.

50. Scully, "The Westminster Dog Show Fails the Animals It Profits From."

51. Bird, "Undercover Video Shows Texas A&M Intentionally Breeds Deformed Dogs."

52. Bekoff, "Why People Buy Dogs Who They Know Will Suffer."

53. I'm also asked frequently if dogs love us more than cats do. The simple answer

is that we really don't know. For more on this, please see Bekoff, "Do Our Dogs Really Love Us More Than Our Cats Do?"

54.   Elise Gatti, email message to author, January 25, 2016.

Chapter Two

1.   "A nose with a body attached" is Frans de Waal's summary of Horowitz in "How Do Dogs Recognize Us?"

2.   A wealth of valuable information about dogs' noses can be found in two books that focus on noses. The first, by dog researcher Alexandra Horowitz, is called *Being a Dog* and the second is by Norwegian biologist Frank Rosell and is called *Secrets of the Snout.*

3.   Horowitz, *Being a Dog*, 29–31. I'm often asked about research that shows that dogs know when their human is coming home. Rupert Sheldrake has done a good deal of research on this question (see, e.g., under "Scientific Papers on Animal Powers" at http://www.sheldrake.org/research) and my friend Lawrence Bosch tells me that Rocket, one of the standard poodles with whom he shares his home, knows when family are coming up the road to visit him regardless of season or if windows are closed or open. I've heard a good number of these stories from people who don't know of Dr. Sheldrake's research. We surely need more research in this area.

4.   For more on conservation dogs, see my interview with Pete Coppolillo, executive director of Working Dogs for Conservation (https://wd4c.org): Bekoff, "For the Love of a Ball."

5.   For more information on these topics, please see Milena Penkowa's book *Dogs and Human Health* and references therein; see also Marucot, "Dogs Can Smell Fear but Can't Detect If You Have Lung Cancer."

6.   "Paintings from the Perspective of a Dog's Nose."

7.   Research published in May 2017 calls into question whether humans' sense of smell is really all that much poorer than that of dogs (Ball, "Don't Be Sniffy If You Smell Like a Dog"). Gallings, "Sight, Hearing, Smell."

8.   Horowitz, "From Fire Hydrants to Rescue Work."

9.   Horowitz, *Being a Dog*, 48.

10.   Hodes, "More Fat, Less Protein Improves Detection Dogs' Sniffers."

11.   Farricelli, "Does Human Perfume Affect Dogs?"

12.   Rosell, *Secrets of the Snout*, 27.

13.   Ibid., 28.

14.   Ibid., 32.

15.   Bradshaw and Rooney, "Dog Social Behavior and Communication," 140.

16.   Ray, "How Does One Dog Recognize Another as a Dog?"; and Autier-Dérian et al., "Visual Discrimination of Species in Dogs (*Canis familiaris*)."

17.   How good is a dog's sense of hearing? 2009. Service Dog Central; http:// servicedogcentral.org/content/node/435

18.   Huber, "How Dogs Perceive and Understand Us."

Chapter Three

1.   Darwin, *The Descent of Man*, 99.

2.   Ibid., 105.

3.   Boult, "Rats Laugh When Tickled."

4.   Caldwell, "Mindfulness & Bodyfulness."

5.   Sarah Bexell, email message to author, November 21, 2016.

6.   Carl Safina, email message to author, October 16, 2016.

7.   "Biology of Fun."

8.   Gruber and Bekoff, "A Cross-Species Comparative Approach to Positive Emotion Disturbance."

9.   Research has shown that dogs growl honestly—they mean what they say especially in serious contest situations—and that humans are very good at understanding what dogs are saying to one another when they growl, women being better than men in correctly classifying these vocalizations. Researchers also discovered that there is more variation in play growls, and perhaps this is one reason why play only rarely escalates into serious aggressive interactions. For more discussion on this topic, see Bekoff, "Dogs Growl Honestly and Women Understand Better Than Men."

10.   *Wikipedia*, s.v. "stabilizing selection," last modified May 7, 2017, https://en .wikipedia.org/wiki/Stabilizing_selection.

11.   These forms of selection are different types of natural selection.

12.   Burghardt, *The Genesis of Play*.

13.   Schaefer, *Religious Affects*, 188.

14.   For more on some classic research on the social and physical development of dogs, please see Scott and Fuller's classic book *Genetics and the Social Behavior of the Dog*; and Fox's *Integrative Development of Brain and Behavior in the Dog*.

15.   Spinka, Newberry, and Bekoff, "Mammalian Play."

16.   Jennifer Miller, email message to author, November 20, 2016.

17.   Rugaas, *On Talking Terms with Dogs*.

18.   McConnell, "A New Look at Play Bows."

19.   Bekoff, "Social Communication in Canids."

20.   Byosiere, Espinosa, and Smuts, "Investigating the Function of Play Bows in Adult Pet Dogs (*Canis lupus familiaris*)."

21. Bekoff, "Play Signals as Punctuation."

22. Bauer and Smuts, "Cooperation and Competition during Dyadic Play in Domestic Dogs, *Canis familiaris*."

23. Norman et al., "Down but Not Out."

24. Smuts, Bauer, and Ward, "Rollovers during Play."

25. Hecht, "Why Do Dogs Roll Over during Play?"

26. Ward, Trisko, and Smuts, "Third-Party Interventions in Dyadic Play between Littermates."

27. Cordoni, Nicotra, and Palagi, "Unveiling the 'Secret' of Play in Dogs (*Canis lupus familiaris*)."

28. Bradshaw and Rooney, "Dog Social Behavior and Communication," 152.

29. Sergio Pellis, email message to author, October 19, 2016.

30. McConnell, "A New Look at Play Bows."

31. Shyan, Fortune, and King, "'Bark Parks.'"

32. Lindsey Mehrkam, email message to author, June 24, 2015.

33. Palagi, Nicotra, and Cordoni, "Rapid Mimicry and Emotional Contagion in Domestic Dogs."

34. Ibid.

35. Bálint et al., "'Beware, I Am Big and Non-Dangerous!'" 128.

Chapter Four

1. Email message to author, March 10, 2016; the author wishes to remain anonymous

2. Krulik, "Dogs and Dominance."

3. Bradshaw, Blackwell, and Casey, "Dominance in Domestic Dogs."

4. Gompper, ed., *Free-Ranging Dogs and Wildlife Conservation*.

5. Hekman, "Understanding Canine Social Hierarchies."

6. L. David Mech, email message to author, February 16, 2012.

7. Mech, "Alpha Status, Dominance, and Division of Labor in Wolf Packs," 1200.

8. Serpell, "Epilogue," 407.

9. Bekoff, "What's Happening When Dogs Play Tug-of-War?"

10. Miller, *Play with Your Dog*.

11. Tracy Krulik is a dog trainer and behavior consultant (http://dogzandtheir peoplez.com). Bekoff, "Dogs, Dominance, Breeding, and Legislation."

12. Tracy Krulik, email message to author, December 22, 2016.

13. Regarding separation anxiety, see Krulik, "Dominance and Dogs."

14. Anonymous email message to author, January 15, 2017.

15. Overall, "Special issue: The 'Dominance' Debate."

16. Ibid., 5.

17.   Michaels, *Do No Harm*; for further discussion, see my interview with Michaels, "A Hierarchy of Dog Needs."

18.   Arnold, *Love Is All You Need*, 6.

19.   Reisner, "The Learning Dog," 214.

20.   Bradshaw and Rooney, "Dog Social Behavior and Communication," 153.

21.   John Bradshaw, email message to author, July 11, 2016.

22.   American Veterinary Society of Animal Behavior, "Position Statement on the Use of Dominance Theory in Behavior Modification of Animals."

23.   O'Heare, *Dominance Theory and Dogs*, 67.

Chapter Five

1.   Pierce, "Not Just Walking the Dog."

2.   Bradshaw and Rooney, "Dog Social Behavior and Communication," 150.

3.   Horowitz, "From Fire Hydrants to Rescue Work."

4.   Unless otherwise noted, the quotes by Anneke Lisberg in this chapter are from a personal email message to the author, November 1, 2016.

5.   Lisberg and Snowdon, "The Effects of Sex, Gonadectomy and Status on Investigation Patterns," 1147.

6.   Caazzo, Natoli, and Valsecchi, "Scent-Marking Behaviour in a Pack of Free-Ranging Domestic Dogs," 955.

7.   Bradshaw and Rooney, "Dog Social Behavior and Communication," 150.

8.   Lisberg and Snowdon, "Effects of Sex, Social Status and Gonadectomy on Countermarking," 757.

9.   Gough and McGuire, "Urinary Posture and Motor Laterality in Dogs," 61.

10.   Caazzo, Natoli, and Valsecchi, "Scent-Marking Behaviour in a Pack of Free-Ranging Domestic Dogs."

11.   McGuire and Bernis, "Scent Marking in Shelter Dogs," 53.

12.   Gray, "Foxes May Confuse Predators by Rubbing Themselves in Puma Scent," 15.

13.   "Sophia Grows."

14.   Greg Coffin, email message to author, November 14, 2016.

15.   Gilbert, *Off the Leash*, 66. For a general discussion on how humans use humor to talk about all sorts of poop, please see Robert, "The Evolution of Humor."

16.   Gilbert, *Off the Leash*, 67.

17.   Horowitz, *Being a Dog*, 17.

18.   Cafazzo, Natoli, and Valsecchi, "Scent-Marking Behaviour in a Pack of Free-Ranging Domestic Dogs," 955.

19.   Bekoff, "Perils of Pooping."

20.   Gayomali, "Dogs Might Poop in Line with the Earth's Magnetic Field"; see also Hart et al., "Dogs Are Sensitive to Small Variations of the Earth's Magnetic

Field"; and Bekoff, "Dogs Line up with the Earth's Magnetic Field to Poop and Pee."

21.   Henry Nichols notes that many different animals show a roughly north-south alignment in different activities, but no one really knows why ("Animal Magnetism.").

Chapter Six

1.   Mary Devine, email message to author, August 25, 2016.

2.   It's been suggested that some people "unmind" animals who are used for food or research in order to distance themselves from what they are doing to these sentient beings; Please see Bekoff and Pierce, *The Animals' Agenda*, for more discussion on this point.

3.   In *Understanding Dogs*, sociologist Clinton Sanders discusses how people "mind dogs" by paying attention to their thought processes, emotional experiences, and unique personalities, and how important this is in developing and maintaining relationships with them.

4.   "Dog Quotations," http://www.crazyfordogs.com/quotes/quotes.shtml.

5.   Cook, "Inside the Dog Mind," interview with Brian Hare.

6.   Hoffman, "To Learn How Smart Dogs Are, Humans Learn New Tricks."

7.   Szentágothai, "The 'Brain-Mind' Relation," 323.

8.   Bekoff, "Dog Smarts."

9.   Horowitz, "Attention to Attention in Domestic Dog (*Canis familiaris*) Dyadic Play," 107.

10.   Harmon-Hill and Gadbois, "From the Bottom Up."

11.   Gorman, "Why Is That Dog Looking at Me?"

12.   Payne, Bennett, and McGreevy, "DogTube."

13.   Coren, "Do Dogs Have a Sense of Humor?"; I do not agree with Dr. Coren that dogs have "juvenile minds."

14.   Bekoff, *The Emotional Lives of Animals*, 57–60.

15.   "Dogs Share Food with Other Dogs Even in Complex Situations."

16.   Cook et al., "Awake Canine fMRI Predicts Dogs' Preference for Praise Versus Food," 1853.

17.   Feuerbacher and Wynne, "Most Domestic Dogs (*Canis lupus familiaris*) Prefer Food to Petting"; also see Bekoff, "Training Dogs."

18.   Bekoff, "Training Dogs."

19.   Arden and Adams, "A General Intelligence Factor in Dogs"; London School of Economics, "Mensa Mutts?"

20.   Coren, "Understanding the Nature of Dog Intelligence."

21.   One study of cats demonstrated they show the same sort of episodic memory

as dogs concerning where they had found food to eat, so for those who like to claim dogs are smarter than cats this study shows that the generalization is false; Briggs, "Cats May Be as Intelligent as Dogs."

22. Anderson et al., "Third-Party Social Evaluations of Humans by Monkeys and Apes."

23. Hyman, "Dogs Don't Remember."

24. Kuroshima et al., "Experience Matters."

25. Fugazza, Pogány, and Miklósi, "Recall of Others' Actions after Incidental Encoding Reveals Episodic-like Memory in Dogs."

26. Ádám Miklósi, email message to author, November 24, 2016.

27. Bekoff, "Theory of Mind and Play."

28. "Clever Dog Steals Treats From Kitchen Counter."

29. Pilley, *Chaser*.

30. Kaminski and Nitzschner, "Do Dogs Get The Point?" 294.

31. Howard, "Here's More Proof That Dogs Can Totally Read Our Facial Expressions."

32. Bekoff, "Dogs Recognize Emotional States Using Mental Representations"; Griffiths, "Dogs Snub People Who Are Mean to Their Owners."

33. Gill and Webb, "Dogs 'Can Tell Difference between Happy and Angry Faces'"; Müller et al., "Dogs Can Discriminate Emotional Expressions of Human Faces"; "A Man's Best Friend."

34. Hrala, "Your Dog Doesn't Trust You When You're Angry."

35. Bonanni, Valsecchi, and Natoli, "Pattern of Individual Participation and Cheating an Conflicts between Groups of Free-Ranging Dogs," 957.

36. Bonanni, Natoli, Cafazzo, and Valsecchi, "Free-Ranging Dogs Assess the Quantity of Opponents in Intergroup Conflicts," 103.

37. Bekoff, "Hidden Tales of Yellow Snow."

38. Gatti, "Self-consciousness."

39. Horowitz, *Being a Dog*, 28.

40. Dahl, "What Does a Dog See in a Mirror?"

41. Arianna Schlumbohm, email message to author, January 13, 2017.

42. A list of some of the animals who have passed the mirror test along with videos can be seen at Pachniewska, "List of Animals That Have Passed the Mirror Test."

43. Zeno Zimmerman, email message to author, January 6, 2015.

44. Rebecca Savage, email message to author, May 26, 2016.

Chapter Seven

1. Rebecca Johnson, email message to author, December 15, 2011.

2. McConnell, *For the Love of a Dog*, 283.

3. Reber, "Caterpillars, Consciousness, and the Origins of Consciousness."

4. For more discussion on comparative studies of animal emotions, please see my book *The Emotional Lives of Animals* and numerous essays that I've written for the *Animal Emotions* blog in *Psychology Today*.

5. Bekoff, "Anthropomorphic Double-Talk."

6. Bekoff, "Anthropomorphic Double-Talk"; Burghardt, "Mediating Claims through Critical Anthropomorphism."

7. Mondal, "Study: Mice Can Sense, Feel Each Other's Pains with a Whiff."

8. Coren, "Do Dogs Have Empathy for Other Dogs?"

9. For a moving and well-informed discussion of canine spirituality and soul, see Root, *The Grace of Dogs*.

10. Christy Orris, email message to author, November 12, 2016.

11. Coren, "Do Dogs Feel Jealousy and Envy?" It is also known that oxytocin promotes social bonding in dogs (Romero et al., "Oxytocin Promotes Social Bonding in Dogs").

12. Stillwell, *The Secret Language of Dogs*, 39.

13. Bekoff, "Dogs Know When They've Been Dissed."

14. Harris and Prouvost, "Jealousy in Dogs."

15. Bekoff, "We Don't Know If Dogs Feel Guilt So Stop Saying They Don't."

16. Morris, Doe, and Godsell, "Secondary Emotions in Non-primate Species?"

17. Bekoff, "Do Dogs Really Feel Guilt or Shame?"

18. Alexandra Horowitz, February 4, 2013, "Spot on, on 'guilt,'" comment on Bekoff, "The Genius of Dogs and the Hidden Lives of Wolves."

19. John Bradshaw, email message to author, January 4, 2016.

20. Schenkel, "Expression Studies on Wolves."

21. Marisa Ware, email message to author, November 4, 2016.

22. Coren, "Long Tails versus Short Tails and Canine Communication."

23. See, e.g., Leaver and Reimchen, "Behavioural Responses of *Canis familiaris* to Different Tail Lengths of a Remotely-Controlled Life-Size Dog Replica."

24. Artelle, Dumoulin, and Reimchen, "Behavioural Responses of Dogs to Asymmetrical Tail Wagging."

25. Quengua, "A Dog's Tail Wag Says a Lot, to Other Dogs."

26. Coren, "What a Wagging Dog Tail Really Means."

27. Feddersen-Petersen, "Vocalization of European Wolves (*Canis lupus lupus* L.) and Various Dog Breeds (*Canis lupus* f. fam.)."

28. Derr, "What Do Those Barks Mean?"

29. Pongracz et al., "Human Listeners Are Able to Classify Dog (*Canis familiaris*) Barks Recorded in Different Situations"; also see Lewis, "The Meaning of Dog Barks."

30. Hecht, "Dog Speak."

31. Coren, "What Are Dogs Trying to Say When They Bark?"

32. Miller, "5 Steps to Deal with Dog Growling."

33. Odendaal and Meintjes, "Neurophysiological Correlates of Affiliative Behaviour between Humans and Dogs."

34. Nagasawa et al., "Dogs Show Left Facial Lateralization upon Reunion with Their Owners."

35. For an excellent summary of this research, see Berns, *What It's Like to Be a Dog.*

36. Berns, Brooks, and Spivak, "Scent of the Familiar."

37. Davis, "Puppies' Response to Speech Could Shed Light on Baby-Talk"; Ben-Aderet et al., "Dog-Directed Speech."

38. Olson, "Dogs have FEELINGS too!"

39. MacLean and Hare, "Dogs Hijack the Human Bonding Pathway," 280.

40. Hathaway, "Dogs Ignore Bad Advice That Humans Follow."

41. Andics et al., "Neural Mechanisms for Lexical Processing in Dogs."

42. Bekoff, "Dogs and Humans Process Sounds Similarly."

43. Carlos, "True Best Friends:"; Bekoff, "'Gosh, My Dog Is Just Like Me.'"

Chapter Eight

1. Dogs also get us out into nature. Renowned photographer Chuck Forsman's dog, Magpie, played an essential role in getting him out into nature as he followed Magpie's curious nose, ears, and eyes in natural and human-made environs, as documented in his 2013 book *Walking Magpie.* See also, on the importance of dogs in our leisure time, Neil Carr's *Dogs in the Leisure Experience* and references therein.

2. Serpell, "Creatures of the Unconscious": see also Wood et al., "More Than a Furry Companion"; and Johnson et al., *Health Benefits of Dog Walking for People and Pets.*

3. "Dog Parks Lead Growth in U.S. City Parks." The website for the Trust for Public Lands (www.tpl.org), where the latter report appears, contains numerous details about many different aspects of urban parks.

4. Information on the history of dog parks can be found in Allen, "Dog Parks"; and El Nasser, "Fastest-Growing Urban Parks Are for the Dogs."

5. Bartram, "All Dogs Allowed"; and Gaunet et al., "Description of Dogs and Owners in Outdoor Built-Up Areas."

6. For a detailed study of an evaluation of off-leash dog parks in which "users were generally satisfied," see Lee, Shepley, and Huang, "Evaluation of Off-Leash Dog Parks in Texas and Florida."

7. Case, "Dog Park People."

8. Estep and Hetts, "Pilgrim Bark Park Provincetown."

9. Heimbuch, "15 Things Humans Do Wrong at Dog Parks."

10. Smith, "Behavior: Dog Park Tips"; see also Gomez, "Dog Parks"; and Ioja et al., "Dog Walkers' vs. Other Park Visitors' Perceptions."

11. Bekoff and Meaney, "Interactions among Dogs, People, and the Environment in Boulder, Colorado." Many people are also concerned about the effect of dogs on wildlife and Sarah Reed and her colleagues discovered that, in Northern California, "the policy on domestic dogs did not appear to affect species richness and abundance of mammalian carnivores" (Reed and Merenlender, "Effects of Management of Domestic Dogs and Recreation," 504).

12. Elise Gatti, email message to author, January 23, 2017.

13. Carrier et al., "Exploring the Dog Park."

14. Howse, "Exploring the Social Behaviour of Domestic Dogs," 2.

15. Ibid., 100.

16. Bekoff, "Social Communication in Canids."

17. Graham and Glover, "On the Fence," 217.

18. Jackson, "Situated Activities in a Dog Park."

19. Siler, "Why Dogs Belong Off-Leash in the Outdoors." A number of people wrote to me mistakenly thinking I wrote Siler's essay; I did not—although I was quoted in it. Bekoff, "Why Dogs Belong Off-Leash."

20. An interesting case of leashed versus nonleashed dogs centers on the Laurel Canyon Dog Park in California, where humans let their dogs off leash illegally to cut down on illegal human activities. The park reverted to a place where dogs and humans could again go (Wolch and Rowe, "Companions in the Park").

21. Bekoff and Meaney, "Interactions among Dogs, People, and the Environment in Boulder, Colorado."

22. Bekoff and Ickes, "Behavioral Interactions and Conflict among Domestic Dogs, Black-Tailed Prairie Dogs, and People in Boulder."

23. Patrick Jackson, email message to author, May 29, 2015.

Chapter Nine

1. Bekoff, "Do Dogs Ever Simply Want to Die to End the Pain?" For further discussion of how to assess whether or not a dog is in pain, see Jessica Pierce's essay "Is Your Dog in Pain?"

2. Geggel, "Anxiety May Give Dogs Gray Hair."

3. King et al., "Anxiety and Impulsivity."

4. Arnold, Love Is All You Need, 6.

5. Milligan, "The Ethics of Animal Training," 212.

6. Pangal, "Lives of Streeties."

7. London, "Should We Call These Canine Behaviors Calming Signals?" In her analysis of the study by Dr. Mariti and her colleagues ("Analysis of the Intraspecific

Visual Communication"), Dr. London, a certified professional dog trainer, notes that the researchers did not report on the rate of de-escalation of an encounter in the absence of a calming signal. However, they did report that in 33 percent of their observations (thirty-six cases) in which dogs did not show any calming signal after receiving an aggressive behavior, they usually increased the distance between themselves and another dog by fleeing or walking away. Dr. Mariti, the senior author of the paper on which Dr. London commented, wrote to me that the reason they did not report the rate was because twenty-four of the thirty-six cases involved a single dog (email message to author, July 5, 2017).

8. In my essay "Dogs: Do 'Calming Signals' Always Work?" I agree overall with Dr. Mariti and her colleagues ("Analysis of the Intraspecific Visual Communication") that their results "suggest that these CSs [calming signals] indeed may have a role in social facilitation and preventing further aggressive behaviors."

9. See Pierce, "Palliative Care for Pets," for numerous references. See also Pierce, *The Last Walk*, and "Deciding When a Pet Has Suffered Enough"; and Klonsky, *Unconditional*. For a discussion of how we mourn various animals, including our companions, see DeMello's *Mourning Animals*. Adam Clark also has a website for dealing with pet loss education and support (www.lovelosstransition.com). For lovely stories about how old dogs can have wonderful lives and about the caring people who selflessly help them along, please see Coffey, *My Old Dog*.

10. Gardner, "Senior vs. Geriatric."

11. Byars, "Boulder Mailman Builds Ramp for Aging Dog along Route."

12. For more information on how to give a blind or sight-impaired dog the best life possible, see Horsky, *My Dog Is Blind*.

13. Jane Sobel Klonsky, email message to author, November 22, 2016. For an interview with Klonsky, please see Bekoff, "Older Dogs."

14. Cici Franklin, email message to author, January 11, 2017.

15. A recent review of different training methods stresses the importance of using positive reinforcement and avoiding positive punishment and negative reinforcement (Ziv, "The Effects of Using Aversive Training Methods in Dogs."); see also Todd, "New Literature Review Recommends Reward-Based Training"; and Michael "Hierarchy of Dog Needs" and *Do No Harm*, which can be purchased at https://gumroad.com/1 /trainingmanual.

16. Information on the Canine Effect can be found at https://www.facebook.com /thecanineeffect/; for wider-ranging discussions on the importance of understanding the different sorts of relationships that are formed between humans and dogs and their complexity, see the books by Donna Haraway in the bibliography.

17. For more advice and suggestions about dog training, see the website www

.ispeakdog.org created by Tracy Krulik, as well as my *Psychology Today* interview with Tracy (Bekoff, "iSpeakDog").

18. Kristof, "Do You Care about a Dog More Than a Refugee?"

19. Singer, *Animal Liberation*, 27.

20. Bekoff, "Valuing Dogs More Than War Victims."

21. Dr. Patty Gowaty, email message to author, August 21, 2016.

22. See, for instance, this summary of some current research: Herzog, "Study Finds Dog-Walkers Have More Bad Mental Health Days!"

23. *Dogs on the Inside*, directed by Brean Cunningham and Douglas Seirup (New York: Bond/360, 2014), DVD; for more on the making of the film, see http://www.dogsontheinside.com/.

24. For a review of animal protection laws in the United States in 2016, see Animal Legal Defense Fund, *2016 U.S. Animal Protection Laws Rankings*.

25. "Study Demonstrates Rapid Decline in Male Dog Fertility."

26. Travis, "Supreme Court: All Dogs Have Value."

27. Goldman, "Success! It's Now a Felony to Abuse Companion Animals in Ohio"; "Ohio Hunter Faces Felony Charges for Killing Man's Dogs"; and Cherney, "Orange-Osceola State Attorney Creates Animal Cruelty Unit."

28. *A Dog Named Gucci*, directed by Gorman Bechard (What Were We Thinking Films, 2015), DVD; see the films official website for more about the film: http://www.adognamedgucci.com; Bekoff, "A Dog Named Gucci."

29. Velarde and Schmitt, "New Mexico Lawmaker Wants to Make Animal Cruelty a Felony"; Orr, "2 Bills Seek Tougher Penalties for Animal Abusers in Wyoming."

30. Fowler, "MS Legislator Pushes Animal Cruelty Bill"; "How Are Animal Abuse and Family Violence Linked?"

31. Brulliard, "In a First, Alaska Divorce Courts Will Now Treat Pets More Like Children"; Paiella; "This Bill to Protect Domestic-Violence Victim's Pets Could Save Women's Lives"; Pacelle, "Federal Court Upholds New York City Ban on Puppy Mill Sales."

32. "Argentina Lawmakers Pass Law Banning Greyhound Racing"; London Assembly, "Time to Review the Dangerous Dog Act."

33. Bird, "Mexico Gets Serious."

34. "Sale of Puppies under Eight Weeks Old to Be Made Illegal."

35. "RSPCA Animal Welfare Prosecutions in Wales Up."

36. Bekoff, "Empathy Burnout and Compassion Fatigue among Animal Rescuers"; "The Vet Who 'Euthanised' Herself in Taiwan."

37. "Dog Fights Prompt 5,000 Calls to RSPCA in Past Decade."

38. Bird, "Dogs Are Worth More Than Mere 'Fair Market Value.'"

39. Pacelle, "Ohio Lawmakers Crack Down on Cockfighting."

40. "Federal Court Rules Police Can Shoot a Dog If It Moves, Barks When Officer Enters Home"; Kassam, "Judge Rules Pet Dogs Cannot Be Treated as Children in Canada Custody Dispute."

41. Kilday, "Universal Cancels Premiere of 'A Dog's Purpose.'"

42. "Animal Cruelty Law Has Governor's Signature, Dog's Paw Print."

43. Lewis, "Breaking News! Vancouver Bans Sale of Dogs, Cats, and Rabbits in Pet Stores"; Wamsley, "In a First, Connecticut's Animals Get Advocates in the Courtroom"; "Vermont Has New Law Banning Sexual Abuse of Animals."

44. Leone, "Brewery Offers 'Pawternity' Leave for Employees with New Dogs."

45. Bekoff, "Censored: Animal Welfare and Animal Abuse Data Taken Offline."

46. Contorno, "'Sarge's Law' Could Bring New Rules for Dog Trainers in Hillsborough."

47. Costello, "Dog Abuse Video Spurs Legislation to License Trainers."

48. Foubert, "Occupational Licensure for Pet Dog Trainers"; information about the Academy for Dog Trainers can be found at https://www.facebook.com/AcademyforDogTrainers/?fref=nf.

49. "Dog Training and Consumer Protection," video, https://www.facebook.com/AcademyforDogTrainers/videos/987644334623619/; also see, for additional information about the Academy for Dog Trainers, https://academyfordogtrainers.com.

50. Carlos, "Even Dogs Have Gotten into the Plastic Surgery Craze."

51. In an essay called "Are There Behavior Changes When Dogs Are Spayed or Neutered," Stanley Coren notes that there can many unexpected and unwanted behavior changes. He summarizes the results of two studies of a large number of dogs that show that, in contrast to what people expect, neutered dogs, both males and females, often show more aggression and increased fearfulness. In contrast, urine marking decreased as a result of neutering. Coren also writes: "Considering the fact that one of the reasons recommended for spaying and neutering dogs is to correct a range of canine behavior problems, Duffy and Serpell's conclusions expose this to be a myth when they say 'For most behaviors, spaying/neutering was associated with worse behavior, contrary to conventional wisdom.'"

52. Bekoff, "Bowsers on Botox."

53. "State Laws Governing Elective Surgical Procedures."

54. Ryan, "Veterinarians in British Colombia Ban Animal Tail Docking and Ear Cropping."

55. McGowan, "Debarking (Bark Softening)."

56. Grossman, "All Dog, No Bark."

57. Ibid.; Council of Europe, *European Convention for the Protection of Pet Animals*; Sweet, "Teen Files Bill to Make Vocal Surgery Illegal."

58. "Actress & Celebrity GUL PANAG Launches the SOUND OF SILENCE CAM-PAIGN!"

59. For more discussion on this topic, see Ganardi, *The Next Social Contract*.

60. Newman, "World (or at least Brooklyn) Stops for Lost Dog."

61. As I noted above, the Animal Welfare Act remains a mixed bag. While dogs and nonhuman primates are considered to be animals, it unbelievable that laboratory rats, mice, and other animals continue not to be considered animals (Bekoff, "The Animal Welfare Act Claims Rats and Mice Are Not Animals"). This is simply absurd and I wonder why aren't researchers who *know* rats and mice are indeed animals speaking out about this idiocy. The science that clearly shows these rodents are sentient beings continues to be totally ignored. Thus, in the 2002 iteration of the Animal Welfare Act we read: "Enacted January 23, 2002, Title X, Subtitle D of the Farm Security and Rural Investment Act, changed the definition of 'animal' in the Animal Welfare Act, specifically excluding birds, rats of the genus Rattus, and mice of the genus Mus, bred for use in research" (Farm Security and Rural Investment Act of 2002, Pub. L. No. 107-171, https://www.nal.usda.gov/awic/public-law-107-171-farm-security-and-rural-investment-act-2002).

62. "Mall Opens Its Doors for Stray Dogs during Winter Storm."

63. Harvey, "Indonesian Charity Finds New Homes Overseas for Unwanted Dogs."

64. More information on the Roots & Shoots Program can be found at the website https://www.rootsandshoots.org.

65. "TEDxDirigo—Zoe Weil: The World Becomes What You Teach."

66. *Encyclopaedia Britannica Online*, s.v. "Biophilia hypothesis," by Kara Rogers, accessed June 30, 2017, https://www.britannica.com/science/biophilia-hypothesis.

Appendix

1. See Bekoff, *Rewilding Our Hearts*, and references therein.

2. Information on the New Guinea singing dogs comes from Janice Koler-Matznick, personal communication.

3. "The Nobel Prize in Physiology or Medicine 1973," https://www.nobelprize.org/nobel_prizes/medicine/laureates/1973/.

4. Sandy McIntosh, "Remembering H. R. Hays."

5. Dale Jamieson and I write more on the topic of integrative ideas concerning ethological questions in our essay "On Aims and Methods of Cognitive Ethology."

6. Bekoff, "Ethology Hasn't Been Blown."

7. Dr. Griffin discovered echolocation in bats as an undergraduate at Harvard University and wrote numerous papers and books on this topic, as well as on bird

migration. He was elected to the National Academy of Sciences based on his groundbreaking research. Dr. Griffin's book *The Question of Animal Awareness*, published in 1976, shocked colleagues because he was considered to be much more of an empirical scientist. I was at some of the meetings where he spoke about his new ideas, and many of his colleagues were incredulous because, at that time, talking about the inner subjective lives and personal experiences of nonhuman animals and consciousness was rarely done, at least in public. Over the years, his ideas were increasingly accepted and some people call Griffin the father of cognitive ethology.

8. Altmann, "Observational Study of Behavior." For more details on different methods of study, see Lehner's *Handbook of Ethological Methods*.

9. "Learning to Speak Dog Part 4."

10. Wynne, "Should Shelters Bother Assessing Their Dogs?"

11. "Most Desirable Traits in Dogs for Potential Adopters."

12. Ádám Miklósi, email message to author, February 11, 2016. For more on the Family Dog Project, see https://familydogproject.elte.hu; you can receive research updates at the website as well. This group also is developing a project called SENSDOG that helps dog owners to collect and analyze behavioral data on their dogs and offers updates oncurrent research (http://sensdog.com/blog/index.php/sample-page/).

13. John Bradshaw, email message to author, February 15, 2016.

14. Bradshaw and Rooney, "Dog Social Behavior and Communication," 152.

15. Luigi Boitani, email message to author, February 7, 2016.

16. Roberto Bonanni, email message to author, February 12, 2016.

17. More information on the Duke Canine Cognition Center can be found at https://evolutionaryanthropology.duke.edu/research/dogs.

18. Stewart et al., "Citizen Science as a New Tool in Dog Cognition Research."

BIBLIOGRAPHY

This list of books covers much of the material I've discussed here from various perspectives. (I don't necessarily agree with everything that's in them. However, it's essential to see what's out there and then decide what fits and what doesn't fit with one's views. As I've stressed here, only positive nondominating methods of training/teaching should be acceptable.) There are numerous books on dog behavior and dog training available, and Dogwise Publishing (www.dogwise.com) and Hubble and Hattie (www.hubbleandhattie.com) regularly publish books for those interested in many aspects of dog behavior, dog training, and dog-human relationships. So, too, does the magazine *The Bark*. James Serpell's edited volume *The Domestic Dog: Its Evolution, Behavior and Interactions with People* is a gold mine for the latest information on numerous diverse topics related to dogs, and *Animal Sentience: An Interdisciplinary Journal on Animal Feeling* (http://animalstudiesrepository.org/animsent/) is an excellent example of the ever-growing amount of comparative research and cross-disciplinary interest on this topic. The website iSpeakDog (http://www.ispeakdog.org) is an interactive tool to allow people and dogs to communicate better and provides a wonderful source for all things dog.

Abbott, Elizabeth. "Dogs (and Cats) without Borders: Frontier Animal Society," *Elizabeth Abbott* (blog), July 14, 2015. https://elizabethabbott.wordpress.com/category/dogs-and-underdogs/.

———. *Dogs and Underdogs: Finding Happiness at Both Ends of the Leash*. New York: Viking, 2015.

———. "Jane Goodall, Rusty and Me." *The Blog* (blog). *HuffPost*. Updated May 14, 2016.

http://www.huffingtonpost.com/elizabeth-abbott/jane-goodall-rusty-and-me_b _7275668.html.

Abrantes, Roger. *Dog Language: An Encyclopedia of Canine Behaviour.* Ann Arbor, MI: Wakan Tanka, 2009.

"Actress & celebrity GUL PANAG launches the SOUND OF SILENCE CAMPAIGN!" You-Tube video, 1:23. Posted by "PFA Chennai." August 2, 2016. https://www.youtube .com/watch?v=j4XCbp83J8c.

Addady, Michal. "This Is How Much Americans Spend on Their Dogs." *Fortune*, August 26, 2016. http://fortune.com/2016/08/26/pet-industry.

Allen, Laurel. "Dog Parks: Benefits and Liabilities." Master's capstone project, University of Pennsylvania, May 29, 2007. http://repository.upenn.edu/cgi/viewcontent .cgi?article=1017&context=mes_capstones.

Altmann, Jeanne. "Observational Study of Behavior: Sampling Methods." *Behaviour* 49, nos. 3–4 (1974): 227–67. http://www.uwyo.edu/animalcognition/altmann1974 .pdf.

American Veterinary Society of Animal Behavior. "Position Statement on the Use of Dominance Theory in Behavior Modification of Animals." 2008. http://www.liabc .com/Articles/dominance_statement.pdf.

Anderson, James R., Benoit Bucher, Hitomi Chijiiwa, Hika Kuroshima, Ayaka Takimoto, and Kazuo Fujita. "Third-Party Social Evaluations of Humans by Monkeys and Dogs." *Neuroscience and Biobehavioral Reviews.* Published electronically January 7, 2017. http://www.sciencedirect.com/science/article/pii/S0149763416303578.

Andics, A., A. Gábor, M. Gácsi, T. Faragó, D. Szabó, and Á. Miklósi. "Neural Mechanisms for Lexical Processing in Dogs." *Science* 353 (2016): 1030–32. http://science .sciencemag.org/content/early/2016/08/26/science.aaf3777.

"Animal Cruelty Law Has Governor's Signature, Dog's Paw Print." *Pocono Record*, June 28, 2017. http://www.poconorecord.com/news/20170628/animal-cruelty-law -has-governors-signature-dogs-paw-print.

Animal Legal Defense Fund. *2016 U.S. Animal Protection Laws Rankings.* http://aldf.org /wp-content/uploads/2017/01/Rankings-Report-2016-ALDF.pdf.

Antonacopoulos, Nikolina M. Duvall, and Timothy A. Pychyl. "The Possible Role of Companion-Animal Anthropomorphism and Social Support in the Physical and Psychological Health of Dog Guardians." *Society and Animals* 18, no. 4 (2010): 379–95. http://booksandjournals.brillonline.com/content/journals/10.1163/156853010 x524334.

"Appetite for Designer Dogs 'Unquenchable,' MSP's Are Told." *BBC News*, May 11, 2017. http://www.bbc.com/news/uk-scotland-scotland-politics-39886045.

Archer, John. "Why Do People Love Their Pets?" *Evolution and Human Behavior* 18 (1997), 237–59. http://courses.washington.edu/evpsych/Archer_Why-do-people -love-their-pets_1997.pdf.

Arden, Rosalind, and Mark James Adams. "A General Intelligence Factor in Dogs." *Intelligence* 55 (2016): 79–85. http://www.sciencedirect.com/science/article/pii /S016028961630023X.

Arden, Rosalind, Miles K. Bensky, and Mark J. Adams. "A Review of Cognitive Abilities in Dogs, 1911 through 2016: More Individual Differences, Please!" *Current Directions in Psychological Science* 25, no. 5 (2016): 307–12. http://cdp.sagepub.com/content/25 /5/307.full.

"Argentina Lawmakers Pass Law Banning Greyhound Racing." *DailyMail*, November 17, 2016. http://www.dailymail.co.uk/wires/ap/article-3946300/Argentina-law makers-pass-law-banning-greyhound-racing.html.

Arnold, Jennifer. *Love Is All You Need*. New York: Spiegel & Grau, 2016.

Artelle, K. A., L. K. Dumoulin, and T. E. Reimchen. "Behavioural Responses of Dogs to Asymmetrical Tail Wagging of a Robotic Dog." *Laterality* 16 (2011): 129–35. http:// www.ncbi.nlm.nih.gov/pubmed/20087813.

Autier-Dérian, Dominique, Bertrand L. Deputte, Karine Chalvet-Monfray, Marjorie Coulon, and Luc Mounier. "Visual Discrimination of Species in Dogs (*Canis famil-iaris*)." *Animal Cognition* 16, no. 4 (2013): 637–51. https://link.springer.com/article /10.1007%2Fs10071-013-0600-8.

Balcombe, Jonathan. *What a Fish Knows: The Inner Lives of Our Underwater Cousins*. New York: Farrar, Straus and Giroux, 2015.

Bálint, Anna, Tamás Faragó, Antal Dóka, Ádám Miklósi, and Péter Pongrácz. "'Beware, I Am Big and Non-Dangerous!'—Playfully Growling Dogs Are Perceived Larger Than Their Actual Size by Their Canine Audience." *Applied Animal Behaviour Science* 148, nos. 1–2 (2013): 128–37. http://www.sciencedirect.com/science/article/pii /S0168159113001871.

Ball, Philip. "Don't Be Sniffy If You Smell Like a Dog." *Guardian*, May 14, 2017. https:// www.theguardian.com/science/2017/may/14/dont-be-sniffy-if-you-smell-like -a-dog.

Bartram, Samantha. "All Dogs Allowed." *Parks and Recreation*. National Recreation and Park Association. January 1, 2014. https://www.parksandrecreation.org/parks -recreation-magazine/2014/january/all-dogs-allowed/.

Bauer, Erika, and Barbara Smuts. "Cooperation and Competition during Dyadic Play in Domestic Dogs, *Canis familiaris*." *Animal Behaviour* 73 (2007): 489–99. http:// psycnet.apa.org/psycinfo/2007-03752-013.

Beaver, Bonnie. *Canine Behavior: Insights and Answers*. 2nd ed. St. Louis: Saunders El-sevier, 2009.

Bekoff, Marc. *Animal Emotions: Do Animals Think and Feel?* (blog). *Psychology Today*, 2009–present. https://www.psychologytoday.com/blog/animal-emotions.

———. "The Animal Welfare Act Claims Rats and Mice Are Not Animals." *Animal Emo-tions* (blog). *Psychology Today*, September 25, 2016. https://www.psychologytoday

.com/blog/animal-emotions/201609/the-animal-welfare-act-claims-rats-and-mice-are-not-animals.

———. "The Animal Welfare Act Claims Rats and Mice Are Not Animals: Why Aren't Researchers Protesting This Idiocy?" *HuffPost*, September 25, 2016. http://www.huffingtonpost.com/entry/the-animal-welfare-act-claims-rats-and-mice-are-not_us_57e7c8b1e4b00267764fc50a.

———. "Anthropomorphic Double-Talk: Can Animals Be Happy but Not Unhappy? No!" *Animal Emotions* (blog). *Psychology Today*, June 24, 2009. https://www.psychologytoday.com/blog/animal-emotions/200906/anthropomorphic-double-talk-can-animals-be-happy-not-unhappy-no.

———. "Bowsers on Botox: Dogs Get Eye Lifts, Tummy Tucks, and More." *Animal Emotions* (blog). *Psychology Today*, March 23, 2017. https://www.psychologytoday.com/blog/animal-emotions/201703/bowsers-botox-dogs-get-eye-lifts-tummy-tucks-and-more.

———. "Censored: Animal Welfare and Animal Abuse Data Taken Offline." *Animal Emotions* (blog). *Psychology Today*, February 6, 2017. https://www.psychologytoday.com/blog/animal-emotions/201702/censored-animal-welfare-and-animal-abuse-data-taken-offline.

———. "Do Dogs Ever Simply Want to Die to End the Pain?" *Animal Emotions* (blog). *Psychology Today*, December 17, 2015. https://www.psychologytoday.com/blog/animal-emotions/201512/do-dogs-ever-simply-want-die-end-the-pain.

———. "Do Dogs Really Bite Someone for 'No Reason at All'? Take Two." *Animal Emotions* (blog). *Psychology Today*, December 5, 2016. https://www.psychologytoday.com/blog/animal-emotions/201612/do-dogs-really-bite-someone-no-reason-all-take-two.

———. "Do Dogs Really Feel Guilt or Shame? We Really Don't Know." *Animal Emotions* (blog). *Psychology Today*, March 23, 2014. https://www.psychologytoday.com/blog/animal-emotions/201403/do-dogs-really-feel-guilt-or-shame-we-really-dont-know.

———. "A Dog Named Gucci: 'Justice Is a Dog's Best Friend.'" *Animal Emotions* (blog). *Psychology Today*, January 11, 2017. https://www.psychologytoday.com/blog/animal-emotions/201701/dog-named-gucci-justice-is-dogs-best-friend.

———. "Dogs and Humans Process Sounds Similarly." *Animal Emotions* (blog). *Psychology Today*, August 30, 2016. https://www.psychologytoday.com/blog/animal-emotions/201608/dogs-understand-what-we-say-and-how-we-say-it.

———. "Dogs: Do 'Calming Signals' Always Work or Are They a Myth?" *Animal Emotions* (blog). *Psychology Today*, June 25, 2017. https://www.psychologytoday.com/blog/animal-emotions/201706/dogs-do-calming-signals-always-work-or-are-they-myth.

———. "Dogs, Dominance, Breeding, and Legislation: A Mixed Bag." *Animal Emotions*

(blog). *Psychology Today*, December 22, 2016. https://www.psychologytoday.com
/blog/animal-emotions/201612/dogs-dominance-breeding-and-legislation-mixed
-bag.

———. "Dogs Growl Honestly and Women Understand Better Than Men." *Animal Emotions* (blog). *Psychology Today*, May 17, 2017. https://www.psychologytoday.com
/blog/animal-emotions/201705/dogs-growl-honestly-and-women-understand
-better-men.

———. "Dogs Know When They've Been Dissed, and Don't Like It a Bit." *Animal Emotions* (blog). *Psychology Today*, July 23, 2014. https://www.psychologytoday.com
/blog/animal-emotions/201407/dogs-know-when-theyve-been-dissed-and-dont
-it-bit.

———. "Dogs Line Up with the Earth's Magnetic Field to Poop and Pee." *Animal Emotions* (blog). *Psychology Today*, January 2, 2014. https://www.psychologytoday.com
/blog/animal-emotions/201401/dogs-line-the-earths-magnetic-field-poop-and
-pee.

———. "Dog Smarts: If We Were Smarter We'd Understand Them Better." *Animal Emotions* (blog). *Psychology Today*, January 11, 2017. https://www.psychologytoday.com
/blog/animal-emotions/201701/dog-smarts-if-we-were-smarter-wed-understand
-them-better.

———. "Dogs Recognize Emotional States Using Mental Representations." *Animal Emotions* (blog). *Psychology Today*, January 13, 2016. https://www.psychologytoday
.com/blog/animal-emotions/201601/dogs-recognize-emotional-states-using
-mental-representations.

———. "Do Our Dogs Really Love Us More Than Our Cats Do?" *Animal Emotions* (blog). *Psychology Today*, February 3, 2016. https://www.psychologytoday.com/blog
/animal-emotions/201602/do-our-dogs-really-love-us-more-our-cats-do.

———. *The Emotional Lives of Animals*. Novato, CA: New World Library, 2007.

———. "Empathy Burnout and Compassion Fatigue among Animal Rescuers." *Animal Emotions* (blog). *Psychology Today*, January 23, 2017. https://www.psychologytoday
.com/blog/animal-emotions/201701/empathy-burnout-and-compassion-fatigue
-among-animal-rescuers.

———. "Ethology Hasn't Been Blown: Animals Need All Help Possible." *Animal Emotions* (blog). *Psychology Today*, December 29, 2015. https://www.psychologytoday
.com/blog/animal-emotions/201512/ethology-hasnt-been-blown-animals-need
-all-help-possible.

———. "For the Love of a Ball: Dogs as Conservation Biologists." *Animal Emotions* (blog). *Psychology Today*, October 26, 2016. https://www.psychologytoday.com
/blog/animal-emotions/201610/the-love-ball-dogs-conservation-biologists.

———. "The Genius of Dogs and the Hidden Lives of Wolves," *Animal Emotions* (blog), *Psychology Today*, February 4, 2013, https://www.psychologytoday.com

/blog/animal-emotions/201302/the-genius-dogs-and-the-hidden-life-wolves
#comment-507763.

———. "'Gosh, My Dog Is Just Like Me': Shared Neuroticism." *Animal Emotions* (blog). *Psychology Today*, February 11, 2017. https://www.psychologytoday.com/blog /animal-emotions/201702/gosh-my-dog-is-just-me-shared-neuroticism.

———. "Hidden Tales of Yellow Snow: What a Dog's Nose Knows—Making Sense of Scents." *Animal Emotions* (blog). *Psychology Today*, June 29, 2009. https://www .psychologytoday.com/blog/animal-emotions/200906/hidden-tales-yellow-snow -what-dogs-nose-knows-making-sense-scents.

———. "A Hierarchy of Dog Needs: Abraham Maslow Meets the Mutts." *Animal Emotions* (blog). *Psychology Today*, May 31, 2017. https://www.psychologytoday.com /blog/animal-emotions/201705/hierarchy-dog-needs-abraham-maslow-meets -the-mutts

———. "Hugging a Dog Is Just Fine When Done with Great Care." *Animal Emotions* (blog). *Psychology Today*, April 28, 2016. https://www.psychologytoday.com/blog /animal-emotions/201604/hugging-dog-is-just-fine-when-done-great-care.

———. "'If Dogs Truly Were Humans They Would Be Jerks.'" *Animal Emotions* (blog). *Psychology Today*, January 3, 2017. https://www.psychologytoday.com/blog/animal -emotions/201701/if-dogs-truly-were-human-they-would-be-jerks.

———. "Is an Unnamed Cow Less Sentient Than a Named Cow?" *Animal Emotions* (blog). *Psychology Today*, February 7, 2016. https://www.psychologytoday.com /blog/animal-emotions/201602/is-unnamed-cow-less-sentient-named-cow.

———. "iSpeakDog: A Website Devoted to Becoming Dog Literate." *Animal Emotions* (blog). *Psychology Today*, March 27, 2017. https://www.psychologytoday.com/blog /animal-emotions/201703/ispeakdog-website-devoted-becoming-dog-literate. An interview with Tracy Krulik, founder of iSpeakDog.

———. *Minding Animals: Awareness, Emotions, and Heart.* New York: Oxford University Press, 2002.

———. "Older Dogs: Giving Elder Canines Lots of Love and Good Lives." *Animal Emotions* (blog). *Psychology Today*, December 1, 2016. https://www.psychologytoday .com/blog/animal-emotions/201612/older-dogs-giving-elder-canines-lots-love -and-good-lives.

———. "Perils of Pooping: Why Animals Don't Need Toilet Paper." *Animal Emotions* (blog). *Psychology Today*, January 14, 2014. https://www.psychologytoday.com /blog/animal-emotions/201401/perils-pooping-why-animals-dont-need-toilet -paper.

———. "Pit Bulls: The Psychology of Breedism, Fear, and Prejudice." *Animal Emotions* (blog). *Psychology Today*, June 2, 2016. https://www.psychologytoday.com /blog/animal-emotions/201606/pit-bulls-the-psychology-breedism-fear-and -prejudice.

———. "Play Signals as Punctuation: The Structure of Social Play in Canids." *Behaviour* 132 (1995): 419–29. http://cogprints.org/158/1/199709003.html.

———. *Rewilding Our Hearts: Building Pathways of Compassion and Coexistence.* Novato, CA: New World Library, 2014.

———. "Scent-Marking by Free Ranging Domestic Dogs: Olfactory and Visual Components." *Biology of Behavior* 4 (1979): 123–39.

———, ed. *The Smile of a Dolphin: Remarkable Accounts of Animal Emotions.* Washington, DC: Discovery Books, 2000.

———. "Social Communication in Canids: Evidence for the Evolution of a Stereotyped Mammalian Display." *Science* 197 (1977): 1097–99. http://animalstudiesrepository .org/cgi/viewcontent.cgi?article=1038&context=acwp_ena.

———. "Some Dogs Prefer Praise and a Belly Rub over Treats." *Animal Emotions* (blog). *Psychology Today*, August 22, 2016. https://www.psychologytoday.com /blog/animal-emotions/201608/some-dogs-prefer-praise-and-belly-rub-over -treats.

———. "Theory of Mind and Play: Ape Exceptionalism Is Too Narrow." *Animal Emotions* (blog). *Psychology Today*, October 9, 2016. https://www.psychologytoday.com /blog/animal-emotions/201610/theory-mind-and-play-ape-exceptionalism-is -too-narrow.

———. "Training Dogs: Food Is Fine and Your Dog Will Still Love You." *Animal Emotions* (blog). *Psychology Today*, December 31, 2016. https://www.psychologytoday .com/blog/animal-emotions/201612/training-dogs-food-is-fine-and-your-dog -will-still-love-you.

———. "Valuing Dogs More Than War Victims: Bridging the Empathy Gap." *Animal Emotions* (blog). *Psychology Today*, August 21, 2016. https://www.psychologytoday .com/blog/animal-emotions/201608/valuing-dogs-more-war-victims-bridging -the-empathy-gap.

———. "We Are Animals and Therein Lies Hope for a Better Future." *Animal Emotions* (blog). *Psychology Today*, December 26, 2013. https://www.psychologytoday.com /blog/animal-emotions/201312/we-are-animals-and-therein-lies-hope-better -future.

———. "We Don't Know If Dogs Feel Guilt So Stop Saying They Don't." *Animal Emotions* (blog). *Psychology Today*, May 22, 2016. https://www.psychologytoday.com/blog /animal-emotions/201605/we-dont-know-if-dogs-feel-guilt-so-stop-saying-they -dont.

———. "What's Happening When Dogs Play Tug-of-War? Dog Park Chatter." *Animal Emotions* (blog). *Psychology Today*, May 6, 2016. https://www.psychologytoday.com /blog/animal-emotions/201605/whats-happening-when-dogs-play-tug-war-dog -park-chatter.

———. "Why Dogs Belong Off-Leash: It's Win-Win for All." *Animal Emotions* (blog).

Psychology Today, May 25, 2016. https://www.psychologytoday.com/blog/animal
-emotions/201605/why-dogs-belong-leash-its-win-win-all.

———. *Why Dogs Hump and Bees Get Depressed: The Fascinating Science of Animal Intelligence, Emotions, Friendship, and Conservation.* Novato, CA: New World Library, 2014.

———. "Why People Buy Dogs Who They Know Will Suffer and Die Young." *Animal Emotions* (blog). *Psychology Today*, February 25, 2017. https://www.psychology today.com/blog/animal-emotions/201702/why-people-buy-dogs-who-they-know -will-suffer-and-die-young.

Bekoff, Marc, and Robert Ickes. "Behavioral Interactions and Conflict among Domestic Dogs, Black-Tailed Prairie Dogs, and People in Boulder, Colorado." *Anthrozoös* 12, no. 2 (1999): 105–10. http://www.tandfonline.com/doi/abs/10.2752/089279399 787000318.

Bekoff, Marc, and Carron Meaney. "Interactions among Dogs, People, and the Environment in Boulder, Colorado: A Case Study." *Anthrozoös* 10 (1997): 23–31. http:// www.aldog.org/wp-content/uploads/2011/04/Bekoff-Meaney-1997-dogs.pdf.

Bekoff, Marc, and Jessica Pierce. *The Animals' Agenda: Freedom, Compassion, and Coexistence in the Human Age.* Boston: Beacon Press, 2017.

———. *Wild Justice: The Moral Lives of Animals.* Chicago: University of Chicago Press, 2009.

Ben-Aderet, Tobey, Mario Gallego-Abenza, David Reby, and Nicolas Mathevon. "Dog-Directed Speech: Why Do We Use It and Do Dogs Pay Attention to It?" *Proceedings of the Royal Society B*, vol. 284 (2017). http://rspb.royalsocietypublishing.org/content /284/1846/20162429.

Berns, Gregory. *How Dogs Love Us: A Neuroscientist and His Adopted Dog Decode the Canine Brain.* Boston: New Harvest, 2013.

———. *What It's Like to Be a Dog.* New York: Basic Books, 2017.

Berns, Gregrory, Andrew Brooks, and Mark Spivak. "Scent of the Familiar: An fMRI Study of Canine Brain Responses to Familiar and Unfamiliar Human and Dog Odors." *Behavioural Processes* 116 (2014): 37–46. http://www.sciencedirect.com /science/article/pii/S0376635714000473.

Beston, Henry. *The Outermost House: A Year of Life on the Great Beach of Cape Cod.* New York: Holt Paperbacks, 2003. First published 1928 by Doubleday and Doran.

"Biology of Fun." 25th anniversary special issue. *Current Biology* 25, no. 1 (2015). http:// www.cell.com/current-biology/issue?pii=S0960-9822(14)X0025-4.

Bird, Susan. "Dogs Are Worth More Than Mere 'Fair Market Value,' Rules Ohio Appeals Court." *Care 2*, December 19, 2016. http://www.care2.com/causes/dogs-are -worth-more-than-mere-fair-market-value-rules-ohio-appeals-court.html.

———. "Mexico Gets Serious: Dogfighting Will Now Be Penalized as a Felony." *Care 2*,

May 1, 2017. http://www.care2.com/causes/mexico-gets-serious-dogfighting-will
-now-be-penalized-as-a-felony.html.

———. "Undercover Video Shows Texas A&M Intentionally Breeds Deformed Dogs."
Care 2, December 19, 2016. http://www.care2.com/causes/undercover-video-shows
-texas-am-intentionally-breeds-deformed-dogs.html.

Bonanni, Roberto, Simona Cafazzo, Arianna Abis, Emanuela Barillari, Paola Valsecchi,
and Eugenia Natoli. "Age-Graded Dominance Hierarchies and Social Tolerance
in Packs of Free-Ranging Dogs." *Behavior Ecology* arx059 (April 2017). https://
academic.oup.com/beheco/article-abstract/doi/10.1093/beheco/arx059/3743771
/Age-graded-dominance-hierarchies-and-social?redirectedFrom=fulltext

Bonanni, Roberto, Eugenia Natoli, Simona Cafazzo, and Paola Valsecchi. "Free-
Ranging Dogs Assess the Quantity of Opponents in Intergroup Conflicts." *Animal
Cognition* 14 (2011): 103–15. http://link.springer.com/article/10.1007/s10071-010
-0348-3.

Bonanni, Roberto, Paola Valsecchi, and Eugenia Natoli. "Pattern of Individual Participation and Cheating in Conflicts between Groups of Free-Ranging Dogs." *Animal
Behaviour* 79 (2010): 957–68. http://www.sciencedirect.com/science/article/pii/So
003347210000382.

Boult, Adam. "Rats Laugh When Tickled—and This Is What It Sounds Like." *The Tele-
graph*, November 12, 2016. http://www.telegraph.co.uk/science/2016/11/12/rats
-laugh-when-tickled---and-this-is-what-it-sounds-like/.

Bowman, A., F. J. Dowell, and N. P. Evans. "The Effect of Different Genres of Music on
the Stress Levels of Kennelled Dogs." *Physiology and Behavior* 171 (2017): 207–15.
http://www.sciencedirect.com/science/article/pii/S0031938416306977.

Bradley, Theresa, and Ritchie King. "The Dog Economy Is Global—but What Is the
World's True Canine Capital?" *Atlantic*, November 13, 2012. https://www.the
atlantic.com/business/archive/2012/11/the-dog-economy-is-global-but-what-is
-the-worlds-true-canine-capital/265155/.

Bradshaw, John. *Dog Sense: How the New Science of Dog Behavior Can Make You a Better
Friend to Your Pet*. New York: Basic Books, 2014.

Bradshaw, John, Emily-Jayne Blackwell, and Rachel Casey. "Dominance in Domestic
Dogs—a Response to Schilder et al. (2014)." *Journal of Veterinary Behavior* 11 (2016):
102–8. http://www.journalvetbehavior.com/article/S1558-7878(15)00198-7/pdf.

Bradshaw, John, and Nicola Rooney. "Dog Social Behavior and Communication."
In *The Domestic Dog: Its Evolution, Behavior and Interactions with People*, edited by
James Serpell, 133–59. New York: Cambridge University Press, 2017.

Brandow, Michael. *A Matter of Breeding: A Biting History of Pedigree Dogs and How the
Quest for Status Has Harmed Man's Best Friend*. Boston: Beacon Press, 2015.

Bray, Emily, Evan MacLean, and Brian Hare. "Increasing Arousal Enhances Inhibitory

Control in Calm but Not Excitable Dogs." *Animal Cognition* 18 (2015): 1317–29. https://www.ncbi.nlm.nih.gov/pubmed/26169659.

Briggs, Helen. "Cats May Be as Intelligent as Dogs, Say Scientists." *BBC News*, January 25, 2017. http://www.bbc.com/news/science-environment-38665057.

Brulliard, Karin. "Americans Are Spending More on Health Care—for Their Pets." *Animalia* (blog). *Washington Post*, November 2, 2016. https://www.washingtonpost .com/news/animalia/wp/2016/11/02/americans-are-spending-more-on-health -care-for-their-pets/.

———. "In a First, Alaska Divorce Courts Will Now Treat Pets More Like Children." *Animalia* (blog). *Washington Post*, January 24, 2017. https://www.washingtonpost.com /news/animalia/wp/2017/01/24/in-a-first-alaska-divorce-courts-will-now-treat -pets-more-like-children/?utm_term=.1ab12e0738a1.

Burghardt, Gordon. *The Genesis of Animal Play: Testing the Limits.* Cambridge, MA: Bradford Books, 2005.

———. "Mediating Claims through Critical Anthropomorphism." *Animal Sentience* (2016). http://animalstudiesrepository.org/cgi/viewcontent.cgi?article=1063 &context=animsent.

Burkhardt, Richard. *Patterns of Behavior: Konrad Lorenz, Niko Tinbergen, and the Founding of Ethology.* Chicago: University of Chicago Press, 2005.

Byars, Mitchell. "Boulder Mailman Builds Ramp for Aging Dog along Route." *Daily Camera*, January 6, 2017. http://www.dailycamera.com/news/boulder/ci_307068 44/boulder-mailman-builds-ramp-aging-dog-along-route.

Byosiere, Sarah-Elizabeth, Julia Espinosa, and Barbara Smuts. "Investigating the Function of Play Bows in Adult Pet Dogs (*Canis lupus familiaris*)." *Behavioural Processes* 125 (2016): 106–13. https://www.researchgate.net/publication/295898387 _Investigating_the_function_of_play_bows_in_adult_pet_dogs_Canis_lupus _familiaris.

Cafazzo, Simona, Eugenia Natoli, and Paola Valsecchi. "Scent-Marking Behaviour in a Pack of Free-Ranging Domestic Dogs." *Ethology* 118 (2012): 955–66. http:// onlinelibrary.wiley.com/doi/10.1111/j.1439-0310.2012.02088.x/abstract.

Caldwell, Christine. "Mindfulness & Bodyfulness: A New Paradigm." *Journal of Contemplative Inquiry* 1 (2014): 77–96. http://naropa.edu/documents/faculty/bodyful -art-joci-2014.pdf.

Carlos, Naia. "Even Dogs Have Gotten into the Plastic Surgery Craze with Botox, Nose Jobs, and More." *Nature World News*, March 22, 2017. http://www.natureworldnews .com/articles/36610/20170322/even-dogs-gotten-plastic-surgery-craze-botox -nose-jobs-more.htm.

———. "True Best Friends: Dogs, Humans Mirror Each Other's Personality." *Nature World News*, February 20, 2017. http://www.natureworldnews.com/articles/35563 /20170210/true-best-friends-dogs-humans-mirror-each-others-personality.htm.

Carr, Neil. *Dogs in the Leisure Experience.* Oxfordshire, UK: CABI, 2014.

Carrier, Lydia Ottenheimer, Amanda Cyr, Rita E. Anderson, and Carolyn J. Walsh. "Exploring the Dog Park: Relationships between Social Behaviours, Personality and Cortisol in Companion Dogs." *Applied Animal Behaviour Science* 146 (2013): 96–106. http://www.sciencedirect.com/science/article/pii/S0168159113000981.

Case, Linda P. "Dog Park People." *The Science Dog* (blog). February 12, 2014. https://the sciencedog.wordpress.com/2014/02/12/dog-park-people/.

Cavalier, Darlene, and Eric Kennedy. *The Rightful Place of Science: Citizen Science.* Tempe, AZ: Consortium for Science, Policy, & Outcomes, 2016.

Chan, Melissa. "The Mysterious History behind Humanity's Love of Dogs." *Time*, August 25, 2016. http://time.com/4459684/national-dog-day-history-domestic-dogs -wolves/.

Cherney, Elyssa. "Orange-Osceola State Attorney Creates Animal Cruelty Unit." *Orlando Sentinel*, July 29, 2016. http://www.orlandosentinel.com/news/os-state -attorney-specialty-unit-20160729-story.html.

"Clever Dog Steals Treats from Kitchen Counter." YouTube video, 1:52. Posted by "Poke My Heart." June 14, 2012. https://www.youtube.com/watch?v=xYBbymUyFwQ.

Coffey, Laura. *My Old Dog: Rescued Pets with Remarkable Second Acts.* Novato, CA: New World Library, 2015.

Contorno, Steve. "'Sarge's Law' Could Bring New Rules for Dog Trainers in Hillsborough, Entire State." *Tampa Bay Times*, February 28, 2017. http://www.tampabay .com/news/humaninterest/sarges-law-could-bring-new-rules-for-dog-trainers -in-hillsborough-entire/2314707.

Cook, Gareth. "Inside the Dog Mind." *Mind* (blog). *Scientific American*, May 1, 2013. http://www.scientificamerican.com/article/inside-the-dog-mind/.

Cook, Peter, Ashley Prichard, Mark Spivak, and Gregory S. Berns. "Awake Canine fMRI Predicts Dogs' Preference for Praise versus Food." *Social Cognitive and Affective Neuroscience* 11, no. 12 (2016): 1853–62. https://doi.org/10.1093/scan/nsw102.

Cooper, Caren. *Citizen Science: How Ordinary People Are Changing the Face of Discovery.* New York: Overlook Press, 2016.

Corbley, McKinley. "Hundreds of Strangers Escort Dying Dog for Final Walk on Favorite Beach." *Good News Network*, November 16, 2016. https://www.goodnews network.org/hundreds-strangers-escort-dying-dog-final-walk-favorite-beach/.

Cordoni, Giada, Velia Nicotra, and Elisabetta Palagi. "Unveiling the 'Secret' of Play in Dogs (*Canis lupus familiaris*): Asymmetry and Signals." *Journal of Comparative Psychology* 130 (2016): 278–87. http://dx.doi.org/10.1037/com0000035.

Coren, Stanley. "Are There Behavior Changes When Dogs Are Spayed or Neutered?" *Canine Corner* (blog). *Psychology Today*, February 22, 2017. https://www .psychologytoday.com/blog/canine-corner/201702/are-there-behavior-changes -when-dogs-are-spayed-or-neutered.

———. "A Designer Dog-Maker Regrets His Creation." *Canine Corner* (blog). *Psychology Today*, April 1, 2014. https://www.psychologytoday.com/blog/canine-corner/201404/designer-dog-maker-regrets-his-creation.

———. "Do Dogs Feel Jealousy and Envy?" *Canine Corner* (blog). *Psychology Today*, June 19, 2013. https://www.psychologytoday.com/blog/canine-corner/201306/do-dogs-feel-jealousy-and-envy.

———. "Do Dogs Have a Sense of Humor?" *Canine Corner* (blog). *Psychology Today*, December 17, 2015. https://www.psychologytoday.com/blog/canine-corner/201512/do-dogs-have-sense-humor.

———. "Do Dogs Have Empathy for Other Dogs?" *Canine Corner* (blog). *Psychology Today*, November 2, 2016. https://www.psychologytoday.com/blog/canine-corner/201611/do-dogs-have-empathy-other-dogs.

———. *How Dogs Think: What the World Looks Like to Them and Why They Act the Way They Do*. New York: Atria Books, 2005.

———. "Long Tails versus Short Tails and Canine Communication." *Canine Corner* (blog). *Psychology Today*, February 1, 2012. https://www.psychologytoday.com/blog/canine-corner/201202/long-tails-versus-short-tails-and-canine-communication.

———. "Understanding the Nature of Dog Intelligence." *Canine Corner* (blog). *Psychology Today*, February 16, 2016. https://www.psychologytoday.com/blog/canine-corner/201602/understanding-the-nature-dog-intelligence.

———. "What Are Dogs Trying to Say When They Bark?" *Canine Corner* (blog). *Psychology Today*, March 15, 2011. https://www.psychologytoday.com/blog/canine-corner/201103/what-are-dogs-trying-say-when-they-bark.

———. "What a Wagging Dog Tail Really Means: New Scientific Data." *Canine Corner* (blog). *Psychology Today*, December 5, 2011. https://www.psychologytoday.com/blog/canine-corner/201112/what-wagging-dog-tail-really-means-new-scientific-data.

———. *The Wisdom of Dogs*. N.p.: Blue Terrier Press, 2014.

Costello, Alex. "Dog Abuse Video Spurs Legislation to License Trainers." *Long Beach Patch*, December 19, 2016. http://patch.com/new-york/longbeach/dog-abuse-video-spurs-legislation-license-trainers.

Council of Europe. *European Convention for the Protection of Pet Animals = Convention européenne pour la protection des animaux de compagnie*. Strasbourg: Council of Europe, 1987. https://www.animallaw.info/treaty/european-convention-protection-pet-animals.

Crosby, James. "The Specific Use of Evidence in the Investigation of Dog Bite Related Human Fatalities." MS thesis, University of Florida, 2016.

Dahl, Melissa. "What Does a Dog See in a Mirror?" *Science of Us* (blog). *New York*, May 23, 2016. http://nymag.com/scienceofus/2016/05/what-does-your-dog-see-when-he-looks-in-the-mirror.html.

Darwin, Charles. *The Descent of Man and Selection in Relation to Sex*. Vol. 1. 2nd ed. New York: American Home Library, 1902.

Davis, Nicola. "Puppies' Response to Speech Could Shed Light on Baby-Talk, Suggests Study." *Guardian*, January 10, 2017. https://www.theguardian.com/science/2017/jan/11/puppies-response-to-speech-could-shed-light-on-baby-talk-suggests-study.

DeKok, Wim. "The Origin of World Animal Day." World Animal Day, September 29, 2016. http://www.worldanimalday.org.uk/img/resource/Origin%20of%20World%20Animal%20Day.pdf.

DeMello, Margo, ed. *Mourning Animals: Rituals and Practices Surrounding Animal Death*. East Lansing: Michigan State University Press, 2016.

Derr, Mark. *Dog's Best Friend: Annals of the Dog-Human Relationship*. Chicago: University of Chicago Press, 2004.

———. *How the Dog Became the Dog: From Wolves to Our Best Friends*. New York: Overlook Press, 2011.

———. "What Do Those Barks Mean? To Dogs, It's All Just Talk." *New York Times*, April 24, 2001. http://www.nytimes.com/2001/04/24/science/what-do-those-barks-mean-to-dogs-it-s-all-just-talk.html.

de Waal, Frans. "How Do Dogs Recognize Us? And Why Do We Love Cats Anyway?" Review of *Being a Dog*, by Alexandra Horowitz, and of *The Lion in the Living Room*, by Abigail Tucker. *New York Times*, November 8, 2016. http://www.nytimes.com/2016/11/13/books/review/being-a-dog-alexandra-horowitz-lion-in-the-living-room-abigail-tucker.html.

Dickey, Bronwen. *Pit Bull: The Battle over an American Icon*. New York: Vintage Books, 2016.

Dodman, Nicholas. *Pets on the Couch: Neurotic Dogs, Compulsive Cats, Anxious Birds, and the New Science of Animal Psychiatry*. New York: Atria Books, 2016.

"Dog Fights Prompt 5,000 Calls to RSPCA in Past Decade." *BBC News*, January 18, 2017. http://www.bbc.com/news/uk-england-38653726.

"Dog Parks Lead Growth in U.S. City Parks." Trust for Public Lands, April 15, 2015. https://www.tpl.org/media-room/dog-parks-lead-growth-us-city-parks#sm.0001n49qvy4vyfoo114gq7j2cqaeg.

"Dogs Share Food with Other Dogs Even in Complex Situations." *Science Daily*, January 27, 2017. https://www.sciencedaily.com/releases/2017/01/170127112954.htm.

"Dog Training and Consumer Protection: What You Should Know." Facebook video, 3:41. Posted by the Academy for Dog Trainers. March 4, 2016. https://www.facebook.com/AcademyforDogTrainers/videos/987644334623619/.

Donaldson, Jean. *Train Your Dog Like a Pro*. New York: Howell Book House, 2010.

Eaton, Barry. *Dominance in Dogs: Fact or Fiction?* Wenatchee, WA: Dogwise Publishing, 2009.

El Nasser, Haya. "Fastest-Growing Urban Parks Are for the Dogs." *USA Today*, Decem-

ber 8, 2011. http://usatoday30.usatoday.com/news/nation/story/2011-12-07/dog
-parks/51715340/1.

Estep, Daniel Q., and Suzanne Hetts. "Pilgrim Bark Park Provincetown: Dog Park Etiquette and Safety Tips." Animal Behavior Associates, Littleton, CO, 2006. http://
www.provincetowndogpark.org/documents/Etiquette.pdf.

Fagen, Robert. *Animal Play Behavior.* New York: Oxford University Press, 1981.

Farricelli, Adrienne. "Does Human Perfume Affect Dogs?" *Cuteness.* https://www
.cuteness.com/blog/content/does-human-perfume-affect-dogs.

Feddersen-Petersen, Dorit Urd. "Vocalization of European Wolves (*Canis lupus lupus* L.)
and Various Dog Breeds (*Canis lupus* f. fam.)." *Archiv für Tierzucht* 43 (2000): 387–
97. http://www.archanimbreed.com/pdf/2000/atoop387.pdf.

"Federal Court Rules Police Can Shoot a Dog If It Moves, Barks When Officer Enters
Home." WISHTV10. December 23, 2016. http://wishtv.com/2016/12/23/federal
-court-rules-police-can-shoot-a-dog-if-it-moves-barks-when-officer-enters
-home/.

Feuerbacher, E. N., and C. D. Wynne. "Most Domestic Dogs (*Canis lupus familiaris*)
Prefer Food to Petting: Population, Context, and Schedule Effects in Concurrent
Choice." *Journal of the Experimental Analysis of Behavior* 101 (2014): 385–405. https://
www.ncbi.nlm.nih.gov/pubmed/24643871.

Forsman, Chuck. *Walking Magpie: On and Off the Leash.* Staunton, VA: George F.
Thompson Publishing, 2013.

Foubert, Elizabeth M. "Occupational Licensure for Pet Dog Trainers: Dogs Are Not the
Only Ones Who Should Be Licensed." Paper presented at the Animal Law Confer-
ence, New York, October 7–9, 2016. http://aldf.org/wp-content/uploads/ALC/2016
/Occupational_Licensure_for_Pet_Dog_Trainers.pdf.

Fowler, Sarah. "MS Legislator Pushing Animal Cruelty Bill." *Jackson Clarion-Ledger*
(MS), December 31, 2016. http://www.clarionledger.com/story/news/politics/2016
/12/31/ms-legislator-pushing-animal-cruelty-bill/95953796/.

Fox, Michael W. *Behaviour of Wolves, Dogs, and Related Canids.* New York: Harper &
Row, 1972.

———. *Integrative Development of Brain and Behavior in the Dog.* Chicago: University of
Chicago Press, 1971.

Frankel, Rebecca. *War Dogs: Tales of Canine Heroism, History, and Love.* New York: Pal-
grave Macmillan, 2014.

Fugazza, Claudia, Ákos Pogány, and Ádám Miklósi. "Recall of Others' Actions after
Incidental Encoding Reveals Episodic-Like Memory in Dogs." *Current Biology* 26
(2016): 3209–13. http://dx.doi.org/10.1016/j.cub.2016.09.057.

Fukuzawa, Megumi, and Ayano Hasha. "Can We Estimate Dogs' Recognition of Objects in Mirrors from Their Behavior and Response Time?" *Journal of Veterinary
Behavior* 17 (2017): 1–5. http://dx.doi.org/10.1016/j.jveb.2016.10.008.

Gallings, Simon. "Sight, Hearing, Smell: The Differences between Dogs and Humans." *TimeHuman* (blog), August 2012. http://timehuman.blogspot.com/2012/08/sight -hearing-smell-differences-between.html.

Ganardi, Wayne. *The Next Social Contract: Animals, the Anthropocene, and Biopolitics.* Philadelphia: Temple University Press, 2017.

Gardner, Mary. "Senior vs. Geriatric: Semantics or Significant?" dvm360.com. December 1, 2016. http://veterinarymedicine.dvm360.com/senior-vs-geriatric-semantics -or-significant.

Gatti, Roberto Cazzolla. "Self-Consciousness: Beyond the Looking-Glass and What Dogs Found There." *Ethology Ecology and Evolution* 28 (2016): 232–40. http://dx.doi .org/10.1080/03949370.2015.1102777.

Gaunet, F., E. Pari-Perrin, and G. Bernardin. "Description of Dogs and Owners in Outdoor Built-Up Areas and Their More-Than-Human Issues." *Environmental Management* 54, no. 3 (2014): 383–401. doi: 10.1007/s00267-014-0297-8.

Gayomali, Chris. "Dogs Might Poop in Line with the Earth's Magnetic Field." *The Week*, January 2, 2014. http://theweek.com/articles/453642/dogs-might-poop-line -earths-magnetic-field.

Geggel, Laura. "Anxiety May Give Dogs Gray Hair." *Live Science*, December 19, 2016. http://www.livescience.com/57254-anxiety-may-give-dogs-gray-hair.html.

Gilbert, Matthew. *Off the Leash: A Year at the Dog Park.* New York: St. Martin's Griffin, 2016.

Gill, Victoria, and Jonathan Webb. "Dogs 'Can Tell Difference between Happy and Angry Faces.'" *BBC News*, February 12, 2015. http://www.bbc.com/news/science -environment-31384525.

Goldman, Laura. "Success! It's Now a Felony to Abuse Companion Animals in Ohio." *Care 2*, September 15, 2016. http://www.care2.com/causes/success-its-now-a -felony-to-abuse-companion-animals-in-ohio.html.

Gomez, Edwin. "Dog Parks: Benefits, Conflicts, and Suggestions." *Journal of Park and Recreation Administration* 31 (2013): 71–91. http://js.sagamorepub.com/jpra/article /view/4549.

Gompper, Matthew, ed. *Free-Ranging Dogs and Wildlife Conservation.* New York: Oxford University Press, 2013.

Goodavage, Maria. *Secret Service Dogs: The Heroes Who Protect the President of the United States.* New York: Dutton, 2016.

Good News for Pets. "Pet Industry Spending at All-Time High: Up $6 Billion," March 24, 2017. http://goodnewsforpets.com/pet-industry-spending-time-high-6 -billion/.

Gorman, James. "Why Is That Dog Looking at Me?" *New York Times*, September 15, 2015. http://www.nytimes.com/2015/09/16/science/why-is-that-dog-looking-at -me.html.

Gough, William, and Betty McGuire. "Urinary Posture and Motor Laterality in Dogs (*Canis lupus familiaris*) at Two Shelters." *Applied Animal Behaviour Science* 168 (2015): 61–70. http://www.appliedanimalbehaviour.com/article/S0168-1591(15)00120-3/abstract?cc=y=.

Graham, Taryn, and Troy Glover. "On the Fence: Dog Parks in the (Un)Leashing of Community and Social Capital." *Leisure Studies* 36 (2014): 217–34. http://www.tandfonline.com/doi/abs/10.1080/01490400.2014.888020.

Gray, Richard. "Foxes May Confuse Predators by Rubbing Themselves in Puma Scent." *New Scientist*, January 19, 2017. https://www.newscientist.com/article/2118444-foxes-may-confuse-predators-by-rubbing-themselves-in-puma-scent/.

Griffin, Donald. *The Question of Animal Awareness.* 1976. Reprint, New York: Rockefeller University Press, 1981.

Griffiths, Sarah. "Dogs Snub People Who Are Mean to Their Owners—and Even Reject Their Treats." *Daily Mail*, June 13, 2015. http://www.dailymail.co.uk/sciencetech/article-3121280/Dogs-snub-people-mean-owners-reject-treats.html.

Grimm, David. *Citizen Canine: Our Evolving Relationship with Cats and Dogs.* New York: PublicAffairs, 2014.

Grossman, Anna Jane. "All Dog, No Bark: The Pitfalls of Devocalization Surgery." *The Blog* (blog). *HuffPost*, November 20, 2012. http://www.huffingtonpost.com/anna-jane-grossman/debarking_b_2160971.html.

Gruber, June, and Marc Bekoff. 2017. "A Cross-Species Comparative Approach to Positive Emotion Disturbance." *Emotion Review* 9 (2017): 72–78. http://emr.sagepub.com/content/early/2016/02/26/1754073915615430.abstract.

Hailman, Jack. "How an Instinct Is Learned." *Scientific American* 221, no. 6 (December 1969). https://www.scientificamerican.com/article/how-an-instinct-is-learned/.

Hallgren, Anders. *Ethics and Ethology for a Happy Dog.* Richmond, UK: Cadmos Publishing Limited, 2015.

Handelman, Barbara. *Canine Behavior: A Photo Illustrated Handbook.* Wenatchee, WA: Dogwise Publishing, 2008.

Handwerk, Brian. "Bees Can Learn to Play 'Soccer': Score One for Insect Intelligence." Smithsonian.com, February 24, 2017. http://www.smithsonianmag.com/science-nature/bees-can-learn-play-soccer-score-one-insect-intelligence-180962292/.

Haraway, Donna. *The Companion Species Manifesto: Dogs, People, and Significant Otherness.* Chicago: Prickly Pear Press, 2003.

———. *When Species Meet.* Minneapolis: University of Minnesota Press, 2007.

Hare, Brian, and Vanessa Woods. *The Genius of Dogs: How Dogs Are Smarter Than You Think.* New York: Plume, 2013.

Harmon-Hill, Cindy, and Simon Gadbois. "From the Bottom Up: The Roots of Social Neuroscience at Risk of Running Dry?" *Behavioral and Brain Sciences* 36 (2013): 426–27. https://www.cambridge.org/core/journals/behavioral-and-brain-sciences

/article/from-the-bottom-up-the-roots-of-social-neuroscience-at-risk-of
-running-dry/D5F6CBA92F64BD0BA87ADF527913E200.

Harris, Christine, and Caroline Prouvost. "Jealousy in Dogs." *PLOS One* 9, no. 7 (2014).
http://journals.plos.org/plosone/article?id=10.1371/journal.pone.0094597.

Hart, Benjamin, Lynette Hart, and Melissa Bain, eds. *Canine and Feline Behavior Therapy*. 2nd ed. Hoboken: Wiley-Blackwell, 2006.

Hart, Vlastimil, Petra Nováková, Erich Pascal Malkemper, Sabine Begall, Vladimír Hanzal, Miloš Ježek, Tomáš Kušta, et al. "Dogs Are Sensitive to Small Variations of the Earth's Magnetic Field." *Frontiers in Zoology* 10, no. 80 (2013). https://frontiersinzoology.biomedcentral.com/articles/10.1186/1742-9994-10-80.

Harvey, Adam. "Indonesian Charity Finds New Homes Overseas for Unwanted Dogs." *ABC News Australia.* January 23, 2017. http://www.abc.net.au/news/2017-01-22/indonesian-rescue-sends-dogs-overseas-in-quest-for-new-life/8192042.

Hathaway, Bill. "Dogs Ignore Bad Advice That Humans Follow." *YaleNews*, September 26, 2016. http://news.yale.edu/2016/09/26/dogs-ignore-bad-advice-humans-follow.

Hays, H. R. *Birds, Beasts, and Men: A Humanist History of Zoology.* New York: G. P. Putnam's Sons, 1972.

Hecht, Julie. "Dog Speak: The Sounds of Dogs." *The Bark*, no. 73 (Spring 2013). http://thebark.com/content/dog-speak-sounds-dogs.

———. "Why Do Dogs Roll Over during Play?" *Dog Spies* (blog). *Scientific American*, January 9, 2015. http://blogs.scientificamerican.com/dog-spies/why-do-dogs-roll-over-during-play/.

Heimbuch, Jaymi. "15 Things Humans Do Wrong at Dog Parks." *Mother Nature Network.* December 2, 2013. http://www.mnn.com/family/pets/stories/15-things-humans-do-wrong-at-dog-parks.

Hekman, Jessica. "Understanding Canine Social Hierarchies." *The Bark*, no. 84 (Winter 2015). http://thebark.com/content/understanding-canine-social-hierarchies.

Herzog, Hal. "Study Finds Dog-Walkers Have More Bad Mental Health Days!" *Animals and Us* (blog). *Psychology Today*, February 1, 2017. https://www.psychologytoday.com/blog/animals-and-us/201702/study-finds-dog-walkers-have-more-bad-mental-health-days.

———. "25 Things You Probably Didn't Know about Dogs." *Animals and Us* (blog). *Psychology Today*, March 13, 2017. https://www.psychologytoday.com/blog/animals-and-us/201703/25-things-you-probably-didn-t-know-about-dogs.

Hetts, Suzanne. *12 Terrible Mistakes Owners Make That Ruin Their Dog's Behavior . . . and How to Avoid Them*. N.p.: Animal Behavior Associates, 2014.

Hirskyj-Douglas, Ilyena. "Here's What Dogs See When They Watch Television." *The Conversation*, September 8, 2016. https://theconversation.com/heres-what-dogs-see-when-they-watch-television-65000.

Hodes, Carly. "More Fat, Less Protein Improves Detection Dogs' Sniffers." *Cornell Chronicle*, March 21, 2013. http://news.cornell.edu/stories/2013/03/more-fat-less-protein-improves-detection-dogs-sniffers.

Hoff, Benjamin. *The Tao of Pooh*. New York: E. P. Dutton, 1982.

Hoffman, Jan. "To Learn How Smart Dogs Are, Humans Learn New Tricks." *New York Times*, January 7, 2017. https://www.nytimes.com/2017/01/07/well/family/dogs-intelligence.html?hpw&rref=health&action=click&pgtype=Homepage&module=well-region&region=bottom-well&WT.nav=bottom-well&_r=2.

Horowitz, Alexandra. "Attention to Attention in Domestic Dog (*Canis familiaris*) Dyadic Play." *Animal Cognition* 12, no. 1 (2009): 107–18.

———. *Being a Dog: Following the Dog into a World of Smell*. New York: Scribner, 2016.

———. "Disambiguating the 'Guilty Look': Salient Prompts to a Familiar Dog Behaviour." *Behavioural Processes* 81 (2009): 447–52. https://www.ncbi.nlm.nih.gov/pubmed/19520245.

———, ed. *Domestic Dog Cognition and Behavior: The Scientific Study of Canis familiaris*. New York: Springer, 2014.

———. "From Fire Hydrants to Rescue Work, Dogs Perceive the World through Smell." Interview by Terry Gross. *Fresh Air*, October 4, 2016. http://www.npr.org/2016/10/04/496417068/from-fire-hydrants-to-rescue-work-dogs-perceive-the-world-through-smell.

Horowitz, Alexandra, and Marc Bekoff. "Naturalizing Anthropomorphism: Behavioral Prompts to Our Humanizing of Animals." *Anthrozoös* 20 (2007): 23–35.

Horsky, Nicole. *My Dog Is Blind . . . But Lives Life to the Full!* Dorset, UK: Veloce Publishing, 2017.

Horwitz, Debra F., J. Ciribassi, and Steve Dale, eds. *Decoding Your Dog: The Ultimate Experts Explain Common Dog Behaviors and Reveal How to Prevent or Change Unwanted Ones*. Boston: Houghton Mifflin Harcourt, 2014.

Howard, Jacqueline. "Here's More Proof That Dogs Can Totally Read Our Facial Expressions." *HuffPost*, February 13, 2015. http://www.huffingtonpost.com/2015/02/13/dogs-read-faces-study-video_n_6672422.html.

"How Are Animal Abuse and Family Violence Linked?" National Link Coalition. Accessed July 13, 2017. http://nationallinkcoalition.org/faqs/what-is-the-link.

Howse, Melissa. "Exploring the Social Behaviour of Domestic Dogs (*Canis familiaris*) in a Public Off-Leash Dog Park." MS thesis, Memorial University of Newfoundland, 2016. http://research.library.mun.ca/11670/1/thesis.pdf.

Hrala, Josh. "Your Dog Doesn't Trust You When You're Angry, Study Finds." Science Alert. May 24, 2016. http://www.sciencealert.com/your-dog-doesn-t-trust-you-when-you-re-angry-study-finds.

Huber, Ludwig. "How Dogs Perceive and Understand Us." *Current Directions in Psychological Science* 25, no. 5 (2016). http://cdp.sagepub.com/content/25/5/339.

Hyman, Ira. "Dogs Don't Remember." *Mental Mishaps* (blog). *Psychology Today*, May 1, 2010. https://www.psychologytoday.com/blog/mental-mishaps/201005/dogs-dont-remember.

Ioja, Cristian, Laurentiu Rozylowicz, Maria Patroescu, Mihai Razvan Nita, and Gabriel Ovidiu Vanau. "Dog Walkers' vs. Other Park Visitors' Perceptions: The Importance of Planning Sustainable Urban Parks in Bucharest, Romania," *Landscape and Urban Planning* 130, no. 1 (2011): 74–82. doi: 10.1016/j.landurbplan.2011.06.002.

Irvine, Leslie. *Filling the Ark: Animal Welfare in Disasters*. Philadelphia: Temple University Press, 2009.

———. *If You Tame Me: Understanding Our Connection with Animals*. Philadelphia: Temple University Press, 2004.

———. "The Power of Play." *Anthrozoös* 14 (2001): 151–60.

Jackson, Patrick. "Situated Activities in a Dog Park: Identity and Conflict in Human-Animal Space." *Society and Animals* 20 (2012): 254–72. http://www.animalsandsociety.org/wp-content/uploads/2016/05/jackson.pdf.

Jamieson, Dale, and Marc Bekoff. "On Aims and Methods of Cognitive Ethology." *PSA: Proceedings of the Biennial Meeting of the Philosophy of Science Association* 1992, no. 2 (1992): 110–24. http://www.journals.uchicago.edu/doi/abs/10.1086/psaprocbienmeetp.1992.2.192828.

Johnson, Rebecca, Alan Beck, and Sandra McCune, eds. *Health Benefits of Dog Walking for People and Pets: Evidence and Case Studies*. West Lafayette, IN: Purdue University Press, 2011.

Kaminski, Julianne, and Marie Nitzschner. "Do Dogs Get the Point? A Review of Dog-Human Communication Ability." *Learning and Motivation* 44 (2013): 294–302. http://www.sciencedirect.com/science/article/pii/S0023969013000325.

Kaminsky, Julianne, and Sarah Marshall-Pescini, eds. *The Social Dog: Behavior and Cognition*. New York: Academic Press, 2014.

Kaplan, Karen. "Dog Domestication Saddled Man's Best Friend with Defective Genes, Study Says." *Los Angeles Times*, December 22, 2015. http://www.latimes.com/science/sciencenow/la-sci-sn-dog-domestication-harmful-dna-20151221-story.html.

Kassam, Ashifa. "Judge Rules Pet Dogs Cannot Be Treated as Children in Canada Custody Dispute." *Guardian*, December 19, 2016. https://www.theguardian.com/world/2016/dec/19/dogs-children-property-custody-canada.

Käufer, Mechtild. *Canine Play Behavior: The Science of Dogs at Play*. Wenatchee, WA: Dogwise Publishing, 2014.

Kilday, Gregg. "Universal Cancels Premiere of 'A Dog's Purpose.'" *Hollywood Reporter*, January 19, 2017. http://www.hollywoodreporter.com/news/a-dogs-purpose-premiere-cancelled-controversy-966354.

King, Camille, Thomas J. Smith, Temple Grandin, and Peter Borchelt. "Anxiety and Impulsivity: Factors Associated with Premature Graying in Young Dogs." *Applied Animal Behaviour Science* 185 (2016): 78–85. http://www.appliedanimalbehaviour.com/article/S0168-1591(16)30277-5/abstract?cc=y=.

Klonsky, Jane Sobel. *Unconditional: Older Dogs, Deeper Love.* Washington, DC: National Geographic, 2016.

Knaus, Christopher. "Greyhound Doping: 51 NSW Trainers Offended after Inquiry Began." *Guardian*, January 26, 2017. https://www.theguardian.com/sport/2017/jan/27/greyhound-doping-51-nsw-trainers-charged-from-may-2015-to-september-2016.

Koler-Matznick, Janice. *Dawn of the Dog: The Genesis of a Natural Species.* Central Point, OR: Cynology Press, 2016.

Kristof, Nicholas. "Do You Care More about a Dog Than a Refugee?" *New York Times*, August 18, 2016. http://www.nytimes.com/2016/08/18/opinion/but-what-if-my-dog-had-been-a-syrian.html?_r=o.

Krulik, Tracy. "Dogs and Dominance: Let's Change the Conversation." *Dogz and Their Peoplez* (blog), January 18, 2017. http://dogzandtheirpeoplez.com/2017/01/18/dogs-and-dominance-lets-change-the-conversation/.

———. "Dominance and Dogs—the Push-ups Challenge." *Dogz and Their Peoplez* (blog), January 16, 2017. http://dogzandtheirpeoplez.com/2017/01/16/dominance-and-dogs-the-push-ups-challenge/.

———. "Eager to Please." *The Bark*, no. 88 (Winter 2016), 39–42.

Kuroshima, Hika, Yukari Nabeoka, Yusuke Hori, Hitomi Chijiiwa, and Kazuo Fujita. "Experience Matters: Dogs (*Canis familiaris*) Infer Physical Properties of Objects from Movement Clues." *Behavioural Processes* 136 (2017): 54–58. http://www.sciencedirect.com/science/article/pii/S037663571630208X.

"Learning to Speak Dog Part 4: Reading a Dog's Body." *Tails from the Lab* (blog). August 29, 2012. http://www.tailsfromthelab.com/2012/08/29/learning-to-speak-dog-part-4-reading-a-dogs-body/.

Lee, Hyung-Sook, Mardelle M. Shepley, and Chang-Shan Huang. "Evaluation of Off-Leash Dog Parks in Texas and Florida: A Study of Use Patterns, User Satisfaction, and Perception." *Landscape and Urban Planning* 92, nos. 3–4 (2009): 314–24. https://www.researchgate.net/publication/223592560_Evaluation_of_Off-Leash_Dog_Parks_in_Texas_and_Florida_A_Study_of_Use_Patterns_User_Satisfaction_and_Perception.

Lehner, Philip. *Handbook of Ethological Methods.* 2nd ed. New York: Cambridge University Press, 1998.

Leone, Jared. "Brewery Offers 'Pawternity' Leave for Employees with New Dogs." WHIO TV, February 17, 2107. http://www.whio.com/news/national/brewery-offers-pawternity-leave-for-employees-with-new-dogs/v7e2jnpbNJtnOopdvqh21I/

Lewis, Lauren. "Breaking News! Vancouver Bans Sale of Dogs, Cats, and Rabbits in

Pet Stores." *World Animal News*, June 30, 2017. http://worldanimalnews.com /breaking-news-vancouver-bans-sale-dogs-cats-rabbits-pet-stores/.

Lewis, Susan. "The Meaning of Dog Barks." *NOVA*, October 28, 2010. http://www.pbs .org/wgbh/nova/nature/meaning-dog-barks.html.

Lisberg, Anneke, and Charles Snowdon. "The Effects of Sex, Gonadectomy and Status on Investigation Patterns of Unfamiliar Conspecific Urine in Domestic Dogs, *Canis familiaris*." *Animal Behaviour* 77 (2008): 1147–54. https://www.researchgate.net /publication/223011377.

———. "Effects of Sex, Social Status and Gonadectomy on Countermarking by Domestic Dogs, *Canis familiaris*." *Animal Behaviour* 81 (2011): 757–64. http://www.science direct.com/science/article/pii/S0003347211000078.

London, Karen. "Should We Call These Canine Behaviors Calming Signals?" *The Bark* (blog). *The Bark*, June 2, 2017. http://thebark.com/content/should-we-call-these -canine-behaviors-calming-signals.

London Assembly. "Time to Review the Dangerous Dog Act." Press release, December 7, 2016. https://www.london.gov.uk/press-releases/assembly/time-to-review -the-dangerous-dogs-act.

London School of Economics. "Mensa Mutts? Dog IQ Tests Reveal Canine 'General Intelligence.'" *Science Daily*, February 7, 2016. www.sciencedaily.com/releases/2016 /02/160207203445.htm.

Lorenz, Konrad. *The Foundations of Ethology.* New York: Springer-Verlag, 1981.

Ma, Lybi. "Take a Walk on the Rewild Side." *Brainstorm* (blog). *Psychology Today*, November 5, 2014. https://www.psychologytoday.com/blog/brainstorm/201411/take -walk-the-rewild-side.

MacLean, Evan, and Brian Hare. "Dogs Hijack the Human Bonding Pathway." *Science* 348 (2015): 280–81.

"Mall Opens Its Doors for Stray Dogs during Winter Storm." Good News Network. January 11, 2017. http://www.goodnewsnetwork.org/mall-opens-door-stray-dogs -winter-storm/.

"A Man's Best Friend: Study Shows Dogs Can Recognize Human Emotions." *Science-Daily*, January 12, 2016. https://www.sciencedaily.com/releases/2016/01/1601122 14507.htm.

Margini, Matt. "What Is It Like to Be an Elephant?" *Public Books*, December 15, 2016. http://www.publicbooks.org/multigenre/what-is-it-like-to-be-an-elephant.

Mariti, Chiara, et al. "Analysis of the Intraspecific Visual Communication in the Domestic Dog (*Canis familiaris*): A Pilot Study on the Case of Calming Signals." *Journal of Veterinary Behavior* 18 (2017): 49–55. http://www.journalvetbehavior.com /article/S1558-7878(16)30246-5/abstract

Martino, Marissa. *Human/Canine Behavior Connection: A Better Self through Dog Training.* Boulder, CO: CreateSpace Independent Publishing Platform, 2017.

Marucot, Joyce. "Dogs Can Smell Fear but Can't Detect If You Have Lung Cancer." *Nature World News*, September 29, 2016. http://www.natureworldnews.com/articles /29386/20160929/dogs-cant-detect-if-you-have-lung-cancer.htm.

Masson, Jeffrey Moussaieff, and Susan McCarthy. *When Elephants Weep: The Emotional Lives of Animals*. Crystal Lake, IL: Delta Publishing, 1996.

McConnell, Patricia B. *For the Love of a Dog: Understanding Emotion in You and Your Best Friend*. New York: Ballantine Books, 2009.

———. "A New Look at Play Bows." *The Other End of the Leash* (blog), March 28, 2016. http://www.patriciamcconnell.com/theotherendoftheleash/a-new-look-at-play -bows.

McCue-McGrath, Melissa. *Considerations for the City Dog*. N.p.: MuttStuff Publishing, 2015. See also the author's blog, *MuttStuff*, at http://muttstuff.blogspot.com.

McGowan, Charlotte. "Debarking (Bark Softening)—Myths and Facts." National Animal Interest Alliance. January 8, 2012. http://www.naiaonline.org/articles/article /debarking-bark-softening-myths-and-facts#sthash.NF3xTGVz.dpbs.

McGuire, Betty, and Katherine Bernis. "Scent Marking in Shelter Dogs: Effects of Body Size." *Applied Animal Behaviour Science* 186 (2017): 49–55. http://www.applied animalbehaviour.com/article/S0168-1591(16)30317-3/fulltext.

McIntosh, Sandy. "Remembering H. R. Hays." *Poetrybay*. Autumn 2000. http://poetry bay.com/autumn2000/sample_autumn27.html.

McPherson, Poppy. "'I Want to Kill These Dogs': Question of Whether to Cull Strays Divides Yangon." *Guardian*, January 19, 2017. https://www.theguardian.com/cities /2017/jan/19/stray-dogs-yangon-myanmar-mass-cull-child-attacks.

Mech, L. David. "Alpha Status, Dominance, and Division of Labor in Wolf Packs." *Canadian Journal of Zoology* 77 (1999): 1196–203. http://www.wolf.org/wp-content /uploads/2013/09/267alphastatus_english.pdf.

Michaels, Linda. *Do No Harm: Dog Training and Behavior Manual*. 2017. https://gum road.com/lindamichaels

———. "Hierarchy of Dog Needs." Del Mar Dog Training. http://www.dogpsychologist oncall.com/hierarchy-of-dog-needs-tm/.

Mikanowski, Jacob. "Wild Thing." *Aeon*, November 28, 2016. https://aeon.co/essays /how-domestication-changes-species-including-the-human.

Miklósi, Ádám. *Dog Behaviour, Evolution, and Cognition*. New York: Oxford University Press, 2016.

Miller, Pat. "5 Steps to Deal with Dog Growling." *Whole Dog Journal*, October 2009. Updated June 8, 2017. http://www.whole-dog-journal.com/issues/12_10/features /Dealing-With-Dog-Growling_16163-1.html?ET=wholedogjournal:e265468:23688 67a:&st=email&s=p_Grabbag031917&omhide=true.

———. *Play with Your Dog*. Wenatchee, WA: Doggies Training Manual, 2008.

———. *The Power of Positive Dog Training*. Nashville, TN: Howell Book House, 2008.

Milligan, Tony. "The Ethics of Animal Training." In *Pets and People: The Ethics of Our Relationships with Companion Animals*, edited by Christine Overall, 203–17. New York: Oxford University Press, 2017.

Mills, Daniel, and Carri Westgarth, eds. *Dog Bites: A Multidisciplinary Perspective*. Sheffield, UK: 5M Publishing, 2017.

Mondal, Pankaj. "Study: Mice Can Sense, Feel Each Other's Pains with a Whiff." *Nature World News*, October 24, 2016. http://www.natureworldnews.com/articles/30571 /20161024/mice-can-sense-feel-each-other-s-pains-with-a-whiff-study-shows .htm.

Morey, Darcy. *Dogs: Domestication and the Development of a Social Bond*. New York: Cambridge University Press, 2010.

Morey, Darcy, and Rujana Jeger. "From Wolf to Dog: Late Pleistocene Ecological Dynamics, Altered Trophic Strategies, and Shifting Human Perceptions." *Historical Biology*, 2016, 1–9. http://dx.doi.org/10.1080/08912963.2016.1262854.

Morris, Paul, Christine Doe, and Emma Godsell. "Secondary Emotions in Non-Primate Species? Behavioural Reports and Subjective Claims by Animal Owners." *Cognition and Emotion* 22 (2007): 3–20. http://www.tandfonline.com/doi/abs/10 .1080/02699930701273716.

"Most Desirable Traits in Dogs for Potential Adopters." *Science Daily*, November 3, 2016. https://www.sciencedaily.com/releases/2016/11/161103151956.htm.

Müller, Corsin A., Kira Schmitt, Anjuli L. A. Barber, and Ludwig Huber. "Dogs Can Discriminate Emotional Expressions of Human Faces." *Current Biology* 25 (2015): 601–5. http://www.cell.com/current-biology/abstract/S0960-9822(14)01693-5.

Nader, Ralph. *Animal Envy: A Fable*. New York: Seven Stories Press, 2016.

Nagasawa, Miho, Emi Kawai, Kazutaka Mogi, and Takefumi Kikusui. "Dogs Show Left Facial Lateralization upon Reunion with Their Owners." *Behavioural Processes* 98 (2013): 112–16. http://www.sciencedirect.com/science/article/pii/S03766 35713001101.

Newman, Andy. "World (or at Least Brooklyn) Stops for Lost Dog." *New York Times*, November 11, 2016. http://www.nytimes.com/2016/11/13/nyregion/world-or-at -least-brooklyn-stops-for-lost-dog.html?_r=0.

Nichols, Henry. "Animal Magnetism: Why Dogs Do Their Business Pointing North." *New Scientist*, December 14, 2016. https://www.newscientist.com/article/mg2323 1040-200-how-animal-actions-are-steered-by-magnetism/.

Norman, K., S. Pellis, L. Barrett, and S. Peter Henzi. "Down but Not Out: Supine Postures as Facilitators of Play in Domestic Dogs." *Behavioural Processes* 110 (2015): 88–95. https://www.ncbi.nlm.nih.gov/pubmed/25217866.

Odendaal, J. S., and R. A. Meintjes. "Neurophysiological Correlates of Affiliative Behaviour between Humans and Dogs." *Veterinary Journal* 165 (2003): 296–301. http:// www.ncbi.nlm.nih.gov/pubmed/12672376.

O'Heare, James. *Dominance Theory and Dogs*. 2nd ed. Wenatchee, WA: Dogwise Publishing, 2008.

"Ohio Hunter Faces Felony Charges for Killing Man's Dogs, Is Fired from Job." KTLA 5. December 1, 2016. http://ktla.com/2016/12/01/hunter-charged-with-killing-mans -dogs-is-fired-from-job/.

Olson, Marie-Louise. "Dogs Have FEELINGS Too! Neuroscientist Reveals Research that Our Canine Friends Have Emotions Just Like Us." *DailyMail*, October 6, 2013. http:// www.dailymail.co.uk/news/article-2447991/Dogs-FEELINGS-Neuroscientist -reveals-research-canine-friends-emotions-just-like-us.html#ixzz4ghiZFCAD.

Orr, Becky. "2 Bills Seek Tougher Penalties for Animal Abusers in Wyoming." *Wyoming Tribune Eagle*, February 2, 2017. http://m.wyomingnews.com/news/bills-seek -tougher-penalties-for-animal-abusers-in-wyoming/article_66d52212-e913-11e6 -ae2e-73ca35a90a16.html.

Overall, Christine, ed. *Pets and People: The Ethics of Our Relationships with Companion Animals*. New York: Oxford University Press, 2017.

Overall, Karen. *Manual of Clinical Behavioral Medicine for Dogs and Cats*. St. Louis: Elsevier Mosby, 2013.

———. "Special Issue: The 'Dominance' Debate and Improved Behavioral Measures— Articles from the 2014 CSF/FSF." *Journal of Veterinary Behavior* 11 (2015): 1–6. http:// www.journalvetbehavior.com/article/S1558-7878(15)00202-6/pdf.

Pacelle, Wayne. "Federal Court Upholds New York City Ban on Puppy Mill Sales." *A Humane Nation* (blog). Humane Society of the United States. March 2, 2017. http:// blog.humanesociety.org/wayne/2017/03/federal-court-upholds-new-york-city -ban-puppy-mill-sales.html.

———. "Ohio Lawmakers Crack Down on Cockfighting, Bestiality, but Give Puppy Mills a Pass." *A Humane Nation* (blog). Humane Society of the United States. December 8, 2016. http://blog.humanesociety.org/wayne/2016/12/ohio-bill -cockfighting-bestiality-puppy-mills.html.

———. "*Rolling Stone* Crushes Puppy Mill Trade." *A Humane Nation* (blog). Human Society of the United States. January 3, 2017. http://blog.humanesociety.org/wayne /2017/01/rolling-stone-crushes-puppy-mill-trade.html?credit=blog_em_010317 _id8700&utm_source=feedblitz&utm_medium=FeedBlitzRss&utm_campaign =humanenation.

Pachniewska, Amanda. "List of Animals That Have Passed the Mirror Test." *Animal Cognition*, April 15, 2015. http://www.animalcognition.org/2015/04/15/list-of -animals-that-have-passed-the-mirror-test/.

Paiella, Gabriella. "This Bill to Protect Domestic-Violence Victim's Pets Could Save Women's Lives." *The Cut*, February 9, 2017. http://nymag.com/thecut/2017/02 /paws-act-aims-to-protect-domestic-violence-victims-pets.html.

"Paintings from the Perspective of a Dog's Nose." Nova Scotia College of Art & Design University News, November 8, 2016. http://nscad.ca/en/home/abouttheuniversity/news/paintingsfromtheperspectiveofadogsnose.aspx.

Palagi, Elisabetta, Velia Nicotra, and Giada Cordoni. "Rapid Mimicry and Emotional Contagion in Domestic Dogs." *Royal Society Open Science*, December 2015. http://rsos.royalsocietypublishing.org/content/2/12/150505.

Pangal, Sindhoor. "Lives of Streeties: A Study on the Activity Budget of Free-Ranging Dogs." *IAABC Journal* (Winter 2017). https://winter2017.iaabcjournal.org/lives-of-streeties-a-study-on-the-activity-budget-of-free-ranging-dogs/.

Pascaline, Mary. "Minnesota Town Elects Dog Mayor Named Duke for the Third Time." *International Business Times*, August 24, 2016. http://www.ibtimes.com/minnesota-town-elects-dog-mayor-named-duke-third-time-2406433.

Paxton, David. *Why It's OK to Talk to Your Dog: Co-Evolution of People and Dogs.* N.p.: printed by author, 2011.

Payne, Elyssa M., Pauleen C. Bennett, and Paul D. McGreevy. "DogTube: An Examination of Dogmanship Online." *Journal of Veterinary Behavior* 17 (2017): 50–61. http://www.journalvetbehavior.com/article/S1558-7878(16)30167-8/fulltext?elsca1=etoc&elsca2=email&elsca3=1558-7878_201701_17_&elsca4=Veterinary%20Science%2FMedicine.

Pearce, Fred. "Down with Data: Sagas Are More Likely to Save Earth." *New Scientist*, January 11, 2017. https://www.newscientist.com/article/mg23331080-500-down-with-data-sagas-are-more-likely-to-save-earth/.

Pellis, Sergio, and Vivien Pellis. *The Playful Brain: Venturing to the Limits of Neuroscience.* London: Oneworld Publications, 2010.

Penkowa, Milena. *Dogs and Human Health: The New Science of Dog Therapy and Therapy Dogs.* Bloomington, IN: Balboa Press, 2015.

"People Living in Cities Will Risk Own Safety to Save Animals." World Animal Protection, July 9, 2014. https://www.worldanimalprotection.org/news/people-living-cities-will-risk-own-safety-save-animals.

"Pet Dogs Help Kids Feel Less Stressed, Study Finds." University of Florida News, May 9, 2017. http://news.ufl.edu/articles/2017/05/pet-dogs-help-kids-feel-less-stressed-study-finds.php.

Peterson, Dale. *Jane Goodall: The Woman Who Redefined Man.* Boston: Mariner Books, 2008.

Petty, Michael. *Dr. Petty's Pain Relief for Dogs: The Complete Medical and Integrative Guide to Treating Pain.* Woodstock, VT: Countryman Press, 2016.

Pierce, Jessica. "Deciding When a Pet Has Suffered Enough." *Sunday Review* (opinion). *New York Times*, September 22, 2012. http://www.nytimes.com/2012/09/23/opinion/sunday/deciding-when-a-pet-has-suffered-enough.html.

———. "Is Your Dog in Pain?" *All Dogs Go to Heaven* (blog). *Psychology Today*, February 3, 2016. https://www.psychologytoday.com/blog/all-dogs-go-heaven/201602/is-your-dog-in-pain.

———. *The Last Walk: Reflections on Our Pets at the End of Their Lives*. Chicago: University of Chicago Press, 2012.

———. "Not Just Walking the Dog: What a Dog Walk Can Tell Us about Our Human-Animal Relationships." *All Dogs Go to Heaven* (blog). *Psychology Today*, March 16, 2017. https://www.psychologytoday.com/blog/all-dogs-go-heaven/201703/not-just-walking-the-dog.

———. "Palliative Care for Pets." Seniors Resource Guide. November 2012. http://www.seniorsresourceguide.com/articles/art01240.html.

———. *Run, Spot, Run: The Ethics of Keeping Pets*. Chicago: University of Chicago Press, 2016.

Pilgrim, Tom. "Children Are Closer to Their Pets Than Their Siblings, Cambridge Study Finds." *Cambridge News*, January 24, 2017. http://www.cambridge-news.co.uk/news/cambridge-news/children-closer-pets-siblings-cambridge-12501590.

Pilley, John. *Chaser: Unlocking the Genius of the Dog Who Knows a Thousand Words*. New York: Mariner Books, 2014.

Pongracz, P., C. Molnár, A. Miklósi, and V. Csányi. "Human Listeners Are Able to Classify Dog (*Canis familiaris*) Barks Recorded in Different Situations." *Journal of Comparative Psychology* 119, no. 2 (2005): 136–44. doi: 10.1037/0735-7036.119.2.136.

Quengua, Douglas. "A Dog's Tail Wag Says a Lot, to Other Dogs." *New York Times*, October 31, 2013. http://www.nytimes.com/2013/11/05/science/a-dogs-tail-wag-can-say-a-lot.html.

Ray, C. Claiborne. "How Does One Dog Recognize Another as a Dog?" *New York Times*, February 15, 2016. http://www.nytimes.com/2016/02/16/science/how-does-one-dog-recognize-another-as-a-dog.html?_r=1.

Reber, Arthur. "Caterpillars, Consciousness and the Origins of Mind." *Animal Sentience*, 2016. http://animalstudiesrepository.org/cgi/viewcontent.cgi?article=1124&context=animsent.

Reed, S.E., and A.M. Merenlender. "Effects of Management of Domestic Dogs and Recreation on Carnivores in Protected Areas in Northern California." *Conservation Biology* 25, no. 3 (2011): 504–13. https://www.ncbi.nlm.nih.gov/pubmed/21309853.

Reid, Pamela. *Dog Insight*. Wenatchee, WA: Dogwise Publishing, 2011.

Reisner, Ilana. "The Learning Dog: A Discussion of Training Methods." In *The Domestic Dog: Its Evolution, Behavior and Interactions with People*, edited by James Serpell, 210–26. New York: Cambridge University Press, 2017.

Riley, Katherine. "Puppy Love: The Coddling of the American Pet." *Atlantic*, May 2017. https://www.theatlantic.com/magazine/archive/2017/05/puppy-love/521442/.

Robert, Christopher. "The Evolution of Humor: From Grunts to Poop Jokes." *Humor at*

Work (blog). *Psychology Today*, November 23, 2016. https://www.psychologytoday
.com/blog/humor-work/201611/the-evolution-humor-grunts-poop-jokes.

Rogers, Lesley, Giorgio Vallortigara, and Richard Andrew. *Divided Brains: The Biology and Behaviour of Brain Symmetries*. New York: Cambridge University Press, 2013.

Romero, Teresa, Miho Nagasawa, Kazutaka Mogi, Toshikazu Hasegawa, and Takefumi Kikusui. "Oxytocin Promotes Social Bonding in Dogs." *Proceedings of the National Academy of Sciences* 111, no. 25 (2014): 9085–90. doi: 10.1073/pnas.1322868111.

Root, Andrew. *The Grace of Dogs: A Boy, a Black Lab, and a Father's Search for the Canine Soul*. New York: Convergent Books, 2017.

Rosell, Frank Narve. *Secrets of the Snout: The Dog's Incredible Nose*. Translated by Diane Oatley. Chicago: University of Chicago Press, 2018.

Rose-Solomon, Diane. *What to Expect When Adopting a Dog: A Guide to Successful Dog Adoption for Every Family*. N.p.: SP03 Publishing, 2016.

"RSPCA Animal Welfare Prosecutions in Wales Up." *BBC News*, March 29, 2017. http://www.bbc.com/news/uk-wales-39423292.

Rugaas, Turid. *On Talking Terms with Dogs: Calming Signals*. Wenatchee, WA: Dogwise Publishing, 2006.

Safina, Carl. *Beyond Words: What Animals Think and Feel*. New York: Henry Holt and Company, 2015.

"Sale of Puppies under Eight Weeks Old to Be Made Illegal." *Guardian*, February 1, 2017. https://www.theguardian.com/world/2017/feb/02/sale-of-puppies-under-eight-weeks-old-to-be-made-illegal.

Sanders, Clinton. *Understanding Dogs: Living and Working with Canine Companions*. Philadelphia: Temple University Press, 1998.

Schaefer, Donovan.. *Religious Affects: Animality, Evolution, and Power*. Durham, NC: Duke University Press Books, 2015.

Schenkel, Rudolph. "Expression Studies on Wolves: Captivity Observations." Working paper. December 27, 1946. http://davemech.org/schenkel/ExpressionstudiesP.1-10.pdf.

Schenone, Laura. *The Dogs of Avalon: The Race to Save Animals in Peril*. New York: W. W. Norton, 2017.

Schoen, Allen, and Susan Gordon. *The Compassionate Equestrian: 25 Principles to Live by When Caring for and Working with Horses*. North Pomfret, VT: Trafalgar Square Books, 2015.

Scott, John Paul, and John Fuller. *Genetics and the Social Behavior of the Dog*. 1965. Reprint, Chicago: University of Chicago Press, 1998.

Scully, Marisa. "The Westminster Dog Show Fails the Animals It Profits From: Here's Why." *Guardian*, February 16, 2017. https://www.theguardian.com/sport/2017/feb/16/the-westminster-dog-show-fails-the-animals-it-profits-from-heres-why.

Serpell, James. "Creatures of the Unconscious: Companion Animals as Mediators." In *Companion Animals and Us: Exploring the Relationships between People and Pets*, edited by Anthony Podberscek, Elizabeth Paul, and James Serpell, 108–21. New York: Cambridge University Press, 2005.

———, ed. *The Domestic Dog: Its Evolution, Behavior and Interactions with People*. New York: Cambridge University Press, 2017.

———. "Epilogue: The Tail of the Dog." In *The Domestic Dog: Its Evolution, Behavior and Interactions with People*, edited by James Serpell, 404–12. New York: Cambridge University Press, 2017.

Shelley-Grielen, Frania. *Cats and Dogs: Living with and Looking at Companion Animals from Their Point of View*. Bloomington, IN: Archway Publishing, 2014.

Shipman, Pat. *The Invaders: How Humans and Their Dogs Drive Neanderthals to Extinction*. Cambridge, MA: The Belknap Press, 2015.

Shyan, Melissa R., Kristina A. Fortune, and Christine King. "'Bark Parks'—a Study on Interdog Aggression in a Limited-Control Environment." *Journal of Applied Animal Welfare Science* 6, no. 1 (2003): 25–32. http://freshairtraining.com/pdfs/BarkParks.pdf.

Siler, Wes. "Why Dogs Belong Off-Leash in the Outdoors." *Outside Magazine*, May 24, 2016. http://www.outsideonline.com/2082546/why-dogs-belong-leash-outdoors.

Singer, Peter. *Animal Liberation*. New York: HarperCollins, 1975.

"Sleep Habits of the Animal Kingdom." *Sleepopolis*, September 30, 2016. http://sleepopolis.com/blog/sleep-habits-of-the-animal-kingdom-infographic/.

Smith, Cheryl. "Behavior: Dog Park Tips." *The Bark*, no. 43 (Summer 2007). http://thebark.com/content/behavior-dog-park-tips.

Smuts, Barbara, Erika Bauer, and Camille Ward. "Rollovers during Play: Complementary Perspective." *Behavioural Processes* 116 (2016): 50–51. http://www.sciencedirect.com/science/article/pii/S0376635715001047.

Sober, Elliott. *The Nature of Selection*. Chicago: University of Chicago Press, 2014.

Solotaroff, Paul. "The Dog Factory: Inside the Sickening World of Puppy Mills." *Rolling Stone*, January 3, 2017. http://www.rollingstone.com/culture/features/the-dog-factory-inside-the-sickening-world-of-puppy-mills-w457673.

Sonntag, Q., and K. L. Overall. "Key Determinants of Dog and Cat Welfare: Behaviour, Breeding and Household Lifestyle." *Scientific and Technical Review of the Office International des Epizooties* 33 (2014): 213–20. https://www.ncbi.nlm.nih.gov/pubmed/25000794.

"Sophia Grows: A Rhodesian Ridgeback Time-Lapse." YouTube video, 1:50. Posted by "Greg Coffin." November 27, 2014. https://www.youtube.com/watch?v=c6eUidLqUAo.

Spinka, Marek, Ruth Newberry, and Marc Bekoff. "Mammalian Play: Training for the Unexpected." *Quarterly Review of Biology* 72 (2001): 141–68. https://www.ncbi.nlm.nih.gov/pubmed/11409050.

"State Laws Governing Elective Surgical Procedures." State Summary Report, American Veterinary Medical Foundation. Last updated December 2014. https://www
.avma.org/Advocacy/StateAndLocal/Pages/sr-elective-procedures.aspx.

Stewart, Laughlin, Evan L. MacLean, David Ivy, Vanessa Woods, Eliot Cohen, Kerri Rodriguez, Matthew McIntyre, et al. "Citizen Science as a New Tool in Dog Cognition Research." *PLOS One*, vol. 10, no. 9 (2015). http://journals.plos.org/plosone/article?id=10.1371/journal.pone.0135176.

Stilwell, Victoria. *The Secret Language of Dogs*. Berkeley, CA: Ten Speed Press, 2016.

"Study Demonstrates Rapid Decline in Male Dog Fertility, with Potential Link to Environmental Contaminants." *ScienceDaily*, August 9, 2016. https://www.sciencedaily.com/releases/2016/08/160809095138.htm.

Sweet, Laurel J. "Teen Files Bill to Make Vocal Surgery Illegal." *Boston Herald*, February 2, 2009. http://www.bostonherald.com/news_opinion/local_coverage/2009/02/teen_files_bill_make_vocal_surgery_illegal.

Szentágothai, J. "The 'Brain-Mind' Relation: A Pseudo-Problem?" In *Mindwaves: Thoughts on Intelligence, Identity and Consciousness*, edited by C. Blakemore and S. Greenfield, 323–36. Oxford: Basil Blackwell, 1987.

Tasaki, Susan. "Trending: Dog-Friendly Housing Associations: Dogs Are Being Written into Residential Master Plans." *The Bark*, no. 84 (Fall 2016). http://thebark.com/content/dogs-are-being-written-housing-development-plans.

"TEDxDirigo—Zoe Weil: The World Becomes What You Teach," YouTube video, 17:24. Posted by "Tedx Talks." January 14, 2012. https://www.youtube.com/watch?v=t5HEV96dIuY.

Tenzin-Dolma, Lisa. *Dog Training: The Essential Guide*. Peterborough, UK: Need2Know, 2012.

Tinbergen, Niko. *The Study of Instinct*. New York: Oxford University Press, 1951.

Todd, Zazie. "'Dominance' Training Deprives Dogs of Positive Experiences." *Companion Animal Psychology* (blog). February 15, 2017. http://www.companionanimal psychology.com/2017/02/dominance-training-deprives-dogs-of.html?m=1.

———. "New Literature Review Recommends Reward-Based Training." *Companion Animal Psychology* (blog). April 5, 2017. http://www.companionanimalpsychology.com/2017/04/new-literature-review-recommends-reward.html.

Travis, Randy. "Supreme Court: All Dogs Have Value." Fox 5 Atlanta. June 6, 2016. http://www.fox5atlanta.com/news/i-team/154610286-story.

Vaira, Angelo, and Valeria Raimondi. *Un cuore felice: L'arte di giocore con il tuo cane* [*A Happy Heart: The Art of Playing with a Dog*]. Milan: Sperling & Kupfer, 2016.

Velarde, Victoria, and Madeline Schmitt. "New Mexico Lawmaker Wants to Make Animal Cruelty a Felony." KRQE News 13. January 25, 2017. http://krqe.com/2017/01/25/new-mexico-lawmaker-wants-to-make-animal-cruelty-a-felony/.

"Vermont Has New Law Banning Sexual Abuse of Animals." *U.S. News and World Re-*

port, June 9, 2017. https://www.usnews.com/news/best-states/vermont/articles/2017-06-09/vermont-has-new-law-banning-sexual-abuse-of-animals.

"The Vet Who 'Euthanised' Herself in Taiwan." *BBC News*, February 2, 2017. http://www.bbc.com/news/world-asia-36573395.

Vilari, Robin Maria. "Tails of Laughter: A Pilot Study Examining the Relationship between Companion Animal Guardianship (Pet Ownership) and Laughter." *Society and Animals* 14, no. 3 (2006): 275–93. http://www.animalsandsociety.org/wp-content/uploads/2016/04/valeri.pdf.

Wamsley, Laurel. "In a First, Connecticut's Animals Get Advocate in the Courtroom." *The Two-Way: Breaking News from NPR*. National Public Radio, June 2, 2017. http://www.npr.org/sections/thetwo-way/2017/06/02/531283235/in-a-first-connecticuts-animals-get-advocates-in-the-courtroom.

Ward, Camille, Rebecca Trisko, and Barbara Smuts. "Third-Party Interventions in Dyadic Play between Littermates of Domestic Dogs, *Canis lupus familiaris*." *Animal Behaviour* 78 (2009): 1153–60. http://pawsoflife-org.k9handleracademy.com/Library/Behavior/Ward_2009.pdf.

Warden, C. J., and L. H. Warner. "The Sensory Capacities and Intelligence of Dogs, with a Report on the Ability of the Noted Dog 'Fellow' to Respond to Verbal Stimuli." *Quarterly Review of Biology* 3 (1928): 1–28. http://www.journals.uchicago.edu/doi/abs/10.1086/394292.

Wild, Karen. *Being a Dog*. Buffalo, NY: Firefly Books, 2016.

Wilson, Edward O. *Sociobiology: The New Synthesis*. Cambridge, MA: Harvard University Press, 1975.

Wogan, Lisa. *Dog Park Wisdom: Real-World Advice on Choosing, Caring for, and Understanding Your Canine Companion*. Seattle: Skipstone Press, 2008.

Wolch, Jennifer, and Stacy Rowe. "Companions in the Park." *Landscape* 31 (2002): 16–23.

Wood, Lisa, Billie Giles-Corti, Max Bulsara, and Darcy Bosch. "More Than a Furry Companion: The Ripple Effect of Companion Animals on Neighborhood Interactions and Sense of Community." *Society and Animals* 15 (2007): 43–56.

Wynne, Clive D. L. "Should Shelters Bother Assessing Their Dogs?" *Dogs and Their People* (blog). *Psychology Today*, August 19, 2016. https://www.psychologytoday.com/blog/dogs-and-their-people/201608/should-shelters-bother-assessing-their-dogs.

Yin, Sophia. *How to Behave So Your Dog Behaves*. Neptune, NJ: THF Publications, 2010.

Ziv, Gal. "The Effects of Using Aversive Training Methods in Dogs—a Review." *Journal of Veterinary Behavior* 19 (2017): 50–60. http://www.journalvetbehavior.com/article/S1558-7878(17)30035-7/abstract.

Index

Note: Page numbers in *italics* refer to illustrative matter. All first name headings refer to individual dogs.

6/18

LUDINGTON PUBLIC LIBRARY
5 S. BRYN MAWR AVENUE
BRYN MAWR, PA 19010-3471